KT CO-BOC 072

Romantic Anatomies of Performance

The publisher gratefully acknowledges the generous support of the Ahmanson Foundation Humanities Endowment Fund of the University of California Press Foundation.

Montante Family Library
D'Youville College

Romantic Anatomies of Performance

J. Q. Davies

UNIVERSITY OF CALIFORNIA PRESS

Berkeley   Los Angeles   London

NOV 26 2014

University of California Press, one of the most distinguished university presses in the United States, enriches lives around the world by advancing scholarship in the humanities, social sciences, and natural sciences. Its activities are supported by the UC Press Foundation and by philanthropic contributions from individuals and institutions. For more information, visit www.ucpress.edu.

University of California Press
Berkeley and Los Angeles, California

University of California Press, Ltd.
London, England

© 2014 by The Regents of the University of California

Library of Congress Cataloging-in-Publication Data

Davies, J. Q., 1973–
    Romantic anatomies of performance / J. Q. Davies.
        pages   cm
    Includes bibliographical references and index.
    ISBN 978-0-520-27939-1 (cloth : alk. paper)
        1. Music—19th century—History and criticism.   2. Music—
Performance—History.   I. Title.
    ML160.D257   2014
    781.4′309034—dc23
                                            2013032716

Manufactured in the United States of America

22   21   20   19   18   17   16   15   14
10   9   8   7   6   5   4   3   2   1

In keeping with a commitment to support environmentally responsible and sustainable printing practices, UC Press has printed this book on Natures Natural, a fiber that contains 30% post-consumer waste and meets the minimum requirements of ANSI/NISO Z39.48–1992 (R 1997) (*Permanence of Paper*).

ML
160
.D257
2014

To My Family

My primitive tongue
is trying to articulate
stone and water,
trees and stars,
naming god in images
that taste of gall and honey.

—DON MACLENNAN (2007)

CONTENTS

ILLUSTRATIONS AND MUSICAL EXAMPLES

FIGURES

MUSICAL EXAMPLES

ACKNOWLEDGMENTS

This book belongs to many hands and many voices. It emerged in the aftermath of a dissertation, the study of a single year—1829—which took me three times as long to complete. No doubt the roots of my interest in performance extend back to my pianistic training in Johannesburg and a life-changing encounter with Pauline Nossel and especially Malcolm Nay, who invested in me and taught me how to work.

Roger Parker set my life as a scholar on its path. He has been an unfailing source of support and is the imagined reader behind much of this text. I thank him for teaching me to write, the opportunities he offered me, and those useful references to the neutering bite of wild boars and human-skin lampshades.

My friend Nicholas Mathew is the world's best interlocutor. His companionship during my time at the University of California at Berkeley has been precious. Mary Ann Smart's generosity of spirit knows no bounds. She read every word of this text several times over and made annotations I have singularly failed to do justice to. I cannot thank her enough for Saturday morning breakfasts, chats in Willard Park, and babysitting.

My colleagues in Morrison Hall all deserve mention. Richard Taruskin's lingering presence in Room 128 has been an inspiration. I am grateful to Jocelyne Guilbault and Steve Feld, Deirdre Loughridge (who helped kick-start the introduction), and particularly Kate van Orden, for red velvet cake. John Kapusta was a brilliant summer research assistant for chapter 5 who focused my interests on voice. Sean Curran was similarly helpful for chapter 4 and assisted on the introduction. I have incurred debts too numerous to mention from others who have taken graduate classes with me, including "Historicism," "Material Romanticism," "Deep Listening," and "Political Anatomies of Voice": Laura Protano-Biggs, Ulrike

Petersen, Adeline Mueller, Robbie Beahrs, Rachana Vajjhala, Leon Chisholm, Tiffany Ng, Emily Frey, Jess Herdman, Tony Lin, and Nell Cloutier. No doubt I am leaving many out. All have my thanks.

Benjamin Walton was a not-so-anonymous reader for University of California Press. His suggestions altered the order of chapters and transformed the argument of the book. I owe to Ellen Lockhart countless bowls of gumbo for her full edit of the manuscript and razor-sharp remarks. Martha Feldman kindly shared her expert thoughts on chapter 5. Mary Francis, Kim Hogeland, Dore Brown, and Sharron Wood shepherded the project through its final stages and put up with my procrastination. An earlier version of chapter 1 appeared as "'Veluti in Speculum': The Twilight of the Castrato," *Cambridge Opera Journal* 17/3 (2005), 271–301. Chapter 2 appeared under Annette Richard's editorship as "Reflecting on Reflex, or, Another Touching New Fact about Chopin," *Keyboard Perspectives* 2 (2009), 55–82.

Of the institutions that furnished assistance, I owe thanks to Gonville and Caius College and its Fellows, who sustained me through my dissertation and awarded a generous research position. Caius laid on a lively intellectual community, an excellent library, an introduction to rowing, functioning computers, palatial accommodations, and crèmes brûlées. Over the years I have received support from the Association of Commonwealth Universities and British Council, the Hellman Fund, the Institute of International Studies, Faculty Research Grants, and the Townsend Center for the Humanities.

John Shepard and the staff of the Jean Gray Hargrove Music Library, as well as the Bancroft Library in Berkeley, deserve credit. Endless trips to Rare Books, Microfilms, Periodicals, Interlibrary Loans, South Front Six, the Anderson Room, and the Pendlebury Library made me a regular for many years at the University of Cambridge Library. In addition I should also thank the old Theatre Museum (National Museum of the Performing Arts) in Covent Garden, the print room of the Victoria and Albert Museum, the British Library, the Bodleian Library, the Public Records Office in Kew, British Library Newspapers at Colindale, Guildhall Library, the City of Westminster Archives, and Senate House Library, University of London. In Paris, I am grateful to the Département de la musique de la Bibliothèque nationale de France, the Bibliothèque-musée de l'Opéra, and Estelle Lambert at the Bibliothèque interuniversitaire de santé. Back in Africa, I wrote the final words of this book on the third floor of the Rhodes Library, at a desk overlooking the streets of Grahamstown, the blinding Eastern Cape heat rising off the shacks of Joza and Makana's Kop. I do not know their names, but I am grateful to the librarians who smiled and let me be.

Closer to home (or should I say on the other side of the world) are my parents. Ma loved me and took me to piano lessons. Dad let me follow my heart. My three brothers, though now far apart, are somehow always with me. Closest is my family. If anyone bore the brunt of these labors it was Sheila, who put up with my nonsense, moved to California, fed me, focused my prose (where possible), and looked after me in my darkest moments. She has been a fiercely loyal and constant source of strength. Our real achievements of the past decade have been Thea and Benedict, who will forever set this book in the light of eternity.

For errors, carelessness, excesses, overelaborations, and omissions, all of the above have amnesty. I alone am to blame.

Introduction

THE SHATTERING OF INSTRUMENTS

In an article for the *Revue de Paris,* the critic Castil-Blaze told the story of how Giovanni Battista Rubini acquired his gift for unmediated expression. The incident occurred in 1831, as the singer forced the sustained B♭ toward the end of "Luna, conforto al cor de' naviganti," the then-famous romance from Giovanni Pacini's opera *Il talismano* (1829). His larynx refusing him, Rubini—egged on by the baying Milanese public—exerted every sinew to overcome the obstacle. He launched a note, the éclat of which had never before been heard at the Teatro alla Scala. Not that its magic came without a price. Rubini felt a break, an inner rupture that would transform his talent forever. A doctor was called as the tenor reeled backstage. It appeared, upon examination, that the singer had broken his clavicle. Healing would take several months, a period far too long for a singer of Rubini's commitments. Accordingly, the tenor asked whether he might just live with the impediment, since brokenness appeared less to have stifled his abilities than unlocked new vocal qualities. To this the doctor admitted that he might, if the injury was not onerous for him. Still backstage, Castil-Blaze—ever the doubting Thomas—touched Rubini's wound for himself, or so he claimed. The critic thus verified a distance of four to five *lignes* (about two-fifths of an inch) between the two parts of fractured collarbone. This was Rubini's fate. He apparently sang thus until the end of his career, creating, in this shattered condition, Elvino in Vincenzo Bellini's *La sonnambula* (Milan, 1831), Arturo in *I puritani* (Paris, 1835), and Fernando in Gaetano Donizetti's *Marino Faliero* (Paris, 1835).[1]

In the same year—1831—similar cautionary tales were told in relation to the most celebrated musical hands of the era, those belonging to Niccolò Paganini. Due to his

1

"laryngeal affection," Paganini would increasingly rely on his illegitimate son and amanuensis Achille to communicate verbally on his behalf. (The violinist's cancerous throat would be the death of him by decade's end.) Since he had no actual voice, the Genovese devil cultivated a figurative voice and a purer order of expression. When one heard Paganini, one did not hear instruments, his Guarnerius violin, or hands. One heard difference. And an erupting body. His singular genius was the result of an abnormal physiology, at least according to the violinist's longtime friend, personal physician, and singer-scientist Francesco Bennati (a figure of importance in the chapters that follow). In May 1831 Bennati challenged the myth that the fingers on Paganini's famous left hand were longer than those of the right. Instead, the doctor noted the elasticity of the ligaments joining wrist to forearm, carpus to metacarpals. He marveled at the way in which the hand's span doubled by some dark magic, fingers bending back laterally with rapidity and violence.[2] For Jules Janin, writing days after the violinist's Parisian debut, this was a hand "splitting itself in two" as it broke between positions. Its savage "dislocations," as Louis-François Lhéritier put it, were born of a youth of tireless instrumental practice.[3] Bennati rejoined that Paganini's hypermateriality was both congenital and acquired: his unique "temperament of being" was the effect of ravaging bouts of measles and scarlet fever as a child. This was why, Bennati reasoned, Paganini's music was so thick with presence; why his sound carried such a fleshy signature; why his skin was alive with sensibility and his expressions charged with "voice." "In his manner of playing, there are no strings, no bow," Lhéritier agreed, "his violin is simply the complement of the great musician, of the man of genius." In short, the critic concluded, "His whole organism merges with his instrument." With broken hands on a crippled violin (a famous in-concert stunt involved breaking strings such that whole pieces had to be played on the low G string alone); Paganini was made the archangel of that quintessentially shattered or damaged nineteenth-century type, "the performer."[4]

. . .

My object of study in this book is twofold: the voices of virtuoso singers and the hands of virtuoso pianists, and, more particularly, configurations of hand and voice in London and Paris circa 1830. This purview honors now well-writ changes in the orientation of historical musicology, its focus being music, not written and read but performed and heard. Its concern for performers and performances rather than composers and great works follows the exemplary writings of Elisabeth Le Guin and Carolyn Abbate.[5] But I want to go one step further and ask what it would mean, not to define voices and hands as mere instruments for music, but to turn the tables: to define "music" instead as an instrument for the induction, even acquisition, of hands and voices. I want to assume an avowedly *realist* stance and ask how bodies are acquired as they are heard, trained, and performed. How does music act in the cultivation of bodies?

The words of Castil-Blaze and Bennati remind us that not everyone was convinced by Rubini's and Paganini's first truly "shattering" performances. The temptation might be to interpret the furious breaking-out of these artists—perhaps the origins of romantic performance?—as a watershed for music, as the birth of "modern piano technique" or "modern vocal practice." How else, after all, to interpret these iconoclastic moments in which great performers tore at mechanism and wrenched it asunder? How else to understand these rifts where mere technique no longer mattered? Where performers were at last freed to truly release? There is surely no more quintessentially historic moment than this, when romantic rebels threw off convention, took contrivance to task, broke their bodies, and let music speak for itself.

Or did they? Castil-Blaze's and Bennati's curious expositions on creative freedom imply that "natural voice" emerges only by force of fatal accident. In the case of Rubini, full eruption was nothing if not violent. (Early nineteenth-century performers, as shall be seen, generally operated outside the assumption that vocal sound automatically externalized character or personality.) The dislocation of hands and breaking of collarbones—so they suggested—was unfortunate, involving techniques as theatrical as any other. What is more, something valuable was lost in the process of exteriorization, precious truths shattered by the specious occlusion of "mechanism." Worse, this at once impressive and brutal manner was contrived in a Faustian bargain, that is, acquired at unreasonable cost. The new manner, they insisted, was unnatural.

THE "SONG OF THE NATURAL BODY"

One prominent champion of "shattering performance" (who had long since forgotten its price) was Roland Barthes, a figure that looms large in any study of nineteenth-century performance. In his classic "The Romantic Song" of 1976, the French essayist exalted the "dark voice" of the opening *andante un poco mosso* in Franz Schubert's Piano Trio in B♭ Major (D.898):

> No excessive notes, no high C, no overflow or outburst into sharps or flats, no shrieks, no physiological prowess. The tessitura is the modest space of the sounds each of us can produce and within the limits of which he can fantasize the reassuring unity of his body. All romantic music, whether vocal or instrumental, utters this song of the natural body: it is a music which has a meaning only if I can always sing it, in myself, with my body: a vital condition which is denatured by so many modern interpretations, too fast or too personal, through which, under cover of *rubato,* the interpreter's body abusively substitutes itself for mine and robs it *(rubare)* of its breathing, its emotion. For *to sing,* in the romantic sense, is this: fantasmatically to enjoy my unified body.[6]

For Barthes, there was nothing more natural than the unifying power of this fantasmatic melody, and this singing that was "better" or at least "sang more" than any individual human voice. "Listening to it I sing the lied with myself," Barthes wrote, "for myself." To listen to this music was to surrender to living desire and to one's "interior body" welling up from within. Schubert's terrifying melody abolished not physical voice but *voices;* its elemental force annihilated such socially contingent classifications as "soprano," "bass," "mezzo," and "tenor." What does it matter who is singing? He wrote that this "natural song" was only incarnated in a historical sense after the disappearance from musical Europe of the castrato, that counterfeit creature vanquished by "a complex human subject whose imaginary castration will be interiorized." "What, then, is this body that sings the lied? What is it, that in my body, sings the lied to me listening?" Most of all, for Barthes, this subterranean sound occurred within: "It would seem that the human voice is here all the more present in that it has delegated itself to other instruments." Its sinister chaos obliterated instrumentality: "Something raises my body, swells it, stretches it," and as the voice of the body reaches full expression, "beats it to the verge of explosion."[7]

Barthes's writings on vocal materiality and expressive presence have been axiomatic for the best and most progressive writing on musical experience since at least the 1990s. His words continue to affect those insisting (quite rightly) upon the bodiliness of music, as well as those insisting (less rightly) on the body's claims to natural subjectivity. His "song of the natural body," in other words, still resonates powerfully in academic circles, embroiled though it has recently become in the most pernicious identity politics. Feminist philosopher Adriana Cavarero, for example, opens her *For More Than One Voice: Toward a Philosophy of Vocal Expression* (2005) by quoting from Italo Calvino's short story "A King Listens": "A voice means this: there is a living person, throat, chest, feelings, who send into the air the voice, different from all other voices." In a fabulous book on divas, Wayne Koestenbaum, not without irony, writes of the cultivated operatic voice as "the furious 'I-affirming' blast of a body that refuses dilution or compromise." More recently, Clemens Risi has quoted Barthes in less self-conscious ways in his clarion call for a phenomenological kind of opera studies, one that surrenders to sensuousness and a "physical concept of voice." "Singing is a physical process," Risi trumpets, "an extension of bodily characteristics into space and an expression of these characteristics."[8]

I am, of course, drawing upon disparate elements in the nascent field of voice studies to make my point, but it seems useful to register how Barthes has been (mis)read and how naturalized his conception of "pure voice" has become. His standard assumption about how expression works is now two a penny when it comes to both scholarly and vernacular conceptions of musical voice. One could cite many examples of the latter by quoting the everyday pronouncements of conservatory vocal coaches and piano teachers. In popular literature, a remarkable case in point is Renée Fleming's biography of her own voice aptly entitled *The*

Inner Voice: The Making of a Singer (2004). For Fleming, one disciplines the self in order to achieve a kind of "universal appreciation that transcends taste." In the introduction to her book she reports being asked to sing "Amazing Grace" at a ceremony at Ground Zero only months after the attacks of 11 September 2001. On the question of why a better-known pop singer was overlooked, Fleming explains, "A trained voice has a kind of innate authority that transmits a sense of strength. We can be heard without a microphone. We sing with the entire body. The sounds that we make emanate not just from the head, but from the whole heart and soul and, most important, the gut."[9] One cultivates one's voice, in other words, in order to apprehend its supernature. That is why "the classical voice" is supposedly so absolute: because it works toward Truth, whereas "popular" voices presumably do not. One (s)trains for a full-bodied sound in order that the emancipated physical body sings rather than the singer.

But do voices necessarily express some hidden somatic presence? Do they really externalize inner personality? Is there only one natural way for bodies to burst forth? One purely biological way for music to reveal itself in unvarnished glory? I wonder whether the question of "how the body works" or "how your particular body type works" is so self-explanatory. Are bodies *just there,* awaiting expressive release? It seems to me that scholars and practitioners have grown too used to equating any kind of individual utterance with a bid for power, or a cry for political representation. The time has come, I think, to question the authority of the primordial song, and to query the claim that there is a biologically objective way to free a voice or master a musical instrument. The conceit of vocal or instrumental freedom, even in the case of such legends as Rubini and Paganini, might prove to be just that—a conceit—so much as the idea of a music shorn of instrumental and stylistic circumstance is. In the end, it may prove invigorating to discover that one can never "crack" technique.

In the chapters that follow I describe the material worlds of 1820s and 1830s performance in high resolution, describing competing styles of vocal and pianistic presentation, standards of training, and notions of health. In addition to investigating how musicians were seen, I also address the ways in which musicians themselves saw their own hands and voices: how they configured them socially, how they related to them, what they felt about them. I do so in ways that betray my effort to write intimate histories, even as I parade the most virtuosic displays of this priesthood of celebrity singers and pianists. The hands and voices of enchanter-performers such as Maria Malibran, Adolphe Nourrit, Sigismund Thalberg, and Frédéric Chopin were more than private property, which is why I pay close attention in these pages to firsthand descriptions of public performances, in addition to the contents of medical treatises, letters and diaries, newspaper and journal reviews, vocal and piano tutors, anatomical atlases, musical scores, and scientific writing. I draw upon these sources in order to evaluate the claims made for the expressive power of myriad "romantic anatomies": the special qualities found in them, the principles beholden to them, the knowledge formed in them, and the solidarities or political antagonisms acquired in relation to them.

My point is that the voices and hands of performers require placement—one has to place one's voice in the body as much as one places piano-playing hands. Materiality itself must be conjured, not only by performer-virtuosos themselves but also by those circles of opinion external to them; bodies themselves must be made sense of in environments of intense social debate. This is to say that the issue of who controls voices and hands is less than self-evident. The claims made upon what hands and voices do might be personal, civic, pedagogical, commercial, aesthetic, educational, and political. In the case of the milieu of Paganini and Rubini, the claimants jostling for control were increasingly medical and biological, as exemplified by the critical cachet of doctors such as Bennati and the attention paid to the physiology of "the species body" in midcentury vocal and piano tutors. Take, for example, Domenico Crivelli's L'arte del canto (London, 1841), published in parallel Italian and English translation, or Félix d'Urclé's Méthode raisonnée du mécanisme de la main (Paris, 1846), of which more in chapter 4. These manuals featured anatomical images of vocal organs and hands, images betraying the burgeoning medical authority given to musical truth. "Here is your body!" these pictures seemed to shout. "Release it!"

MATERIAL ROMANTICISM

The "romantic" of my title, Romantic Anatomies of Performance, belies that word's traditional musicological association with otherworldliness, unconscious fantasy, and ecstatic dematerialization. New work by (for example) Emily Dolan, Benjamin Steege, Deirdre Loughridge, David Trippett, and historian of science Lorraine Daston suggests that the "romantics," whatever their own denials, were also arch-materialists, heavily invested in science, objectivity, and technology.[10] "Performance" needs qualification too, since it suggests the opposite of dematerialization: incarnation. I do not think that bodies or voices are performed. They are acquired, theatrical, and real. And it takes effort to make them work for the norm, or to cultivate them according to regulatory ideals. Anyone who has trained in music knows that one cannot simply stage the self in the moment, or even easily reiterate that posture repeatedly until—one day—the sideshow sticks.[11] It takes time to achieve any state of grace.

The word "performance" has—unfortunately—accrued pejorative meanings, meanings that suggest one has a body that one activates as if to iterate a fiction, where really that body is—at every point—just as mediated as real. "When we study conceptions of the body," historian of medicine Shigehisa Kuriyama argues, "we are examining constructions not just in the mind, but also in the senses."[12] Kuriyama implies that the expressive competence required for music making requires a corporeality that is both artful and actual, shaped from the outside in as well as the inside out. To be marked as exemplary, bodies require habituation to the most painstaking forms of musical conduct, to "health," passion, and control. This is why they are at once so real and so elusive. All physical truths require cultivation, even the most unlikely ones. They do not exist by themselves.

For just as there is no such thing as unmediated embodiment, there is likewise no such thing as ecstatic musical disembodiment. The most imaginative musicological scholarship on operatic and instrumental performance in the eighteenth and nineteenth centuries still tends to frame musical performance in terms of these enraptured binaries: as a battle between the forces of matter and spirit, text and improvisation, technique and expression, subject and object, act and text, performer and work, phenomenal and noumenal, voice and silence, presence and erasure, materiality and transcendence. Elisabeth Le Guin's call for a "carnal musicology" and Carolyn Abbate's construal of voice have been rightly influential in this regard.

My definition of voice, however, renovates Abbate's conception somewhat. In my unromantic view, voice does not stand for agency, as "sheer sound . . . that may be perceived as modes of subjects' enunciations," or as the metaphoric "voice of freedom."[13] Instead I define voice neutrally, as vibrating air, but vibrating air that is recognized as particular political and physical articulations of body. The material force of voice is no less explicit than in Abbate's model, though this physicality— far from self-evident—is socially and ideologically contingent. Like Abbate, I am interested in the ways in which sounds, by virtue of their being recognized as voices, necessarily furnish knowledge of a body. I would only add that this body is no primordial essence because it offers up a whole panoply of potential expressive truths, all of them available to assiduous cultivation, placement, and discrimination.

As such, the following chapters do not restore the voices of nineteenth-century performers, "unsung" or not (though they certainly recover their "vocal anthropologies").[14] I make no attempt to rescue the materiality of the performer or return bodies to reality. Neither will I be exposing the truth behind long-held fantasies of "Western disembodiment," or giving voice to the voiceless. Nor will I claim to be healing the scourge of mind-body dualism, or setting our souls to right, by my new drastic or carnal methodology.[15] Equally, it has not seemed useful to oppose the vagaries of romantic fiction with the hard evidence of modern fact, in ways pertinent to the careful research of Susan Rutherford and Dana Gooley, two fellow scholars pursuing nineteenth-century singers and pianists.[16]

One of the difficulties in dealing with romantic musicians involves the skein of anecdotes and half-truths that available sources present to inquiry. The lies run deep in the case of women virtuosos, who seldom find representation in the archive other than as male fantasies. A well-worn tactic available to social history in particular has been demythologization; historians have pushed hard to find evidence of individual hardship rather than effortless glory. Their strategy has involved the backbreaking work of debunking propaganda, unmasking the facts behind the glittering veils of performance, and exposing the grim truths of practice, travel, failure, and everyday life. Yet the problem with recovering "lost voices" from the distant past is that these working artists were in business not merely *in spite of* but *because of* nineteenth-century legends of virtuosic triumph. When it comes to "genius," fact and fiction were necessarily confused, as both Rutherford and Gooley will attest, to the extent that it seldom proves possible to separate the quotidian from the spectacular, the embattled entrepreneur from the erotic fantasy.[17] I have resisted the urge to "let voices be heard again" or to recover the suffering body from beneath the ideology (as if such a thing were possible). Instead of the standard coming-of-age story where fiction is opposed with fact, or where disembodiment is countered with embodiment, I have chosen a story about embodiment and reembodiment, one where historical agents are seen to achieve more than merely constraint or freedom.

BETWEEN THINGS

This study confounds the cultural history of hands and voices and addresses middle zones. First, alternate chapters switch between the worlds of virtuoso singing and those of virtuoso piano playing, less in the spirit of *interdisciplinary* than old-fashioned *indisciplined* inquiry.[18] The voice-hands juxtaposition works less to separate out than to move against traditional distinctions between vocal and instrumental music. The book thus navigates between opera and "music" studies, between invisible (voice) and visible (hands), mostly in order to stress how concerns of "voice" mattered to both.

In addition to drawing connections between singers and pianists, I have located this study on the lucrative London-Paris musical circuit rather than fixing it according to some falsely stable notion of geographical "context." I have waded into the English Channel (La Manche, if you are French) in order to act against purely nationalistic models of musicological explanation. The straits between Calais and Dover were well enough traversed, to be sure, in ways that eased the flow of sheet music, instruments, debates about music, performance styles, and musicians. The briefest glance at diplomatic wrangles over performers, the commercial operations of cross-border music publishing, or such multinational enterprises as the piano-manufacturing industry loosens disciplinary moorings further. The idea of "context" or "the social" has proved an immovable object in scholarly vocabulary, being used to refer to a kind of scenic frame against which historical events are taken to be acted out. Following Bruno Latour, I take "the social" in the earliest sense of the term, referring less to some permanent biological or national background than to the humble bonds of "association." Any association, Latour points out, may form in the name of shared interests across ethnic, language, or geographical barriers and may overlap with multiple other assemblages.[19]

This said, the networks of pianists and singers trafficking between Paris and London addressed themselves to a diverse range of local associations. These iterant musicians—Spanish, Austrian, Italian, Polish, Prussian, Hungarian, Swiss—encountered two very different constellations of audiences. The King's Theatre in London, for example, was an entirely different institution from the Théâtre Italien in Paris. Yes, these two elite venues for Italian opera both received financial backing from the same *directeur-entrepreneur* (Émile Laurent) in the 1829 season and shared its resources. And, yes, the musical seasons of each city were often interlinked. By the mid-1830s, for example, Jean-Pierre Laporte, Laurent's former frontman in London and manager of the King's Theatre, secured the availability of the season's best singers by delaying his opening night to February and then to March, a measure taken in order to dovetail with the end of the fashionable winter season at the Opéra, the premier venue for the burgeoning field of French-language opera in Paris.[20] But the social and aesthetic politics of each setting—the Opéra, King's Theatre, and Théâtre Italien—though symbiotic, remain barely comparable. The meanings ascribed to music could diverge considerably, as evidenced, for example, by the contrasting fate of such a singer as Rubini, who was less the subject of controversy in Paris than in London.[21] More intimate venues such as Hanover Square, the King's Theatre Concert Room, the Parisian salon of exiled Milanese princess Cristina Belgioioso, or the hall of the Conservatoire—as one might expect—flaunted even more specific characteristics, characteristics that are not so easily generalized or conflated.

In chapter 1 I describe the "romantic anatomy" of Giovanni Velluti, a favorite of Stendhal and Rossini (who had written *Aureliano in Palmira* for him in 1813). The castrato appeared on the main stage of the King's Theatre, a venue that held the legal monopoly on Italian opera in London. (The building was the centerpiece of John Nash's grand scheme of Metropolitan Improvements; between 1816 and 1818 Nash oversaw the widening of Pall Mall, extended Charles Street into the Haymarket, opened the Royal Opera Arcade along the west side of the theater, and erected imposing façades and colonnades along three fronts in Palladian style.) Velluti's hostile reception in the radical press provides a useful starting point for the argument. Serious male reviewers in particular condemned his "vile" vocal manner in phantasmic or nightmarish language. I select several overlapping critical frameworks—histories of psychology, vocal physiology, listening practices among sections of the nobility, shifting stylistic expectations, and debates over conceptualizations of voice—in order to explain why the castrato was forced from the operatic stage. Having made links between castration and emerging ideas of "the subconscious," I review the contemporaneous scientific work of James Rennie, Charles

Bell, and William Lawrence. The latter two scientists in particular were at the forefront of reformulating vocal knowledge and authorizing a highly gendered conception of vocal function in ways that imperiled the category of the Italian castrato. In their hard-nosed account, vocal sound served genetic law, biological process, and stricter sex binaries. A survey of the castrato's affected vocal manner-isms as the hero of Morlacchi's *Tebaldo e Isolina* and his reception from 1825 to 1829 makes emerging codes of nineteenth-century physiological realism plain. Velluti suffered a historical fate that throws "modern" assumptions about natural vocality into powerful relief.

The second chapter proceeds from the 1837 doctoral dissertation of Chopin's best friend and flatmate in Paris, Jan Matuszyński. I discuss the relationship between the medical student's view of the "sympathetic system" and the musician's assumptions about keyboard technique and touch. Matuszyński's observations about autonomic action, motor memory, and reflex action made important contri-butions to Parisian debates. The chapter outlines historical conceptions of the sympathetic nerve and examines Matuszyński's ideological and institutional affili-ations. (He moved between his life with Chopin on the boulevard des Italians and the Left Bank—including the world of the Faculté de médecine and the bohemian student district to the east of the exclusive Faubourg St-Germain.) I focus upon the musician's idiosyncratic approach to pianistic touch and bring the work of both Matuszyński and Johann Nepomuk Hummel into focus; each was closely engaged with the question of how bodies learn to "play by themselves." An analysis of the Étude op. 25, no. 3 pulls the strands of inquiry together, applying period models of pianistic functioning to an affective comportment assiduously cultivated by inti-mates of Chopin's elite Parisian circle.

The category of the diva, now a familiar stereotype in the musical firmament, did not descend to earth in full-fledged glory. Rather, as chapter 3 shows, her entry was uncertain. The twinned voices of the legendary Spanish-French soprano Maria Malibran and her Prussian rival Henriette Sontag sparked a popular craze for two-soprano duets in the 1829 London-Paris season. The virtuosic two-soprano idiom that they perfected, in other words, was associated with the identification of the diva in ways that had little to do with the codes of diva conduct later so firmly bound to the stereotype: narcissism or selfish individuality.[22] In London the pair performed at the Argyll Rooms, a building remodeled and opened in 1820 as part of Nash's improvements.[23] These Sontag-Malibran performances were remarkable for the way in which women from the audience, dressed in florid fashions, were invited to sit among male orchestral players. The language chosen by early critics to describe the singers was remarkable for its use of organic and commercial met-aphors. On the one hand, reviewers were drawn to images of flowers or perhaps mated birds in flight. On the other were references to the commerce and con-sumption of Regent Street, as in the singers' jewel-like ornaments or the polish of their doll-like performances. By the mid-1830s, the Sontag-Malibran idiom had grown sinister, as conservative critics in particular attacked the sensuous immorality of the sound of "the diva."

Chapter 4 describes a concert at which audience members clustered around Sigismund Thalberg's piano in order to gawk at his beautiful hands. (His famous three-hand technique was on display at the Hanover Square Concert Rooms, the elegant late eighteenth-century assembly rooms off Regent Street that had once hosted J. C. Bach, Haydn, and Hummel.) The chapter suggests that changes in listening practice—the "transformation in behavior" so frequently vaunted of increasingly silent audiences in this period—initially had less to do with attentive listening than attentive looking.[24] These pages trace the strands of Frédéric Kalkbrenner's pianistic legacy through the careers of two of his pupils, Thalberg and Marie Moke Pleyel. The most celebrated pianist of the late 1820s, Kalkbrenner was important as much for his music as for his exemplary hands, their form being an index of his character and his eloquence in improvisation. Kalkbrenner's popularization (in tandem with Johann Bernhard Logier and his business partner Ignace Joseph Pleyel in France) of such orthopedic devices as his so-called Hand-Guide—a wooden rail placed over the keyboard to "correct" pianistic deportment—served his purposes admirably. The chapter aligns emerging notions of "pianism" with the popularization of orthopedic medicine in 1830s London and Paris in the name of middlebrow "correction." (Significantly, Berlioz, Moke Pleyel, and Chopin began their Parisian teaching careers at so-called orthopedic institutes around 1830.) Thalberg endorsed his own orthopedic device in the 1840s at a time when he was turning from virtuosic improvisation to a career as a "serious" classical musician.

The penultimate chapter clarifies the book's position on indistinct gender differentiations between male and female voices in this period. First, I isolate the bari-tenor, so named by Bennati and perfected, apparently, by Bergamasque *tenor serio* Domenico Donzelli (creator of, among other roles, Bellini's Pollione in *Norma*). Second, I describe the rival *voix mixte*. According to Bennati this "mixed voice" was nonexistent, though it was famously used by French patriot and tenor Adolphe Nourrit, creator of Néocles in Rossini's *Le Siège de Corinthe* (1826), Aménophis in the revised version of *Moïse et Pharaon* (1827), the title role in *Le comte Ory* (1828), and Arnold in *Guillaume Tell* (1829). Nourrit was the leading light of the Salle Le Peletier, a venue opened in 1821 for the Paris Opéra after the fatal stabbing of King Louis XVIII's nephew on the steps of its former home. Nourrit was also the first Masaniello in Auber's *La Muette de Portici* (1828), Robert in Meyerbeer's *Robert le Diable*, Eleazar in Halévy's *La Juive* (1835), and Raoul in Meyerbeer's *Les Huguenots* (1836). I compare the vocal anthropologies of the baritenor and *voix mixte*, both voices construed here as political cultivations and useful analytical means by which to explore social worlds. The chapter goes in search of voice and finds a plethora of fully objective ways to find bodies in voice, and no single truth—a menagerie of materialities for a menagerie of voices. Nourrit's *voix mixte* in particular became a focal point for the cultivation of a specifically male and conservative sense of body. His performance of the trio in act 2 of *Guillaume Tell* in particular became a rallying cry, particularly in view of the contrasting style of Gilbert-Louis Duprez in this same passage.

Chapter 6 reconstructs Liszt's shifting experience of his hands. "Franz Liszt, Metapianism, and the Cultural History of the Hand" begins by describing Liszt's method of playing octaves with "dead" or "dissociated" hands. Later I examine the many anecdotes that describe Liszt as playing as if in defiance of materiality, as if with dislocated fingers, lame or cut fingers, or only three fingers on each hand. These stories point to a "sacralization" of keyboard-playing hands. Newly fraught ways of relating to manual action betray cultural anxieties about the physiological life of these ever more powerful creative agents. Liszt's influential pedagogical methods, developed in the early 1830s, relied on fingerings and hand positions chosen not on the basis of five-digit realities, the vagaries of particular pianos, or any other visible contingency. Rather, the virtuoso set his sights on deep cognitive functions, privileging both the external purpose of the musical work and the physiological personality of each student. Liszt sought out music-religious experiences. He began to think in transformational ways, working beyond instruments, scores, and even his own fingers.

To say that this final chapter contradicts the findings of previous ones would be to artificially oppose the worlds of materiality and ideas, something I am keen to avoid. Rather, these closing pages reinforce my observation that piano-playing hands had become so musically eruptive by the 1830s as to require zealous ideational control. The myth (which Liszt himself promulgated) of his own transfigured approach to the keyboard around 1832 was a response to the manual intractabilities that he found materializing before his very eyes. His compositional avant-gardism, disdain of method, lack of "fixed position," and hyperbolic performing manner at the piano were conditioned by his own search for a "purer" corporeal state. As much as Rubini or Paganini, in other words, Liszt was condemned to work out his own tragically beautiful ideology in the flesh and blood of everyday life.

"Veluti in Speculum"

The Twilight of the Castrato

"BENEATH MY WINDOW"

On the night of 15 May 1829, Felix Mendelssohn had a nightmare about Giovanni Battista Velluti, the last great operatic castrato. Velluti's voice had been in the German's head since that afternoon, when they crossed paths at a concert at the Argyll Rooms on Regent Street in London. There he had heard the "poor wretched creature," as he called him, sing an aria by Bonfichi and a duet with Henriette Sontag, Mayr's "Deh! Per pietà" from *Ginevra di Scozia*. The singing of the "confounded" Italian "so excited my loathing," Mendelssohn remembered, "that it pursued me into my dreams that night."[1] Three days later the young composer-performer was at his desk at 103 Great Portland Street writing to a friend. Outside he again spied the castrato going about his chores. "Velluti," he wrote, "is just passing beneath my window." His simple observation seemed to pinpoint the cultural position of a singing species that would not go away.[2]

This was the fate of the castrato: he haunted cosmopolitan European culture, lurking just below its "window." When the critic for the *New Monthly Magazine* heard Velluti's London debut as Armando in Meyerbeer's *Il crociato in Egitto* and his opening accompanied recitative, "Popoli dell'Egitto," in 1825, he wrote that they "came upon the ear like the spectral moan of an unearthly being."[3] The critic's language, as we shall see, was fired by a press dispute instigated by the *Times* in relation to this performance. A year later, the *New Monthly Magazine* rejoined that Velluti's Armando "had to us something unearthly in it." "On seeing the thin, tall form tread the stage in armour, we felt a sensation which we cannot describe," the writer mused. "It seemed as if we saw a spirit glide before us."[4] The male soprano, for this critic, was a "twilight figure," encountered as if one were inhabiting a dream. It was little consolation that Meyerbeer had composed Armando for and in collaboration with Velluti.

In Paris, Honoré de Balzac constructed the hallucinatory world of *Sarrasine* (1830) around the specter of the castrato's presence. The novella was probably written with Velluti in mind, the singer having visited Paris in April 1825 on his way to London.[5] "I was deep in one of those daydreams," the now-famous story opens, "which overtake even the shallowest of men." By way of explaining the strange wealth of the De Lanty family and the "fragile machine" who lives in their midst, Balzac's narrator tells the tale of a castrato and a young sculptor named Sarrasine. While in Rome, the Frenchman falls madly in love with the singer, believing him a woman. Sarrasine's error is revealed too late, only after he has desired too much. The story ends when Cardinal Cicognara, the castrato's patron, has the dangerously unstable sculptor murdered in order to protect his prize singer. As events unfold, it becomes clear that the source of the De Lanty's wealth is the shadowy half man who now lives in their mansion. The "real" backdrop for this story of extravagance, deception, and death—told in terms of reminiscence and metaphor—rests on his unsettling provision.[6]

The generation of Balzac and Mendelssohn, in other words, imbued the figure of the castrato with its phantasmic charge.[7] Donning my psychoanalytic cap, I might claim that this generation pressed the whole notion of castration into its psychological or culturally repressed sphere. This would be the argument of Mladen Dolar's *A Voice and Nothing More* (2006), which—in well-rehearsed Freudian style—links our "fascination" for vocal sound to castration. (Dolar defends psychoanalytical notions of "the object voice" by describing it not in the Derridean sense as productive of fantasies of self-presence, but as always already differentiated—as proof of subjective lack.)[8] Beguiled by this uncanny sense of voice, I could argue that castration anxiety emerged as *the* founding moment of adult sociability and subjectivity at the time of Mendelssohn's dream.[9] (The word "subconscious" in the English language, after all, was apparently first used by essayist Thomas De Quincey as late as 1823.) Such a position might seek out early articulations of the phallus as causative principle not only for gender differentiation but for the whole possibility of intersubjective desire. Mendelssohn's eerie encounters with Velluti thus might be taken to foreground the birth of Dolar's castration complex and the historical experience of castration as social death. Via his voice, psychoanalysis might say, castration emerged as the ghost haunting the symbolic order of "modern" culture.

Let me put this in less overwrought ways. How best to explain why the castrato became anathema? Why did Mendelssohn have this dream? Why was it at these specific moments that the castrato became not only unpopular but impossible? As Martha Feldman, Suzanne Aspden, John Rosselli, and many others have shown, unease over the castrato (as a symbol of luxury, effeminacy, popery, and artifice) was as old as the castrato himself.[10] These singers suffered constant vilification for different reasons at different times by different communities and commentators. Velluti, moreover, achieved his fair share of praise in the 1820s, even from such reform-minded critics as Richard Mackenzie Bacon, who lauded his chaste delicacy. In 1827 the *Atlas* reported that demand for them had actually redoubled in Rome recently under the tutelage of maestro Sogatelli.[11] Male soprani were feted even beyond the nineteenth century, as the career of long-standing Sistine Chapel castrato Alessandro Moreschi proves. On the one hand, attacks on Velluti continued a long and often xenophobic tradition. On the other, a clear fault line opened up for an increasingly authoritative (and authoritarian) coterie of opinion formers in 1820s London, the castrato becoming unnerving enough to provoke apprehensions of nonbeing.

In what follows I first propose a series of theoretical frameworks to explain this historical slippage, exploring the abjection of not only Velluti's vocal sounds, but also those of the female contralto musico. The insights reached are then tested against the reception of Velluti's performances in Regency London. His public appearance provoked trenchant reactions, reactions of such pleasure and disgust as to throw theoretical conclusions into sharp relief. Finally, I reconstruct Velluti's vocal manner via a single musical number, an aria from Francesco Morlacchi's opera *Tebaldo e Isolina,* using the rich documentation of the castrato's interpretation of that number in García *fils*'s singing treatise *Traité complet de l'art du chant* (1840–47). My analysis reads Velluti from the point of view of his harshest critics, hearing "the twilight of the castrato" both in Morlacchi's score and the singer's "otherworldly" appearance in it. Velluti's vocal manner was physical—inevitably so. Yet for his detractors, castration spelled failure, even "disembodiment." The overripe materiality of these sounds sickened.

BIOLOGY SINGS

One way to characterize the castrato's fall from grace would be to survey developments in vocal science, as Gregory Bloch has done.[12] Velluti passed "beneath the window" when the issue of vocal placement was under urgent review. In the 1820s, studies of vocal function largely continued in traditional vein. Scientific discussion still invariably hinged on the fragile question of whether the vocal apparatus best resembled a wind, string, or reed instrument. In Paris, physician Félix Savart's widely read "Mémoire sur la voix humaine" (1825) revived ancient Galenic wind analogies by concluding that a hunting whistle proved the best resemblance to the vocal organ. In London, it was more usual to describe "a double mechanism," as James Rennie did in his natural philosophy of that same year. Rennie followed Balthasar-Anthelme Richerand in naming a wind-string apparatus, his identification confirming the human voice's perfection in relation to lower, inflexible instruments.[13] Charles Wheatstone described the vocal chords as a vibrating reed attended by an ever-modifying larynx, which, trombone-like, shifted the column of air by continually shortening or lengthening its tube. A still oft-cited statistic in London was John Barclay's early-century enumeration early in the century of all possible movements of the organ: fifteen pairs of muscles capable of upward of 1,073,841,800 combinations and, in cooperation with the seven pairs of the larynx, 17,592,186,044,415.[14] To be clear, this was an apparatus of fabulous profusion. The cultivated larynx dispensed "airs" of precision and very little essence. The equivocation of this fluctuating, variable body—deviation—is what made it human.

The wind-string-reed debate lost focus after 1830, however, as physiologists and comparative anatomists jockeyed for vocal control. (A sign of this loss in Paris was physician Pierre Gerdy's claim that no analogy did the human voice justice—thus the futility of building artificial larynxes or replicating its sounds mechanically.)[15] Liberal-minded reformers in London preferred their voices congenital. Charles Bell's "Of the Organs of the Human Voice" of 1832, for one, fixed voice as the *principium individui,* as the song of subjectivity. At once endorsing string-wind theories and wiring voice into the respiratory and nervous systems, the first professor of physiology at King's College London sourced vocal sound at the four principal nerves of throat and neck. Bell thus "unraveled" the functions of the entangled laryngeal nerves, associated voice with a "variety of offices," and multiplied to infinity the number of possible movements. The physiologist thus linked vocal sound to individual will. (This was years before the emergence of the idea that voice externalizes agency, that the voice is the signature of some fixed sexual identity, or that "having a voice" is a natural-born right, as much as the democratic right to vote.) In Bell as in Wheatstone—whose acoustic work on timbre opened the way to the later classification of so much vibrating air by sex, race, and native vocal type—the invisible worlds of the respiratory, muscular, and (later) reproductive systems were brought to the forefront of vocal research.

As early as 1832, pioneering American physiologist Robley Dunglison professed to hear age and sex in "the *timbre* or stamp" of each individual. In Paris, Marc Colombat de l'Isère (of whom more in chapter 5) echoed the work of Guillaume Dupuytren, who, early in the century, had dissected the corpse of a eunuch in order to test the variable sympathetic relation between voices and "noncontiguous" anatomical parts such as the larynx and testes. (It was only by mid-century, as we shall see, that "the sexual system" appeared, less a *sympathetic influence upon* than a *reproductive source for* voice.)[16]

Already in 1819, London-based surgeon William Lawrence heard voice as a function of the species. For him, men and women were complementary sexual beings. His bifurcated view led him to launch a stinging attack on still-prevailing Aristotelian "one-sex" models, where women were construed falsely as a "degradation and imperfect copy of the constitution of man, while, in fact, she is the most essential part of the species." In his strong "two-sex" view, all existence bore the essential chemistry of sexual difference. A result was "the increased depth and strength of the tone of voice" at a boy's coming of age, that "strength" being useful to their "natural" function as provider-protectors of the family.[17]

Lawrence thus construed male puberty, in line with his politics, as revolution, *pace* thinkers who thought of maturation as slow and fluid, as in eighteenth-century naturalist Georges de Buffon's famous view that manhood arrived only at around thirty years of age. When boys became men, for Lawrence, they moved aggressively to the masculine ideal. Woman, "in advancing towards the age of puberty, departs from her primitive constitution less sensibly than man." From this fateful moment, anatomy was destiny, sex was fixed at the organs of genera-tion, voice was established by function, hermaphrodites were freaks, and castra-tion was fatal. If "biology" (a word Lawrence helped to establish) determined the physical and moral life of the organism, there was no place for such "degraded" or "equivocal" individuals as castrati. Lawrence quoted the republican French phi-losopher Pierre Jean George Cabanis to make his point: "Eunuchs are the vilest class of the human species: cowardly and knavish because they are weak; envious and malignant, because they are unfortunate." These *lusus naturae* were subhu-man, since "mutilation separates him in a manner from his species; and the fatal event, which deprives him of the most agreeable relations established by nature, between beings of the same kind, almost extinguishes in his breast the peculiar feelings of humanity."[18]

One way to read Velluti's reception, therefore, would be to say that the biologi-cal determinism of these men worked to exclude him. All human process (vocal production included) was being folded into the great qualitative world of genetic law and animal function. New bodily codes, new musical behaviors, new physio-logical realisms, and a strict sexual dimorphism were being proscribed. (It must be said that Lawrence's "manly" proscriptions hardly went unchallenged; his "materi-alist" ideas were forced underground in 1819, when his much-debated *Lectures on Physiology, Zoology, and the Natural History of Man* had to be withdrawn after accusations of blasphemy.) These truths implied novel techniques of vocal identi-fication, where listener-viewers listened beyond subdivision—indeed, beyond quantitative or rhetorical questions of musical skill, technique, cadences, graces, shakes, divisions, ornament, and nuance. The long view suggests that Lawrence's ideas eventually won out, imperiling the figure of the Italian castrato by pressing him beneath "species" conceptualizations of "man."

There are other ways to characterize these developments: to venture that scien-tific norms only shadowed trends in music rooms, concert halls, and opera houses. In general terms, it seems clear that a new art of "the voice" was establishing itself in competition with much older and still-elite disciplines of Italian song. Where usually vocal sounds were prized for their purity, polish, and science (as for the castrato), now the voice was grainy, powerful, and individual (as for the prima donna). The basics had altered: when singers sang, they were heard less to echo fixed moral, ideal, or mimetic states—or at least not always. Rather, they appeared to express something elusive—a physiological presence—from deep within. In these instances, to continue this line of argument, song was encountered less as the *representation* of a myriad of affections or passions present, visible, and real to each individual than the *presentation* of inscrutable personality.

In this conception, the vocal organ was less the means of expression than its source. What occurred (to borrow from psychoanalytic discourse again) was an ennoblement of geno-song (the voice organic and immanent) over pheno-song (more poetic, grammatical, or cultivated articulations).[19] A biomedical view, or what Elizabeth Grosz calls the "species body," gained traction: what was important was not so much pure, unfettered vocal *emissions*.[20] A raw, powerful, and charged *extraction* was preferred.[21] Certainly, descriptions such as that of Angelica Catalani in 1829, as "a Pythoness expanding with inspiration . . . her very impatience of the [orchestral] accompaniment shows the fullness and force of her conceptions, anxious for melodious birth," would have been unthinkable only twenty years earlier.[22]

Where creation was experienced thus—as (female) procreation out of the natural order rather than as an ex nihilo act of (male) creation—so the castrato was driven under. His fate is difficult to sketch in ways less general than this. If anything, the temptation is to advance to a third stage of abstraction: to suggest links between experimental formations of "the voice" (as an object of artistic and scientific knowledge) and formations of "the body" as at once the subject and object of the nineteenth-century human sciences.[23] On the basis of the history of physiological approaches to vocal sound, at least, it seems that experience of "the voice" was powerfully bound to functional notions of inner life—an indication perhaps of the success of soft power and the middlebrow call to political self-regulation or individuation. The elevation of what physiologist at the Faculté de médecine de Paris François Magendie, in 1816, disparagingly called the "voix native" to the status of the goal of the singing arts (in such vocal tutors as Giuseppe Concone's *Introduction à l'art de bien chanter* of 1845) was certainly dramatic.[24]

After all, "romanticism"—as is commonly observed, particularly in literary studies—involved privileging orders of inborn difference (relativistic, nationalistic, individualistic, historicist, racialistic, and gendered) over "Enlightenment" principles of the universal. Yet to imply by this observation—as is frequently done—that the "romantics" suddenly discovered their own bodies or found their individual voices is to miss the point. It might prove better to speculate, following Alan Richardson, that a new conceptualization of "man" found its first articulation in the long nineteenth century, one ordered less according to theories of shared intellect, morality, or language than in relation to the shared condition of embodiment.[25] This naturalized sense of humanness, one might claim, threw the category of the male soprano into disarray.

The Musical World confirmed the projection of this singing species below language when another castrato, Paolo Pergetti, visited London in 1844. This was at a time when, as the writer put it, even "the negroes of the British dominions have been placed in the class HUMAN." Only chained consonants could do Pergetti's performance justice: "Sbgrmld—vxgspl—zb—tdpmbg—qz."[26] This class of being, in other words, was unspeakable. As Balzac put it, the castrato was a "creature for which the human language [had] no name, a form without substance."[27] Cut off from the emerging truth, his unnatured vocalizations no longer made sense. Human expression could not still be reflected or exchanged in the manner of hard currency. No longer belonging to cultivated nature, vocal sounds now cleaved to physiology, to the physical organization of the brain-mind and the materiality of consciousness and emotions.[28] This earthly frame was not to be done away with or denied; the individualized "body" was to be imagined as definitively and all-embracingly human.

BEFORE "THE VOICE" SO-CALLED

The 1820s were pivotal in these processes. Important changes in vocal technique were taking hold; alternative schooling methods were being tested across Europe. In the previous century, singers trained in fine elocution and messa di voce spent their hours of practice acquiring sounds, skills, and qualities. They built expression from the ground up, softening the organ, unraveling its individualities, smoothing away brute distinctiveness, and setting aside such impediments as texture, timbre, and personality. What *l'arte del canto* aimed at was pure, unmodified vowels in all parts of the range, vast expressive scope, unhindered volubility and flexibility, and the cultivation of imperceptible shifts between sounds—most of all, between chest and head voices. The *London Magazine* toed the old-fashioned line in 1825 when it lauded the "artificial formation" of Velluti's tone. "His *portamento* is exact," it wrote, "no taint of nose, mouth, or throat, is discoverable in its production; nothing can be more perfect or more finished; there are no roughnessses, no inequalities."[29]

Denis Diderot, hardly the most obvious writer to cite in defense of castration, had famously made the development of nonindividuality the highest objective of art. In "The Paradox of Acting" (1773–77), an essay published only in 1830, he listed the attributes of the actor graced with "the gift of mimesis." "Perhaps it is just because he is nothing," Diderot argued, "that he is before all everything. His own particular form never interferes with the shape he assumes."[30] The finished actor, like the finished singer, only found true form, the philosopher found, once he had been emptied of self. To be the echo of every passion was to wipe the slate clean and to attain to a moral absolute: total insignificance. Nothingness was the actor's guarantee of perfection, and it could be achieved only with devotion, sacrifice, and long periods of discipline and privation. Every aspect of self had to be abstracted away.

In a musical sense, the ne plus ultra of the ideal formed in the voice and figure of the castrato. Not only was he subject to the rigors of the *conservatorio*. Such a nonperson was ideal precisely because originary significance had been taken from him as a child. Since adult adjuncts had been cut away, he was free to cultivate or acquire a *vox perfecta* from a nascent position of "first things." Via a small act of violence, his body had been opened to every oratorical possibility. Hypostasized as an object, his figure—this house of the living artwork—had a nonidentity liberated from self. Living at the zero-point of subsistence, castrati, it was widely reported, had weak heartbeats, poor eyesight, and almost no pulse and they lacked blood pressure. Medically, their susceptible temperaments, pale countenances, enervated sensibilities, and absence of inner heat bore out their variability of being. John Ebers, who was manager of the King's Theatre from 1821 to 1827, reported how sparing Velluti was "in the pleasures of the table; a cup of coffee and a little dry toast form his breakfast, and his other meals are in proportion."[31] Compare this to Malibran, who, it was reported, lived on breakfasts of oysters and port.[32] If in the eighteenth century castrati had generally been vilified as the ultimate in overblown luxury, by the nineteenth they were usually portrayed by their antagonists as pale, inanimate, threadbare beings.

In its best sense, castration was not only a reversion to a life of prepubescence (Velluti was regularly castigated in the press for his infantile temper and childlike personality); it also freed the singer to acquire an instrument attuned to all shades of expression. A physical refinement had taken place that was not so much an act of mutilation as an opportunity to produce without hindrance, to lay aside and start afresh. As if to memorialize his conversion, a long poem in the *Examiner* in 1825 hearkened back to Velluti's "second baptism" as a child.[33] More beautiful than woman, the *evirato* had seen his ability to procreate exchanged for an ability to become somebody else in an ex nihilo act of (male) creation. His capacity to impersonate, to be everything, gave him—from a positive point of view— tremendous virility. Far from sacrificing *potentia generandi,* he might acquire godlike status, so endowed was he with the power to create from nothing. More soberly, his model would be Hermes, the genderless messenger-god who merely carries, at no stage interfering with the swift execution of his task. The castrato's vocal flights served lofty functions, bearing texts effortlessly into the ears of listeners. If not the bearer of letters, then the castrato was his own sign system—the voice of logos—part of an empty grammatical system awaiting signification or meaningful drawing-together. More pointedly, he might embody music itself. In 1828 the *Athenaeum* made clear that Velluti was "a being with a soul breathing nothing but music."[34]

It was not for nothing that British critics made ironic reference to Giovanni Cipriani's motto, still displayed above the Covent Garden stage when they brought the last operatic castrato into question: "Veluti in speculum" (literally, "as in a mirror"). Even in the 1820s it was understood that the singer-actor had honed his art precisely in order to mirror truth. All in all, the soprano in perfect form—Velluti at his best—was the blank that signifies, inviting his audience always and everywhere to inscribe their passions back on him. The true reflection of every figure and every form, Velluti echoed those sharply defined "varieties of the voice" so beloved of such writers as Rennie—the tenderness of the *aria cantabile,* the dignity of the *aria di portamento,* the caprice of the *aria di mezza carattere,* the impetuosity of the *aria parlante*—without distortion.[35] The listener sang through him, as it were, his passions sung back to him through another mouth. *Pace* modern erotic notions of the castrato, he was not in the classical sense an object of desire, nor of repulsion. He in no way expressed himself or some inner sex, impulse, or feeling. Rather, he expressed others' feeling, or, more widely, that economy of universal emotions. To be all, to acquire all, one must first make oneself nothing.[36]

THE OPAQUE FORM OF THE FEMALE CONTRALTO

If the castrato fell beneath the window of culture around this time, then roughly the same may be said of the other eminently neoclassical figure of the era, the female contralto. Were a date to be chosen, these formidable women could be said to have taken center stage at opera houses in Italian states around 1806. This year witnessed the retirement of the charismatic Milanese castrato Luigi Marchesi (who inspired such forgotten masters as Niccolò Antonio Zingarelli, Giuseppe Nicolini, Simon Mayr, and Angelo Tarchi) and the debut, in Verona, of Adelaide Malanotte, Rossini's first Tancredi. (Of the castrati, only Girolamo Crescentini in Paris and Velluti remained in the top flight.)

The contralto both resembled and was dissimilar to the castrato (each, in fact, could be called a "musico").[37] Descriptions of womanly character in the first two decades of the century continued to imagine her as a degenerate or passive homology of the male. Her ability to impersonate depended on a certain involuntary blankness, a mimetic flatness that smoothed over her as yet indistinct vegetality and predisposed her to artifice and playacting in the manner of the castrato, a figure now on his last legs. Although her vocal sounds were never fully as imitative, they did preserve what Rossini called the castrato's "ideal and expressive" legacy.[38] So, in one sense, women took up where the male musico left off. In another, they were more than merely his stand-in, more than a substitute for an unproductive masculine type: they were a point of arrival, a privileged new subject position in culture.[39]

Shifts in notions of human sexuality, however, have obscured the significance of her historical achievement by positing this woman as a transitional figure separating the age of the castrato from what came to be known as "romantic opera." From the point of view of the future—from the perspective of the 1830s—the voices of these women were ambiguously sexed and, frankly, unattractive. Singers such as Rosmunda Pisaroni were not yet "fully woman" in the contingent sense of Sontag or Malibran, who rose to fame during the late 1820s. Even during the attractions of Sontag and Malibran, in any event, voice types were classified not according to some preconceived notion of body type but according to pansexual standards of absolute beauty. As late as 1830, Bennati—who was a specialist more in the anatomy of singing than in the matter of Paganini's left hand—identified three voices in human existence. (A full examination of Bennati's observations will occur in chapter 5.) These voices were separable by range only: soprani sfogati, tenors-contraltini, and basses-tailles.[40] The ear, nose, and throat specialist's sexual blindness, betrayed here in a paper given to the Académie des sciences, replicated the time-honored models of the ancients. Bennati could not shake the weighty traditions of the past. He had studied singing, after all, under the great castrato Gasparo Pacchierotti.

Whereas audiences would throw texts, poems, or sonnets at Pisaroni, flowers—organic, natural objects (as well as sonnets to be sure)—would fall at the feet of the first modern divas. The first time that wreaths and bouquets were thrown at the Théâtre Italien in Paris was for Malibran's Desdemona in Rossini's Otello on her season debut of 31 March 1829. This at least was according to the Havanese aristocrat of Creole extraction, singing enthusiast, and leading salonnière in the city Maria de las Mercedes Santa Cruz y Montalvo (better known as la Condesa de Merlin).[41] In May of 1835 in London, the practice was novel enough for the Times to recommend instead "a shower of cabbage-leaves" for Giulia Grisi's Elvira (Bellini's I puritani). "This practice, which a few contemptible sycophants have introduced among us within the last four or five years," the writer complained, "is an exceedingly silly one, and not at all in harmony with English notions and English customs."[42]

Even Giuditta Pasta, never a contralto in the strict sense, perpetuated the classic ideal, particularly during her peak in the early to mid-1820s.[43] As long as she held court, the femme grecque ideal of le code Rossinien would remain. Critics hailed her as the ultimate animate artwork. The Quarterly Musical Magazine and Review's description of the pose she took while listening to Leicester (Curioni) in Coccia's Maria Stuart, Regina di Scozia on 7 June 1827 was typical: "The attitude was so perfect—was taken with such slow and solemn stillness, and kept with such immovable beauty, that we never recollect to have seen such a personification of the attributes and effects of sculpture; and if art is employed in the imitation of nature, here it seemed as if nature had been turned towards sculpture for her model and authority."[44] Metamorphosing from one attitude to another, Pasta—according to Stendhal—copied the sculpted poses of the actor de' Marini and of Viganò's principal ballerina, Pallerini.[45] Her style was perfectly matched to the firm plasticity Rossini scripted into his characters.

Like every musico before her, Pasta was an impersonator. While her woman-ness was not in doubt, her genius hinged on an ability to hide it. She was of that malleable sort of sex that was in no way significant to her acting parts. Her per-formance *en travesti* mobilized this essential mutability; intrinsic personal beauty was of no matter. When Mary Wollstonecraft Shelley wrote to the *Examiner* in 1826, she took the opportunity to point out what she felt to be Pasta's chief short-coming. The style of "Velluti's pupil," the author of *Frankenstein* argued, "wants the 'touch of nature.'" For Shelley, Pasta's gender was not variable enough, her "local and arbitrary modes of expression" falling short of the "generosity" and "sentiment attached to [Velluti's] person." Shelley thus both protested the language used by the newspaper to attack Velluti and chided republican men for their unnatural stance on sexual difference. (She had firsthand knowledge of Lawrence's misogynistic "two-sex" idea, the surgeon being her personal physician and a close friend of her husband.)[46] John Ebers disagreed in relation to Pasta in 1828: "There is no percep-tible effort to resemble the character she plays; on the contrary, she enters the stage [as] the character itself; transposed into the situation, excited by the hopes and the fears, breathing the life and the spirit of the being she represents."[47]

Similarly, in *Rose et Blanche,* a novella cowritten by George Sand and Jules San-deau in 1831, the protagonist recognizes Pasta only at the beginning of the last act of *Tancredi.* Rose lets out a cry of surprise: "This handsome warrior—this was a young woman who shook the pale Rose—here was the revelation! Tancredi was Judith Pasta."[48] Such surprise was echoed in the *Examiner* when it hailed Pasta's Nina:

> Her voice is veiled. . . . She is of the Bolognese school of art—no glancing lights, no meretricious expression, no extravagance, no violent contrast,—she goes straight on to her end, and arrives at it. She does not shine in parts, but in the aggregate impression—the whole is well-balanced, continuous, firm. . . . She gives herself entirely up to the impression of her part, loses her power over herself, is led away by her feelings wither *[sic]* to an expression of stupor or of artless joy, borrows beauty from deformity, charms unconsciously, and is transformed into the very being she represents. She does not act the character—she is it, looks it, breathes it . . . her whole style and manner is perfect keeping, as if she were really a love-sick, care-crazed maiden, occupied with one deep sorrow, and who had no other idea or interest in the world.[49]

Stendhal too was obsessed by Pasta's plasticity, the way she projected the *bello ideale,* the *pacatezza* (sedateness) of her phonation, and her arcane, "celestial beauty."[50] What was most celebrated in her art was her ability to deny the self and breathe every character into life. Not so much a creation from within nature, Pasta perfected nature from without.

In the 1820s the sublimated beauty of this ideal followed in the footsteps of her older siblings, the ailing female contralto and castrato. Pasta's song, her elevated speech, was no longer absolute, at least for her critics in London. Both the sounds she made and her *en travesti* tendencies could be off-putting. To "express manly sentiments of love and attachment in the acute sounds of the additional keys," in anything "additional" to the male register, the *New Monthly Magazine* wrote of her Tancredi in 1826, was "preposterous and ridiculous, whether such sounds proceed from eunuchs, or from females in male disguise." (Audience expectations and critical language were very different elsewhere; in north Italian urban centers, for example, hardly a twitter of protest was heard in view of contralti until much later in the century.) The London critic continued, "Let us have Nature; let us have all that Nature will afford for our enjoyment—mental or physical. What is beyond, is evil."[51]

ATTACKS ON THE CONTRALTO IN LONDON

Pasta left London on 2 August 1828 after a disastrous year dogged by illness, Sontag mania, and performances of Armando in *Il crociato* that failed to live up to Velluti's precedent.[52] The editor of the *Harmonicon,* William Ayrton, summed up the season by observing that "Pasta's magnetic powers have deserted her, and none but Madlle Sontag has drawn the crowd."[53] The *Athenaeum* of that year complained that her voice "is still naturally defective, naturally so, especially in its lower tones, which are not only husky, but so weak, that some will scarcely pass the orchestra to the nearest ear in the pit."[54] Even Pasta fell victim to the vogue for charged, powerful singing. Nine months later, around the time of Mendelssohn's nightmare, she was plying her trade in far-off Milan.

As listeners in London preferred "natural song," so the squat physicality of those female contraltos bequeathed to cosmopolitan Europe by the 1810s—Malanotte, Grassini, Pisaroni—became disconcerting. Pisaroni being engaged at the King's Theatre in 1829, the *Harmonicon* chose her benefit night to criticize "her hard masculine voice" when she sung Arsace opposite Sontag's Semiramide. "With a full consciousness of her merits," the critic confessed, "we always witness her performance with pain."[55] Harriet Granville made a nastier assessment of her in a letter to her sister in 1827:

> On Saturday we had Pisaroni, magnificent, wonderful, entraînante, electrifying Pisaroni. Hideous, distorted, deformed, dwarfish Pisaroni. Add it up, dearest Sissee, divide, subtract, multiply, it is capable of all for it is marvellous. She has an immense head, a remarkably ugly face. When she smiles or sings her mouth is drawn up to her ear, with a look of a person convulsed with pain. She has two legs that stand out like sugar tongs, one shorter than the other. Her stomach sticks out on one side of her body, and she has a hump on the other, not where stomachs or humps usually are, but sideways, like paniers [sic].[56]

The desire to "divide, subtract, multiply," to locate Pisaroni in terms of her "singing parts," threw her undeniable vocal excellence into disarray. The great contralto's technique of forcing her mouth to the left on high notes—a style discussed in detail by Bennati—became curiously injurious to her success.[57]

Many other singers suffered the trend for operagoers to listen for natural conditions in the voice. When Velluti was appointed director of the King's Theatre in 1826, he engaged one of his protégées, Giovanna Bonini, as prima donna. No doubt he looked forward to singing "Ravvisa qual alma" with her. This celebrated duet was the highlight of the 1824 Florentine version of Meyerbeer's *Il crociato in Egitto* and one of the castrato's showpieces. A rondò finale for Armando had ended the original Venetian version of the opera, which had premièred only eight weeks before this second production. In Florence, the presence of Adelaide Tosi meant that Meyerbeer and Velluti favored a duet to the original rondò. In London a year later, the castrato having shipped the set designs, costumes, and music over from Florence with Meyerbeer's blessing, Maria Caradori-Allan had partnered Velluti in this climactic moment to great acclaim.[58] The *New Monthly Magazine* exalted the blend of Caradori's "clear tones" with the castrato's "penetrating soprano." "Let [the] duet with Velluti at the very conclusion of the opera be listened to," the critic enthused, "and no more be said."[59] Before the King's Theatre revival of 1826, in other words, the duet's reputation was second to none.

With Bonini in tow, however, the number faltered, the problem being that, as Richard Bacon put it, the prima donna was "old, exceedingly plain, and took snuff." In the duets Velluti had taken to forcing her to "stand through the scene with her eyes fixed on his face, and if possible with both her hands in his, that she might be guided in her performance by his slightest look or movement."[60] An extraordinary passage in *London Magazine* lambasted this sycophantic gesturing. Reading her body through her voice, the critic found Bonini's muscular lyricism painful to experience; watching her sing was like watching the most elemental emission:

> The severe struggle with which she draws a thin and wiry note *ab imo pectore*, and the awkward pain with which she delivers herself of it, can only be likened to one operation in nature. She obviously labours under a vocal constipation. The pencil of Cruikshank can alone do justice to the distress of the poor Signora in the popular duet in the finale of the Crociato. We cannot describe the effect of Velluti, with his tall figure bending over the little lady, and holding her up by the hand as if to lift her over the gamut, as a careful father lifts little miss over the gutter; then, when the time comes for the high note, the manager seems to coax, wheedle, and encourage her for a violent squeeze; the hand is carried up by jerks to its highest possible elevation, and the voice appears, by some curious attraction, to follow it, and at the critical moment no one but the artist we have named can do justice to the awkward anxiety of the struggling Prima Donna's countenance.[61]

This harsh form of natural-physical attack on singers—castratos as well as female contraltos—became routine in the late 1820s, not only in satirical print but also in pictures. The engraving "An Italian singer, *cut out* for English amusement;

FIGURE 1. Louis Marks's depiction of Velluti. © The Trustees of The British Museum.

or, Signor Veluti *[sic]* Displaying his ~~Great~~ *parts*" circulated in 1825. The military officer in the center of the picture exclaiming, "Do you not think he's a well made man!" is probably the Duke of Wellington, one of Velluti's keenest fans. In radical culture, the political explanation typically given for the success of the castrato in the 1820s was that he serviced the repressive tastes of the ruling elite. "Cut out" for their amusement, he was seen to mirror and exemplify aristocratic dandyism and effeminacy. The *Times* made clear that although Velluti might preen the feathers of the higher orders, he was below the tastes of "the manly British public."[62] In figure 1 Louis Marks (a contemporary of satirist George Cruikshank) depicts the castrato showing off "his parts" (displaying a manuscript in his right hand). Something vital, it is clear, is missing from the scene. As the lady standing in the back row with her lorgnette points out, Velluti is "not quite" complete.

THE PROCREATING EUNUCH

In London, at least, the castrato was dogged by this awareness of the fundamental lack at his core. Those thin features, smooth, glistening skin, pale and beardless features, high, narrow shoulders, arched back, rounded hips, and fine wrinkles ringing the eyes all covered over the nagging void. For reformist writers, as we have seen, the castrato lacked the basic materials from which to create. He possessed an engrossing strangeness that thrust him outside the human, an emptiness that made him seem at once animal and machinelike. The *New Times* condemned Velluti for attacking "the manliness of our [British] national character." The writer continued, "He stands forward as living evidence of the lamentable extent to which human nature has been degraded in order to satisfy human sensuality. . . . It is not to be borne with patience, that for the sake of such an exhibition, the mind of a young and virtuous female should be exposed to the consequences of dangerous curiosity and vicious insinuation."[63] Since the first principles of production were missing, any creative generation on the eunuch's part was unthinkable.

Velluti's detractors wanted to expose his lie, to strip him down and uncover his deception. There they would find not that he was nothing, but rather that he was something, a terrible something-without. His was a figure of tremendous repressed pain; his outward form muffled a screaming silence. Because of his mutilation, in an inhuman twist, he was apparently barred from protesting the injustice he had faced; vocal resistance was pathetic, shrill. Shorn of biology, his was a reality of pure, acid pain (of the kind later revealed in Wagner's Klingsor, a role originally conceived for the castrato Domenico Mustafà).[64] In the 1820s Velluti's voice began to recall a gutless past of old mores, powdered exteriors, and false-faced aristocrats in court shoes.

In the midst of the hype surrounding Velluti's public debut and the first London performance of *Il crociato in Egitto* in 1825, the *Times* orchestrated a full-blown press war.[65] On the morning of the English premiere (30 June), the newspaper printed a stinging denunciation. "Some savage," the *London Magazine* reported, "took the trouble to translate the brutal article in *The Times* of the Thursday, and sent it to Velluti" just before curtain-up.[66] The public took up the newspaper's goading, having not witnessed a vocal species of this type since the days of the second-rate appearances of Neri and Roselli in 1800. As the *Examiner* put it, they "anticipated a disturbance."[67] The King's Theatre was packed with the most fashionable of patrons that evening. A party dining at Apsley House led by the Duke of Wellington was in attendance, as was the extravagant Lord Maryborough and "a lady for whom we feel too much compassion to mention her name" (as the *Times* put it; this was probably Byron's ex-lover, Lady Caroline Lamb, who was separating from her husband in June and July.)[68]

A delay of several minutes as the scene was prepared heightened the mood of anticipation before Velluti's entry. Armando's ship eventually docked in the port of Damietta and the castrato timidly stepped down the galley to "mingled applause and disapprobation." The *Times* reported how he "trembled excessively" before bowing "respectfully to the audience." "The most profound silence reigned in one of the most crowded audiences I ever saw, broken on his entering by loud applauses of encouragement," wrote Lord Mount Edgcumbe. "The first note he uttered," he recalled from his box, "gave a shock of surprise, almost of disgust, to inexperienced ears." Ebers recoiled at the "preternatural harshness" of Velluti's first words, which jarred "even more strongly on the imagination than on the ear." The *New Monthly Magazine* detected in the shrillness of his voice an "extremely nervous state" brought about by having to oversee two last-minute rehearsals the previous day. "The most grave of Velluti's supporters," the *Times* rejoined, "could not conquer their inclination for laughter." Velluti responded to an attempt to encore the famous first-act trio, "Giovinetto cavalier," by reentering the stage in an attitude of humility. An uproar ensued, led by those wishing to sabotage the repeat. "Certain imitations of his voice, proceeding chiefly from the gallery," the *Times* observed, "defeated the intention." "For a few moments he appeared overwhelmed, and as if crouching for mercy," the *London Magazine* added, "but, after a short time, he drew himself up and folded his arms, with the air of one whose sprit was roused by unjust and barbarous treatment." Taking "Caradori by the hand, he stepped forward, cast a most imploring look towards the audience . . . and retired." By the final act, the gallery had taken to singing back to him in mocking high catcalls whenever he made his entry. After a long and eventful night, the curtain finally fell in a tumult; the house emptied in anticipation of the ballet.[69]

The mob in the gallery mimicked his voice as if to interpret these sounds as the cause or symptom of some terrible illness. "A hero, a valiant crusader, a soldier, a victor, and a lover, venting his emotions in a squalling treble, singing of valour and glory as it were in a consumption, and making love in a feeble voice, higher than the mistress of his affection," the *Examiner* complained, "was more than we could well endure."[70] When he sang, he recalled only the slicing of the knife, that formative moment in his youth.[71] "There was something in the voice of Velluti," the *Times* reported, "which, mingled with the reflection on his situation, really set the teeth on edge; and people were heard to suck up the breath as if in pain."[72] Reviewing the 1826 production of *Il crociato*, the *London Magazine* found it "painful to our sense of hearing to listen to Velluti's singing, as it is to our sense of sight to see a man standing insecurely on a dizzy height." The vertigo of having to deal with the constant deferral of "natural" resolution was particularly unbearable when the castrato's voice apparently cracked momentarily. "The Signor frequently loses command of his voice," the critic explained, "and bitterly does it then grate on our musical nerves, like the scraping of a slate pencil, or the chromatic performance of a grinder on the edge of a saw."[73] Whereas, according to an oft-repeated anecdote, in the eighteenth century the castrato's voice was greeted with cries of "Viva il coltello!" (Long live the knife!), now there were shouts of laughter—in the reform-minded press at least. The *Atlas* critic complained that he had tried to educate his ear by persevering "night after night" with Velluti, having expected "by repeated doses to cure our nausea." But in vain: "The more our ears took in," the critic admitted, "the more we sickened."[74]

What made many listeners queasiest was Velluti's epicene gender. Talk among his detractors had it that he was attempting to pass himself off as a woman. Censorship in the papal states of a backward Italy, it was thought, had forced these poor simulacra into existence. This was also the Balzacian view: that the eunuch was a creature desperately seeking fulfillment as a female. Why else would Velluti display what the *Harmonicon* described as such "morbid antipathy" toward the fairer sex?[75] The fact that he had been a lady-killer in his prime was now long forgotten. Only dim memories remained of him fleeing Milan in the wake of Rossini's *Aureliano in Palmira* (an opera written in 1814 for him) after a scandalous affair with a young lady of good standing (recorded in accounts of Velluti's biography as the Marchesa Clelia G—).[76] In ten years his voice had become both mocking and jealous of the sex he secretly admired. The prima donna's excess of life and proximity to nature accounted for his every display of envy, competitiveness, and misogyny.

The "woman issue" dealt several damaging blows to Velluti's career, particularly after his engagement as director of the King's Theatre. In the wake of his benefit of that year, Velluti neglected to hand bonuses to the women in the chorus. Hauled before Middlesex County court on charges of "sordid and grasping conduct," the castrato was foiled by the articulate plea of one of the young women, the timely intervention of Pasta on behalf of the chorus, and what the judge described as Velluti's own "trumpery defence."[77] During the dispute, the press took the opportunity to both leap to the aid of the oppressed and jump on Velluti. For at least one commentator, the "extraordinary brevity" of the girl's petticoats on any given night at the opera was the most obvious measure of the director's "screwing down" and exploitative tendencies.[78] He was not reengaged at the King's Theatre the following season.

Velluti's reputation as antiwoman was not improved by his championing of Bonini. "If Signor Velluti had his way," the *Atlas* remarked in reference to the chorus dispute, "we should not see a woman on the stage, unless one, perhaps, as old and as ugly as original Sin."[79] Elsewhere, in a review of Bonini's Cenerentola, the same critic found it hard to believe that the hero would fall for "a lodging-house char-woman." "If the Prince wanted a maid of all work to scrub and scour his palace," the correspondent explained, "he could not have made a more prudent choice."[80] Also in that year, *London Magazine* protested at the decline of "the Star of Venus" at the opera and savaged the "brace of effete old women, whose voices do not gain even by comparison with the manager's."[81] Since attractive women had disappeared under Velluti's management, the opera house was becoming a confusing place. Edward Holmes commented on the 1826 production of *Aureliano in Palmira* with Bonini as Zenobia, Queen of Palmyra, and Velluti as Arsace:

Madame Bonini wore an immense sword by her side, which she, on certain occasions, drew, and carried about the stage in the stirring attitude of a kitchen poker. Her use of this substantial tool reminded us of Cinderella. . . . At the conclusion of the second scene of the Aureliano, and before the third began, a figure nearly six feet high, clad in robes of virgin-white, and wearing a fine black bushy beard, came on and sung for a good space. . . . The party in question may be a gentleman; for really, as things are ordered now at the Opera, there is no making out the sexes. The gentlemen look very lady-like, and the ladies are so hard-favoured, that we no longer know how to distinguish the one from the other. They ought to be labelled like decanters, for fear of mistakes.

The virgin-white figure without the label was, of course, Velluti.

The lobby against effeminacy, dandyism, extravagant male attire, and cross-dressing became powerful and vocal by the late 1820s. "Let your dress be as cheap," warned Tory radical William Cobbett in his *Advice to Young Men* of 1829, "as may be without *shabbiness*."[82] Given his lavish dress, Velluti became an easy target for scorn. The proscription of vocal finery, ornament, and display attended the proscription of lace and embroidery in men's clothing. Several melodramatic imitations of him appeared in London theaters. J. Russell, for example, played Arionetti in *The Son-in-Law* at Drury Lane, making, the *Courier* noted, "a capital imitation of Velluti in a Recitative. . . . Every species of theatrical ingenuity had been resorted to, for the purpose of rendering the outward appearance of Mr Russell as feminine as possible: his very plain face was carefully rouged; full flowing ringlets fell upon his high shoulders, a timid step and childish gait."[83] The *Examiner* pulled apart the castrato's ladylike crusader garb in *Il crociato*. The hero's "lank face, hid up in a helmet with a most injudicious bow of white satin ribbon on the tip of his chin," the radical paper summed up, "seemed to have been dressed up by his enemies to look as ridiculous and effeminate as they could make him."[84] Such imprudence was not becoming of a self-made man. The worst thing about Velluti—mean, arrogant, and excessively interested in sartorial splendor—was that he was a female substitute. He made women despicable, undermining them at every opportunity. Worse still, he corrupted desire for them by poisoning the male imagination. In *Sarrasine* Balzac has the sculptor despairing, "I shall forever think of this imaginary woman when I see a real woman." Screaming at this fake feminine object, he chokes, "Monster! You who gave life to nothing. For me, you have wiped women from the earth."[85]

FROM POETIC TO HERMENEUTIC LISTENING

To construe sex in this way is to tune into a different way of knowing. The vocal source, for such listeners, is no mere instrument, no mere bodily appendage to be isolated and played. Rather, the vocal organ obeys the drives of an invisible, even inaudible kind. What becomes fascinating for many an audience, no matter who the singer, is to extrapolate backward, from the sonority heard to the situation of the expressive body that generated it. Poetic or intellectual eloquence is no longer at issue. Turning from what has become "superficial," audiences increasingly read sounds as traces of something else, as symptoms of an a priori nature, expressions of a truth that has come before.[86] For them, this is a game of identification, a way of discriminating (embodied) difference. As ever, listener and performer possess and breathe into each other in a sensual, physical way. But a new level of absorption, of deep listening, is required to generalize first a sounding physiology and then a living cause. Now that vocal sounds are heard as a form of evidence, a desire to identify—a hermeneutic curiosity—begins to characterize their reception.[87]

What this implies is that the listener engages every aural faculty in locating "the voice" behind the acoustic veneer. Since this elusive and largely inaudible singularity is powerful, it impinges on its hearers, crying out for interpretation. Thus critics, physiologists, and natural historians begin to sexualize this presence. Identifying a gendered charge in production, an obvious derivative of listening for its biology, became a prime preoccupation in these decades. The paradigmatic argument of the century would be Charles Darwin's in *The Descent of Man*, wherein he claimed that the vocal organs had evolved in mankind as a way of propagating the species by sexual selection. "Throughout the animal kingdom at large, the commencement of reproduction," Darwin observed, coincides with an "unusual vivacity of every kind, including vocal vivacity."[88] The drive to song was engendered (in this view) by desire, biology, and animal magnetism. Virtuosity—and here the stock nineteenth-century operatic heroine comes to mind—only added to the vivacity of the preternatural cry. The throat, in other words, was "revealed" to have a sexual density proper to its bio-evolutionary function. More than any nonreproductive body part, *it* was heavily sexual.[89]

MUSIC AND THE ORIENTAL MACHINE

A range of historical evidence invites reconstruction of Velluti's vocal manner. Fortunately this great survivor left behind him one of the most complete records of his school's methods of performance. That he rubbed shoulders with Rossini and Meyerbeer allows his style to be compared with more familiar singers and practices. Add to this that the castrato helped Manuel García *fils*, son of the tenor and brother of Malibran, publish a detailed guide to the performance of an aria from Morlacchi's *Tebaldo e Isolina* and the evidence mounts (see figure 2).[90]

"Caro suono lusinghier" occurs in the last act of the opera, which Morlacchi had composed in 1822 for Velluti in the role of Tebaldo. In the preceding scena, a suicidal Tebaldo despairs of his separation from Isolina and fears her dead. As

FIGURE 2. "Caro suono lusinghier" with Velluti embellishments. Manuel García *fils, Traité complet de l'art du chant* (Paris and London, 1847–51), 2: 100–103. The measure numbers are my additions. Reproduced by permission of the Bibliothèque nationale de France.

FIGURE 2. (*continued*)

FIGURE 2. *(continued)*

events turn toward the romanza, he thinks he hears her strumming a harp. The sound of this offstage instrument encourages him to recall the first time he heard her song, the moment he fell in love with the daughter of his mortal enemy. This recollection dates back to an episode that Gaetano Rossi described in the long *introduzione* to his libretto, which set the scene for the main action. "Caro suono lusinghier," in other words, hearkened back to a moment preparatory or external to the operatic plot—to a framing narrative, where Tebaldo unwittingly lost his heart to the voice of Isolina.

The song was adjudged the most engaging of the opera. Ebers recalled how it "enchained" and "enthralled" in London, not only because of Morlacchi's evocative use of the orchestra, but also because of the visual spectacle accompanying the music. Its moonlit scene, Ebers wrote, bound the audience, "as it were, by a spell." A pale light was called for from the King's Theatre technicians to "deepen [the music's] sombre and unearthly aspect." The moon, hovering against the backdrop, appeared as a thinly disguised metaphor; it symbolized the position of the protagonist, the half-lit environment mirroring Velluti's sense of abstraction. Music played its part too. Diegetic gestures abounded: the offstage harp, the musical form of the romanza, the return to a recollected performance. It was as if Tebaldo's aria had been cut off from the main narrative: a suboperatic song. "While this scene is displayed, which seems to *paint* the silence of night even to the eye," Ebers wrote, "the full orchestral accompaniment is hushed—the flute and the harp alone are heard to prelude the mournful air that breaks from the lips of the melancholy warrior."[91] The stillness of the scene presented an inactive twilight world to the audience, where nothing (new) was happening. Events had been suspended on the surface, as if to simulate the haze of a dream.

Musically, the most striking feature of Tebaldo's song is its harmonic stasis. The romanza is in two stanzas, the first beginning at measure 9, the second at measure 39. Overall, the harmony moves within a spectacularly narrow orbit; background interest is subordinated to foreground ornament. Apart from the briefest dominant arrivals at bars 27 and 54, there is hardly any harmonic movement. Mirrored phrases (like those at bars 19–20 and 21–22), fragmented appearances of the theme (bars 31–35 in the flute and bars 59–63), and repeated cadential echoes in the tonic (mm. 18–23; mm. 36–39; mm. 48–51 and mm. 64–70) extend the form and preserve the mood of suspense. The stiltedness is particularly remarkable in the first stanza (mm. 9–38), with its interrupting pause marks and unmetered sections of vocal display (mm. 18–25).[92] The propulsion of an *andante mosso* will come only at bar 39 with the words "Caro suono lusinghier." Yet Velluti's embellishments showcase a vocal range of nearly two and a half octaves, from the singer's low E♭ ossia (bar 47) to high A♭ in bar 50.

For the first nine bars the absent Isolina plays a simple dominant seventh sweep on her harp. We can imagine her audience holding its breath in anticipation of the melody. But instead of a singing voice as expected in measure 9, a parlando section ensues, with the cantabile played by a flute. For a full thirty bars Velluti merely apostrophizes beneath and around this tune. We are in Tebaldo's mind, the flute a surrogate for the lost voice of Isolina. Her imagined song begins with three phrases ending on dominant fermatas, reinforcing the tonal hovering. Only the forte cadence brings resolution (upbeat to measure 16), although the cadential echo sung by Velluti nullifies its grounding effect, with an asymmetric fifth phrase shorn of accompaniment and meter (m. 18).[93]

In this tentative first stanza the castrato has been subtracted from the scene; dramatically he is trying to make sense of a song heard in his head. It is as if the real world of Isolina's aria is offstage; the castrato is reduced to commenting on a memory, observing an intrusion from the past. The stage is set on the other side of the musical experience, in the dark space of listening rather than in the light of performance. Here Tebaldo joins his audience; the actor is reduced to directing his and their experience of the action. As the flute plays the opening melody, Velluti interprets it as "the sound of love" (il suono d'amore), his identification of this voice in measure 18 registered in melismas "performed by supple movements of the throat." He makes the identification, in other words, in an alienated or estranged style of vocalization. Similarly, when he first recognizes the love-object—the sound of the flute—he utters "lo conosco" (I know it) in "tones from the outside," in a covered timbre (m. 11). The implication is that he is external to experience, that his voice is partially missing. Unable to speak or sing of love directly, he must comment from the still, enigmatic world of his subconscious.

As if to reinforce the sense of an onstage subject being spirited away, Tebaldo's romanza appears as a kind of shadow aria. From the first statement of the melody Velluti's voice is cut away—compensated for by the missing Isolina, this "real" diegetic sound, this sound of earthy femininity. His voice has been mis- or displaced. There is a real sense in these opening lines that the audience must listen for an absence, something that has passed. When Velluti finally answers the flute with "Caro suono lusinghier," when he finally arrives at his beginning, he has been preempted; an excuse has been made for him. Once the music reaches the second stanza at measure 39, he merely repeats a preexisting melody. When the flute echoes his "Caro suono" with a melodic summary of the two phrases that have come before, the line has been divided or split into octaves (m. 42). Velluti's response is to sing "dolce ognor mi scendi al cor" in "tones imitating an echo" and smorzando (m. 46). Tebaldo's vocal statement here is a sad reflection of what it means to be "touched sweetly by love." Melodically, moreover, he is in tatters; he has entered the aria only on the occasion of its embellished repeat. The castrato's failing subjectivity has been scripted into the score; only a mutilated commentary, an echo of Isolina's original, remains.

In the 1820s "Caro suono lusinghier" owed much of its popularity to the way in which Morlacchi underwrote the onstage subject's castration. Velluti's lack of agency is also dramatized in such bizarreries as the flute-voice clashes (F♮–F♯/ F♯–G♮) from the end of measure 28, the hemidemisemiquaver echo in measure 48, and the offbeat forte stresses in measure 52. All these reinforce his sense of stylization; his removal from the musical scene is striking. After all, the romanza itself was about absence, a fact that no doubt excused the thinness of the castrated sound as expressive rather than pathetic. The refrain that "will never more return" (non mai più ritornerà) in the concluding bars must have been poignant for audiences in the late 1820s. We can imagine listeners drawn to Morlacchi's dramatization of the castrato staged in the twilight of his career, attracted as much as repulsed by the smooth wailing of his voice. All in all, "Caro suono lusinghier" appeared as a way of integrating the castrato's outdated micromanaged aesthetic into an emerging expressive framework, where expiry and expiration (literally, if you take Velluti's audible expirations into account) were drawn on as a dramatic resource.[94] The castrato was heard as if in a dream, in the same "virtual" way Mendelssohn experienced him on the night of 15 May 1829.

Velluti's style of performing Tebaldo, as exemplified in García's tutor, hearkened back to a bygone era, an era before the individuality of the singer was expressed according to inner timbre.[95] Here was a time in which personality was expressed via spontaneous selections from the vocal armory: a learned technical palette with preparations, formulas, and other "parts of speech." Minute gradations of *smorzature, rinforzi, gruppetti, mordenti, trilli, appoggiature, mezzotinte,* and *sfumature* were called forth to etch the precise emotion. A myriad of *chiaroscuro* and *ombreggiamento* effects added to the innumerable modifications in tone quality. Never once was the purity of the vowel disturbed. Here was music to elevate, educate, and ennoble, "felt within the soul," as Rossini would have it, and a material body free of vulgar essence.[96]

In many ways, even now, the performance markings and ornamental finery are disturbing. From the point of view of modern practice, it is debatable whether a historically informed restitution of Velluti's style is musically useful or desirable— not to speak of ethical. One of the assumptions of authentic practice is that "correct" performance makes for a pleasant, wholesome encounter. In the case of Velluti, the stench of antiquity that hangs over his manner is on the contrary disengaging. There are places in history, this being one, that are perhaps best left alone. (Even the most open-minded of us would surely never assent to the castration of Italian boys?) This music is not ours.

For Velluti's critics, as we have seen, such an accretion of signs was equally affected, even sickening. All these inflections added up to little more than empty whimpering. More disconcerting for the modern ear was all that soft moaning, the sniveling half breaths, the fussy silences, the supple movements in the throat, the audible exhalations, the thrilling "jerky inhalations" of air, the echo effects, glottal sounds, sustained consonants, sobs of passion, snuffed finishes, constant diminuendos, mooching swells, the lack of brio—the refined whining, sighing, and panting. This school's miniaturist aesthetic had no breadth of vision. It felt effete in the way it evaded cultural work, swooping pusillanimously from one note to the next. (These sounds, of course, were far from disembodied; it was just that the kind of body given to them had become difficult to ingest.) This *canto di maniera*—this mannered style—possessed little organic power, conviction, or direction. There was hardly anything there, as if the thoracic cavity, the vocal carriage, had been hollowed out. Everything happened externally, in the always already of a boyish throat. If sound issued from the castrato's languorous body at all, far from being *expressed*, it seemed to be *emitted* accidentally. It was as though the voice was secreting or discharging passively. The music had nothing to do with *expression*— natural self-expression—in the modern sense.

On one level, Velluti was animal, "a reptile to be loathed," as the *Examiner* suggested, with a voice like a "peacock's scream"; on another, he was machine. The artificiality of his acting drew repeated comment, the *Atlas* being troubled by the "incessant jerk of the head, like a mandarin in a china-shop."[97] *London Magazine* linked his style to singing machines and steam engines:

> If we could imagine an automaton as skilled in singing, as Roger Bacon's fabled clock-work head was in speaking, we can fancy that the effect would be similar; for the precision with which Velluti executes the most difficult passages, can only be compared with that of a piece of machinery, and the likeness would hold good also in respect of an occasional want of modulation in his highest tones, and a certain grating sharpness of finish. Some pieces of music he performs exactly as a steam-engine would perform them, if a steam-engine could be made to sing, taking each note with unerring accuracy, and taking each by a separate impulse, instead of floating on the gamut as less perfect singers commonly do.[98]

The end of the passage is interesting. When Velluti did receive praise, it was usually because he avoided "connecting the sound with another by whooping, hectic slides," as the *New Monthly Magazine* put it in 1826. The technique of vocalization referred to here is foreign to the modern ear, although it is plain that such sliding across notes was expected, particularly of castrati. The practice of connecting tones microtonally, though Velluti was chaste in his use of it, was fresh enough in the memory to be described in García's tutor in 1847. *Portamento di voce* or the related *agilità di portamento*, García suggested, was indicated by what we would today interpret as a legato slur, as in measures 54, 48, or 36 of Morlacchi's aria for Velluti. Both Bacilly (1669) and Tosi (1723) describe a similar *portamento* or *port de voix* as a style of "sliding" or "dragging" one note into another. García was clear that the serpentine line implied by this pre-nineteenth-century indication "revolts a man of taste."[99] This winding, phonetic genus, although on its way out, was nevertheless lodged in the vocabulary of mid-nineteenth-century song. Stendhal's description of Velluti's voice as a "terra incognita" was not idle. The castrati were always best made sense of in terms of an ethnography of song.[100]

Tebaldo e Isolina failed miserably when Velluti presented it in London in 1826. The *New Monthly Magazine* found it tiresome and complained at "the abundance of subjects in the minor mode," "dissonant harmonies," "diminished sevenths with inversions without end," and "chromatic modulations of the deepest die":

> The ear soon grows tired of a continued succession of *larmoyantes* melodies, and lugubrious harmonies. . . . Such *lympomania* is perhaps more endemial here than anywhere else, as may be inferred . . . from the numerous gloomy subjects daily poetised upon among us. . . . Patrons of the woeful, whose bliss are groans and tears, have a delightful treat prepared for them in Morlacchi's music of "Tebaldo e Isolina," especially when moaned out in the lugubrious and impure intonation of Signor Velluti.[101]

A pall of decay and gloom seemed to hang over Morlacchi's music when the castrato discharged it via his "sickly" body. The *Examiner* called it "a thing of shreds and patches" and "a mere cobweb in composition." "All is cut and frittered away," the reviewer argued, "in a constant succession of unmeaning flourishes."[102] The sound seeped like vapor from the singer's tall, gothic form. At least one caricature related this Tebaldo to another "freak," a certain Claude Ambroise Seurat, who was being exhibited at the Chinese Saloon. This emaciated Frenchman—the so-called *l'anatomie vivante*, "living skeleton," or *cupidon français* of 94 Pall Mall—lived off Velluti's continued celebrity, or so most of the public understood. "The gaunt frame and awkward gait of Velluti," the *Examiner* concluded, "looked like an embroidered skeleton with a spangled death's hand, aping the hero and the lover."[103]

In the end, "the painted sepulchre," as the *Times* labeled him, concealed a deception fundamental to everything—death. Bizarrely, though he was at least forty-four in 1825, *London Magazine* introduced him as being "no more than twenty-four years of age."[104] He was apparently both old and young.[105] His lack of center emptied him of history, made him a relic or corpse with the opera house his tomb. "Were I to scour your body with this blade, would I find there one feeling to stifle, one vengeance to satisfy?" Sarrasine asks the eunuch in Balzac's story. "You are nothing," he rages. "If you were a man or a woman, I would kill you."[106]

Velluti arrived for his final season in London on 11 April 1829. He was no longer welcome at the opera. Instead he earned his living teaching the wives and daughters of the *haute ton* at his Singing Academy on Regent Street (the School of Cant, as it was affectionately known). Occasionally he would venture into public to perform, although by the end of the season he was reduced to singing English concert airs, such as Thomas Welsh's "Ah! Can I Think of Days Gone By."[107] A plan he brokered (which garnered the support of the Duke of Wellington and the ballet master D'Egville) to turn the Argyll Rooms into a venue to rival the King's Theatre came to nothing in 1830 when the building burned to the ground. Broken and dispirited, the castrato returned to Italy, where he patched together appearances in *Tebaldo e Isolina* (Lugo di Romagna, 1830), *Il crociato in Egitto* (Brescia, 1830; Florence, 1833), *Aureliano in Palmira* (Brescia, 1831), Nicolini's *Il conte di Lenosse* (Venice, 1831), and an Italianized *La muta di Portici* (Venice, 1831). For all intents and purposes, however, the writing had been on the wall during those last days in London. At the close of the 1833 season he retired to a quiet villa on the banks of the Brenta near Venice.[108] There, as if to make peace with the natural laws that had put paid to his career, he spent his final thirty years as a gentleman farmer, communing with the fields and flowers.

2

Reflecting on Reflex

A Touching New Fact about Chopin

POLISH DISEASE

The organ of the ear sometimes provokes very bizarre sympathetic movements, which, in all probability, have their source in the ganglionic system. . . .

I know a distinguished pianist, of tremendously nervous temperament; he often has trouble urinating and is often subject to all possible trouble *[toutes les peines du monde]* without being at liberty to satisfy his needs; yet whistling or a few chords on the piano frees this obstruction in an instant.

The intimate connection existing between the human ear and the abdominal viscera by the sympathetic nerves permits these organs to have a significant influence upon the organ of hearing.[1]

These words formed part of an argument made by Jan Matuszyński behind the great gated colonnades of the École de médecine in Paris on 16 August 1837. The school was a celebrated institution, the foremost of its kind in Europe. The occasion was the oral exam of a doctoral thesis entitled "The Influence of the Sympathetic Nervous System on the Function of the Senses." A jury of two professors and two proctors in gowns and mortarboards guarded the solemnity of the event. For young initiates, such trials were the crowning achievement after four years of medical training. Largely symbolic, they marked entry into the establishment—literally, in the case of Matuszyński, as he would join the faculty in the years to come. One hundred copies of his thesis, issued by the school, were printed for circulation among benefactors, colleagues, family, and friends.[2] Among these last, probably in situ to witness the occasion, was the graduate's closest companion, former school- and flatmate, the "distinguished pianist" himself, Frédéric Chopin.

Matuszyński's proud moment had been long in coming. Seven years earlier the student had cut short his degree in Warsaw to enlist as a medic in the November Uprising against Russian occupation. Later in 1831, when the insurrection failed, he slipped across the German border and enrolled for a second academic stint at the University of Tübingen. A study of *plica polonica* (Polish plait)—a rare condition of the scalp involving the strange growth of matted hair thought endemic to Polish sensibility and the nervous-magnetic emanations that swirled around the ethnic cranium—suggested itself. By 1834 Matuszyński had published a monograph on the malady, this several years before its Chopinesque thematization in Honoré de Balzac's *L'Initié* (*The Initiate*).[3]

Balzac's novella, set in 1836, tells the story of a young do-gooder, Godefroid, who is moved to assist an impoverished aristocrat, the former prosecutor general under the restoration. The plight of the nobleman, bunkered in a squalid Parisian apartment, is peculiarly affecting in view of his half-Polish daughter, Vanda. For medical reasons, the proud retiree and widower keeps this frail, mysterious girl in ignorance of his indigence. Selling his books and saving where he can, the Baron maintains one room of their lodgings in determined luxury. He and her son thus shield Vanda's exquisite sensibility and propensity to nervous attack from the terrible destitution of the outer rooms.

In a memorable episode, Godefroid enters the apartment to find pale-skinned, bed-ridden Vanda—a "singular and mysterious creature"—at the harmonium: "The patient seemed to him transfigured by the pleasure she felt in making music; her face was radiant, her eyes were sparkling like diamonds." She flung herself "upon the little organ as a starving man flings himself on food" to render Rossini's famous "Dal tuo stellato soglio":

> Vanda made a sign to her son, who placed himself in such a way as to press with his foot the pedal which filled the bellows; and then the invalid, whose fingers had for the time recovered all their strength and agility, raising her eyes to heaven like Saint Cecilia, played the "Prayer of Moses in Egypt," which her son had bought for her and which she had learned by heart in a few hours. Godefroid recognized in her playing the same quality as in Chopin's. The soul was satisfied by divine sounds of which the dominant note was that of tender melancholy.[4]

In so many words, Balzac embroidered stories of Polish vulnerability and pitiableness that were by then familiar, tales of a proud but ultimately pathetic piano-playing people.

But not even Polish plait could keep Matuszyński in southwestern Germany forever. By 1834 new challenges had presented themselves, and in spring of that year (probably early June) he traveled to Paris to renew a friendship he had maintained since his youth. There, having registered on the unfortunately named rue des Boucheries (Street of the Butchers), where the School of Medicine stood, the trainee-physician wrote back to his brother-in-law in Poland: "I am living with [Frédéric Chopin] at No. 5 rue de la Chaussée d'Antin. This street is a little far from the medical school and the hospitals but I have strong reasons for staying with him—he means everything to me."[5] Matuszyński settled quickly into Parisian life. He and Chopin probably played music together (Matuszyński was a talented flautist) and went out regularly, attending the theater and dining on the boulevards nearby. As every Chopin scholar knows, the pianist found Matuszyński indispensable to his moral, mental, and physical well-being. No one had such intimate knowledge of Chopin's precarious sensibility.

As early as 1831, in the last of three celebrated letters written from Vienna before Matuszyński's life as a political exile, Chopin had asked for his friend's complicity in a case of compassionate deception: "I am unwell but I don't want my parents to know. Everyone asks what is the matter with me. I am out of spirits . . . [and] have a cold in the head. Anyhow, you know what is wrong with me. . . . Why am I desperately lonely today? Why can't you be here with me at such an awful time? . . . Embrace me, for I love you more than my life—write as often as you can."[6] These are famously tender words—excruciatingly so, as much for what they conceal as they suggest. Matuszyński had been Chopin's confidant in confessions of love. In 1836, they apparently formed a pact to choose wives; later that year, the pianist officially witnessed his friend's marriage to Thérèse Bouquet, his own proposal to Maria Wodzińska having failed.[7]

What happened next hardly needs rehearsal. A little more than a year after his medical exam—in the winter of late 1838—Matuszyński began to present signs of tuberculosis. A slow, stereotypically pathetic process of proud Polish capitulation was thus set in motion. Four years later Chopin arranged for his closest friend—coughing blood, a shadow of himself, bankrupt, and his marriage destroyed—to move to George Sand's apartment on rue Pigalle. In April 1842, the story goes, Chopin experienced a prequel of his own death. Sand recorded how Matuszyński "died in our arms after a slow and cruel agony that caused Chopin as much suffering as if it had been his own. [Chopin] was strong, courageous, and devoted, more so than one would have expected from such a frail being. But when it was over he was shattered."[8] Thus, far from home, two brothers-in-arms at last went their separate ways.

Such stories are poignant. Most of us, aided by years of cultural training, can usefully supply some suitably Chopinesque soundtrack to such narratives. But why rehearse them? Why this need to weep for Poland? To make Jan Matuszyński's intimate knowledge of his flatmate's medical history explicit? So that we might better imagine touching scenes of two men bending over a chamber pot, one whistling gently into the other's ear? Now is the time, I suppose, when we hold our collective breath in anticipation of some thrilling musical release. A technical analysis, perhaps, in which we reveal all about Chopin's cascading runs or showers

of notes? A new explanation for the composer-pianist's evasion of public performance? A new meaning for the "Raindrop" prelude? What we have here is a new
fragment of Chopiniana. These do not come around often. The composer apparently had a problem with urinary retention, readily relieved by a few well-chosen
chords on the piano.

LETTING GO?

There are serious issues to deal with here. What are we to do with such an awkward
addition to our knowledge? How might such information be said to contribute? As
I hope I've suggested, not everything unearthed need be useful. There are truths—
and this seems a good example—that we might not want to know, since their effect
is not so much to assist as to despoil the musical imagination. In this case, should
we always cheer when scholars (such as myself) emerge from the archive bran-
dishing some new idea, some glistening fact wrenched from ignorance? What
gives these questers—with all their sticky romantic zeal—the right to venture into
these forbidden places anyway? Is nothing sacred?

Worse about this "little fact" is the excitement it is likely to generate among
such musical-medical bio-pathographers as Ganche, Barry, Franken, and O'Shea.[9]
Chopin studies has its own special branch devoted to the great man's litany of ill-
nesses. According to an article in one recent medical journal, Chopin's complaints
included hemoptysis, fevers, gastrointestinal soreness, diarrhea and abdominal
pain (particularly after eating fatty pork), vulnerability to heatstroke, infertility,
arthralgia, effort intolerance, shortness of breath, productive cough, delayed
puberty, and so on. A sample of the cocktail of causes of death recently proposed
is more impressive still: "pulmonary tuberculosis, hypogammaglobulinemia,
mitral stenosis, allergic bronchopulmonary aspergillosis, tricuspid valve incompe-
tence, Churg-Strauss syndrome, pulmonary hemosiderosis, pulmonary arteriov-
enous malformation, cystic fibrosis and alfa1-antitrypsin deficiency."[10] How unfortunate that we must add yet another ailment to the list.

Since I am no doctor, these big medical words mean little to me. My sense,
however, is that their chief effect is to fortify the once commonsense hypothesis
that Chopin's failing body—the fragile life of heart, lungs, nerves, fingers, pelvic
floor—in some way grounds the divine charm of his music. All this science propa-
gates the age-old metaphysics: this obsession with infirmity replays time and again
the legends that the pianist "had been dying his whole life long"; that he was only
ever barely alive; that (weighing less than a hundred pounds) he was hardly ever
here; that he "enjoyed suffering"; that he was "as permanent as his cough"; or that,
as Ignaz Moscheles is supposed to have observed, "he resembled his music."[11] Here,
again, is a discourse struggling to reconcile the mortal life of the man with the
immortality—divinity, even—of his music.

In what follows I recuperate this "little fact" for Chopin studies, all the while avoiding the assumption that historically informed analysis necessarily amplifies the pleasures of musical experience. (This difficult medical truth, after all, makes the very idea of "playing Chopin" or standing in for Chopin awkward, so much does it estrange our sense of this beloved music.) Instead, my intention is to pursue a period sense of "touch." Initially the chapter reads Matuszyński's thesis in terms of the strange history of early Parisian physiology. Matuszyński's explorations provide precious insights, insights into a near-forgotten emotional anthropology that encourage us to get to know and love "Chopin" in newly intimate ways. The medical student enjoyed exclusive knowledge of the exquisite habitus so assiduously cultivated by his friend. This affective sense drew both into an elite community or circle of feeling in 1830s Paris. The student's enthusiasm for the physiology of sensing, tact, or touching, in other words, will be aligned with a pianistic practice, musical community, and affective comportment Chopin knew well.

ON THE SYMPATHETIC NERVE

Matuszyński's "The Influence of the Sympathetic Nerve on the Functions of the Senses" was in fact a work of considerable bravery. It addressed a topic of physiological inquiry that was of critical importance to researchers of this era. Matuszyński's concerns, moreover, were in no way remote from the interests of such nonspecialists as Frédéric Chopin. In the history of the neurological sciences and sensibility, the keyboardist at his or her keyboard had always been a subject of urgent interest. The question of how bodies learned to "play by themselves" with what we might today call "motor memory" had been crucial to the field of animal economy since at least the 1740s. Somatic intelligence, automatic action, the ideas of thinking with sensibility and of playing by feel: this is what Matuszyński's thesis was about. His work tackled the problem of sympathetic or automatic movement, organic self-regulation, unconscious bodily activity, and apparently "rational" yet involuntary movement. Crucial to his thesis, too, was the question of how this all squared in the 1830s with newly pregnant notions of agency, volition, and selfhood.

Matuszyński's thoughts were forged in the fire of intense scientific debates enveloping the so-called "grand sympathique" (great sympathetic nerve) in the 1820s and '30s. Since the work of Parisian neuroanatomist François Magendie, whom Matuszyński cited as an authority early in his dissertation, fashionable conceptions of this complex of ganglia and plexuses spiraling down and around the spine had faced radical challenge. The experimental brand of neurophysiology pioneered in this period had in fact gone so far as to question whether the "great sympathetic" was even a nerve. More provocatively, as we shall see, Magendie had queried whether this nervous core had anything to do with sensibility, sentience, consciousness, sympathy, or—that great unquantifiable and for him no-longer-useful category of scientific inquiry—life.[12]

The introduction to Matuszyński's thesis divides the debate neatly. On the one hand, as he saw it, were second-generation *idéologues,* a group he himself identified with. They were thinkers who saw in the dense, all-traversing nerves of the spinal ganglia nothing less than a portrait of sentience itself, a picture of living, animate materiality. Physicians aligned to the group followed Pierre Jean George Cabanis, Balthasar-Anthelme Richerand, and particularly Xavier Bichat, the same Bichat who had spent the winter of 1801–2 (legend has it) holed up in the morgue at the Hôtel-Dieu dissecting some six hundred corpses. For Bichat, the "autonomic," "vegetative," or sympathetic system constituted not one but several interlacing nervous systems, a rich tapestry of semiautonomous "lives" existing independently of the higher cerebrospinal system. There was the life of nutrition, the lives of digestion, circulation, secretion, and perspiration, each with its own distinct "little brain" or ganglion near the sympathetic trunk (see figure 3).

Bichat argued that there was as much contrast between the tissues of the cerebellum and their white, dense cerebral nerves as there was between each "little (spinal) brain" and their tiny, red-gray, soft, innumerable nerves. On the basis of this homology, he theorized a great division at the core of human experience. All vertebrates, he proposed, lived "two lives": *une vie animale* (involving the centered experience of a brain-mind) and *une vie organique* (involving the decentered life of the sympathetic system). On one hand was the clear light of volition or rational activity, registering sense through the sense organs and responding thoughtfully to external percepts. On the other was the twilight of unceasing, everyday secretion, digestion, circulation, perspiration—a visceral automatic system maintaining the body in natural check.[13]

Such a diffuse vision of *le moi* would have been seditious—anarchic, even—had it not been tempered by powerful counterconceptions of organic sensibility. Particularly for Bichat's followers, the sympathetic system was also a strong unifying agent that supplied form to the whole. Key to this unifying concept were the body's vital properties, (supposedly) immanent in all organs, fibers, membranes, cartilage, and so on. All tissue was liable to life, sensibility being understood here as the material basis for consciousness. Bichat himself had spent long hours classifying every mode of vitality on the basis of every variety of human tissue. For months he soaked, baked, and boiled human matter and dipped it in acids and alkalis, becoming in the process the first thinker to apply the word "tissue" to the somatic weave. What Bichat discovered for the body was an irregular space of charged material sensibility, a homogeneous geography of physicalized feeling, a traffic of animate tissue that connected all masses and volumes. His assumption was that this fluctuating space of sensation was held together on the basis of a vital traffic of sensible matter regulated at the sympathetic center.

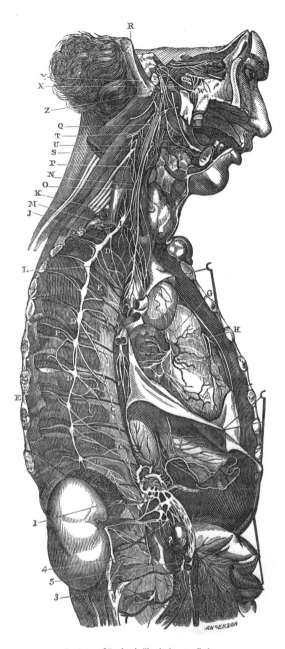

FIGURE 3. A view of Bichat's "little brains," the sympathetic nerve imagined as a line of ganglionic nodes or "stars" running parallel to the spine. H. H. Sherwood, *The Motive Power of Organic Life* (New York, 1841), 64. Courtesy of the Marian Koshland Bioscience and Natural Resources Library, University of California, Berkeley.

Such a replete conception of tissular life spilled powerfully into the work of Matuszyński's mentors at the School of Medicine. François-Joseph-Victor Broussais, probably the leading member of the senior faculty, was so devoted to sympathetic unity that he positioned himself against Bichat's theory of absolute ganglionic independence in the 1820s. For him, as for many physicians in the decade (including J.J.C. Legallois, Johann Christian Reil, and Johann Lobstein), the "empire of the great sympathetic" (as Broussais called it) was too vital to relegate to automatic life alone.[14] To seal his point, Broussais made several bold intellectual moves. First, he located *le moi* not in Bichat's cerebrospinal sphere but in ganglionic feeling (in digestion, secretion, perspiration, and nutrition). As such, Broussais made primary that which had been secondary in ways that explained why the lower self supervened in the organism at times of stress. His second move anticipated Matuszyński's dissertation exactly, as we shall see. Here, like Matuszyński, he argued against Bichat's assumption that the senses—touch, sight, taste, smell, and hearing—operated only in relation to the higher sphere. External sensation, he countered, was very much part of organic life. Third, Broussais demonstrated the extent to which this lower self asserted its authority in the life of the brain-mind. Citing instances of headless chickens and brain damage, Broussais argued that although the brain-mind might desire certain outcomes, it lacked direct control of even the most basic of muscular motions. "I can positively affirm," Broussais wrote in the 1830s, "that the capacity of regulating the muscular movements, or manual dexterity, or dexterity of any kind, [bears no] relation at all to the cerebellum."[15] The cognitive center, in other words, was not the first, primary, or principle agent of "reason" in the human body.

Such an inversion would have been anathema had it not resurrected dusty, old-hat notions of the body: ideas about the body's endless coordinations and undulations, ideas about so-called "reflex" action pioneered in the 1740s, and conceptions of sympathetic fluxions to and from the spine derived from the 1750s. The word *sympathy*, indeed, drew from ancient wells. The Hippocratic doctrine of the sympathies held that all parts of the body were connected, not by tissues or physical substance as for Broussais or Bichat, but by immaterial psychic principles (which explained why the organs could act in "consensus"). Here the elaborate line of spinal entanglements acted as the source of all sensibility, as the *sensorium commune*, the great meeting place where sense was registered and reactions willed. Life itself circled this spinal imperium, to the point that Broussais, as late as 1828, could still explain all contagion—all disease—on the basis of delicate disturbances in the sensible equilibrium. Interpreted as such, disease was merely the symptom of internal antipathies, which unbalanced the symmetry of the whole. (In 1828 alone, twenty-seven million leeches were imported into France to countermand, by bloodletting, the increasing debility of the citizen body.)[16] For Broussais, as for Matuszyński, the "sympathies" unified inner and outer life; they threw Bichat's neat "two lives" notion into peril; they posited the ideal of a body harmonized internally and externally with itself, a body open to the delirious wonder and richness of the sensory and tactile world.[17]

Time-honored though these ideas were, Broussais drew fierce criticism in 1837, as Matuszyński well knew. A new breed of skeptics, Magendie at their lead, had attacked the quantitative language still widely used to describe sensible life. The "new physiology" broke from the old ecologies, arguing that there was no material evidence for "sympathy." Via a series of brutal experiments, mostly on greyhounds, Magendie argued that there was little to prove that the ganglionic nerve had anything to do with life. That the "great sympathetic" had no observable function merely furnished evidence for his much more urgent contention that sensibility and contractility, far from being diffused throughout the organism, were qualities localized in the neuromuscular system.

Life, indeed, was other than the *idéologues* imagined. For Magendie, it had nothing to do with tissue or visible matter. Life was in the beyond—the self, if anything, was a by-product of invisible physiological functions. As one of Magendie's staunchest and most powerful supporters at the Académie des sciences, naturalist Georges Cuvier, put it, "Life is a continuous vortex. . . . The actual matter of the living body will soon be there no longer, and yet it is the depository of the force that constrains future matter to behave in the same ways as it. Thus the form of these bodies is more essential to them than their matter, since the latter changes incessantly while the former is conserved, and moreover it is the forms that constitute the differences of species, and not the combinations of matter."[18]

This take on an immaterial, regenerating self must have been provocative for Matuszyński, but he wasn't about to bite the hand that fed him. Eschewing experimental ignobility, he followed the higher-minded Broussais in stressing "the intimate rapport" that he saw binding the sympathetic nerve to the five organs of sense. *Pace* Magendie, in other words, the sympathetic nerve had everything to do with life. As Matuszyński saw it, the body achieved its healthy balance on the basis of a mysterious *sympathie intime* centered in this *region précordiale,* which maintained the form and texture of organs. The proof of this was to be sought in persons of extreme delicacy such as Chopin. In these subjects, the liaisons occurring between auditory nerves and organs, he argued, were intimate and readily identifiable. Thus surveying the literature, he was able to cite reports of young girls suffering epileptic fits at the sound of tolling bells (Samuel-Auguste Tissot in *Traité des nerfs et leurs maladies,* 1778–80), a man driven mad by the sound of the organ, a lady who, according to Jean-Jacques Rousseau, could not hear any species of music without laughing, a friend who suffered attacks of *frémissement* (tremulousness) when touching the harp, a woman who fainted on hearing vocal polyphony. Everyday evidence might be cited: the rasping physiological effect of chalk on blackboard, files on metal, tearing paper, the "asphyxiating" sound of sweeping, or the rustling of silk fabric. And then, of course, there were the delicate nerves of his closest friend, that "distinguished pianist."[19]

Matuszyński, in other words, theorized a sympathology, with the body a delicate harmonic array extending into and outward from the spinal nerve. He saw the internal organs—arranged centrifugally in consort—perpetually communing and imitating each other. The conformity of the viscera to affections and inclinations bore witness to the miracle of sensory impressions combining in life-giving association. Here Matuszyński emphasized that the sympathetic nerve was not merely a passive reflector or deflector of sensory life. More than this, it was an active agent, a primitive center that interpreted sensation back to the tissular whole. It had a sentient personality that modified every percept it received. The finesse of one's experience of the sensory world had everything to do with the creative presence of the sympathetic nerve.

THE HISTORY OF TOUCH

Matuszyński's curious conception of touch was perhaps most relevant to the concerns of Frédéric Chopin. For the medical student, as we have seen, one of the most important tasks of the sympathetic nerve was to rouse the flow of secretions. But the purpose of liquid emanations of all kinds was not merely to dispose of unwanted bodily waste. More than this, fluids acted to make sensible life vivid. Light perspiration on the skin of nerve-sensitive fingers, for example, could be indispensable to the subtle transmission of the felt impressions of outside agents.[20] Crucial to Matuszyński's thinking here was the question of how one could access the body, and how sensory traffic was mediated. To be clear: impressionability depended on the film of moisture lining the membrane between inner and outer worlds. And it was the spinal nerve that controlled the degree to which the world passed through this film before dissolving into the sea of inner life. The sympathetic system supplied an individual's sensibility with its distinctive temperament and somatic touch.

From a modern point of view these ideas may seem curious, but they were shared by nearly all physiologists of the era. Even Magendie seems to have agreed that oily secretions in the hands sharpened the intensity of human experience, and this despite the fact that, in the 1820s, the neuroanatomist worked tirelessly against the outmoded *idéologue* assumption that touch was the highest of the senses.

Physiology had to wait for the work of German experimentalists Ernst H. Weber and Johannes Peter Müller before sympathetic notions of permeable corporeality were challenged. Until Weber dipped each of his fingers into boiling water in 1834, bodies were still generally seen to act in sensitive sympathy with their environments.[21] Immersing all parts of the hand in combination—phalanges, thumb, then forehead, ears, lips, eyelids, cheeks—proved the point still further: that each body part possessed specific nerve energies, and each had its distinct way of registering and dealing with sense. Indeed, it was only after such experiments that it became possible to think that sensations are perceived not by transmission but by interpretation.[22] As Müller summarized, "The sensation of touch in our hands makes us acquainted, not absolutely with the state of surfaces of the body touched, but with changes produced in the parts of the body affected by the act of touch. . . . If we lay our hands upon a table, we become conscious, on a little reflection, that we do not feel the table, but merely that part of our skin which the table touches."[23]

The modern truth that sense is subjective, that human beings never feel *things* but merely their *sensoriums* engaging such things, was evidently a provocative claim to make in this milieu. Figures 4 and 5 illustrate the extent to which this provocation altered the construal of touch in early-century anatomical atlases.

FROM "TOUCHING" TO "TOUCH"

Touch, as every musicologist knows, was the spine of Chopin's conception of method and musical style. "The goal is not to learn to play everything with an equal sound," Chopin wrote in the sketches of his unfinished piano method. "It seems to me, a well-formed technique [is one] that can control and vary [*bien nuancer*] a beautiful sound quality." His students, famously, learned "sound" before all else; facility or velocity came only after the achievement of a uniquely sensitive or inimitable sonority at the instrument. Scholars have long argued that Chopin looked beyond questions of evenness or the equalization of fingers. Independence was never as important to him as the so-called "individuality of the fingers." "For a long time we have been acting against nature by training our fingers to be equally powerful," he continued in his method sketch. "As each finger is differently formed, it's better not to attempt to destroy the particular charm of each one's touch but on the contrary to develop it."[24] "Everything is a matter of knowing good fingering," Chopin concluded, before adding, "Hummel was the most knowledgeable on this subject."

Johann Nepomuk Hummel was indeed a venerable forebear, though he is now generally remembered for his gruff temperament and the diamond rings that adorned each of his "spidery fingers."[25] The Viennese artiste, *pace* his quirky modern reputation, was nothing if not influential in his day—particularly for Chopin, who had met him in the Austrian capital in 1830. Like Chopin, Hummel taught economy of movement: a quiet hand, calm deportment, tranquil wrist, and passive arm. Chopin had in fact followed his predecessor by recommending that the pianist's hand be turned outward, although for Chopin the hand's pivot finger was the

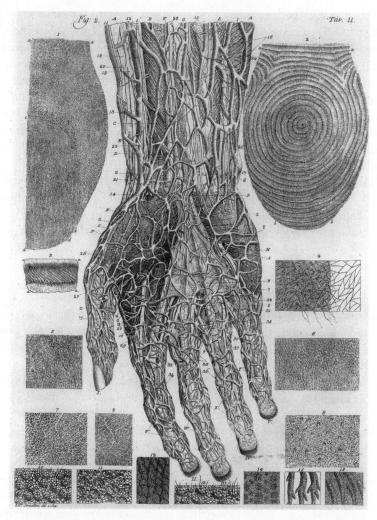

FIGURE 4. Paolo Mascagni, *Tavole figurate di alcune parti organiche del corpo umano* (Florence, 1819), Tav. II, Fig. 2. This atlas image, like many of the 1820s, is beholden to Bichat's conception of the sensible hand, fully open to the external world via tactile–tissular gateways. © BIU Santé (Paris).

index finger (dividing the hand) rather than Hummel's thumb. Furthermore, instead of counseling students to close the hand à la Hummel on C–D–E–F–G (thumb and forefinger pinching together), Chopin proposed a new "first position," with the sensitive tips opened on E–F#–G#–A#–B.

This insistence on ease and economy, for Hummel as for Chopin, had one aim:

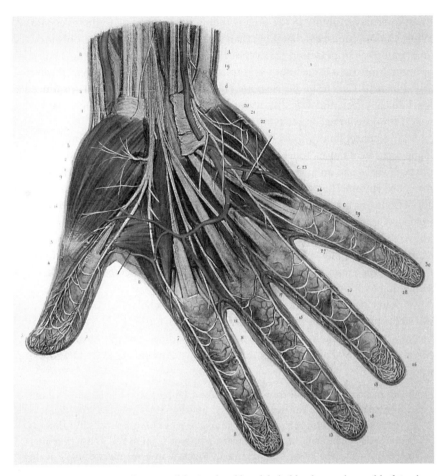

FIGURE 5. A neuromuscular view of the insulated hand, beholden less to the world of tissular sense than to internal function and form. Jean Baptiste Marc Bourgery, *Traité complet d'anatomie de l'homme* (Paris, 1844), 3: Pl. 61. © BIU Santé (Paris).

to open the acquiescing body to the finesse of its sensory environment—to the instrument and to the room. Qualities of clarity and evenness were important. But at base, the urgent point of order was the nervous sensibility of the student and the vital perspicuity of each finger. Acuity, sensitivity, susceptibility: all these had to be inculcated into the pianist's automatic habits. The tissues of the fingers, in other words, were to be animated—less as active shapers or molders of tone than as receptors, as fine receivers of the most delicate physical impressions. One can only achieve "every gradation of touch," Hummel pointed out, after acquiring "the finest internal sensibility in the fingers themselves, extending to their very tips."[26] When Chopin counseled that more than three hours practice per day only induced *abrutissement* (stupefaction by overwork), he was in fact rehearsing Hummel's opinion. More than three hours, Hummel had warned in his *Complete Theoretical and Practical Course of Instructions* (1828), dampened the spirit, produced a mechanical effect, and was disadvantageous to the performer—particularly, one would suppose, to his or her sympathetic nerves.[27]

Such a conception of touch—its principle being to cultivate an immense catalogue or array of finger "touchings" rather than seeking out *the* one, modern, metapoetic "tone"—had an ancient pedigree. On the most superficial level, the titles of many pre-Hummel keyboard methods display their queasy (for modern tastes) ideas about feeling or touching keys for all to see. Witness, for example, the English title of François Couperin's *Art of Touching the Clavecin* (1717) or castrato Niccolo Pasquali's *The Art of Fingering the Harpsichord* (1765), with its gamut of touchings *(legato, staccattisimo, sdrucciolato, tremolato)*, or even Muzio Clementi's *Introduction to the Art of Playing on the Piano Forte* (1801). For modern taste, the discomfort seems to have something to do with that awkward preposition "on."

Chopin's ideas about touch, in spite of the stories scholars tell themselves, were not so far removed. *Carezzando* (stroking the keys), *touché lourée (porté* or *portamento), touché vibratoire, piqué, détaché, porté,* and *lié* were all known to him. Of *carezzando,* fellow Polish émigré and keyboardist Antoine de Kontski wrote near midcentury:

> By this manner of touch the *sound* of the piano acquires a vibration so sensitive and so agreeable that one can no longer say, as was said formerly, *"The Piano is an instrument on which it is impossible to sing or move [anyone]!"* . . . It is thus up to the Artist to animate this instrument so cold; it is up to the Artist to render the instrument capable of singing and to touch it in a manner to make it do what he wants, that is to say, make it sing, cry, growl, and so on. All this is thus in the manner you want, and the instrument will obey at once, thanks to the combination of pedal, of touch, and especially of the amount of sensibility possessed by him who plays. For whoever wants to move those who listen to him must himself be moved, must himself vividly feel what he wants others to feel. Thus these two things in tandem, *touch* and *sentiment,* make the music irresistibly stirring.[28]

Such pianistic ideals involved freeing vital matter to be itself—liberating the life of the fingers. Thus Chopin's continual pleas with his students for *souplesse* and those insistent refrains: "You must sing if you wish to play"; "You must sing with your fingers"; "Music ought to be song."[29] "As many different sounds as there are fingers," Chopin reiterated in his unfinished *Méthode.*[30] If such words were not so familiar, they might seem curiously anthropomorphic, this tendency to conceive each phalange, this human substance, as though alive, as if breathing from the wrist.

Scholars, in other words, do a disservice to Hummel when they assume his work to be engineered for rationalizing or equalizing the fingers only, as a kind of modern gymnastics. Muscular training—building pianistic physique, power, or technique—had little to do with it. Rather, the *Complete Theoretical and Practical Course* addressed itself to its user's sensibility, or—to be precise—to his or her sympathetic system. The plethora of exercises covering every conceivable combination of finger and hand movement, as Leslie Blasius has argued, was less the result of Hummel's mild insanity than evidence of his determination to further the acquisition of fine inner sensibilities.[31] The willful concerns of modern pianism—those familiar invisibles, "weight," transference, pressure, intensity of sound, even our modern sense of that word *touch*—were not qualities to be prized in this system. In fact, quite the opposite. It was only later that it became possible to think that the hand should imprint rather than feel, that it might mold, sculpt, form, or "express" rather than "sense" its way over and across the keys. The word *touch* did not yet refer to the one forceful and poetic quality thrust upon the instrument by only the most gifted pianists. Rather, for Hummel, as for his predecessors, the ideal was to "form the hand," to purify the playing of merely subjective properties, to do away with intentional impurities, and to cleanse the playing of volition. The pedagogue's object, in short, was to transform performance—as far as possible—into the spontaneous effusion of the student's pure sympathetic temperament.

This may be a grand claim, but a host of historical evidence backs it up. Since the 1740s at least, as I have signaled, the keyboardist at play had become a key trope in scientific explications of automatic action. Famous descriptions of the human body as a vibrating harpsichord, by Diderot, for instance, in his conversation with d'Alembert in 1769—or, indeed, by Chopin with Fontana (a mutual friend of Matuszyński) late in life—are too familiar to rehearse here.[32] Suffice it to say that for these thinkers complex reflex or involuntary action did not come from within, as the product of some innate or rebellious somatic power. Rather, sympathetic movements were learned; sensibility was trained by both its host and its environment to act in apparently willful ways. For keyboardists, then, to educate the sympathetic weave was to release the will from the necessity of overseeing every bodily action. This in fact was the idea: to do away with impurities altogether. What we would today call "touch"—they apparently agreed—only implied lack of cultivation.

Take these words, written in 1749 by the English philosopher and so-called father of associationism, David Hartley:

Suppose a person who has perfectly voluntary command over his fingers, [were] to begin to learn to play upon the harpsichord: the first step is to move his fingers from key to key, with a slow motion, looking at the notes, and exerting an express act of volition in every motion. By degrees the motions cling to one another, and to the impressions of the notes . . . the act of volition growing less and less express in the time, until at last they become evanescent and imperceptible. . . . Whence we may conclude that the passage from the sensory ideal or motor vibrations which precede, to those motory ones which follow, is as ready and direct, as from the sensory vibrations to the original automatic motions corresponding to them, and consequently, that there is no intervention of the idea, or state of the mind, called will.[33]

Two years later, in 1751, Robert Whytt, whose work on the sympathies was so important, wrote:

A great variety even of the voluntary motions are many times performed, when we are insensible of the power of the will exerted in their production. . . . Thus a young player upon the harpsichord or a dance is, at first very thoughtful and solicitous about every motion of her fingers, or every step he makes while the proficients or masters of these arts perform the very same motions, not only more dexterously, and with greater agility, but almost without any reflexion or attention to what they are about.[34]

In his chapter "Sensibility and Memory" in *La Logique* (1780), French philosopher Étienne de Condillac, whose ideas became so dominant in the postrevolutionary era, concurred:

Every day my fingers acquire more facility: and finally they follow, as if by themselves, a sequence of determined movements; and they follow it without effort, without the necessity of my paying attention to them. Thus it is that the organs of the senses, having acquired different habits, move by themselves without the soul having any longer to watch continually over them in order to regulate their movements.[35]

No sense of horror; no fright at the absence of will; no unease about the idea of releasing "predetermined" habits: such insouciance would be impossible only a few decades later.

According to Blasius, the manual to fully realize such associationist principles in practice and set Parisian trends was Louis Adam's 1798 textbook for the newly formed Conservatoire, *Méthode ou principe général du doigté pour le forte-piano,* a true document of its postrevolutionary context. As Jan Goldstein has argued, the French Revolution represented something of a triumph for materialist philosophies of the sort under examination here. Around the turn of the century, a comprehensive scheme of institutional establishments aimed at regulating the automatic activity of the citizen body. For the aims of the Revolution to succeed, environmental reforms needed implementation, from the founding of a system of national secondary schools (the *écoles centrales*), to the annual cycle of revolutionary festivals, to the renaming of street signs (intended to excite patriotic thoughts and sentiments), to the institution of such influential public establishments as the Conservatoire. Like Hummel's *Course,* these public measures aimed at the education of sensible function. By directing "the chain of ideas," the *idéologues* assumed, the populace would acquire the habits of sympathetic interdependence. Sense organs, nerves, imagination, and somatic memory were to be enthused to the task. The ideals of mutual feeling and transparent sociability depended upon it.[36]

THE AEOLIAN HARP

The highly strung and yet sensorially aware posture suggested by such high-minded ideals inevitably recalls Chopin's delicacy before his Pleyel. The pianist's susceptibility to his environment was legendary. Take his obituary printed by the *Revue et gazette musicale de Paris:* "[He was] so superhumanly sensitive that everything in this world became a torment to [him]; the least contact was like a wound, the least noise like a clap of thunder, and the slightest whiff of a rose like a fatal poison."[37] Schumann's famous description of Chopin's performance of the A♭ étude from op. 25 only fortified the myth: "Imagine an Aeolian harp possessing all the scales, and an artist's hand combining these with all kinds of fantastic embellishments, but always with an audible deep ground bass, and in the treble, a softly flowing cantilena—and you will have some idea of his playing."[38]

Schumann's appeal to the familiar period metaphor of an Aeolian harp—imagining a being wholly enlivened with and by its world—was no doubt intended to intimate some impression of Chopin's calm sensitivity. It was no accident that the critic recalled the "artist's hand"—not his person—controlling the étude's apparently automatic opening A♭ arpeggiations. Georges Mathias, a pupil of Chopin's after 1838, imagined his master's extraordinary sensibility similarly: "Chopin as a pianist? First of all, those who have heard Chopin may well say that nothing remotely resembling his playing has ever been heard since . . . . the exultation, the inspiration! The whole man vibrated! The piano became so intensely animated that it gave one shivers."[39]

Descriptions of quivering nerves and sentient materiality seem common enough in the Chopin literature. Charles Rosen, for one, has written that in Chopin études, for the first time the emotion of the music and body of the performer become coequal, such that when pain is expressed, "the hand literally feels the sentiment."[40] The growing market for keyboard studies in 1830s Paris presumably reflects the burgeoning appeal of Rosen's aesthetic of presentification, this need to provoke high sensibility in aching flesh. That the emotion felt in these studies is not so much mental as physical makes them, in other words, Chopin's best and most "mature" contribution to the romantic aestheticization of pain.[41]

But the myth that Chopin was only ever "barely in existence" is, as Jeffrey Kallberg has suggested, largely the ideological work of his late and posthumous reception.[42] Chopin himself lived long enough to benefit both artistically and financially from the invention of this shy, pained, nocturnal creature, reminiscent, in Liszt's words, "of the unbelievable delicacy of a convulsive blossom poised on a stem—a cup divinely coloured but so fragile that the slightest touch will tear it."[43] It was only by the late 1840s, Kallberg suggests, that the infirmity of this "oyster sprinkled with sugar" (as Liszt's mistress, Marie d'Agoult remembered him) became consistently interpreted as a symptom of his "hardly there" existence. Because it seemed to explain his music in some way, acquaintances and critics, in other words, increasingly began to imagine him as if he had never truly been alive.

This Chopin had not always been available, as I have implied, simply because sickliness has such a long and complex history. To be sure, illness had been *en vogue* in Parisian salon culture for some time, at least since it became embroiled in old eighteenth-century ideas of nervous cultivation. And an infirm physiognomy might not necessarily signify absence or incorporeality. Before the 1840s, suffering seemed generally fashionable for precisely the opposite reasons. Around the time of Matuszyński's exam, more often, the pain you experienced might be interpreted as evidence—proof, even—of a very present situation of being. (It is worth registering the extent to which highbrow affliction was always cultivated as a mark of social distinction.) The influential philosopher and self-observationalist Maine de Biran famously wrote, "It is only unhealthy people who [actually] feel themselves existing." For Biran, a thinker whose impact on the cautious liberalism and doctrinaire ethos of the July Monarchy was considerable, as Jan Goldstein has demonstrated, pain might be the only reason you know you're alive. To feel pain, in other words, was to experience an enviable intensification of life. To be ill was potentially to be among the very few members of an increasingly "faceless" 1830s Paris that in fact truly existed.[44]

Such was the canon of the unhealthy. And its lingering cultural and political cache, evidence suggests, provoked affective practices that deliberately incited low-level suffering, at least in emigrant salon culture. Take the case of a close friend and patron of Chopin, Princess Cristina di Belgioioso-Trivulzio, famous for the green-blue tinge of her skin, revolutionary Italian connections, and her relish of the fashionable poison *Datura stramonium,* which she took to fire the nerves and stimulate "feeling." In the milieu of her rarefied salon, it seemed, persistent physical discomfort was useful for the ways it promoted that inimitable inner sense of the fragility of life. The excruciating intimacy of the letters exchanged between Chopin and Matuszyński, to cite another example, only confirms the value of physical discomfort and intense emotion to elite political sociability in early 1830s Paris.

THE "NO FOURTH FINGER" ÉTUDE

The music Chopin had in his head as he witnessed Matuszyński's defense in August 1837 was hardly immune to such principles. Only a few days after the exam—in

October 1837—the pianist's op. 25 études were published in Paris. These pieces, reconceived by Clara Wieck and Liszt in the 1830s as public "concert studies," explicitly cultivated the students' centers of feeling. Oriented around single hand shapes, small motivic figures, and motoric or automatic patterns, implementing finely balanced formal symmetries and long slurs, they explicitly engaged the pianist's performative or automatic routines. Not that the études were alone in this. All practice and performance—polonaises, impromptus, scherzos—served the perpetuation of Chopin's affective habitus, that sense of handedness, though in perhaps less conspicuous ways. Even the most allegedly "heroic" of Chopin's scores, after all, do not necessarily exclude the possibility of a tactile comportment in tune with Matuszyński's physiological assumptions.[45] This said, the medical student's vision of hands fully open to sensory environments, his claims about the sympathies, touch, and nervous sensibility, take on acute importance in light of such pieces as the F-major étude. op. 25, no. 3. What kind of body—what kind of *moi*—might this score commend?

At once apart and bound to the other pieces in the set, the F-major study begins and ends ambiguously. The music is introduced with an upbeat C, a note that continues the three postcadential Cs intoned pianissimo to end its predecessor in F minor. At the close of the study, prefiguring the ensuing piece in op. 25, are three concluding reverberations, also reserved and hushed. This time they are repeated chords broken off from the body of the piece by their midpiano homophony. The dissipating whir of the music, before this soft conclusion, has already ascended via swift trills into a generic Chopinesque close (reminiscent of the Nocturne in C Minor, op. 48, no. 1), which gently whips the right hand up and off the keyboard. The ascending fourth (C–F) in the alto of the final chords, the descending fifth (C–G) in the bass, and the repeated upper As, though, belong equally to this study as to the first intervals heard in each hand to begin the ensuing étude in A minor.

What is remarkable about these final moments, however, is not so much their open-endedness, or the study's susceptibility to its external setting. More important is that these last measures are the only three wherein the use of the pianist's fourth finger (in the right hand, at least) might properly be recommended for use (in view of Chopin's ideal). In this sense, it is significant that the first French edition score of one of Chopin's pupils, Camille O'Meara (later Mme. Dubois), should indicate the fingerings as shown in figure 6.[46] These final measures, significantly, are the only ones where the rhythmic figure that motivates the study is no longer active, and where the hands seem finally to reconcile with themselves. Ring fingers on either hand, in other words, are not necessarily required for any of the preceding measures—sixty-nine of them! Chopin's famous complaint—"All I have left is just a big nose and an *undeveloped* fourth finger"—might of course explain this quirk (these words appeared in a letter to his friend Fontana ten days before his famous Manchester appearance).[47] But the fourth fingers' absence is probably

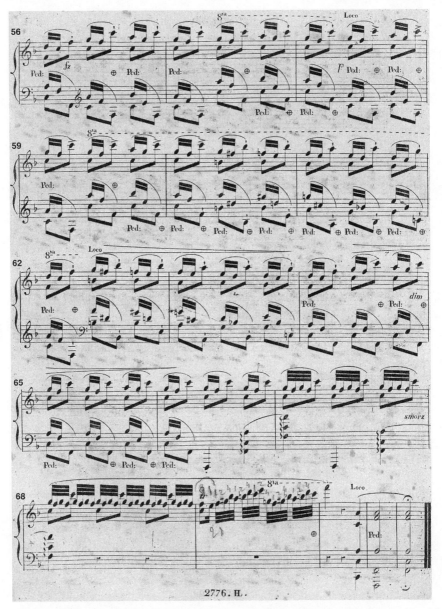

FIGURE 6. Chopin's Étude op. 25, no. 3, coda, with fingerings at m. 69, probably in the composer's hand, from the Dubois–O'Meara score. Frédéric Chopin, *Études pour le piano* (Paris, 1842), 35v. The measure numbers are my additions. Reproduced by permission of the Bibliothèque nationale de France.

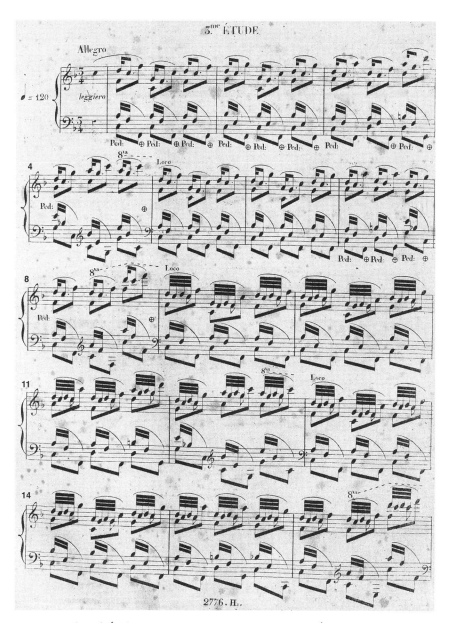

FIGURE 7. Chopin's Étude op. 25, no. 3, mm. 1–16. Frédéric Chopin, *Études pour le piano* (Paris, 1842), 34r. Reproduced by permission of the Bibliothèque nationale de France.

more the result of this: that the F-major study is merely an extraordinary example of Chopin's intention to cultivate the tactile and sonorous personality of each finger. Each finger (besides the fourth), in fact, must find its own special sensibility within the fractured texture.

Most obviously, the étude is generated by a repeating "ricochet" figure for both hands, the rhythmic cadence of which suggests a reflex movement (figure 7). The eight fingers needed here divide into four pairs of two, each pair tracing intervals that recoil against each other. In the right hand, the outer digits (one and five) outline a lyrical rebounding melody in octaves, which opens up a tender fourth in the first bar, a fifth in the second, and a sixth in the third before reaching out to an octave interval in the fourth. Fingers two and three, meanwhile, subtly blur the reverberating C of the left hand (the same C that suggested the piece into existence in the first instance). This reverberating C, always retiring and returning on first beats, is in fact sustained in some form as late as measure 24, when—dissolving and subtly shifting gear—an F♯ reverberation begins to supply its place. Always playing against the inside-outside pair in the right hand, meanwhile, is the laterally shifting left hand, the thumb and forefinger of which are shifted away from the lower fingers and their bass undulations.

The sense of vibrating stasis conjured in the opening of this study is largely sustained by that C pedal offset by the gentle tonic offbeats of the left hand's fifth finger. Crescendos at measures 4 and 8 prolong the hovering uncertainty, urging the fingers to play across the four-plus-four, answer-response phrases. Measures 9 to 16 simply repeat the opening eight measures. But these are now "lost measures." The mirror effects of the competing digit-pairs are embellished with shiver-trills in the central finger-pair of the right hand. An auxiliary voice stressing C emerges from this shimmering texture—notated with down-stems—suggesting an inside-out version of the rebounding right-hand melody. This memory of the opening has the effect of distancing the player even further from her hands. The echo sounds suggest self-consciousness, as if the performer were listening to herself, or merely observing the automatic action of fingers performing a long, learned, involuntary movement.

Taken as a whole, the study may be felt as one glorious sympathetic reflection, or rebounding motion, in three parts. The piece's most striking feature, as many musicologists have observed, is the B-major restatement of the theme at the core of the piece at measure 29, harmonically as remote as you can get from F major.[48] One would perhaps expect that such an audacious in-and-out tritone movement (dividing the octave symmetrically) would generate a mood of "distance" in this middle section. The opposite is in fact the case. When B major explodes into action at measure 29, the transposed "false recapitulation" that ensues is more grounded than both the opening tonic statement and its later reprise (m. 49). The left hand has now been rewritten as a simpler span, making the dynamic easier to achieve

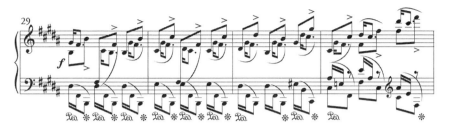

MUSICAL EXAMPLE 1. Chopin's Étude op. 25, no. 3, the "A section" from m. 29. Frédéric
Chopin, *Études pour le piano* (Paris, 1842), 34v.

(see example 1). More than this, its pulsating D♯s lend this middle section a far
weightier first-inversion feel than before. The displaced accents in the right hand,
coinciding now with the bass tonics, both nullify the effect of the bar line and
reinforce rootedness. What we hear in this study, harmonically speaking, is not so
much an A–B–A form as a reverse B–A–B structure (all admitting that the B-major
theme is exactly mirrored in both flanking sections).

This said, Chopin divided the study in a subtler way than I have so far suggested. He appeared less concerned with these great harmonic surges than with
the reverberating Cs and F♯s mentioned earlier. In the score, changes of key signature (mm. 29 and 45) segment the 72-measure study in an impeccably symmetrical
way (28 + 16 + 28). The division to notice is at measure 45. It is here, four bars
before the F-major reprise, that the C reverberation shifts back into focus as an
inner voice in the right hand. Chopin's palindromic conception, which softens the
effect of the final F-major recapitulation (its *sforzandi* and introductory diminuendo notwithstanding), once again highlights the vitality of this B-major nucleus.
It is around this nerve center that the outlying material reverberates, as if rebounding inward and outward from it.

The way in which this inward-outward reflex is managed only adds to the pianist's sense of delicate poise. In broad terms, the transitions into and away from B
major might be said to involve a whole-tone progression (as Salzer has argued)—
C–B♭–A♭–F♯–E–D–C—which at halfway stage (reaching F♯), diverts and explodes
into the 16-measure core just discussed. This harmonic surge toward B major, as
the surge away, occurs in three 4-measure sections, each with a 2-measure statement and its 2-measure sympathetic echo. Measures 17 to 20 initiate the scheme,
the middle voice of the right hand leading the fifth finger of the left through a
parallel C–B♭–A♭ harmonic shift. The final pair of these bars echoes the first a tone
down. For the following four measures (21–24), the mode of reflection becomes
registral and dynamic. This time the bass leads, briefly escaping the whole-tone
pattern by slipping a half step to G. (The parallel fifth and octave shifts are dis-

guised with deft prolongations.) The final mirror effect (before the *ritenuto* and B major)—written over an F♯ bass now—is achieved by voice exchange. Here the melodic outline traced by the thumb of the left hand (mm. 25–26) is commandeered by the thumb of the right in measures 27 and 28. Meanwhile, the bass in these slowing and expanding bars imitates (at the octave) what the right-hand thumb had played in the previous statement.

Exactly equivalent scenes of sympathy and antipathy perpetuate the whirl back to F from measures 37 to 49: the F♯–E–D movement pauses to reflect on C♯ (m. 41), settles a clear dominant on C (m. 45), and reenacts the uninhibited, "automatic" reprise. After this (our "lost bars" are now truly lost), an extraordinary coda ensues, which in itself might be read as a muted sympathetic echo of all that has passed before (bars 56–72). This section too has three parts (B–A–B), including a five-bar reverberation-codetta to end. Once again, the symmetry is ingenious. For twelve beats an undulating tonic-dominant pattern plays with registral and dynamic reflections. For the next twelve, somehow, B major and the memory of the piece's nervous center returns to the fingers, again in such a way as to keep the sense of double focus (the last six beats echo the first six an octave below). The tiny twelve-beat reprise that ensues recalls the shiver-effects of the "lost measures" for its final six beats. But inevitably, these last sounds, reverberating around C, spin into a trill, as if the sensible energies of the sympathetic nerve were finally losing shape and dissipating away.

AWKWARD ENDINGS

What has happened here? Despite my best efforts, the "new fact" has again led to uncomfortable conclusions. Readers may object that this chapter has only succeeded in reducing a Chopin étude to a form of complex autonomic activity, a kind of physiological "secretion." My analysis, perhaps, makes too little distinction between musics performed and bodies playing it. (One might counter that there is no aspect of musical activity, produced or heard, that is not embodied.) Worse, it has repathologized Chopin. Where once the Romantic impulse had been to interpret his music as the expression of a supposedly semimortal being, now his music merely recalls his this-worldly body, perhaps less pained, but still afflicted. The same hypersensitive composer-performer remains, although now (at least) the hypersensitivity involves a materially or historically situated *moi.*

This étude, I have suggested, provided elegant Parisians with an instrument for the induction of cultivated feelings, the text being used for the pleasurable exploration of an elite political comportment. The score, in other words, served in the acquisition of a life-world, where tactile pleasures and autonomic routines could be cultivated as physical "proofs" of high-class sentience. As a script for the animation of sympathetic life, the text educated sense. Its musical scenes of bounding and rebounding movement, autonomic echoes and replies, sympathy and antipathy, and repetitions and reverberations acted for the vivification of the student-pianist's sympathetic faculties. Enlivening the life of the fingers, the score projected the student's body into an improvisatory whirl. Thus the symmetry of the deft move from the world of external sense to the intimate core and back again. This music, in short, was originally played in relation to a richly vitalist experience of body. Its refinement can be read as a measure of the extent to which matters of intense susceptibility and refined deportment coming under pressure in Chopin and Matuszyński's milieu. What we have with the publications of these scores is an argument for the truth of intelligent matter, for the value of a finely tuned ethic of social conduct. At once avant-garde and conservative (indeed, antidemocratic), this music related, in intimate ways, to one of the most extreme takes on localized somatic agency, "individualized" or sentient fingers, as has ever been conceived.

Balance and pain (though perhaps not illness) are still properly at the core of Chopin's reception and his world, I think. But I wonder whether all the talk of breathless metaphysics has obscured something palpable in the pianist-composer's scores: that there is a material effect, something needlingly physical about them, perhaps related to the cool low-level pain that practice and performance brings. It is a music, finally, that we may find argues insistently for our own fragility, for our own materiality, and for our beholdenness to the automatic life of our bodies.

3

The Sontag-Malibran Stereotype

The word female (femina) seems to derive its etymology from the word family (familia) since woman is the common centre of all families, the source of the generations of men, and the universal link of human beings. She gives life, and she leads to death; her purity is the great support of morality, and the very ground-work of society; and her profligacy enervates the courage of men, and depraves the morals of the community. Possessing equally the power of good and evil, of love and hatred, of pleasure and pain, she becomes the vis insita, *the regulator, and the perturbing force in the whole system of human nature. . . . A being so feeble is, even from the very debility of her organisation, more liable to adopt every impression, to lend herself to all the sensations of the heart and mind, and to increase their energy and elevation by means of her exquisite sensibility.*

From this endless pliability of the female character, and the imitative quality annexed to it, as well as that extreme versatility which complies with every modification of manners, arises a contradictory creature, which is incapable of definition, and distinct discrimination. With women every thing is easy, variable, fleeting.

ÉTIENNE DE JOUY (ETHNOLOGIST, HERMIT, FORMER POLITICAL
PRISONER, AND LIBRETTIST OF ROSSINI'S GUILLAUME TELL)

LONDON

Just before two o'clock on the afternoon of 30 May 1829 there was a rush at the doors of the Argyll Rooms, a suite of four spacious apartments on Regent Street, in central London. Carriages drew up along the arcade (John Nash's recent design); attendants hustled up and down making way for their employers. Most of the fashionables pressing on the entrance were women who, having paid ten shillings and sixpence at the door, had their coats removed as they climbed the stairs to the main chamber. Those who had obtained copies of the fashion journal *La Belle Assemblée* probably stole a march on their rivals: they entered the Argyll's strange parallelogram-shaped concert room in short-sleeved rose satin dresses *à la Circassienne*. Convent crosses and cordons of embroidered flowers were also de rigueur

66

for the season. If brave, one might even try a headdress in rose crepe adorned with ostrich feathers. The boxes and parterre were already overflowing. Patrons might perhaps overhear talk of Turner's views of England and Wales, which were being exhibited around the corner in the Egyptian Hall at 22 Piccadilly.[1] The less fortunate, denied entrance for want of proper seating, arranged refunds at the door and doubtless contemplated the tedious journey home. In the bustle, it was unlikely that too many noticed the giant mythological figures—"discreditably painted," so one critic judged—adorning the walls of the 713-seat venue.[2]

The *Times* reported of the second concert that the room was "so exceedingly crowded that it was found necessary to accommodate some of the company with seats in the orchestra."[3] Whether this measure was strictly necessary or not, seating ladies among the instrumental players had a striking visual effect. Had the critic recalled his review of Giuseppe de Begnis's benefit on Thursday morning, 21 May, he would have remembered that this arrangement was no mere emergency measure. On that day too, the Italian basso buffo had given a concert at which "a great number of ladies [had] sat amidst the performers in the orchestra." An explanation suggested itself: "The *coup d'oeil* from thence to the pit, which was almost exclusively occupied by ladies dressed in the gayest attire of the season, and wearing satin hats of various colors, ornamented with flowers, was of the most picturesque description that can well be imagined."[4] By 30 May, nine days after the experiment was first tried, the practice of adding delicate female touches to the male orchestra had been more or less established. Seating women among the instrumentalists, in short, was not only the pragmatic response to a lack of seating. The innovation added attractive feminine color to an otherwise traditionally uniform and masculine space.

Similar scenes characterized each of the "grand morning concerts" cohosted by Velluti and Thomas Welsh in mid-1829. Welsh relished the phalanx of fashion in his chambers: he was a music seller, ex-bass, proprietor, and principal shareholder of the Regent's Harmonic Institution, a music publishing company attached to the Argyll Rooms. The forty-eight-year-old Velluti, struggling in his career as a theatrical singer, as we have seen, operated a singing academy out of the same building. As ever, the "shadow with lorn eyes," as a poet in the *Examiner* had recently called him, haunted the scene; the castrato was probably on board with the proprietor right from the planning stages of the series.[5] The band put together, now filing into the room, was made up of members of the Philharmonic, the Ancient Concert, and disaffected members of the King's Theatre orchestra. (Many of this last group had recently been fired in a pay dispute.) Led by violinist Franz Cramer and "conducted" from the piano by George Smart, the group was a force to be reckoned with. For the star-studded performance of 30 May, Velluti had signed the twenty-year-old Felix Mendelssohn to make his performing debut in London. (Only twelve days earlier, you will recall, the castrato had "passed beneath the window.")

Mendelssohn played Weber's *Konzertstück* for piano and orchestra, op. 79, a piece that would become one of Liszt's war-horses. The Belgian violinist and future husband of Malibran, Charles de Bériot, performed variations of his own composition; Mademoiselle Blasis sang a Pacini aria and duet with Alberico Curioni (the tenor who would create Orombello in Bellini's *Beatrice di Tenda*, 1833); two new German singers on the scene, Franz Rosner and Amalia Schütz, presented arias in their native language. The sensation of the season, Maria Malibran, introduced a piece composed for her by Bériot.

But the real coup of Welsh's series was the engagement of Henriette Sontag for Velluti's concerts (11, 15, 22, and 30 May). The German siren had taken time off from her hectic schedule, probably to care for a child she had borne in secret toward the end of 1828 (the father being Count Rossi, Sardinian ambassador to The Hague). The unofficial press version of the scandalous story, potentially libelous since Rossi faced a shameful disinheritance, was that Sontag had slipped on a cherrystone in her boudoir. Reports suggested they had been married in secret two years earlier, the count having obtained a cabinet order from George IV to indemnify his union with a minor.[6] Rumors ran wild as to the truth of her situation. "She no longer has such a pretty waist," Malibran jibed on 8 September.[7] Even as the German Nightingale reappeared in Paris at the Théâtre Italien on 29 January 1829, she soon receded into obscurity after a showdown with Malibran's *Tancredi* on 31 March 1829. Versions of her plight, meanwhile, were elaborated to incorporate orange peels rather than cherrystones. (Orange selling, according to its long-standing associations in London theaters, suggested prostitution.) And if Sontag was promiscuous, then Rossini had been her pimp, Théophile Gautier once deriding the maestro as "an orange tree spontaneously producing its round, golden fruit."[8]

Since her final appearance in a Paris production of *Tancredi*, Sontag had used some of her free time to make an advance tour to the English capital. This was already weeks before the commencement of what Ayrton at the *Harmonicon* called a "fast and loose engagement" in 1829 with Laporte, the aforementioned comanager of the King's Theatre and representative of the London interests of the director of the Théâtre Italien in Paris. On arrival, according to the *Quarterly Musical Magazine and Review,* the soprano found that Laporte's main attraction for the 1829 season, Malibran, was not in full cry. Engaged as *prima donna assoluta* for the season, Malibran had not made a good journey across the Channel, and opinion had cooled after her debut as Rosina in Rossini's *Barbiere* on 21 April.[9] So when Laporte learned of Sontag's arrival, he tracked her down and engaged her for a run of concerts he was putting together with harpist Nicolas Bochsa. In the contract presented to her, Laporte sought to close a deal that would prevent her appearance at any venue other than his own. He was so confident of securing her compliance in this that he even began to advertise her debut for 28 April 1829 in the light blue luxury of the King's Concert Room, a newly refurbished chamber attached to his main auditorium.[10] The move was premature: Velluti and Welsh had made a counteroffer behind his back with terms favorable enough to seal her acceptance, delay her entrance on the King's main stage until 5 May (as Angelina in *Cenerentola*), and keep her (for the moment) from Laporte's jealous grasp.[11]

In the wake of the Sontag intrigue, Welsh's concert series attracted widespread publicity—not all of it complimentary. In the *Harmonicon*, Ayrton complained that "the music selected is, for the greater part, of that insipid, mawkish kind, which the singers, aided by a few tasteless people of influence, are at present forcing, not down the throats, but into the ears of such of the public that are passive, and allow themselves to be drugged by the wretched stuff of Nicolini, Bonfichi, Mosca, Pacini, &c. &c."[12] Richard Bacon at the *Quarterly Musical Magazine* disagreed, arguing in retrospect that "the concerts [Welsh] gave were by far the finest of the season, whether the variety and elevation of the talent employed, the solid excellence of he compositions performed, or the superiority of the orchestra be considered. The public heard there Sontag, Malibran, and Velluti, with the richest combination of talent in every department. . . . While the concerts at the opera concert room entailed a loss upon the proprietor, Mr Welch's [*sic*] increased in attraction and success."[13] Unusually for morning concerts, every one of Velluti's events had been sold out.

The third and fourth concerts in Velluti's series were near-identical with one another. On both 22 and 30 May, the audience was large and predominantly made up of women. There were some insignificant differences. On 30 May Rosner sang Don Ottavio's "Il mio tesoro" from *Don Giovanni* as "Tränen vom Freund getrocknet"; this was in contrast to his London debut the previous Friday, when he had performed a *scena* from *Der Freischütz*. At the later concert, Velluti was "in charming voice" and sang what the *Times* described as "a beautiful composition" ("Ah che forse" by Giuseppe Nicolini) "with spirit as well as delicacy above all praise," a statement in defiance of those critics of chapter 1 who insisted he be retired. It was also Sontag rather than Malibran who rendered the week's highly embellished aria by Mercadante ("Del mio pianto") and "performed new miracles." This time Mendelssohn replaced a young German pianist, Edward Schultz, who had played a set of Henri Herz variations on "Ma Fanchette est charmante" from Boieldieu's *Angéla* (1814). Mendelssohn preferred a work that the *Times* described as "a description of a soldier's farewell to his mistress." The pianist was a revelation, not only producing "a powerful effect" in the march's crescendo, but performing all four of Weber's movements entirely from memory, an unheard-of feat in 1829. At this concert Velluti sang alongside Sontag in "Questo cor" from Rossini's first opera, *Demetrio e Polibio* (1812).

None of this detail would be worth mentioning, of course, did it not whet the appetite for the main attraction. The headline act in each case was the final face-off between Malibran and Sontag. On 30 May, this number was the stunningly virtuosic two-soprano duet from Rossini's *Tancredi,* "Lasciami, non t'ascolto." On 22 May the duet's partner piece brought the program to a climax: "Ebben a te: ferisci," from the same composer's *Semiramide.*[14] So blistering was the performance that Velluti arranged for its repetition at two extra concerts. The first was his own benefit of 9 June. The second occurred six days later for the benefit of organizer-in-chief Welsh. At this final event, Sontag and Malibran brought down the curtain on a dazzling 1829 season on Regent Street by singing both of Rossini's showpieces.[15]

Two concerts, two duets sung by two *prime donne:* the Sontag-Malibran infatuation of 1829 was adjudged—whatever the subsequent rulings of history—as the greatest concert phenomenon of the age. The authority of their fused sound was certainly provocative. In Paris, for example, this double sonority inspired the first uses of the word *diva,* a one-off creature very different from the familiar trope now so beloved of opera houses and music conservatories. The remainder of this chapter argues that the success of their stereotype betrays the extent to which "many-voicedness" was increasingly being feminized across Europe. Sontag and Malibran themselves no doubt resisted the emerging status quo, not by identifying voice with sex, but by placing expression in their highly dynamic nervous systems. Rather than buying into an essentialist concept of voice, in other words, these women deployed a tactic of vocal dispersal. If anything, Sontag and Malibran themselves worked against the conservative idea that they sang for women, or that women sang with only one voice. For many, their sound suggested biological indeterminacy and a dangerous sensuality. It was just that they had to contend with social conventions and, in particular, male critics, who framed even their equivocality in powerfully gendered terms.

PARIS

A lavish display of dress, a blaze of candlelight, perfumes; so many pretty arms, and lovely shoulders; bouquets, the entrancing melody of Rossini's music, Ciceri's paintings! I am carried right out of myself!

STENDHAL, *SCARLET AND BLACK*

The Sontag-Malibran *engouement* dated back to 27 January 1829 in Paris. Sontag had reappeared at the Salle Favart as Rosina, a role suited to her ravishing soprano sfogato and ease of execution. The winter had been particularly bleak at the Théâtre Italien, and many Italophiles had deserted their time-honored wateringhole in despair of ever finding sustenance. That evening, Malibran could be seen in her loge on the third tier. During intermission, according to one anecdote, Rossini appeared onstage and announced that he had left Malibran in tears in her box despairing that she would ever match such perfection and purity of execution.[16] Actress Katherine Bauer remembered Malibran whispering, "My God! Why does she sing so beautifully!" as Sontag delivered her part.[17]

Rumors began to circulate among the dilettanti suggesting that Sontag and Malibran had been brought together at a private concert. Some said their meeting had been organized by the Condesa de Merlin, the Afro-Cuban noblewoman whom we met briefly in the first chapter. A plot had apparently been hatched at her salon, where *Tancredi*'s "Fiero incontro" was called for unexpectedly: "[The pair] stood gazing at each other with a look of distrust and confusion; but at length the closing chord of the introduction roused their attention, and the duo commenced." Merlin remembered that at the final cadence "they joined hands, and, inclining affectionately towards each other, they interchanged the kiss of friendship with all the ardour and sensibility of youth."[18] Others would speculate (inaccurately) that Fétis had effected their first reconciliation after unpleasant scenes of rivalry at the King's Theatre. He remembered how he had first accompanied them at the piano in *Semiramide*'s "Ebben, a te: ferisci" at Lord Saltoun's house: "It was the first time those two voices had rung together; and the effect of this [duet] was indescribable, for both the two great singers, each striving to out-sing the other, severally attained a pitch of perfection higher than any they had reached before."[19] Yet another implausible account had the wit, bon vivant, and Russian consul general, Chevalier George de Benkhausen, introducing them on the turf of Epsom Races over champagne and Gunter's ice cream: "They gazed one instant at each other, another instant and their hands were clasped, and a tear glistened in the eye of the daughter of the South, who was passion's essence, whilst a deeper tint mantled the cheek of the more reserved German.... Thus for the first time met the two greatest musical geniuses of the age."[20] Some even claimed it was Rossini himself who had first played the keyboard introduction to "Ebben, a te: ferisci" for them at some fashionable house. In "Giorno d'orror!," the story went, their voices "united, or rather melted into one another with incomparable smoothness." Moving into the *tempo di mezzo*—while Sontag was singing "T'arresta. Oh Dio"—"Rossini cried 'Oh! That was beautiful!' embraced them both and pushed them together, but Maria stepped back and Sontag turned away."[21]

Contrasting though they were, these anecdotes carried similarities. First, it seemed important that some (usually male) figure lurked behind the pair's coming together. Second, it seemed necessary that the singers' vocal relationship be mirrored physically. Theirs was an intense personal rivalry caught up in a circle of estrangement and reconciliation. Induced to pull apart, they would continually be brought together to embrace and make up. These scenes of intimacy and loathing, this back-and-forth movement, made for a dynamic that—like the *vocalismo d'agilità* that formed in their throats—was always in flux.

Four months before Velluti's series in London, the love-hate relationship between Sontag and Malibran was finally staged for the public. Laurent had advertised them together for 15 January at the Théâtre Italien but repeatedly postponed their appearance in order to fire expectation. Exactly a month later, on 15 February

1829, the *directeur-entrepreneur* finally bowed to public pressure. The occasion was his benefit, and he took the opportunity to double ticket prices. Later that year, the *Times* of London published a "retrospect," recording that this date caused an "epidemic" in Paris.[22] Exacerbated by a burgeoning and newly active musical press, such cults of celebrity—described here in terms of metaphors of mass illness or popular delusion—could scarcely have been anticipated. The public divided into two camps. Three-fourths of the dilettanti and most of the fashionable world became committed Malibranistes; the remaining aristocrat savants, musicians, and cognoscenti were Sontagists.

In these early days the papers favored the "Koeniglichsaalkammersangerinn," as one journalist called her, whose throat was "a veritable compendium of vocal fiorature *[sic]*": "Sontag, with that sort of *aplomb* which the consciousness of superior ability as a vocalist could not fail to give her, went through the part of *Amenaïde*, which seemed to have been almost purposely written for her clear and easy vocalization, with great success."[23] A reporter for the *Morning Chronicle* who witnessed the Parisian spectacle enjoyed seeing Malibran in trousers: "The crusader's garb is moreover extremely welcoming to her person; and her portraiture of the youthful hero is thus rendered in all respects a dramatic personation of the most engaging interest." "The prevailing light, graceful, and airy character of the music belonging to the part of Amenaïde recommend it no less as a favourable specimen of Mademoiselle Sontag's talents," the reviewer continued, "than do different qualities recommend *Tancredi* for the display of Madame Malibran's." The reviewer then braced for the opera's showpiece: "The great gem of the performance is the duet 'Lasciami!—non t'ascolta', in which the voices of Madame Malibran and Mademoiselle Sontag blend together with a strain of the richest and most delicious melody."[24]

Heated debates raged over Spanish cigarettes at the Café de Paris. Tempers frayed over ices at Tortoni's, that center of Italophile dandyism. The great Rossini acolyte and critic Paul Scudo remembered a war so fierce "between the imperious Juno and the blonde Venus that they could not remain together in the same room. . . . Their stupendous jealousy manifested itself by malicious cadenzas and rockets of sound . . . which inflamed their hearers. Now it was the Trojans burst all bonds, and now the Greeks. The parterre rose and fell like the waves of the sea under the touch of the divinities of Olympus." For Scudo, this clash of deities brought about "the most glorious—the culminating epoch of the *Italiens* in Paris."[25] The Salle Favart was revived.

Had they an eye for it, opera scholars would probably view the Malibran-Sontag *engouement* as at once fashionable and unfashionable. Fashionable, because the years around 1830 saw an important though perhaps uneasy reinvigoration of the once amorous musico-soprano idiom in Italian and French opera. The more familiar examples of this Indian summer occur in Donizetti's *Elisabetta al castello di*

Kenilworth (1829), *Anna Bolena* (1830), *Ugo, conte di Parigi* (1832), and *Maria Padilla* (1841); and, of course, Bellini's *Norma* (1831). They are unfashionable, in addition, because scholarship tends to consider those supposedly austere moments of *canto fiorito* (literally, flowered or flowery song) at their peak in *Semiramide* as old hat by the late 1820s; in fact, they were shopworn even by the standards of the early 1820s, when Rossini still composed for Italian theaters. As Heather Hadlock has put it, "Giorno d'orror!" seems at once backward- and forward-looking.[26] The vocal writing, she argues, points toward the past, but also to lush two-soprano duets like Bellini's "Mira, O Norma" in operas of the 1830s. Was this double focus and the paradox Hadlock describes a by-product of the Sontag-Malibran success in the concert hall? Did these singers inspire the belated—shall we say "romantic"?—tendency to preserve old two-soprano styles as were formerly prized by Rossini's audience at La Fenice? The question of whether these two-soprano conventions were adaptable to same-sex dramatic environments (as exchanges between sisters, rivals for love, and mothers and daughters) was certainly fraught.[27]

A GENDERED EMERGENCE?

A surviving piano score offers a rare glimpse of Malibran and Sontag in combined voice. In autumn of 1829, Ignaz Moscheles published a piano reduction of "Ebben, a te: ferisci" in his *Gems à la Malibran II*. Although not a full transcription, the score was based on the moment when the twinned sopranos were first heard in London, perhaps even on a set of manuscript parts prepared for the occasion by Moscheles himself. Prefaced by a brief arrangement of "Crudel! Perche finora" from Mozart's *Figaro*, "Ebben, a te: ferisci" dominated the second of his two-volume collection of "dramatic fantasias" re-creating memorable Malibran moments for the piano-playing amateur. What makes this score valuable for modern research is an inscription prominently displayed on the title page: "with the admired embellishments & cadences, as sung by Mad. Malibran."[28] The volume's importance is immediately recognizable in another way, too, as a measure of how freely Sontag and Malibran altered the weave of Rossini's text. Beneath the concessions Moscheles made to meet the requirements of the bourgeois pianist, these pages conceal not so much performances as compositions. Feminist appeals to the live power of "pure voice" aside, these interpolations do not merely redecorate pauses or ornament repeats in formulaic ways. In a hard physical sense, rather, the doubled artistes rework the (Rossinian) melody from the opening notes of their parts, creating—as we shall see—"in unison."

Moscheles's benefit concert took place not at the Argyll Rooms but at the King's Concert Room on 8 May 1829. Besides his own Symphony in C, op. 81, and a performance of a piano fantasy entitled "Sir Walter Scott's Favourite Strains of the Scottish Bards," Moscheles programmed and then "conducted" this key Sontag-

Malibran squaring-off. Given the license taken by performers, authoritarian-idealists in the press corps were piqued. The *Times* of the following day attacked Moscheles for performing keyboard arrangements of what it assumed were Rossini highlights. The reviewer conceded, however, that the big attraction—the "Ebben, a te: ferisci"—"was listened to with great delight."[29] Ayrton, at the *Harmonicon,* was of two minds as to the merits of the exhibition. He noted that Malibran had used this concert to perform "not 'Di tanti palpiti' properly so called, but what can only be considered as variations on it; and thus substituted her own tinsel for the sterling air, with a self-complacency that we never before saw equalled." In Ayrton's formulation, the severity of the "damage" done to Rossini's original was matched only by the extent of the overhaul done on the final showstopper. He could allow, on one hand, that the *Semiramide* duet had been sung "with charming effect." On the other, he bristled that "the last part of this was so altered by the *concetti,* that it was difficult to trace the author's notes."[30]

At the heart of the Sontag-Malibran version, of course, was the duet's illustrious andante, "Giorno d'orror! E di contento!" In Rossini's opera, in the original dramatic context, incest has just reared its ugly head, as Arsace (performed *sans travesti* by Malibran in concert performance) has been revealed as the long-lost son of Sontag's Queen Semiramide. In this horrific moment of mother-child recognition, the Babylonian queen binds vocally to a character she once tried to seduce and marry. Pressed into his mother's arms, at the crucial moment Arsace embraces Sontag in parallel thirds ("Arsace si getta fra le di lei braccia, esso la stringe con trasporto; restano abbracciati"). Drawn into an acoustic circle, the singers express not so much the rapture of the maternal bond as the moral dread of sexual attraction for each other. The identification of the mother in this scene ("Ma sei mia madre ancor") is striking for the way it sets up a renovation of the aging musico-soprano idiom (conventionally associated with erotic love) by turning it into a sexually charged and socially "dangerous" two-soprano expression of "natural" consanguinity.

Moscheles's "transcription" is notable for its key scheme. In Rossini's original, the music sifts into four harmonic broad areas—I am borrowing Basevi's anachronistic "solita forma de' duetti" (two kinetic-static pairs divisible as *tempo d'attacco*–cantabile/*tempo di mezzo*–cabaletta): E–G/E–E.[31] The Sontag-Malibran equivalent, by contrast, avoids tonal closure and is senseless in purely musical terms: F–G/G–Eb. (Rossini's already brief *tempo di mezzo* appears as a somewhat nonsensical four-bar accompaniment figure in Moscheles's reduction.) Since such transpositions cannot be justified in terms of ease of keyboard performance, it is likely that they represent accommodations made for singers—and fairly routine ones at that, since more drastic alterations than these were common in operatic practice of the day.[32] The vocal styles of both Malibran and Sontag are equally discernable in the transcription.

"Giorno d'orror!" was apparently transposed for Sontag. It matched her tessitura perfectly ("she is very fond of singing in G").[33] Her voice was in its element,

MUSICAL EXAMPLE 2. Double cadenza preparing for the *tempo di mezzo* in *Semiramide*'s "Ebben a te: ferisci." See Ignaz Moscheles, *Gems à la Malibran: A Dramatic Fantasia for the Piano Forte II, with the Admired Embellishments & Cadences, as Sung by Mad. Malibran* (London, 1829).

particularly as it broached the end of this slow movement. Of all the allures in these duets, both of which featured at Welsh's benefit of 15 June, the *Courier* singled out this passage for comment:

> The beautiful duet Giorno d'Orrore *[sic]* seems now identified with the names of Sontag and Malibran; being concertante throughout, it is well chosen for the mutual display of their powers; neither can be said to play an inferior part, and in the contest, as it were, between them, they produce an effect of which no person who has not heard them can form an adequate conception. The delicious cadences of their own introduced at the end of the andante are executed as tastefully as they are written.[34]

In the Sontag-Malibran version, the most commented-upon part of this cantabile, and indeed of the whole duet complex, was the final double cadenza anticipating the *tempo di mezzo*. Moscheles's piano reduction, according to the *Athenaeum,* "skilfully imitates Malibran's double cadences in Giorno d'orrore" (see example 2).[35]

Evidence suggests that Malibran authored this cadenza in a sketchbook she used for preparing ornaments, variations, gestures, facial expressions, and other details of her parts. The *Athenaeum* hailed her work in June:

Double cadences, either by a voice or an instrument, or by two voices, are almost invariably the dullest and worst arranged things possible; but, upon this occasion, the cadence of Sontag with Malibran was perhaps the most beautiful feature of the performance, not only as regarded the execution displayed, but the excellent arrangement of the passages, musically speaking; and especially let it be remembered, that it was the *composition* (for it deserves that denomination) of Malibran herself! The orchestral performers seemed to be inspired by the excellence of the singers, and the whole was exceedingly delightful, and highly superior to any previous performance of the same description.[36]

A classic Malibran trait, exemplified in Moscheles's score, was to insert improvisations into the text at unconventional points, as in the Sontag-Malibran performance of *Tancredi*'s "Lasciami, non t'ascolta." In 1836, Castil-Blaze remembered that Malibran "would combine and note down points [of embellishment] in her duets." "We all recollect the pauses Mme. Malibran inserted in the three duets in *Tancredi*," he remembered in the *Revue de Paris*. "She put in the best of them with Mlle. Sontag, and the tradition of them has remained."[37] Registering these free insertions fully, the singers would follow Malibran's tendency by singing slowly and deliberately. "*Tancredi*'s 'Lascia mes' [sic] had been sung more brilliantly than we ever remember to have heard it executed before," the *Athenaeum* recorded in 1829, continuing, "We were particularly struck with the effect it produced by the slowness with which they sang it, and exquisite taste in which all the introductions were made."[38] John Ruskin, who probably saw Malibran as a teenager in Paris in 1835, also recalled that she "sang at least one-third slower than any modern [late nineteenth-century] cantatrice."[39] The pace of this cadenza, in other words, would have added to the breathless intoxication of the performance.

In the *tempo d'attacco* of "Ebben, a te: ferisci," to return again to *Semiramide*, Moscheles's reduction suggests that Malibran marked out the word "madre" (mother) by inserting an option (a pause for unmetered embellishment) above the word's first appearance as a melisma. Only fifteen measures into Arsace's second subject, this would both break Rossini's line and dramatize the terrifying connotations of that phrase "mia madre ancor" (still my mother).

Malibran's tendency to throw accents into her voice ("convulsive shrieks" and "violent gesticulation") is also in evidence here—"small, piqued notes which are thrown out from time to time like a ball in flight, as in the first two measures of example 3.[40] In critiquing her "impulses of a wild and disorderly nature," the *Times* wrote, "Malibran displays a certain energy; she likewise shows occasional sparks of fire . . . which her admirers call *inspirations heureuses,* [but which] are little better than fits and starts; they break upon the audience like sudden claps of thunder, through a quiet and unruffled atmosphere."[41] Such small assertions of the prima donna's power were allied to her ability to leap between tessituras. Malibran's skill in this regard suggests itself forcefully in Moscheles's reduction. Although she

MUSICAL EXAMPLE 3. The keyboard part of Moscheles, *Gems à la Malibran* mapped against the vocal line as reproduced in Gioacchino Rossini, *Semiramide: Melodramma Tragico in Two Acts. Libretto by Gaetano Rossi. A Facsimile Edition of Rossini's Original Manuscript*, 2 vols. (New York, 1978), 2: 316r–v.

would probably be described as a mezzo in modern terms, her voice featured an upper extension—a third octave. Such range and power was shown off to its fullest extent when it alternated suddenly between dramatic *melodie lunghe* and agile flourishes.

Sontag's style is equally evident in the Moscheles transcription; the Prussian's gift for ascending and descending chromatic scales, for example, is borne out in the score's stretto. Sontag's chromatic talents were second to none. Having heard her sing Desdemona early in 1829, the critic for the *Journal des débats* reported that he had erased all memory of the performance other than one rising scale. Castil-Blaze's extraordinary words appeared just hours before Sontag (as Amenaïde) and Malibran (as Tancredi) first crossed swords at the Théâtre Italien:

> I'll never forget the sensation I felt during the victorious, rapidly rising chromatic scale written by Rossini that ends the second act of *Otello*. All the most famous Desdemonas had cheated there before, but Mademoiselle Sontag sang it with such force and freedom that I bounced on my bench. From that moment I have passed my complete *Otello*. Go ahead, criticize this singer on the rest of the role, say that she is inferior to her estimable challengers, fine. It doesn't matter. I have my chromatic scale.[42]

Such a physical response to music exemplified a dilettantish erotics of listening, which came to its climax in what we might call this age of Sontagmanie. (Velluti, as we have seen, both suffered and reveled in this sense of voice.) "When Mademoiselle Sontag runs up or down a chromatic scale," the *Times* mused across the English Channel in September, "the metallic vibration of her voice, the perfect clearness of her articulation and of the sound she utters, satisfy every ear."[43] Chopin—who shared her exquisite sensibility, as we have seen—wrote that "her diminuendi are non plus ultra, her portamenti wonderful and her scales, particularly ascending chromatic, excellent."[44] The physical effect of her sliding scales, in other words, titillated many an ear.

THE BIRTH OF "THE DIVA"

Critics made clear that since their appearance in tandem, neither Malibran nor Sontag was sufficient to stir up excitement on her own. They needed each other. If Malibran lacked Sontag's class, naïveté, flexibility, and charm; Sontag apparently lacked Malibran's volume, range, intelligence, and drama. But together, each brace of coloratura—both "Fiero incontro" and "Ebben, a te: ferisci" are intensely virtuosic—enhanced the effect of its blazing counterpart. This "twoness"—two voices singing two duets—was definitive. Twisting and circling around its twin, each voice depended on the breath of the other.

Critics in London hailed the Sontag-Malibran phenomenon as emblematic of the entire 1829 season.[45] As the *Quarterly Musical Magazine and Review* recalled:

> This season—it was not Sontag—it was not Malibran—it was not both that would attract if they sung only single songs. "The only thing going" was to hear them in the duets, "Fiero incontro" from *Tancredi*, and "Ebben, a te: ferisci" from *Semiramide*—and certainly the two was thus far right—a more perfect performance was never heard, and it is questionable whether any two voices ever went so well together, and whether any two singers ever sung with such generous rivalry, not to distinguish each to herself.[46]

One trope tickled the popular fancy in particular: the idea that the twin sopranos sang from the same throat. The comments in the *Athenaeum* in June on the slow *a due* in *Semiramide* were typical: "After witnessing every species of vocal performance in this country, from the days of Mara in the year 1800 to the present period . . . nothing has been heard so finished, so beautiful, or so interesting; in the immediate duet parts, every breath, every aspiration, was given so simultaneously and so perfectly, that the two voices seemed to be actuated by one person only."[47] A May issue of the *Herald,* to cite another example, printed that "the principal attraction of [a King's Theatre evening concert] was a duetto by Rossini [from *Tancredi*], which was executed by Madlle. Sontag and Madame Garcia in the most *delightful unison!*" (The *Harmonicon* satirized this impossibility as a critical faux pas a few days later.)[48]

This fused-person notion took varied forms. In every case, an important double meaning or irony was brought into focus. Although the sopranos' mutuality could lift them into stratospheric realms, it also brought them down to the most basic levels of visceral experience. It was as though this original plus its double made for a sensuous presence that was in effect twice real. Two copies of the same, in other words, were interpreted to be more, not less, real than one.

Another feature of criticism was the appeal to explicitly sexual imagery. The desire to register female difference (via physiology, nervous electricity, and so on) was apparently overwhelming in the case of the Sontag-Malibran *dédoublement.* These florid womanly scenes often appeared useful to the bourgeois project of strengthening absolute sexual oppositions between male and female. The popularity of this twinned sound, in other words, hinged on its usefulness to the wider political project broached in chapter 1, where voices were heard to be powerful sexual markers. The vocal organs of Sontag and Malibran, in this sense, became subject, as Thomas Laqueur might put it, to the emerging "biology of incommensurability."[49]

An extraordinary passage appearing in the *Athenaeum* bears this out as it describes the Sontag-Malibran slow movement from *Tancredi,* "Ah! come mai quell'anima." The words register a moment of primordial female creation, not merely an act of making but of remaking, of making over from a base, preexisting materiality. What is striking for the reviewer is vocal biology, the sexual charge of the sound apparently inhering in moments of mutuality and free play:

Nothing can exceed the sweetness of the union of these two voices. No instruments, prepared by the first art, ever attained a more perfect and reciprocal nicety of tone. No birds "sitting upon the forest's midmost tree" poured forth notes more silvery and flowing. And, to carry to the highest possible degree of beauty this common and equal charm, art and industry have been diligently employed to adapt themselves each to the other; so that their ornaments and variations are like the flights of mated birds; their wings are spread together and twinkle in the air—they rise or sink, and float here and there, in circles or angles, or straight onwards; but still inseparable as at first, their pinions keeping the same aerial track, their bodies almost commingled. Their duets are like a succession of the sweetest of earthly sounds heard simultaneously with their echoes, and, in the minute cadences and florid interpolations, the effect of these quick reverberations is almost miraculous.[50]

The *Athenaeum*'s appeal to John Keats is striking. The phrase "sitting upon the forest's midmost tree" evokes the fourth book of *Endymion,* a poem famously savaged in the English press on its publication in 1818.[51] This "vulgar" piece retold the Greek myth of a mortal shepherd's quest to gain the love of the virgin moon goddess Cynthia. In a notorious subsection Keats replays Endymion's séance with the goddess, now disguised as an Indian maiden "sitting beneath the midmost forest tree." Endymion asks for a song as he leaves. "Let me have music dying," he entreats. Thus for the *Athenaeum* the importance of the miracle of mated birds: as Sontag and Malibran fold into each other, so the listener is witness to something animal. Yet this language is also mixed with words suggestive of distance, with the familiar romantic appeal to far-off echoes and dying tones.

Metaphors echoing the *Athenaeum*'s free association on "commingled bodies" recur time and again in male critical writing of the time. Images of flight, processes of revealing, women showing themselves, and talk of "art in all its nakedness" repeat in many contexts. We are used to the idea that nineteenth-century ideologies of female domesticity attempted to suppress or control the threat of female sexuality. But perhaps in this light, as Sally Shuttleworth has argued, we should pose the question the other way around: "Why, at this specific historical period, should women have been perceived as being in possession of a disruptive sexuality which needed to be disciplined and controlled?"[52] In *Massimilla Doni* (1839), Balzac has a character revel in the promiscuous flow of such "sheer music." A kind of spontaneous ovulation occurs, only a few years after Karl Ernst von Baer first described this in women in 1827:

> The roulade is the highest expression of art: it is the arabesque adorning the most beautiful room in the house: a little less and it is nothing; a little more and everything is confusion. Performing its task of reawakening in your soul a thousand ideas that lay dormant, it takes wing, it flies through space, sowing in the air seeds which are gathered by the ear and blossom within the heart. . . . It is deplorable that the masses have forced musicians to make their expression depend on words, on factitious elements—admittedly they would not be understood by the masses. The roulade is therefore the only point left to the friends of pure music, those who love the art in all its nakedness.[53]

Such a defense of vocal virtuosity—this image of a roulade "sowing seeds"—seems peculiar to modern tastes. Yet Balzac's spirited vindication of the *roulade de bravoure* is more than merely playful.

The first vernacular use of the term *diva*—in Paris—originally referred to the virtuosic twinning of Sontag and Malibran. According to the *Trésor de la langue française,* Gautier appropriated the word from the Italian in order to describe the heroine-sorceress of his early long poem "Albertus," set in 1829 and published as the climax to his *Poésies* a year later. She appears in transfigured form: "A very pearl of love! Great eyes, almond-shaped, at times most German in their sweetness tender, at times flaming with Spanish heat; two glorious mirrors of jet that make one wish to gaze within them one's whole life long. Her voice's tone more sweet than nightingale's lay; Sontag and Malibran, whose every note doth thrill and in the heart awake a secret note . . . —a miracle, a dream of Heaven!"[54] We will return again to this gothic poem, and Gautier's appropriation of and reference to the Sontag-Malibran stereotype. But for the moment, it is enough to situate this "diva" historically, this double-voiced apparition at once real and fantastic, Spanish and German, sexed and transcendent, animal and illusion, dangerous and ideal.

Much of our modern sense of "the diva," I have elsewhere argued, is indebted to Gautier and his immediate circle.[55] The social stereotype is familiar enough: the diva is a creature who has been made to live her reality as she would live onstage—as melodramatic, emotional, and capricious as her pseudoexistence as Art would dictate. In Gautier's mind, the original divas were at once sacred beings and useless commodities. Gautier's enthusiasm for *l'art pour l'art,* to be sure, was hardly of the high moralizing sort so conspicuous of later ideologies of aesthetic autonomy. For if this "diva" was transcendent, she was also conceived as the pleasurable object of low-bohemian hedonism. For Gautier, the new goddess of song had arisen as a kind of antiestablishment weapon, implemented in order to combat gray bourgeois doctrines of sexual normalcy. However normal they may appear to us today, in other words, the first divas (as envisaged by Gautier) were dangerously heterogeneous. They unleashed their eruptive voices against the status quo.

"SHE JUST SINGS"

Women don't know what they are saying, that's the whole difference between them and me.

JACQUES LACAN

A view of the beginnings of the "diva" recommends a return to the high-resolution scene so nonchalantly sketched at the beginning of this chapter. Thus far I have suggested that an important cultural or historical emergence took place at the time of these Argyll Room concerts, inaugurated in elaborate scenes of bodily display. Via Sontag, Malibran, a doubling, a flower-laden concert in a strange parallelogram-shaped room, the "diva" has been seen to take on a formidable authorial voice. Yet Mendelssohn recalled at this concert being "highly amused to see bonnets agitated at every little cadenza, which to me and many critics brought to mind the simile of the wind and the tulip-bed."[56] Such offhand remarks may suggest "floriculture" (in the words of historians of botany and woman's writing) and the possibility of other, less eulogistic narrations.[57] After all, the word *fioriture*, according to etymologists, was naturalized as a French term in 1823 when Stendhal used it for his famous Rossini biography, the English equivalent entering soon after in the early 1840s. In one way, yes, by doubling, there may be a sense in which—symbolically at least—this fused voice becomes raw and powerful.[58] But there are several provisos attached to this social rising.

Let me be blunt: the "diva" enters so-called romantic opera as a way to diffuse its meaning. As she moves out from under the shadow of the castrato and then the female contralto musico in these years (the backstage presence of chapter 1's Velluti is poignant), her doubling might be impressive, but her subjectivity is presented in the terms of dual processes of combination and dispersal. At the height of the Sontag-Malibran infatuation, the ideal vocal object—a singing voice now worshiped—apparently undergoes a loosening of origin. At the moment cultural narratives begin to orbit around her, so this powerful double voice transfers outside itself into the mouth of another of the same. In other words, the sonorous fabric, so miraculously fused, now also—if we take a less approving (Mendelssohnian) perspective—splits down the middle.

How, then, was this replication regulated? The final pages of this chapter will set out the ways in which this "diva" represented here was "undone," to use a word opera scholars were once drawn to. Initially I will make a brief survey of some of the general ways in which Malibran and Sontag together tended to be discursively disassembled in this milieu. The chapter will veer, in other words, toward a survey of the myths and half-truths that envelope Sontag, and then switch to concentrate on Malibran and the legends that effectively smother even the remotest possibility we might entertain of recovering "the way she really was."

THIS DISPERSED SENSE OF WOMAN . . .

Several factors served to undo "the diva." First, as we have seen, her sonority was split. And a lingering prejudice—most famously articulated at least fifty years earlier by that great "lover of knowledge," Denis Diderot—added to this social sense of its dispersal. "Nature is like a woman who enjoys disguising herself," the encyclopedist theorized, "and whose different disguises, revealing now one part of her and now another, permit those who study her assiduously to hope that one day they may know the whole of her person."[59] Women, in other words, were apparently disposed to playacting. And for Diderot, the female tendency to impersonate rather than just be herself betrayed a fundamental poverty of character. Unfathomable as a singularity, she only appeared by displacing her person elsewhere. To know her, then, was to study her vicissitudes.

A cursory glance at the popular and critical reception of both Malibran and Sontag will confirm that neither figure was permitted a life outside music. In most obvious ways, they were unknowable in themselves. Instead they were identifiable primarily in operatic parts such as those of Cenerentola, Rosina, Euryanthe, Donna Anna, Norma, and so on. After meeting Malibran in the summer of 1833, Bellini wrote, "Throwing her arms around my neck, she said to me in the most exalted transport of joy, with those four notes of mine: 'Ah! m'abbraccia!' (from the final scene of *La sonnambula*) and said nothing more."[60] The singer was incapable—such anecdotes saw to it—of escaping the stage.

Bellini's story exposes a third aspect of this voice's undoing: that both singers could apparently communicate only in vocalise. Alphonse de Lamartine, for example, demarcated Malibran's sole sphere of utterance when he wrote, "She was music, or even better, poetry in the form of a woman."[61] Having seen Malibran's Norma in Bologna, the American author Nathaniel Willis remarked how the "Siren of Europe" seemed possessed by her vocal line: "The incomparable creature sang with a fullness, an abandonment, a passionate energy and sweetness that seemed to come from a soul rapt and possessed beyond control with the melody it had undertaken."[62] In *Musurgia Vocalis,* Isaac Nathan, a composer and friend of Byron, spoke of her as "this fable of music" in terms of the eighteenth-century poet Thomas Gray's encomium, "thoughts that breathe and words that burn." He imagined that she was "a transfusion of nature in all her varieties into the delicious sounds:—for she feels what she sings, and she sings, what she feels."[63]

Her electric body sang even when her lips were closed. A German writer who saw Malibran in the winter of 1831 in Paris explained, "She did not only sing with her mouth. Every limb of her body sang. The sounds shot out in sparks from her eyes, from her fingers: they streamed from her hair. She was singing even when mute."[64] She oozed singing: her hair, eyes, and fingers. She seemed woven together acoustically. Gautier wrote simply, "She was music."[65] And he made a similar reduction of Sontag: "Sontag! ... when we were young ... the beauty of Mademoiselle Henriette Sontag was something so *spirituelle,* seemingly, to us, so far elevated above common mortality, that reason was the slave of sensation—a double entrancement of the eye and ear.... To describe her powers minutely would occupy too much space, but they are all summed up in one short sentence. Sontag *sings!*"[66]

In the critical imagination, then, both sopranos had apparently surrendered themselves to their spontaneously careening voices. They had control neither of their exalted bodies nor of what their voices might do.

WHO WAS HENRIETTE SONTAG?

Berlioz experienced Sontag similarly. It was useless trying to make a summary of her. She just sang—effortlessly, like an automaton:

> On she carols, higher and higher, like a lark at "heaven's gate," so soft, so clear, so wonderfully distinct that, like the silver bell from the altar, it is heard through the pealing organ. But her principal merit, in our eyes, is the absence of "rant"—the substitute of genius—in any shape whatever. She always SINGS, and does not depend on mere strength of lungs—erroneously called "power." She never strains her delicate organ—that sweet instrument so susceptible of every shade of expression.[67]

This "incarnation of song," as the *Harmonicon* called her, never forced or made faces. She was just so. Her voice made sense of her.[68]

Allied to the resonance of Sontag's body was the sense of her instrumentalization. Although often worshiped for the motorized quality of her singing, this "idol" was frequently criticized for it—particularly as it impinged on her style of ornamentation. Her Rosina, for some critics, suffered from such exacting displays of the "flexibility of her organs": "It is true, she imitated also the defects of these [musical] instruments [in "Una voce poco fa"], namely, that of repetition, as, on four different pauses, she used precisely the same cadence. This she seems to have learnt from instrumental performers."[69]

Her vocal organs—and there *were* many—were to be played upon. She sang, as the *Athenaeum* explained, "with a precision, rapidity and delicacy of execution that has caused her, not inaptly, to be compared to a living musical snuff-box."[70] Her hypostatization was not so much the result of her voice being restrained as the result of it being set free (as it had been made to turn back and repeat itself). Magazines marveled at this level of automation. All signs of physical exertion had been pressed beneath her perfect skin. "Her evolutions through the mazes of sound," one writer noted, were at once spontaneous and preconceived. It was as though she were being played on by some external force. If you watched her chest—many were prone to—you would not catch her breathing:

> Not only were all passages alike to her, but she appropriated some that were hitherto to belong to instruments—to the pianoforte and the violin for instance. Arpeggios and chromatic scales, passages ascending and descending. . . . There is a firmness and neatness that appertain to the piano forte, while she will go through a scale, staccato, with the precision of a bow. . . . The ear is never disturbed by a harsh sound— the notes trickle and sparkle like the diamond drops of the brightest fountain. Every thing is rendered clear and liquid by solution. . . . She appeared to sing like a bird, from impulse, and to feel whilst she inspired delight. There was no distortion, not even the heaving of her bosom was visible.[71]

She seemed, then, both doll-like, a piece of machinery (hard and shiny) and a natural being (liquid and seductive). Not surprising that she came to fame in the

1820s, the era of the first female shop assistants in Paris and London, of the Royal Opera Arcade on the Haymarket, of the moving panorama and the mobile gaze of the flâneur. Idle fashions were cultivated for Indian shawls, Egyptian cashmere, hashish, handkerchiefs, perfumes, oysters, cafés, and satanism. This was the era of the open display of goods, fixed pricing, the seductive show of merchandise, the first open bazaars (early forerunners of modern department stores), ready-made clothing, and bad taste. In such an environment Sontag was set out as the classic commodity. Paul Scudo, for example, likened his experience of hearing her to visiting a jeweler:

> In the magnificent casket of vocal gems which Sontag displayed every night before her admirers, we especially remarked upon the brilliancy of her trills, which sparkled like rubies on a velvet ground. Each note of those long-descending spirals stood out as if it had been struck isolatedly, and attached to the following note by an imperceptible and delicate solder, and all these marvels were accomplished with a perfect grace, never disfiguring her countenance by the slightest sign of effort. Her charming figure, her fine limpid and soft eyes, her elegant form and her stature, springing and supple as a stem of a young poplar, finished the picture and completed the enchantment.[72]

The singer here responded to her customers' scrutiny by displaying wares, by turning and spinning her voice, allowing it to be seen from all sides. What price for such vocal brilliance? There was nothing true, nothing real, in the play of surfaces passing before you. A form without substance, as the physician Augustus Granville argued, she was of the moment: "a pretty thing—a pretty singer, a pretty *bijoux* [sic], and nothing more."[73]

Pursued by fantasies of possession, Sontag was available everywhere. In Vienna, one of her satin slippers had been stolen by youths and used to drink champagne. In Frankfurt, men untied the horses from her carriage in order to pull it themselves.[74] In Berlin, army officers fought duels over tickets to see her at the opera house. In Spandau, Ludwig Rellstab, the eminent music critic, spent three months of 1827 in prison after satirizing Sontag's relationship with a diplomat.[75] She was both visible and desirable; she tantalized—availability is key here—and evaded acquisition at the same time.

As if to confirm her commoditization, the singer captured the attention of lithographers everywhere. Dealers such as J. Brocker and Albert Hoffay of London ran a roaring trade in the reproduction of her image.[76] Though many craved to hear her sing, many also seemed to desire her silent, as the *Athenaeum* did in 1828: "Her face has ever been truly German, but of that fair and pleasing order so frequently met among the Bourgeoisie, near Frankfort. Waiving our critical functions for a while, we often regret, notwithstanding her beautiful teeth, the professional necessity for opening her lips at all: it puts to flight a delicious and sweet-tempered expression, which the finest tones of her voice can never banish from our remembrance."[77]

If Sontag's ubiquity in the shadowy world of 1820s pornography is anything to go by, the *Athenaeum* was not alone in desiring her silence. Pisanus Fraxi's *Bibliography of Prohibited Books* indexes several appearances of her, *The Virgin's Oath; or, the Fate of Sontag,* printed for G. Cannon around 1828–30, being a particular example. This banned "historical drama" billed itself as "a picture of unbridled lust and licentiousness, unparalleled in history." In its pages the true-life figure of Prince Leopold (the uncle of Princess Victoria and future king of Belgium) bribes one of the singer's attendants to drug her. When she is unconscious, the prince enters her boudoir, cuts her dress from her with a pair of scissors, and satisfies his lust. Not appeased by this first ravishing, he has his way with her a second time. And as she regains consciousness, the nobleman finds to his delight that her wakened body is still softly acquiescent and surrendering.[78]

Though the authorities suppressed its circulation, this libelous material perpetuated the fantasy of Sontag's passivity. Mimesis being proper to her, she displayed a pliancy that was based not so much in naïveté as in a basic promiscuity of character. She was equally at home as any of the girl-types that were being identified in illustrated manuals of womanhood in the 1820s, such as Piers Shafton's *Female Character Illustrated* of 1829.[79] All stereotypes were natural to her: the working-class seamstress, the courtesan, the *lorette* (the young *danseuse*), the laundress, the flower seller, the *modiste,* the *grande horizontal.* She represented every aspect of femininity.

Sontag's body threatened to dissociate in sympathy with her cascading voice. Louis Borne, for example, could not listen to her without dismembering her mentally: "I could not see and hear her at the same time," he explained, "and I had to think of her points of excellence one by one, together, in order to arrive at the sum of her worth."[80] Critics such as Borne felt a compulsive need to make shopping lists—teeth, foot, mouth, jaw, eyes, nose, hair, arms—so as to arrive at her best sum. Her foot, for instance, was famously picked out by Granville. "I would say that her foot is the prettiest thing imaginable, if her hands were not prettier still," the doctor began. "She is faultless as to teeth, which the sweetest smile imaginable, for ever hovering round her mouth, sets off at every warble in all their glory." If any part made sense of her voice, it was her hair: "Her *chevalure,* between auburn and *blonde,* is magnificent."[81] Writers cultivated an infatuation with her body parts as if they bore no relation to her living person. Four such lists from the period appear below:

Mademoiselle Sontag is stated to be nineteen years of age; she cannot exceed one or two-and-twenty. She is of a middling stature and inclining to embonpoint. Her hair and complexion are fair, her eyes blue, with that kind of Roxaline nose—the *nez retroussé,* which often gives the appearance of great vivacity . . . Her mouth is well made . . . and it is lined by a set of teeth, the beauty of which she does not conceal. Her countenance indicates good temper, and is extremely pleasing. . . . Her hand and arm are beautiful, and her foot is not unworthy of the encomiums lavished on it. Her carriage is not objectionable.[82]

She was about one-and-twenty; of the middle status, and round and plump in the figure, with beautiful hands and arms, and a foot not unworthy of the admiration it had met with. She had light hair, a fair complexion, and blue eyes, which made her altogether very English-looking. She had a pretty mouth, embellished with a fine set of teeth, and a sweet and good-humoured countenance.[83]

She is exactly the height of the Medicean Venus, what the moderns call the middle height: her figure, though slight, has the full proportions of womanhood: her skin glows with the soft tint of the China rose; her arms and hands are faultless; her ankle, revealed by the short petticoat that of the "Danzatrice"; the foot, one for which the glass slipper would be too large. Who can describe her face? The soft, pouting lips of infancy, the delicate features, the large, melting blue eye, the finely turned oval face, enshrined in a cloud of golden curls.[84]

No one can deny, however, that Mademoiselle Sontag has a figure of great symmetry,—a fine open countenance, expressive blue eyes, perfectly regular teeth, a beautiful hand, and a smile of the greatest imaginable cheerfulness and good-nature; and yet, notwithstanding all these, the union produces only a pleasing and pretty woman.[85]

Sorted into "a pleasing and pretty woman," Sontag, in the end, accumulated into a list of disparate fragments. For idealist critics, she amounted to very little of substance. A "fluttering, unstable, whimsical little creature," Edward Holmes called her in 1828, "with a pleasant quality of voice, [but] with small quantity of tone" unsuited to lyrical, long-breathed passages.[86] Le Globe was obsessed with her "je ne sais quoi vaporeux, ce gazouillement indéterminé est quelque chose de délicieux."[87] Wordsworth wrote famously of "the spotless ether of a maiden life," a category Sontag exemplified. From her beginnings, this creature of lace and feathers proved "how divine a thing / a Woman may be made."[88] At the dawn of such "epidemics" of celebrity—such as Byronmania and now an even more virulent strain of Sontag-manie—the brilliance of her accomplishment was perhaps flaunted too much. Like the commodity form she most personified for many male admirers, she was enthroned as a fantasy object, powerful, but only in a sense that was dissipate or diffuse.

MALIBRAN SWIMS LIKE A FISH

Malibran perpetuated an image quite unlike Sontag's, although there was at least one important similarity. She, too, had a disparate character—a not-altogether-centered artistic personality—although in her case the fragments that came together were never so easily made sense of. Unlike Sontag, Malibran was seen to have a wildness about her, an organization that did violence to the poise of her profession. In a letter to her first husband in 1827, Malibran described her daily activities as a mishmash: "I eat like an Ogre, I drink like a drunkard, I run like a deer, I swim like a fish, I sing like a siren, I ride horseback like Napoleon (the late) and I sleep like a woodchuck."[89] Not so much diffuse as divided, Malibran's constitution split violently into dissonant registers. Her "voice" was the same. Rather than disintegrating, it painted in stark, acerbic colors; she had a way of altering her tone timbrally, shifting between registers and shading them to suit her parts.

Her style of acting underscored this apparent vocal abundance. In April 1829, the *Times* was struck by "the frantic terror" of her Desdemona (played on 25 April) in the second scene of act 2: "Again we find her in transports of an ungovernable despair, falling on her knees, dragging herself in that position over the stage to excite her father's pity, tearing her hair, and abandoning herself to all the excesses of an ungovernable grief." In September, the same correspondent attacked her "loose and unsettled" style, writing that her Desdemona "resorts to all those shifts of low mimicry, such as running from one side of the theatre to the other, falling on her knees, tearing her hair, dragging herself over the stage with shrieks of anguish and despair, rolling about, scratching the walls with her nails, and so forth."[90] Clawing at walls and walking on her knees, Malibran predisposed herself to criticism as dispersed, lowbrow, and *en vogue*. Audiences in general found her "shuddering" to look at. The "servility" of Malibran's imitation of Pasta's Desdemona, the *Times* concluded, "was slightly covered by some deviations in the style of the melodramatic exhibitions at the Boulevard Theatres."[91]

Imitating these crude forms, Malibran signed toward her own nondescript sense of self. She was prone to bouts of hysteria, and her doctors struggled to make sense of her fainting fits and periodic catalepsies. Those in the know speculated that she suffered from "la bougette," an inability to keep still. In *A travers chants*, Berlioz described an incident in which, during a concert performance of Beethoven's Fifth Symphony, she had to be carried from the auditorium suffering convulsions.[92] Not so much hyperactive as formless, Malibran, as a Milanese newspaper made clear, was of spurious human parentage, "not descended from Adam": "La Malibran is neither beautiful nor ugly; she has something not descended from Adam, something that is the result of what we wish and imagine. Everyone sees her differently. She has a face that is rather elongated, but delightfully so, a nose that is almost aquiline, a mouth immense in delight, and two great big flashing black eyes that a nail couldn't put out."[93] What made Malibran's style reminiscent of Sontag's *gazouillement indéterminé* was this shapelessness, although hers was of a deep, impenetrable order that seemed—as in this passage—to lodge in her eyes.[94] She became an altogether different creature in the imagination of each of her spectators.

Singing, for her, was like internal combustion. Simply adorned in white with jet-black hair falling over her shoulders, she took the stage as an incandescent object. Sound seemed to pass through her transparent frame, insinuating itself into her pale features. Lamartine wrote of "her beauty, which shone through her frail tissue like light through alabaster. One felt that one was in the presence of a being whose fabric had been eaten away by the sacred fire of art."[95] She seemed to be burning, as if her insides were raked over by flames.

Given that she was imagined in this way, it is perhaps unsurprising that she ended up the way she did. Legend has it—and this, of course, is the most famous outworking of the Malibran myth—that her voice killed her. As Jules Janin eulogized, "She was consumed by a double passion, drama and song, which she obeyed unto death." In September 1836, already in failing health, Malibran succumbed to high B♭ trill at a music festival in Manchester (she was singing another two-soprano duet—from Mercadente's *Andronico,* with Maria Caradori). Having achieved this note, she staggered out to the wings, collapsed, and, with terrifying shrieks, began to lose consciousness. A week later she was dead and crowds were clamoring to see her corpse.

What was prized in her voice in the years leading up to this "perfect" concert was a certain fleshy or deathly kind of vocalization that slowed down the vocal line and imparted a nervous edge to the sound. Malibranists came by the thousands precisely to witness the inner consumption of her form, to hear her wasting away.

Notwithstanding this compulsion to imagine her consumed from within, most critics understood this prima donna to be not so much dissipating as dismantling. She more than any other approached the accolade most often heaped on Pasta, that she was "encyclopaedic." In 1823, Stendhal had famously praised Pasta for "both her voices," that is, her ability to sing passages in both head and chest tones. Because her tone was "not all moulded from the same metallo," he repeated, she had "two voices."[96] Following the teachings of her father, Manuel García, Malibran developed similar subdivisions: the ability to alternate between a somber or covered tone where the larynx remained fixed, and a clear sonority where the larynx followed the voice in its ascent. The predilection to redescribe "voices" as "registers" was only just beginning to be explored in the 1820s (as we shall see in a detailed discussion of Bennati's contribution to the history of vocal register in chapter 5). As we are beginning to see, important changes were taking place in the history of voice as its mechanism was categorized in terms of invisible biological and anatomical process. The vocal organs would have to adapt to a bewildering array of physical comportments, suitable to all sounds *(sons grave, la voix laryngienne, sons aigus, la voix surlaryngienne, voix mixte),* styles of singing *(canto spianato, canto fiorito, canto declamato, canto di agilità, canto di maniera, canto miniato, canto di bravura),* and taxonomies of singer *(soprani sfogati, soprani parfaits, soprani-acuti,* lyric sopranos, coloratura sopranos, etc.). Everything vocal was being recategorized, if only to underline the sense that "voice" no longer referred to the myriad sounds available to a well-cultivated organ, but rather that "the voice"—this enigmatic signature—had somatic subsections and acoustic regions, a whole geography of parts.

If Pasta had two voices, Malibran famously had three. In other words, her extraordinary vocal equipment, under the *emplois* system of the Théâtre Italien, equipped her for the jobs of more than one category of singer. The proprietor of the Italian Theater in Paris, Edouard Robert, for instance, was prepared to pay her the salary of three employees in September 1829 since he observed she was both a serious and comic soprano, as well as a contralto: "We need her absolutely and at all costs, because in point of fact she fills three roles, serious soprano, buffo, and contralto, and as for talent you really have to keep in mind that she is unique in the world."[97] Bellini famously embellished this well-rehearsed notion to explain why she lived three times as intensely as any of her contemporaries. In a letter of 27 February 1835 to her, he wrote, "I adore you and your miraculous talent, as well as your graceful and lively person, not to mention your three souls (because you have that many, and not one like all other women)."[98] To this day, thanks to Lamartine, Malibran's disparate sense of self remains etched onto her tombstone. At her disinterment and reburial in Belgium around 1843, her second husband, Bériot, erected a small mausoleum with a statue of her by Guillaume Geefs. Predictably, the sculptor depicted her not as herself but as one of her most famous alter egos, Norma. Lamartine contributed the poetic inscription, basing his alexandrine verse on Bellini's three-souls motif:

> Her name as a woman was beauty, genius, love,
> Written into her eyes, her Heart, and her voice,
> This soul belonged to heaven under three forms.
> Cry, earth, and you heavens, welcome her three times.[99]

To bind Malibran's God-given talents to such Trinitarian subdivisions, of course, was to suggest that she was divine. And it is in this sense—this sense that she was "more than human"—that it seemed right that she share the stage with Sontag.

DUPLICITY

Having divided the Sontag-Malibran pair, we now return to the scene of feminine display with which we began: two virtuosos flanked by women patrons wearing ostrich-plumed turbans, and an aging castrato in the wings. We have seen how Sontag and Malibran appeared to disperse into each other. According to such critics as Gautier, this order of vocality represented, on a somatic level, a duplication of bodies, one that involved not so much duplication as duplicity—and "duplicitous" is an important word here. The diva is twice. Her coupling suggests three things: that her voice is split (she forks in two); that she is without site (she lacks a starting point); and that she is not only herself.[100]

Yet despite the split system of mediation, her impossible sonority carried power. The stereophonic voice was certainly no mere social ornament, as was the case with the young Sontag at her height in the mid-1820s. In the age of the contralto or the castrato, in general, vocal sound had been prized for its "finish," "polish," "completeness," or "purity." For an increasing number of listeners, these sounds possessed a charge; they were shocking. Thus, lifted out of history, vocal sound was heard to contain a biology. If audience members had once been fascinated by the faithfulness of a singer's impersonation of a character (by the skill with which she concealed herself while in role), they now directed their attention elsewhere: to the involuntary ways in which the diva's supposedly essential nature—placed under pressure—leaked or spilled into her vocal parts. Most importantly, this powerful voice—one that was diffuse, embodied, polyglossic, and would flare up and supersede that of the castrato or contralto musico—was qualified as decidedly female.

In the 1840s, protofeminist Margaret Fuller hailed that essence in the vocal sounds of women singer-geniuses:

> The electrical, magnetic element in woman has not been fairly brought out at any period. . . . Women of genius, even more than men, are likely to be enslaved by passionate sensibility. The world repels them more rudely. . . .
>
> Those who seem overladen with electricity, frighten those around them. "When she enters the room, I am what the French call hérissé," said a man of petty feelings and worldly character of such a woman, whose depth of eye and powerful motion announced the conductor of the mysterious fluid. . . . Such women are the great actresses, the songsters.[101]

A formidable electricity, in other words, inhered in a prima donna's nervous system (Malibran's electric death again comes to mind), particularly when this invisible physiology was forced to act under extreme pressure or nervousness, or forced to sing on instinct.[102]

Predictably, this "essential woman"—magnetic, aristocratic, and frightening—was under moral attack from the very first Sontag-Malibran performances. Already at the 8 June Philharmonic concert of 1829, Edward Holmes showed disdain for their "Ebben, a te: ferisci": "Defend us from a contest for the supremacy of roulades between two fashionable lady singers! The harlequinade of both was clever—the notes clearly touched, the intonation exact, the graces and decorations well remembered; but if the end of music be answered by such singing as this, music is despicable."[103] After hearing Bellini's *I Capuleti e i Montecchi* two years later in Florence, Berlioz recorded his contempt for the convention of "two feminine voices . . . produc[ing] those successions of thirds." He attributed their popularity to the Italian "public of sybarites, who were attracted by sweet sonorities as children by lollipops."[104] In Gautier's aforementioned "Albertus," the hero is eventually seduced and destroyed by the double-voiced witch-turned-enchantress. The "diva" leads to damnation, as Gautier's hero finds when the creature "melts" beneath him while he is making love to her. "A foul hag with green eyes" materializes: "Her bones showed plain under withered breasts, and her ribs stuck out of her sides."[105]

For moralists as for hedonists, therefore, the sensuality of this sonority was encountered with mixed fear and excitement. Whether or not you enjoyed it, the *dédoublement* of the dark Spanish allure of Malibran with the flaxen-haired grace of Sontag piled fascination upon fascination. Gautier's frankly anarchist agenda, of course, led him to embrace rather than decry its social threat. But that was typical of the Frenchman's exaggerated way of thinking, his avant-garde bohemianism obliging him to worship such impossibly fused alchemies as the Sontag-Malibran craze celebrated. What we are confronted with in relation to this fused sonority— if we excavate it in the terms of its social reception—is the articulation of a strange kind of vocal essentialism, one that was Rossinian and operatic in derivation, allied at once to an emerging ideology of autonomous art and to prevailing cultures of high sensibility. The great vocal *engouement* of 1829, in the end, was an example to those who dared to imagine what might happen when voice obeyed raw function alone, when, freed from the artificial categories of communication, voices were unleashed to go their own way.

4

Boneless Hands / Thalberg's
Ready-Made Soul / Velvet Fingers

HANDS CLAP HANDS

Dressed in severe black with a white cravat, Sigismund Thalberg made his London debut on 9 May 1836. The Swiss-born pianist played at the Hanover Square Concert Rooms, only a block to the west of the 1829 triumphs of Sontag and Malibran. He entered just before 9 P.M., flanked by immense reflective mirrors, glass chandeliers, and an audience on crimson-cloth benches. At Regency events, we know by now, only the most obdurate critics failed to listen with their eyes—which makes this glittering occasion a case of déjà vu. A rendition of the milieu's favorite instrumental piece—Beethoven's Pastoral Symphony under "conductor" George Smart—was still fresh in the ears of the men of the Philharmonic Society.[1] Later that week, the *Spectator* would remember how Beethoven had "peopled his scene with mirthful sports and rustic pastimes: he made the air vocal with the 'plaint of rills,' the murmur of the woods, the song of birds: Nature, gay and happy Nature, animate and inanimate."[2] The visual imagination had been stirred, second, by Tamino's "Portrait Aria" from *Die Zauberflöte*, sung twice in Italian by Russian "ténor contraltino" Nicola Ivanoff (the same whose bizarre facility in a low supplementary "voice," termed "contre-basse" by Manuel García *fils*, had inspired Bennati to a memoir on the subject).[3] Mozart would be heard once more in act 2, though the placement of "Non più di fiori" from *La clemenza di Tito* (Thomas Willman on obbligato basset-horn), the program warned, would depend on the speed of Maria Malibran's coach trip from Drury Lane. (When the singer did arrive at 11 P.M., according to the *Atlas*, she showed both "signs of fatigue" and energy enough to "*Rossinize* the commencement of her song by some cadences from *Tancredi*.")[4] Thalberg was third on the program, performing a "Grande Fantaisie" without orchestra.

Thalberg's solo event was unprecedented at these concerts, the society having banned nonensemble displays.[5] It was so unexpected, according to the *Spectator*, that the room fell into confusion—instrumentalists usually vacated the room when not required. Instead, having heard the pianist at Saturday's rehearsal, the players hustled for a better view. "Thalberg played (contrary to usual custom here) without any orchestral accompaniment. The orchestra presented an unusual appearance as he entered it. Every performer was unemployed, and it is the habit of those who are so to retire into the adjacent room: but, on this occasion, the only movement of the band was from the left wing to the right: the principal performers were clustered around the pianoforte, and the rest stationed themselves so as to command a view of the instrument."[6] The instrument, according to the *Sunday Times*, was a "magnificent" seven-octave Érard, one that would probably travel with Thalberg on tour in anticipation of late-century commercial practice.[7] Érard's new patent metal brace—its *barrage métallique*—was on show, boasting newfound durability and stability of temperament, and what Chopin disparagingly called its "ready-made" tone.

Thalberg decided against having Érard's instrument pushed out front, however, as had occurred when Henri Herz—the "Semiquaver King"—had performed his *Introduction, Variations, and Rondo* two seasons previously.[8] Thalberg chose instead to sit within the orchestra, as Smart had when "presiding at piano" for Beethoven. This decision was probably another effect of confusion. Like any "conductor," Thalberg was fixed to appear without remuneration. His unexpected solo had reopened the old wrangle over whether musicians "at piano" should receive payment, a question that was answered in this case by the gift of tickets and silver plate a month later.[9] The *Spectator* again:

> When Herz played, the pianoforte was removed, in order to enable the audience to discern his feats of legerdemain—his ups and downs—his crossings and weaving, and all the fooleries with which he contrives to gull the simpletons of this metropolis. Herz's exhibition is not only addressed to the eyes, but to the eyes of the ignorant: conscious that he has little worth *hearing*, he is doubly anxious to be seen. Thalberg seated himself at the instrument where and as he found it; and a very few bars had passed before we were satisfied that no common mind impelled the firm, brilliant, and rapid finger that glanced over the keys. . . . His playing, had nothing frothy and claptrap about it—nothing for mere trick or display.[10]

The *Atlas* reported that Thalberg, before plunging into his B-minor *Grande fantaisie*, op. 22, without score, improvised an "unostentatious prelude (some chords in C minor sustained in the right hand, with a delightfully characteristic moving accompaniment in the left)."[11] As per convention, Thalberg extemporized here to test his Philharmonic audience. August Lewald, for one, described earlier that year how "the young wizard's eyes frequently wander round the circle of listeners" at a performance at Ferdinand Hiller's highbrow salon on the rue Saint Florentin in Paris.[12] Hummel recommended similar introductory preludes in his celebrated 1828 piano tutor, "to look in the faces of his auditory to see how they take what he gives them."[13] These improvisations could be manipulative. The *Atlas* of 1836 went on to describe how Hummel "tenderly experimentalizes with a contrapuntal subject, and, if the girls look desponding, instantly turns off into a tune that makes every bonnet rhythmical."[14] "He does very wisely to play alone," the *Morning Post* added in view of Thalberg's rehearsal for the Philharmonic—an occasion more amenable to female attendance than the main event—"for then he can display the command he possesses over the instrument."[15] "The very circumstance of the pianoforte being heard without instruments," the *Atlas* reported of Monday evening, "added zest to the occasion."[16]

Such scenes of concert ogling became ubiquitous at Thalberg's London performances of 1836 and 1837, as we shall see. They were brilliant occasions. The audience would fall into a wide-eyed "trance" or "unbroken silence," becoming "bewitched." The *Court Magazine* recalled of the Philharmonic occasion that "the succeeding duet was scarcely listened to, so powerful was the fascination which M. Thalberg threw over the whole audience." (Ivanoff and Henry Phillips sang an Italianized version of the grief-torn Tell-Arnold duet from Rossini's *Guillaume Tell*, which will receive close attention in chapter 5.)[17]

The cause of the stupefaction was Thalberg's so-called "three-hand technique." A religious silence customarily attended his patented moment of transubstantiation, the incarnation of Thalberg's phantasmic third hand.[18] Famously, this invisible hand—a metaphysical "tenor" played covertly by the thumbs—incarnated a cantus firmus at the most unlikely moments: amid swirling textures of leaping octaves, rushing arpeggios, cascading thirds or scales. A voice from nowhere would emerge amid chaos of heavenly proportions, "the idea around which all the others gravitate," wrote the *Gazette des salons* in 1837, "which, trained like planets around the sun, form rapid eddies, but never eclipse the great center of light."[19]

From mid-1837 the most famous disembodied melody—Thalberg himself—would materialize at the most religious moment in the score of his Fantasy on themes from Rossini's *Moïse*, op. 33, which introduced the hushed act 3 Israelite prayer as shown in figure 8. Two years later, Schlesinger published Thalberg's well-named miniature "Mi manca la voce," the melody again from *Moïse*, on three staves, pioneering an innovative way of notating the third invisible hand. That same year, the inaudible *innere Stimme* famously haunting the second miniature of Schumann's *Humoreske*, op. 20, was printed alike in its first Viennese edition.

This said, in his debut season Thalberg was mostly lauded as a four-handed pianist, as in Jean-Pierre Dantan's celebrated twenty-fingered statuette of him. It was only at another Philharmonic performance of a year later, on 12 June 1837, that the *Moïse* fantasy in fact began to steer the composer-pianist's career (after yet another,

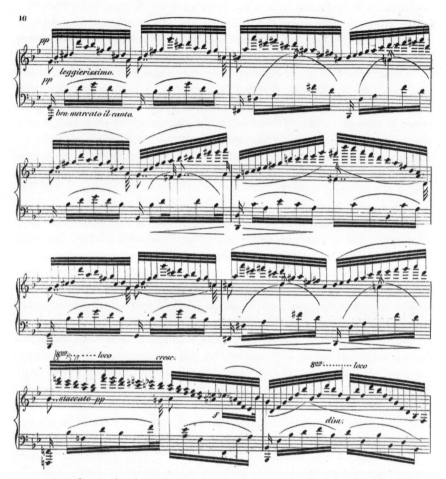

FIGURE 8. A phantom hand sounds the melody in *Fantaisie pour le piano, sur des thèmes de l'opéra Moïse de G. Rossini, composé par S. Thalberg, oeuv. 33* (Paris, 1832), 14. Reproduced by permission of the Bibliothèque nationale de France.

this time "38-minute," rendition of Beethoven's Pastoral Symphony).[20] Early descriptions of quadruplication rather than triplication attended Thalberg's performances of the *Grande fantaisie* at his 1836 arrival on the cosmopolitan scene. (The appropriately named *Le Phalange* hailed "cette incroyable multiplication des doigts et des mains" in 1842.)[21] The *Musical World* wrote of the *Grande fantaisie* early in 1837:

> At one time we meet with a distinct melody for the right hand accompanied with *tremando* harmonies for the same hand, whilst the left is employed in the most playful coruscations of demisemiquavers which are rendered the more dramatic by the

startling octave with which they commence. Here there are four distinct features to develop,—and it is in the extraordinary power which this performer possesses of dividing his hands as it were into four parts, and producing from each a distinct and essentially different quality of tone, that he so overwhelms his auditors with astonishment and admiration.[22]

This power to "divide" the hand, to isolate and differentiate regions of the hand, to cultivate polydactyly, or to incarnate third or fourth hands heralded what Robert Schumann begrudgingly called "the epoch of Thalberg."[23] As early as March 1836, *Le Ménestrel* hailed a "new art" incomparable to anything yet heard.[24] "The piano playing of the present day, to tell the truth," admitted Liszt acolyte Wilhelm von Lenz by 1852, "consists of Thalberg simple, Thalberg amended, and Thalberg exaggerated: scratch what is written for the piano, and you will find Thalberg."[25]

Piano tutors in the "epoch of Thalberg" promulgated "division of fingers" in line with the pianist-composer's demonstrations, anatomizing, cutting up, or etherealizing the hand, apparently in order to diffuse materiality and cultivate "voice." The *Méthode des méthodes de piano* (1840) of Thalberg's greatest supporter, for example, lavished attention on exercises training the hand to play two or three textures at once, by "voicing" the finger or finding "sa qualité plus ou moins moelleuse."[26] Written in collaboration with one of Thalberg's teachers (Ignaz Moscheles), François-Joseph Fétis's metamethod summed up the insights of every tutor the critic could find since C. P. E. Bach, at the same time as it divided hands into regions. Fétis's "end-of-history" method and critical opinions intensified the enthusiasm for Thalberg in cosmopolitan Paris. In London, meanwhile, listeners clustered around the musician's Érard like moths surrounding a flame in 1836. Whatever the divisions of hands—three, four, five, or six—they seemed inexorably drawn to the voice they heard behind the glittering arpeggios.

Another example: a week after his Philharmonic debut, on 21 May, Thalberg staged a Saturday morning concert in the light-blue elegance of the "great concert room" attached to the King's Theatre. The audience was select and the program sparse (for the period): arias and duets; Malibran and her partner Charles de Bériot improvising a piece for voice and violin on "Le Songe de Tartini"; Thalberg playing his *Huguenots* Fantasy, Second Caprice, and *Grande fantaisie*. The *Morning Herald* hailed Thalberg for his failure to hire a band, given the "scraping, jingling, and blowing which invariably attends an orchestral concert." The correspondent went on to extol the caliber of the listener-viewers, who were free to roam the performing area, as at the most elite salons: "The presence of most of the distinguished amateurs and professors, who ranged themselves around the space usually occupied by the performers, gave to the affair more the appearance of a reunion of artists and guests, than of an assemblage of persons who had deposited their half guineas for the privilege of being seated there."[27] A first glimmer of critical disaffection for such high-minded "hand gazing" emerged that week in the pages of the *Athenaeum*. (The author was probably Henry Chorley.) Here, the critic urged Thalberg to show off less and eschew melodies from "flimsy" "popular operas" in the hope that he would "be able to forget his two amazing hands a little oftener."[28]

Thalberg appeared only sporadically after his own concert in 1836, a painful whitlow having gathered on one of his fingers. But both his emotional final appearance of the year and his debut London appearance of 1837 inspired yet more awe-bound episodes of hand watching in London.[29] For Berrettoni and Bennett's benefit concert—again shorn of band at the same venue—the *Morning Post* reported that Thalberg's "plaintive" minor-key *Romance et hymne national russe, varié pour le piano* "seemed to be a farewell lament, and we are sure it was so felt by both the audience and the host of eminent professors who crowded around him."[30] More spectacular crowding still attended his first London appearance the following year. The event was the annual Monday benefit of Anglo-Italian violinist Nicolas Mori. The papers hailed it the most sensational concert of the year.[31]

An epic five-hour program was planned for 8 May 1837. The concert featured "a galaxy of talent," according to the *Musical World*, with Thalberg "the lion of the evening." The orchestra was, in the words of the *Morning Herald*, "the strongest ever brought together in London—we rather think it stronger than the Philharmonic."[32] No fewer than ten double basses and forty violins crowded the main stage of the Italian Opera House. The adjoining King's Concert Room proved too cramped to host Mori's spectacles—and spectacles they were. "At an early hour on Monday evening," wrote the *Musical World*, "all the seats and standing room in the pit and gallery were occupied; every stall owned a possessor; and the boxes throughout the house were in requisition."[33] Critics could only highlight key moments. Thalberg's future father-in-law and voice coach, Luigi Lablache, afflicted with a cold, "croaked" through a duet with Antonio Tamburini, though he managed "a very plump FF . . . which is a note lower than we remember to have heard him venture in public." "Thus, like another *Falstaff,*" the *Atlas* added, "this jolly, good-humored personage turns 'diseases into commodity.'" (The bass would profit from affliction once more in 1843 when he underwent a jawbone operation in Paris, a procedure that apparently "produced a favorable [artistic] effect.")[34] The orchestra was erected on the operatic stage and "set off by appropriate scenery and well-disposed lights," according to the *Atlas*, in anticipation of a partial performance of Nicolas Charles Bochsa's *Voyage Musical* for harp and orchestra. (This piece was originally set with twenty-two stage scenes painted by the King's Theatre's scene painter, William Grieve, and tableaux vivants by local ballet master Coulon. Bochsa was alone in being "ruthlessly hissed," both because of a scene-shifting "hitch" and his disgraceful moral reputation: he was an escaped convict, condemned forger, con man, bigamist, thief, and—horrors!—harp virtuoso.)

At the head of Mori's concert—still with lingering scenery—was Beethoven's Fifth, Sir George once again "conducting," probably from Thalberg's Érard. Not all the critics were pleased. The *Morning Herald* argued that, although the "masterwork" contained "many *palpably* noble passages," Mozart's Jupiter would have been more rewarding, the Fifth being mere "*caviare* to the mass."[35] As for the *Atlas,* the problem was less Beethoven's (who was God) than the venue's (which was large). For while "the unusual crowd of performers" caught the eye, the ear had two reasons to complain:

> One reason is that the instruments are placed most unfavorably for effect in the depths of the stage (the violins in particular sounding as though muted); another, that among the crowd who here figure as instrumentalists are many who, though their services may swell the amount of noise, certainly contribute little to exalt the general purity of execution. For mere scenic effect we grant that any man who can hold a fiddle, picturesquely is to be patronized; at the same time, when the business at hand is Beethoven's symphony in C minor, artists of this caliber should be enjoined to keep their instruments as quiet as possible.[36]

Thalberg's season premiere, in other words, overflowed with onstage instrumentalists. The *Musical World* was struck by their facial expressions once the pianist really began to play: "The interest of the whole audience; the crowding of professors around the instrument; the deep silence . . . It was a curious sight the other evening to observe the countenances of so many talented professors who surrounded him while he was performing some of his wonderful passages from the *Huguenots*. They appeared scarcely to believe their eyes."[37] Such professorial ogling got so out of hand that the *World of Fashion* decided to censure the whole process. Springing to the defense of "ladies," the critic voiced the frustration of those necessarily barred from orchestras and up-close views of Thalberg's dazzling fingers. "We would wish to draw the attention of those who have the management of these concerts to the circumstance, that is [when] the persons who are standing on the orchestra are allowed to crowd round the pianoforte while Thalberg is playing, it is quite impossible for ladies who are seated at any distance from the performer to observe at all how the different passages are fingered; we heard many ladies complaining much of the unfairness of the proceeding, and hope in future to see it rectified."[38] Such awe of fingering, the accomplishment of the artist, and what was "seen," in other words, lingered in concert practice deep into the 1830s.

Striking in the case of Thalberg was how serious male attention actually narrowed when the object ostensibly on view—as a third or fourth hand or a clandestine voice—was difficult to see. "It is in vain for us to attempt to describe what cannot be conveyed by the pen of an ordinary mortal," wrote the *Morning Herald* when *Moïse* was premiered in London three days after Mori's concert (17 May 1837), "since, even while one looks and hears the wonders of these performances, they seem at the very moment to be utter impossibilities."[39] *Moïse* may have been a limit case. The *Morning Post* wrote about this performance in the King's Concert Room that the piece's effects "baffle all attempts at description."[40]

In evidence here is a historical moment when listeners relinquished making visible sense of what they were hearing. This point of aversion, of course, may not have been merely the result of the miraculous advent of superhuman hands or of a virtuosity impossible to emulate. More likely, listeners turned their eyes for social or moral reasons, because of an ideology that declared art beyond seeing, or that made it vulgar to look. The convergence of such aversions with new scientific intuitions, which found that different sense nerves communicated different nerve energies, is striking. The so-called Bell-Magendie law, which was gathering currency in London as much as it was in Paris by the mid-1830s, theorized an absolute separation between the activities of seeing and hearing. The senses, in this scientific conception, conjured several parallel and mutually exclusive "life worlds," worlds that had little to do with one another. Arguably, the experience of these conflicting aural and visual worlds lodged the emergence of ever-purer ideals of listening, and ever-higher theologies of art, into the unyielding bedrock of romantic truth.

This chapter will attempt to shed light on that bedrock by returning to the glittering surface and the strange picture of crowds jostling to glimpse Thalberg. Was he really such a braggart? Might there be a sense in which the pianist's art had a strong public ethic, involving as it did the effort to display, in keyboard-playing hands, the signs of accomplishment? Thalberg, it seems, was a musician at once quotidian and superhuman, faddish and immortal, garish and immaculate, depending on the politics of the spectator. His case apparently rested on nothing less than the question of whether or not he had a soul, on what it meant, frankly, to be alive. In what follows, I wend my circuitous way back toward the scenes with which I began, the intention being to emerge with a less jaundiced view of Thalberg surrounded by his many admirers.

MUMMY MEN

By 1840 the critics who could not bear any looking at all were—predictably— German. Take Schumann, for example, who oozed vitriol for the atrocity he called "finger-music," music that belonged to the display of hands. The editor of the *Neue Zeitschrift für Musik* was initially ambivalent about Thalberg, "the matador of the drawing room."[41] More squarely in Schumann's crosshairs from the outset were Frédéric Kalkbrenner, Herz, and J. B. Cramer. (Cramer sported "aristocratic, long, thin fingers," according to Moscheles, with "beautifully-shaped nails.")[42] Kalkbrenner, in particular, was a disgrace: he had been the most celebrated cosmopolitan virtuoso at the time of the Orléanist succession in July 1830. Schumann's attack on arguably the first-ever keyboard fugue written explicitly for left hand alone—the "Four-Voiced Fugue" first published in his *Méthode pour apprendre le piano-forté* (1831)—was typical:

> While playing Kalkbrenner's four-part one-handed fugue, I thought of the excellent [Anton] Thibaut, author of the book, *On the Purity of Music* [1825], who told me that once, at a concert given by [J. B.] Cramer in London, a polite Lady Somebody, an art amateur, actually rose, against all English convention, and stood on tiptoe to stare at the artist's hands. The ladies near her imitated her example, until finally the whole audience was standing; and the lady whispered enthusiastically into Thibaut's ear: "Heavens, what trills!—what trills! And with the fourth and fifth fingers!—and with both hands at once!" The whole audience murmured in accompaniment "Heavens! What a trill! What trills!"[43]

Such gratuitous exhibitions led Schumann to wonder, later in the essay, whether "a race of freaks could arise in the world of artists, with one finger too many on each hand," an eventuality that he hoped would shock audiences out of their compulsive gawking.

Mocked for his "femininity," Kalkbrenner also drew scorn for being past his sell-by date. Heinrich Heine found that the virtuoso had ossified by 1843. "His lips gleam still with that same embalmed smile that we observed on the face of the Egyptian pharaoh," the poet wrote, "whose mummy was unwrapped at the museum here recently." Giving credence to the rumor that Kalkbrenner avoided England because of its antibigamy laws—the pianist reputedly preyed on his fairer students—Heine prodded at "his elegant mien, his admirably attired form, his polish and sweetness, his whole candied sugar cake exterior."[44] Mendelssohn could not stomach him either, calling him a "little fish patty" or "an indigestible sausage."[45] Shopworn beauty, Egyptian, and freak, Kalkbrenner was so prehistoric by 1839 that, reviewing both books of the *25 Grandes études* (op. 145), Schumann decided that the pianist was less mummy than granny. "Scarcely anything to be found but dry formulas, beginnings, or remains," wrote the German, "the picture of an old, once beautiful coquette." The problem was in plain sight, according to Schumann, since "Kalkbrenner himself acknowledges that he has devoted a great part of his life to the mechanical cultivation of his hands."[46]

MEN OF VISIBLE ACCOMPLISHMENT

The vicious marginalization of "hand cultivation" in the 1840s obscures Kalkbrenner's early century accomplishments. In the previous two decades the virtuoso had been a figurehead for the massive commercial expansion of the pianoforte industry, sheet-music production, and the standardization of pedagogical systems in Paris, London, and elsewhere. Kalkbrenner was a *chef d'école*, to be sure, the early century establishment figure par excellence. A partner in the firm of Pleyel, he developed a system of performance that at once inspired and benefited from the firm's highly sensitive instruments. (His Pleyel—an instrument especially innovative in the area of cross-stringing—was often described as a sensible extension of his nervous system.) Kalkbrenner was the standard-bearer for a veritable pianistic code disseminated across Europe and beyond, on a commercial scale comparable to the rolling-out of Napoleon's Civil Code. Along with pianos and sheet music, of course, went the social accomplishments and practical disciplines associated with them. His achievement consisted of nothing less than the invention of that creature we today call "the pianist." His students, in addition to Thalberg, Chopin, and Stephen Heller, included the foremost women performers of the century, Marie Moke Pleyel and Arabella Goddard. And he attained all of this by celebrating the hand in Aristotelian terms as "the instrument of instruments."[47]

The hand, in this neoclassical conception, was exalted. Its wondrous intricacy was prized as the most obvious physical measure of man's moral and intellectual superiority. In *De anima* Aristotle had famously proposed that "the soul is as the hand"—that is, the soul is seen in the hand, and the hand's actions were "soulful" in the sense that they manifested the mind. "Man has a far more accurate sense of touch than other animals," explained Aristotle, "for which reason he is also far more intelligent than they."[48] At the threshold of experience, hands wove inner and outer together, confounding expression and impression, passion and compassion, body and soul. The "instrument of instruments" was thus legible to the world. Its significations echoed natural, philosophical, and intentional truths. In short, this hand was a sign, and it acted in signs. The work it performed, the language it spoke, its very physiognomy was always "engaged to" or "on behalf of." Signs, indeed, had been etched into it since biblical times (as in palmistry). The gestures and shapes of fingers (chirognomy) had been subjects of study at least since Johann Kaspar Lavater's *Physiognomische Fragmente* (1775–78) or Gilbert Austin's *Chironomia, or a Treatise on Rhetorical Delivery* (London, 1806).[49] The French would say the hand was "en gage," thus the idea of "giving one's hand in agreement"—as in handshakes or salutes—for binding contracts and ideas of unbreachable commitment, precedent, tradition, patrilineal authority, or obligation. It signified the clutch of the invisible past on the visible present, responsibility to forefathers, and rule or law *(le droit).*

The science of chirognomy, young in the 1840s, claimed that the character of men was mirrored in the form of their hands and fingers. The founding father of the science was Captain Casimir Stanislas d'Arpentigny, a close friend of Frédéric Chopin in the late 1840s. The former military officer and author of *La Chirognomie* (1839) was "witty and amusing" according to the Pole. A companion of Alfred de Musset, he spent many hours at George Sand's "phalanstery" at the Square d'Orléans (the court just below Montmartre, where apartment holders included

Chopin, Kalkbrenner, Pierre-Joseph Zimmermann, George Sand, Manuel and Charlotte Marliani, Jean-Pierre Dantan, Alexandre Dumas père, Louis and Pauline Viardot, Antoine Marmontel, and Charles-Valentin Alkan). The erudite d'Arpentigny, who dyed his hair green, summarized the neo-Aristotelian view best when he extolled "the part which is played by our hands upon the theatre of our existence, when we consider that there exists scarcely a single incident of our lives in which the hand is not the prime agent, the apparatus whereby we practically live, move, and have our being."[50]

This instrument of instruments could be a weapon of finesse for well-practiced men. Kalkbrenner was certainly one of these: a trained military aide-de-camp, deadly with the lance, a master tactician, art collector, agriculturist, and sportsman. He was fluent in Latin, French, and German and educated in geography, ancient and modern history, and astronomy. This piano executive, and *homme du métier* was the father of modern octave playing. He revolutionized the use of the left hand, had a passion for mathematics and medicine, and made good on the foundations of Clementi and Adam.[51] In other words, Kalkbrenner arguably brought the neoclassical conception of the hand to its highest ascent in European history. The period of the virtuoso's celebrity witnessed an epidemic of "method-fever," a concentration on piano-playing digits in Europe as never experienced before or since. To lay fingers before the eyes, extending them into space as much as space extended into them, was a demonstration, if ever there was one, of how humans were woven into the world, and the world into them. Palpable here, too, in this concentrated work on the care and deportment of fingers, was the culmination of a long eighteenth-century trend toward the untwisting of the keyboard-playing hand. (As chapter 6 will show, the situation shifts in the later century for such pianists as Liszt, for whom the experience of the hand was less instrumental than relational.)

In this sense, the history of the keyboard tutor charts the rise and fall of the hand as the "instrument of instruments," as *the* motive element in worldly affairs. Keyboard manuals as early as Carl Philipp Emanuel Bach's *Essay on the True Art of Playing Keyboard Instruments* (1753–87) had already proposed a formal "SCHOOL based on nature," where the "natural shapes of the hand and the keyboard teach us how to use our fingers," and where the old moral prejudices against the outer digits were acted against.[52] Bach, of course, did not discard earlier practice completely—that mobile, idiosyncratic hand that twisted, turned, writhed, and danced in keeping with the music it played. The "French" love of finger substitution was still solidly in practice for Bach, as was single-finger repetition in scale passages, and what *The True Art* called *üntersetzen* (turning of the thumb), or *überschlagen* (the crossing under and over of second, third or fourth fingers).[53] The thumb and fifth, in particular, carried ancient stigmas, as did *la mano sinistra,* or the left hand in general. The earliest instruction manuals, such as Girolamo

Diruta's *Il transilvano* (1597), warned against the immanent moral qualities of fingers: how "good" fingers might only play "good notes" (accented ones) and "bad" fingers "bad" ones (unaccented notes). (Prominent thumbs were potentially seditious because they carried archaic associations with power, the thumbs of forgers and subversive writers being amputated as late as the sixteenth century in England.)[54] The earliest printed tutors—those from the later sixteenth century—were hardly methods in any modern sense anyway, since, instead of training "mechanism," they educated keyboardists in the arts of improvisation, notation, embellishment and intabulation.[55]

General evidence suggests a steady aestheticization of the keyboard-playing hand after C.P.E. Bach, and the systematization of myriad local practices into what that composer-musician called a "True Art." Suffice it to say that the encyclopedic late-century texts of Daniel Gottlob Türk (*Clavierschule*, 1789), Jan Ladislav Dussek (*Instructions on the Art of Playing the Piano Forte or Harpsichord*, 1794), Johann Peter Milchmeyer (*De wahre Art das Pianoforte zu spielen*, 1797), and Pleyel-Dussek (*Méthode pour le piano forte*, 1800) perpetuated the trend toward what I call "the Universal Hand"—that is, a hand of perfect rationality, democratized fingers, and uniform tranquility. In the 1790s tutors had formulated exhaustive rules for figured bass, tasteful ornament, and fine execution, leading students to "play with their ears," to listen and learn as they practiced. The music examples they printed were not so much "exercises," in the sense of later conservatory tutors, as they were exemplifications of what a knowledgeable hand might do. As encyclopedias for natural practice, they facilitated naming and knowing.[56]

These large instruction manuals, such as Türk's, aimed less at manual gymnastics than at the acquisition of knowledge. When the student sat herself before such texts, she expected to be enlightened; she looked forward to displaying her hand before society as an emblem of her creativity and accomplishment. Even as late as the 1820s, in fact, many primers still introduced "basic reading" or the "general laws of music" at the same time that they taught fingers to play (although these theoretical introductions were increasingly truncated). The familiar first-chapter image of "the gamut," far from being an injunction to practice morning scales, was more akin to a bookish grammar lesson. Rudiments laid the foundation: staves, clefs, note naming, key signatures, time signatures, rhythm, rests, accidentals, ornaments, and so on. Practical exercises thus functioned principally to inculcate knowledge. The keyword in this system, to repeat, was *engagement,* the philosophy being to engage theoretical knowledge to manual activity, to tie the student-apprentice to precedent, to draw eyes away from hands toward printed page, and to bind learning to doing.

The same was true for the generation of Louis Adam, Kalkbrenner's teacher at the conservatory, as well as such early century luminaries as J. B. Cramer, Daniel Steibelt, and Muzio Clementi. Instead of beginning with score reading, the first lesson in each of these tutors presented the student with her right hand in five-finger position. Here the hand became the alpha and omega of keyboard music and instruction. This was the principle: to fix manual habits, correct technique, standardize pedagogical practice, inculcate one (only one!) system for fingering, demystify thumb and fifth, ensure smooth shifts between hand positions, prevent unnecessary twisting of arms or hands, instill economy of movement, and equalize all ten fingers on both hands in terms of power and independence. In short, the idea was to instrumentalize hands, to form them as an uncomplicated effusion of the soul, to extend them into the keys, to cultivate perfection, eliminate insufficiencies, and reveal grace in "true position." The tutors of Kalkbrenner's teachers and contemporaries (particularly that of Johann Nepomuk Hummel, published in 1828) do precisely this: they imagine a student of absolute plasticity, where the aim is to acquire every means of beautiful doing.

The master-hand of Kalkbrenner was arguably the highest exemplification of the Aristotelian model. Here was a man who had devoted a lifetime to the cultivation of his hands. His beautiful hands were famed for their "enchanting touch—unbelievable evenness and mastery" (as Chopin put it), rapidity of finger, delicacy and grace in ornaments, free and decisive touch, motive control, supple wrist, bold declamation, "perfect finger," and the smoothest, definitive *jeu perlé*. (Schumann countered that "the pearl never floats on the surface; it must be sought in the depths.")[57] In December 1831, Chopin met Kalkbrenner daily, his mentor being "superior to all the pianists I have ever heard": "Herz, Liszt, Hiller and the rest," Chopin wrote, were "nobodies compared with Kalkbrenner."[58] The pedagogue-virtuoso encouraged his students, on memorizing a passage, to place a looking glass on the desk so that the hands might be watched from all angles.[59] Audiences were also invited to gaze, to marvel at the spectacle of perfect hands gliding effortlessly across the keys. (According to Václav Tomásek's 1840s autobiography, it was Jan Dussek who first positioned the piano so as to display his profile and a side-angle view of his hands for an event in Prague.)[60] Ever the omniscient technician, Kalkbrenner brought *stile brillante* pianism and *stile brillante* extemporization to its zenith, with glistening streams of right-hand arpeggios, scales, passagework, figurations, sequences, expressive formulas, and florid, chromatic double-note runs of every variation. His intoxicating modernity heralded a new era of both hedonism and military precision. "The piano for Kalkbrenner is a slave," the *Musical World* of 1839 quipped, "well regulated, and accustomed to obey."[61] Ernst Pauer remarked that he commanded his fingers like a "well-drilled company of soldiers."[62] The effect of such a remarkable engagement of theory to practice was paraded for all to see.

Kalkbrenner's hands, furthermore, were proof of the exemplary accomplishments of the Paris Conservatoire. The eloquence of his improvisational style evinced visible erudition: docility of body, symmetry of pose, effortless precision, and devotion to system. Indeed, his art of the body was the beau ideal of a highly theorized discipline of keyboard practice. Simplicity was key, a fact communicated eloquently in his 1831 correspondence with William Ayrton in relation to arrangements for the latter's English translation of his *Méthode* (using documents now preserved in British Library.)[63] As we shall see, Kalkbrenner instructed that the body should enter a machinery of power, a regime engineered for an endlessly perfectible ideal—the soft wax of the hands would be improved and "simplified" so as to achieve a legible eloquence. He sought to free distortion, have students play only from the level of the keys, correct students' fingering, emancipate their thumbs, equalize all ten fingers, and cleanse the body of impurity. "My principle," declared the master in the English edition of his method, "is to form the hands before the eyes"—in other words, to shape them merely by overseeing their motions.[64]

Such a mania for system implied a love of accumulation. Kalkbrenner's "alphabetic" approach followed enlightenment models of language learning or instruction in the arts of rhetoric. The student was to accrue one by one (in elementary order) a "complete" social grammar at the same time as she shaped the *mollesse* of her hand merely by beautifying its actions. An armory of expressive quantities was thus prepared: figures, topics, sequences, expressive manners, affects, style types, the whole panoply of key-area conventions. Good principle was assembled in natural array: the laws of the five-ruled staff, scales, signatures, keys, intervals, note values, meter, dynamics, trills, gruppetti, grace notes, minor modes, phrasing, attack, fingering, and targeted exercises. In his posthumous *Traité d'harmonie,* for example, Kalkbrenner instructed that pupils memorize key signatures in relation to visible parts of their own bodies. (He thus located theory haptically, in ways that recalled the use of such ancient mnemonic aids as the Guidonian hand). His études prepared for the display of every technical figure: diatonic and chromatic scales, thirds, sixths, octaves, repeated notes, stretches, held notes, cadences, trills, sequences, passages in contrary motion, and so on.

If quantities were to be thus accrued, personal qualities had to be smoothed away. The finished student, in his estimation, was a pianist free from impediment. She was a pupil liberated from vulgar individuality. Every display of feeling would ideally be an echo of universal emotions present and real to each auditor, not merely evidence of some singularly dark or inscrutable artistic personality. Freed from "expression," the pianist would shine with moral excellence. Her hand would be the instrument of her soul, and it would act to stimulate ever-novel musical effects and varieties of sentiment.

Students were not merely trained in music but instructed to glitter in public, to be, as Kalkbrenner was, "as polished as a billiard ball." When Stephen Heller was "straightened" *(décrotté),* for example, the pupil reported that Kalkbrenner castigated him as much for his French pronunciation, low pitch of speech, deportment, seriousness, and shyness as for any pianistic fault.[65] The law was absolute: rules governed even Kalkbrenner's thoughts on "expression and nuance" in the *Méthode*. Rising scales or passages were played crescendo, descending passages diminuendo; the longest note in a measure was stressed; melodic phrases ended with a ritardando; higher notes were played louder than lower ones, and so on in impeccable order. Kalkbrenner himself pondered why so many found such "pedantry" stultifying, a fact noticed by Henri Blanchard in his 1838 review of the third edition of the *Méthode* and this "last expression of the large, noble and beautiful school of Clementi."[66] Experience and the classic model of Diderot and Talma, Kalkbrenner declared, confirmed the rectitude of precedent.

Kalkbrenner's polish was nowhere more evident than when he performed his trademark *Effusio Musica*, op. 68, a stylish fantasy that stunned cosmopolitan audiences in the late 1820s. Written in the style of Hummel's celebrated op. 18 Fantasy in E-flat Major, the *Effusio* was well known to Mendelssohn. The music critic of the *Athenaeum*, Henry F. Chorley, recalled how the young Felix and Fanny used to vie "with each other which could best execute a certain difficult left-hand passage" in a prestissimo section toward the end.[67] By 1829 the twenty-minute fantasy was used to judge "la rectitude de la pose de la main" for women pianists undergoing their final exam at the Paris Conservatoire. (The men, significantly, played Kalkbrenner too: his First Concerto in D Minor, op. 61).[68] The *Effusio*, to be sure, showcased a scintillating variety of style types and affective idioms, modulating rapidly between keys in order to explore the gamut of topical regions within a bold fast-slow-fast arch. As the author of a long analysis of the work appearing in the *Quarterly Musical Magazine and Review* put it, "Every difficulty is introduced which is possible for the hands to execute."[69]

Figure 9 presents a snatch of the central "slow movement," and a glimpse of what Antoine Marmontel, a fellow resident with Chopin at the phalanstery on the Square d'Orléans, called Kalkbrenner's "grande variété de style et de forme, souvent de l'inspiration et toujours une main ferme, sûre d'elle-même, traduisant la pensée dans la langue musicale la plus correcte."[70] The "tender" cantilena echoes a formulaic Rossinian F-major "aria di cantabile." As per the lingua franca (what Italian opera scholars call the "lyric prototype"), it begins with a pair of corresponding four-measure phrases (the second a tone higher) before the standard swerve through two medial phrases (two-measure sequences inflecting the "first movement" D major) and a florid segue back to the tonic. The "aria type" works well for Kalkbrenner. First, it allows the pianist to display his singing fingers and, in the closing phrase, his double thirds, then Pleyel's double escapement action (with accelerando repeated notes) before his skills in the obligatory cadenza. (Here Kalkbrenner follows Rossini in writing out improvisations.) For the pianist, what is expressed here (and later, when the melody is repeated in ornamented form) is control and imagination in a standard

FIGURE 9. The operatic "slow movement" of Kalkbrenner's *Effusio Musica* (Paris, 1823), 14. Reproduced by permission of the Bibliothèque nationale de France.

aria form. Such a conventional frame, of course, provides a bold contrast with the *Effusio*'s brooding written-out prelude (eventually cadencing in C♯ major), a "symphonic" D-major first theme (making rhetorical features of four-note motives and rapid-fire hand crossings), and the canon in octaves immediately preceding the cantabile (begun in E major!). The encyclopedic approach to sentiment was typical for Kalkbrenner, as was the abundance of rhetorical formulas, virtuoso figurations, and extended passages of ornamentation. The pianist "effused" this armory. Kalkbrenner's fame indeed rested on his facility to shuttle between the diverse languages that he had acquired and to exhort his listeners to be as worldly as he was. As *Le Pianiste* put it in 1833, "Watch Kalkbrenner as he touches the piano.—It is not without reason that I say 'watch,' because he never betrays, either in his body or his face, the immense difficulties passing beneath his fingers. Kalkbrenner est *l'exécutant-modèle.*"[71]

The most misunderstood part of Kalkbrenner's immense nineteenth-century legacy, of course, was his notorious "hand-guide," also known as the chiroplast. This orthopedic device—a wooden rail placed horizontally above the keys—had its own complementary manual, the best-selling *Méthode pour apprendre le piano à l'aide du guide-mains*, op. 108 (1831), dedicated to "all the conservatories of music of Europe." In Pierre-Joseph Zimmermann's class in Paris, the "shaper" was systemically in use throughout the 1830s and beyond. (Such pianists as Charles-Camille Saint-Saëns via Camille-Marie Stamaty were students of the method.)[72] By the fourth edition of November 1845, Kalkbrenner could claim the sale of thirty-one thousand copies of the manual in Paris alone.[73]

Two years previously, the chiroplast had attracted the attention of Schumann, who was predictable in his denunciation: "In Paris, you encounter whole generations of Kalkbrenner pupils. You can subdivide them: beginners, ur-beginners, and ur-ur-beginners. The female component of the city's population is largely a product of Kalkbrenner's muse. They have all been weaned at his method's breast, and have suckled life, strength, and fingering from it. Their hobbyhorse and plaything is the famous Hand-Guide."[74]

In the preface to his *Méthode*, Kalkbrenner emphasized that the chiroplast was not so much an instrument of torture as a device for correction. He told the story of the genesis of the machine in the context of his battle against "deformity." Louis Adam, Kalkbrenner's teacher and Zimmermann's predecessor at the Conservatoire, had long worried about the misshapenness of his pupil's fifth finger. The tension in fact became so injurious to him at the point of playing cadences—Kalkbrenner was famed for his long extemporizations at the moment of pedal points—that it "made the hand seem maimed." Kalkbrenner grew so perturbed by this misshapenness, according to the tale, that one day he seized an old armchair and sawed off one of the legs. In so doing, he invented the first wooden rail, which he bolted horizontally to the keyboard in order to support his arms. The apparatus (a simplification of Johann Bernhard Logier's London device) thus soon found itself applied particularly to womanly hands, relieving unsightly strain and beautifying the fingers in preparation (one presumes) for perfect marriage.[75]

ORTHOPEDIC FORM

The existence of such devices betray the strange alignment of pianistic method and orthopedic medicine in the 1820s and '30s. Both sets of practices—musical

and therapeutic—shared a common commitment to well-made limbs, moral rectitude, and forming the body "before the eyes." Because they improved *mobility* in
both physical and social terms, both shared solid middle-class pretensions. Practitioners in each case tapped into an emerging popular market: the commercial
culture of the July Monarchy and Paris in particular, with its middlebrow aspira-
tions of self-improvement. As Constance Malpas has pointed out, orthopedic
medicine represented far more than itself in this milieu.[76] In 1830s Paris, at least,
it was a groundswell movement with strong political affiliations, bound to
the proper social balance and public symmetry of postrevolutionary France.
Orthopedic medicine experienced a considerable boom at the time of the
July Revolution, most schools in France employing some sort of extension bed
by the end of the decade. Although it initially flourished in unregulated ways outside the "clinic" or "hospital medicine," in 1835—in the season of Thalberg's first
success—a move was made to open a space for it in the medical establishment.
The orthopedic method, as if to moderate its aims, thus expanded to embrace a
widening array of cosmetic malformations, and noninvasive "gymno-orthopedic"
techniques. Traction devices or mechanical extension beds, to be sure, were not
entirely on a par with Kalkbrenner's chiroplast. Yet, as we shall see, to treat a
patient for skeletal deviation was not so far from conducting a piano lesson in this
milieu.

Extraordinarily—these are little-known facts—Frédéric Chopin and Marie
Moke Pleyel (the most celebrated of Kalkbrenner's pupils) taught piano at exclusive private orthopedic establishments in the 1830s. Moke's case is better known.
The young Hector Berlioz fell hopelessly in love with her while they both made
their living teaching music at the Institution de Mme. d'Aubrée with its attached
Établissement orthopédique in the Marais. This "pensionnat de demoiselles,"
which moved to the rue de Harley in 1824 and added an orthopedic wing in 1829,
was an infirmary set in quiet gardens. The probity of its reputation was second to
none: Janin, Sainte-Beuve, Hugo, and Lamennais were frequent visitors; Dumas's
sister was a pensionnaire, as was Adèle Huet (Janin's wife from 1841);[77] Ary Schef-
fer taught painting[78] and Berlioz guitar; and a large English clientele attended.
Those admitted underwent "straitening" in the fullest sense: executive schooling
in religion, deportment, gymnastics, language, literature, arithmetic, writing, history, geography, and music. Activities were conducted under the strictest surveillance in order to inculcate in the girls "la douceur, la docilité, l'égalité de caractère,
l'esprit d'order et d'application."[79] The 1834 prospectus named as its two extramural
piano teachers Madame Polmartin, a "belle et noble" pianist famous for her visible
accomplishments ("ses beaux cheveaux, sa taille élégante, son pied mignon, sa
main blanche, ses oreilles fines"),[80] as well as "M Hertz." (This was either Jacques
Herz, Marie's first teacher, or his famous brother, Henri Herz, inventor in 1836 of
the notorious finger strengthener, or "dactylion.")[81]

The story goes that, around mid-March or early April 1830, Ferdinand Hiller asked Berlioz to act as his *postillon d'amour* at d'Aubrée's, a go-between passing letters to the nineteen-year-old Moke. The volcanic Berlioz, however, soon either broke his friend's trust or was seduced by his *séraphin,* depending on your version of the story. Berlioz biographers record a frantic physical affair. According to David Cairns, the "superficially fascinating but brittle, vulgar, self-seeking nymphomaniac" barged into the composer's teaching room at d'Aubrée's to announce her desires. Later the pair would elope to Vincennes briefly on 6 June 1830 to make love, before Moke dumped Berlioz to marry her piano teacher's business partner. Since adolescence, the *pianiste* had been her family's chief breadwinner after the failure of her father's interests in Belgium and the sale of her mother's Dutch lingerie shop on the rue du Faubourg-Montmartre. As Berlioz put it, Moke "set my senses on fire till all the devils of hell danced in my veins."[82]

Chopin, meanwhile, was listed as a teacher at "the finest and most successful orthopedic institution in all France" around 1834. The illustrated prospectus of the Institut orthopédique de Paris records Chopin as the instructor of "perfectionnement de piano" (Anson taught "piano," Massart, probably the great Belgian violinist Lambert Massart, "accompagnement").[83] The institute was housed in the Château de la Muette near the Bois de Boulogne in Passy, a stately home owned by none other than Pierre Érard, piano manufacturer and recent inheritor of the Érard dynasty after his uncle Sebastian's death in August 1831. Pierre rented the grand park, pavilion, and two buildings (one for each sex) to physician Charles-Gabriel Pravaz, who wished to expand his mother-in-law's boarding school for girls nearby, and to powerful director Jules Guérin, owner-editor of the pioneering *Gazette médicale de Paris.* When Érard discontinued the lease in 1841, the château (which the family had purchased in 1818) became one of the most important venues of nineteenth-century music history. It was the location of legendary Sunday-evening parties hosted by Madame Érard, Spontini's sister; Rossini spent his final years nearby; Wagner and Rubinstein were frequent visitors; and Thalberg apparently used La Muette late in his life as his chief Parisian residence.

Back in 1834, the Institut orthopédique provided instruction in Italian song, English, Italian, and Latin, painting and drawing, gymnastics, and the piano. The prospectus promised that use of the institute's personalized orthopedic braces would be compulsory: "For all lessons, students are placed in *appareils,* or supported by belts and corsets such as to preclude any interruption in treatment."[84] Correction by music, in other words, was supplemented by such "suspension" machines as the swan brace, which was illustrated for the great orthopedic atlas of the era, *De l'orthomorphie* (1828), by Pravaz's great teacher at Montpellier (see figure 10). Jacques-Marie Delpech was the "father of the science of orthopedics," famed for his legendary "maison de redressement," which he began in a suburb of the city before being shot by an apparently malaligned patient on 28 October 1832.

FIGURE 10. Jacques-Marie Delpech's apparatus for a straight spine and erect head (after a similar English device by John Shaw), illustrated in *De l'orthomorphie* (Paris, 1828), plate 68. © BIU Santé (Paris).

The Passy institute was heavily indebted to Delpech, he having popularized less retributive forms of posture, as perhaps *"la pianiste suspendue"* suggests (what does it mean to be gently directed by a swan?). Guérin too built his name on exposing the abuse of mechanical or "permanent extension" and organizing against the unregulated practice of popular orthopedics. Yet he was not exactly the least invasive of therapists. New York surgeon Valentine Mott remembered paying a visit to the gardens of Passy in 1834. He watched Guérin's knife "untwisting, as it literally does, the most misshapen, and revolting, and convoluted mass of deformity," cutting at forty-three muscles and tendons, until the patient was "stretched out upon the table in his natural shape," free from pain, and without having shed a drop of blood. For Mott, the delicate division of tendons proved that orthopedic practice was the future of medical endeavor. Most impressive was how Guérin might "unbind the fettered limbs, restore symmetry to the distorted form, give mobility to the imprisoned tongue, and directness to the orb of vision."[85]

Whatever Guérin's approach to righting the body, he generally favored the *redressement* of muscle over bone, and a form of modern ortho-gymnastics that preferred the indirect benefits of physical, nutritional, spiritual, moral, and social education over the direct manipulations of mechanical extension. Orthopedic endeavor was, in any event, on a slippery slope by the late 1830s, as Guérin's surgical excesses and tirades against extension imply. The trend, in other words, was less toward the old visible beatification of the outer body (and bone structure) than toward fortifying its invisible inner qualities. Musculoskeletal "health," musculature, a toned body, regular exercise, and nutrition had become preoccupations in the modern style.[86]

Under such conditions, as we shall see, the whole question of the orthopedic significance of piano playing became the subject of lively debate. It was already so for swan-obsessed Delpech: was piano playing good or bad for you? In the old language, an elegant Pleyel might yield visible orthopedic improvements. Such benign traction, indeed, was an elegant means of fine-tuning the body, of smoothing away disequilibrium, and of tending to the hand's poise and elegance. The more physiologically oriented opinions of the 1840s, however, speculated the reverse: that to engage with the instrument for twelve to thirteen hours a day, as Kalkbrenner recommended, was injudicious (Chopin inclined to this view).[87] Even if one was neutral on the subject, it might not seem so admirable to seek the hand's absolute apex of beauty so assiduously. To play at the highest level, modern pianists were increasingly compelled away from visible accomplishments. Instead of "forming the hand," virtuosos were drawn to "deform" or better "transform" the hand—to have it act against itself. For these reasons pianistic hands were increasingly bound, clamped, or levered into extraordinary positions so as to achieve a permanent state of transfiguration.

PES ALTERUS MANUS: BACK TO THALBERG

The famous pianistic Thalberg-Apparat sought exactly this.[88] Instead of untwisting or directing the action of the performing body in the tradition of Delpech's and Kalkbrennner's guides, Thalberg's 1846 *assouplisseur* turned on the hand, directly undermining its ontology. Unlike the old cosmetic finger shapers, the device that

Thalberg began recommending to his students responded to the most up-to-date insights of the increasingly prestigious science of human anatomy. The inventor, Félix Levacher d'Urclé, in fact, developed the Thalberg-Apparat in close consultation with the foremost physiologists of the era: Jean Cruveilhier and the professor of anatomy at the Faculté de medécine de Paris, Joseph-Alexandre Auzias-Turenne. The author counseled that musicians, instead of training the hand to be eloquent in several musical languages, step back from the instrument. The first principle of piano playing was to get to know "given" conditions: to know one's hands. As such, the *Méthode raisonnée du mécanisme de la main,* which accompanied d'Urclé's device, was a "nouvelle méthode" (in Berlioz's words) in name only.[89] Stripped of theoretical adornments, the tutor made no mention of keys, durations, scales, arpeggios, exercises, pianos, or even music. Any engagement with theory, music making, or visible work with the keyboard was now a waste of time, since the *"appareil orthopédique"* reduced by "twenty times" the manual labor habitually required of the instrument.

Such an approach to playing imagined the hand as inherently inexpressive. The hand here presented a dynamic space of divisions and resistances, a shifting geography of knotted muscles, tendons, fasciae, bands, medians, torsions, oppositions, transversions, and tensions. It had regions (dorsal and palmar) crisscrossed by extensors, flexors, and ligaments. Its *affaiblissements* were not simply to be smoothed away. The old cosmetic project to equalize the fingers was doomed because of concealed *relations* or "intimate rapports" operative within the hand. As d'Urclé explained, the unseen natatory ligament in particular (first described as *la bande transversale* by Jean Baptiste Marc Bourgery in the 1830s) forced a marriage between fingers three, four, and five (the "brides correlative"), which encumbered affective display.

Scientific observance of the inner hand, in other words, evinced that piano playing was frankly "antinatural." For d'Urclé, performance set up "un combat sera ouvert entre l'action de la volonté et la resistance des expansions."[90] The only way to solve the conflict, in his view, was to apply the *assouplisseur:* to distend the hand. Pianists were encouraged to work less on their fingers than on the relations or muscles between them. They were asked to pressure the hand into a state of deliverance by focusing on dynamic invisibles. Berlioz, in his laudatory review of Thalberg's apparatus, enthused over what he hoped would be the "debridement" of the hand, his vision being that d'Urclé's technology would free performers from their ignoble preoccupation with mechanism. New techniques of distension, in other words, promised to unbridle materiality and abnegate garish display.

Thalberg too soon longed for more than the shopworn parade of symmetrical bone structure. His famous *L'Art du chant appliqué au piano* (1853) advocated against the invasive corrections of orthopedic pianism. Instead, this tutor advanced a mode of modern "body management" that involved unrelenting surveillance and a deep knowledge of the biological life of one's hands. "Let [pianists] listen well to their own performance, question themselves, be severe in judging themselves," Thalberg wrote. "In general," he continued, "they work too much with their own fingers, and not with sufficient intelligence."[91] Here was a pedagogy geared more to sensory acquisition than to the management of two preexisting biological presences. In order to find the "voice" of nature, Thalberg counseled that pianists not so much "strike" the keys as "knead" them. The metaphors useful to his quest were significant—"pressed as though with a boneless hand *[main désossée]* and fingers of velvet." The hand's energies, in other words, were to be released by circumventing muscle and bone.

Such an imperative—to make of the (boneless) hand an idea—reflected the most recent research developments in "philosophical anatomy" and osteological research, particularly that of Auzias-Turenne. If Auzias-Turenne had contributed scientifically to the Thalberg-Apparat—he endorsed d'Urclé in a letter dated 23 January 1846—by the end of the year his fascination with the hand and its place in the human body had only intensified. On 28 December 1846 Auzias-Turenne gave a groundbreaking lecture to the Académie des sciences, wherein he presented his contribution to the now forgotten discipline of intermembral or serial homology.[92] Following a practice pioneered by the great comparative anatomist Félix Vicq d'Azyr in 1774, Auzias-Turenne laid out the bones of a beautiful human skeleton before him, in the illustrious tradition of Galen, Chaussier, Sömmerring, Mechel, Cuvier, Bourgery, de Blainville, Flourens, and Cruveilhier. Like Vicq d'Azyr, Auzias-Turenne could only marvel at the wondrous unity of man's organic composition. He extolled the ways in which God had established harmonious relations between the superior and anterior parts of the human frame. The elegant similitude of shoulder blade (scapula) and pelvic bone (ilium) was remarkable, as were the ways in which the bones of the hand were repeated in those of the feet (as per the old adage "pes alterus manus"), the arm bone found isomorphic parallels in the thigh, and so on. The young anatomist, in other words, displayed the body in ways that laid bare the marvelous symmetry of man. Man's natural preeminence was mirrored in the harmony of his frame.

Placing right leg (Fig. 1) alongside right arm (Fig. 2), however, Auzias-Turenne encountered a nagging noncorrespondence, which would throw the great classical science into peril (see figure 11). Vicq d'Azyr himself had noticed how, when laid out, the forearm's radius and ulna crossed in ways that belied their resemblance to the fibula and tibia of the lower leg. Also nagging was that the knee looked forward while the elbow projected backward. To undo such unbeautiful *croisements,* Vicq d'Azyr first turned the upper arm (humerus) outward. This maneuver caused an arrangement where the higher joint of the right thighbone faced inward, while that of right arm now looked outward (Fig. 3). Ingeniously, Vicq d'Azyr then amended the dissimilitude by swapping right arm with left arm, thus proposing a

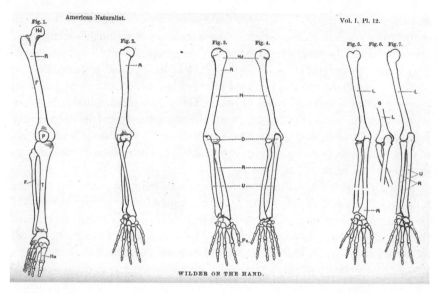

FIGURE 11. The problematic leg-arm homology illustrated in Burt G. Wilder, "The Hand as an Unruly Member," *American Naturalist* 1/8 (October 1867), 414–23; 1/9 (November 1867), 482–91; and 1/12 (February 1868), 631–38, plate 12, 490. Courtesy of the Marian Koshland Bioscience and Natural Resources Library, University of California, Berkeley.

new homology: a transposition to the opposite side of the body, where the right arm corresponded with the left leg and the left arm with the right leg (Fig. 4). But whereas Vicq d'Azyr, Cruveilhier, Bourgery, and others were happy to leave it there, Auzias-Turenne remained unconvinced. He was bothered by that unruly left hand, with its thumb now at variance with the design of the right foot, a flaw that for him required yet another homology. Thus before the members of the academy he severed the right hand from its arm by hacking through radius and ulna with a blade, uncrossed these bones, and glued them back together in parallel so the whole would correspond in the way that the science required (Figs. 5–7). By surgical intervention the young anatomist disengaged the hand from a once homologous order, as if to suggest that it no longer made sense in view of the old natural unities. The hand, in this conception, was unhinged. No longer an instrument of the soul, it appeared as if disengaged from the body, its conformation at odds with the form of the whole.

THE QUESTION OF THALBERG'S SOUL

Such a turn from visible beauty brings Thalberg squarely back into view. As noted in the prelude to this chapter, many of Thalberg's popular and professional listeners took frenzied pleasure in looking. The throng of musicians surrounding his Érard apparently read the actions of Thalberg's piano-playing hands as visible manifestations of moral rectitude. But, as was so often the case in this age of fledgling music criticism, such high-minded behavior was at variance, as much with nascent ideologies of art as with nascent "realist" conceptions of the body. A new moralizing breed of journalist saw things differently: eye candy was neither to be countenanced nor stomached. Even those moralist-critics who supported Thalberg held that his genius had little to do with any obvious visible engagements with the music. Apparently for such writers, *pace* all the rambling spectators, there was nothing much to see other than an unflappably cool exterior, Thalberg's patented brand of emotional disengagement, and hands apparently released to a purely musical task. For the critics, then, "detachment" was Thalberg's strength, his bodily economy apparently inviting audiences to listen for invisible qualities. It was the melody played by his unseen third hand—the music that he apparently *did not* play—that most charged his performances with "soul."

In Paris, the most ardent disciple of the "inspirited Thalberg" was Joseph d'Ortigue, the liberal Catholic writer who will reappear as an important critic of Italian vocal styles in my next chapter. On hearing the musician in March 1837, the critic-theologian cheered that it was impossible to tell where the pianist's left hand began and right hand ended, so perfect was the action of his apparently fingerless hands.[93] In London, two months later, having witnessing the ignoble crowd of instrumentalists encircling Thalberg's Érard at Mori's 1837 benefit, the *Atlas* claimed that "a feeling so deep and beautiful may be detected in the pressure of fingers that caress the keys and make the piano give out its most beautiful sounds that herein we have the secret of the enchantment. The charm is simplicity. Thalberg has a soul, and no common one."[94] The *Morning Post* agreed a month later, especially when Thalberg appeared half dead. With "languid step, and rather bloodless cheek," Thalberg scarcely seemed to be awake, and yet his powerful soul writhed in audible tumult.

> In the very tempest and whirlwind of the passion which he creates, he himself seems tranquilly intent upon what he is doing, but nothing more. He appears to make no extraordinary exertion. He does not plunge up to the shoulders in the pianoforte, as I have seen some men *almost* do. He holds his hands level with his wrists, and from the wrist all the force of his touch appears to come. The shoulder muscles seem as quiescent as if he were asleep. But his soul—his soul must be all awake, to produce such music.[95]

For Thalberg's enthusiasts, the disconnect between what was heard and seen was the wellspring of his allure. The way that this pianist watched his hands suggested that he was not wholly responsible for them.[96]

For the influential Fétis, Thalberg's sangfroid was less a sign of cultivation than a mark of seriousness. It was a mark separating "la musique de pensée" from "la mécanique des doigts." In his pioneering 1 March 1836 review of Thalberg in *Le Temps*, Fétis could not believe his eyes. Or rather he realized that it was pointless to look.[97] In a tailspin, he explained that he'd endured a twenty-four-hour fever trying to fathom Thalberg's first Parisian benefit at the Salle Ventadour. Fétis's "stupefaction" centered on a quasi-religious revelation: a "new art" and a "powerful voice" that had transfigured what for him had formerly been a dull instrument. (The piano was now an "orchestra" or perhaps a celestial "organ.") In thrall to his own brand of German idealism, Fétis heard in Thalberg's voice the expression of a unitary and indivisible *moi* of the sort identified in the haute bourgeois political philosophy of his guru Victor Cousin. In Fétis's eyes, the pianist's performance bore witness to nothing less than the truth of a veritable Cousinian *fait intérieur,* an immaterial and ready-made soul to match the "ready-made" sound of the thousands upon thousands of iron-braced Érards now increasingly heard in bourgeois homes. Thalberg had chosen to evince his "soul," furthermore, in service of ready-made music. His performance of Hummel's Septet for Winds, Strings, and Piano, op. 74, for instance, demonstrated how much he was "born to render the thoughts of the great musician that he was interpreting with absolute perfection."[98] Even in the newly ascendant genre of the opera fantasy, Thalberg betrayed his inborn *moi* by the way he reinspirited ready-made melodies, distinguishing himself as *the* faithful "classical" pianist *avant la lettre.*[99] These grand performances stood out in relation to the "banal queue" (as one writer put it) of the now defunct "air with variation." This was a music, Fétis explained, beyond music, "animated by six hands and an ardent soul."[100]

Fétis's enthusiasm for Thalberg of course stemmed from his politics. For him, the pianist was the model of self-government, one that, in the words of liberal statesman and politician François Guizot, was "internal" rather than external to society. For believers such as Fétis, Thalberg's talents proved him the paragon of male bourgeois subjectivity. The musician was the "archangel" of the middling doctrinaire compromise wary of absolute monarchical power on the one hand and mob rule on the other. Indeed, in the new juste-milieu, power was no longer displayed in the singularly beautiful body of the sovereign. Instead, in this constitutional monarchy, power was ideally invisible and impersonal. If despots had once ruled by their brazen instruments, the solidly moderate body politic of the future was to be founded according to the anonymous relations of a diffuse bureaucracy. The ideology of "the given"—of biological truths and man's inborn *moi*—was thus fundamental to the physiological integrity of the modern state. The new regime of "the normal," indeed, would be a regime of self-observation, muscular health, and self-restraint. It was one perfectly in tune with that invisible Cousinian theology of "the True, the Beautiful, and the Good."[101]

AGAINST MANUAL LABOR: THE CRITICAL
COUP DE MAIN

Antiestablishment critics, however, disagreed with the Fétisian assessment of Thalberg, especially when they saw wide-eyed audiences hustling for a better view. The problem, apparently, was less Thalberg's style than the way in which his fans just kept on looking. Since he could detect no soul, since he heard no "voice," Ludwig Rellstab, for example, borrowed the language routinely used to lampoon Kalkbrenner in 1842: "Thalberg's art is like a harmoniously developed, exquisitely beautiful body without soul; everywhere we find symmetry, firmness, repose, grace and strength; yet it does not possess that charm which a high spiritual nature lends to the body."[102] Other Germans such as Wilhelm von Lenz, scoffed at "la *plastique* de Thalberg," his "cold perfection," his commercial success, his "Olympian purity," and his operatic Italianisms and pedantry. Like Kalkbrenner, Thalberg's particular body politic (his dressage) lacked machismo: "[Thalberg] debases art to the level of fashion, reproducing, in one word, the 'hermaphroditism' of the *l'artiste-homme du monde*, of the aspiring social-pianist, created in our times, and already much perfected."[103] Thalberg's sexlessness, in the ears of these critics, was of a mechanical sort, reminiscent perhaps of the meek femininity of the first women typists, a social type conceived in 1842 to serve the first generation of "type-composing machines" or "type-setters."

The type-writing secretaries of figures 12 and 13 would arguably carry Kalkbrenner's legacy of precision and perfect execution deep into the nineteenth century and beyond (Herz, after all, was nicknamed "the stenographer"). The "distributing machine" of Young and Delcambre of London (1842), for example, was built on the model of a cottage piano, as were the word-processing inventions of the same year by Clay and Swedish entrepreneur Captain Rosenberg in Paris. These skeuomorphs—at once musical instruments, "composing machines," church pews, and weaving looms—betrayed the extent to which the old pianistic beau ideal had been feminized. The portrayal of women in both images illustrates the extent to which on-the-spot creative improvisation had been silenced. To cultivate beautiful hands, to engage them in religious devotion to scores, was to devote oneself to the compliant reproduction of male texts.[104] After all, according to the ubiquitous education manuals for the fair sex, there was nothing so ladylike, nothing so docile or visibly obedient, as a well-made hand.[105]

Thalberg proved strangely prone to accusations of "type-writerliness," despite his metaphysical "voice." The *Times* threw a second serious critical salvo at the musician-composer when its critic returned to Hanover Square for the pianist's second Philharmonic appearance in 1836. "From some hidden and mysterious cause," Thomas Massa Alsager complained, Thalberg had been made "an absolute idol" by the public. Most unfathomable was his "cold" choice to play without

FIGURE 12. Young and Delcambre's type-composing machine illustrated in *Mechanics'*
Magazine, Museum, Register, Journal, and Gazette 36/985 (25 June 1842), 497. Reproduced
by kind permission of the Syndics of Cambridge University Library.

orchestra, since "the monotony of the [single] instrument palls upon the ear" in a
way that reminded the reviewer of a "musical snuff-box, or the mechanical wonders of Flight and Robson's repertory."[106] Alsager was a leading proponent of "serious" listening in London. Alsager's friends in the city would in fact cause more
trouble for Thalberg in 1842 when George MacFarren the younger and James William Davison hissed the virtuoso's attempt at an encore at a Philharmonic concert

FIGURE 13. Rosenberg's composing machine in "Des Claviers typographiques," *L'Illustration* (25 March 1843), 59–61, 61. Courtesy of Doe Library, University of California, Berkeley.

on 13 June 1842, before "talking loud, and flirting with female friends." The same orchestral band, who had once gathered to gawk at Thalberg's hands, now gathered to defend their hero, who had performed not one but an unprecedented two solos at this Philharmonic appearance. At the ensuing Saturday rehearsal at Hanover Square on 26 June 1842, there was a fracas as Felix Mendelssohn sat down to try his second piano concerto. On entering the room, MacFarren and Davison were greeted with such a volley of jeers and shouts of "Turn them out!" that Mendelssohn leapt back from his instrument.[107]

In the end, predictably, the voice that hissed loudest and last was Franz Liszt's. In Liszt's famous public spat with Fétis over the *Grande Fantaisie* in January of 1837, "the Ostrogoth" was again likened to a machine. Here, Liszt compared Thalberg to the 1821 "componium," Dietrich Nikolaus Winkel's mechanical improviser, which used an early algorithmic form of artificial intelligence. Schumann would follow Liszt by observing that Thalberg "made music, like the trumpeter in [Friedrich] Kaufman's Museum in Dresden, blown through the air, not through the soul."[108] Thalberg's soullessness, for Liszt, was evidenced by the score of the *Grande Fantaisie*, which he denounced as a "decomposition" of "magisterial boredom." The fantasy boasted structural integrity, yes, but not of a sort to be proud of: "Des arpèges, partout des arpèges, rien que des arpèges! Quelle merveilleuse unité!" If there was life in this music, Liszt confessed that he lacked the ear to recognize it.[109]

Fétis struck back at Liszt by invoking one of his typically grand pianistic metan-arratives. He argued that (in the light of eternity) it was Thalberg (not Liszt) who was the true avant-garde, the prophet-pianist of a new "epoch of transformation." Liszt, after all, would inspire his own machine: around 1840, according to the *Wiener Courier*, a Parisian inventor named Curille invented an automaton, a man-nequin that performed an apparently "perfect" facsimile of the virtuoso playing two of his studies.[110] By the end of his spat with Fétis, in May, Liszt had resorted to asking who the critic was to talk and where, exactly, he got his "impossible" view from nowhere. Mocking selfish delusion, the composer-pianist quoted the illustri-ous Catholic philosopher Blaise Pascal—"le *moi* est haïssable" (the self is loath-some)—to put Fétis in his place.

The debate, in other words, boiled down to what counted as "soulful." Liszt's self-effacing politics, after all, was defined in rebellious opposition to "the normal." He opposed Fétis's bourgeois faith in the *vérité* of some supposedly immanent Cousinian "self," some apparently noncontingent, God-like objectivity. The indi-visible self emerging beneath Thalberg's fingers, as far as Liszt could tell, was a ruse, a commercial trick conjured by vain slight of hand. For if Thalberg found expression in the concretization of one authentic "voice," Liszt's catholic socialism expressed itself in more equivocal ways. The selfless pose of the "Thalberg Hongr-ois," as *Le Ménestrel* called him, betrayed a body that was more than merely a representation of only one "soul," if such a thing could be said to exist.[111] Rather, as we shall see, Liszt aspired to consecrate himself as the temple of "the world soul." His hope was to be the universal representative or Humanitarian-Apostle of not *one* voice but "an infinity of voices," as Berlioz put it, "born beneath the fingers."[112]

5

In Search of Voice

Nourrit's Voix Mixte, *Donzelli's Bari-Tenor*

LOSING VOICE

Historians still remember the year of Gilbert-Louis Duprez's return from Italy as the year when the Paris Opéra fell into "triste décadence."[1] A dark veil descended in 1837, when a long-favored artist-citizen was forced into exile: Adolphe Nourrit, legendary singer, idol of the Salle Le Peletier, and former inspiration for a host of high-profile Rossini and Meyerbeer roles. Duprez made his Parisian debut as Arnold in Rossini's *Guillaume Tell*—a signature Nourrit role—on 17 April. The new tenor's entry heralded a new era of political self-interest, or so they said. Not only the Opéra but Paris itself was passing away—"our Paris, the Paris where we were born," as the Goncourts lamented some years later.[2]

Those circles of friendship, which had been an organizing principle for conservative liberal elites since long before the July Revolution, were unraveling; the networks of intimacy—those cautious doctrinaire alternatives to the hierarchic social architecture of the prerevolutionary era—were weakened. Assailed by factionalism, cultural life itself was dulled, enfeebling the *amitié* of bohemian life and socialist phalansteries as so enthusiastically attended by Nourrit on the rue Taitbout. Salons, too, were losing their luster. The boudoirs of Madame Apponyi, the rooms of Comtesse de Merlin, and the political activity of the Faubourg Saint-Germain: these havens of exclusive and often liberal intimacy no longer thrived.

The old socialities were going the way of the elite ideal in which *citoyens capacitaires* were threaded together, not by top-down obligation or force but by close personal attachment and elective affinity. Things were changing even on the street, where once men walked arm in arm, held hands, and poured out their private affection in touching love letters: "I have missed you," "I love you," "Embrace me," Nourrit wrote to male friends such as August Féréol.³ A new Paris was apparently being born, a world of suspicion and market capitalism. This was the dawn of Balzac's *la vie parisienne*, characterized by *flânerie* and anonymous theater going, free-press journalism, draconian theatrical censorship, increased police surveillance, criminality, selfish pleasure, and the telegraph. It was the dawn of private luxury, the inalienable natural right, and lawyers—a France "without faith, without love, without excitement, without glory," as Virginie Ancelot wrote. Once it had abolished intimacy, according to François Guizot, connoisseur of beautiful friendship and minister of public instruction from 1832 to 1837, the new *mondanité* would have but one axiom: "enrichissez-vous."

Louis Quicherat, childhood intimate and biographer of Nourrit, pointed accusingly at the director of the Opéra, Henri Duponchel, who had apparently concocted the fiction of "the new species of tenor" and erected the Duprez-Nourrit *échafaudage* merely to generate profit. A stench of business hung over the "système materialiste" of this "little yellow man," a man who dressed more like an undertaker than a theater director, as Heine observed.⁴ Already in 1840, Ange-Henri Blaze reported that the Opéra had become "an enterprise without direction, without unity, without system, surrendered to the hazards of fortune." "What had become of those singers," Blaze complained, "whose individuality merged into the ensemble?" (He had Nourrit in mind.)⁵ In his memoirs, Berlioz called Duponchel a "monophile." Léon Escudier thought the former *metteur en scène* "a director of indisputable incapacity." Quicherat remembered an administration of press bribery and *claquerie* to the extent that applause would occur *before* cadences; in short, it was a system propagating the kind of rampant individualism that made nuanced French art impossible.⁶ "The Opéra," wrote Heine in 1837, "has become reconciled with the enemies of music." The Salle Le Peletier was "a sahara of music."⁷

All the complaints of the *salonnières*, however, could not undo Duprez's success. *La Presse* used the example of the "new tenor" both to question Nourrit's masculinity and attack the high *voix mixte*. "For our part," the correspondent wrote, "we have a horror of those little fluted falsetto notes, that make one doubt the virility of he who produced them, and prefer, as in modern drama, to hear a man's voice from a man's chest." Frédéric Soulié hailed Duprez as a straight shooter. His unfussy style and declamatory energy expressed an "ever-present, rich, liberal voice, which retracts nothing, conceals nothing and says everything, without fear of what it has to say." Théophile Gautier swooned over Duprez's purity of timbre, sonority, "plenitude," sobriety of ornament, restrained acting style, and "religious devotion" to the "beauties of the score."⁸ The simple trustworthiness of his sounds evinced personal freedom and artistic autonomy, though critics such as Blaze found them "insufferably uniform." "In sum," wrote Charles Maurice in 1837, Duprez sang in "a chest voice, and always a chest voice, oblivious to dramatic situation, to the shifting emotions of the scene, or to national taste."[9] If his voice struggled to blend effectively in ensembles, it was unassailable in Italianate recitatives and solos. According to Quicherat, it was for selfish reasons that Duprez reinstated Arnold's "Asile héréditaire," the andantino opening the fourth act of *Guillaume Tell*, which Nourrit usually omitted.[10]

Even such friends of Nourrit as Joseph Mainzer and Joseph d'Ortigue had to admit "the revolution," conceding Duprez's superiority as "a singer" in order to defend their champion's preeminence as "an artist." D'Ortigue wrote that, unlike Duprez, Nourrit was not really a singer at all. He was "a man with a moral purpose."[11] While Duprez reveled in *le chant pour le chant,* Mainzer argued, he was overshadowed by his predecessor's skill in pantomime or masterminding a character. Duprez's talents were purely musical, self-seeking, Italian, and meaningless. "Instead of singing a sentiment or an idea," wrote Hippolyte Fortoul that year, the Italians "sing nothing but sounds. This, to tell the truth, is the great reservation that we have for Duprez."[12] Mere singers, in short, were too wedded to "the absolute value of the notes," too careless of words, too enamored of the dark mysteries of sound, and too reckless of French. In "Asile héréditaire," according to former singer Auguste Laget, Duprez sang the lines "J'appelle en vain, douleur amère! J'appelle, il n'entend plus ma voix!" as "Ch'appelle en fain, touleur amère! Ch'appelle, il n'entend plus ma foix!" In 1838, the *Journal de France* railed against Duprez's "rude" mouth, with its strange way of pronouncing the letter *r*. His *s*'s, according to *La France,* tended to hiss.[13]

Nourrit famously felt the homogenizing force of Duprez's voice—a voice that will become a protagonist of this chapter—when he traveled to Naples in early 1838 to rebuild his career from scratch. Turning his back on a glorious past, Nourrit resolved (as Blaze put it in 1839) to "hollow out the registers of his voice." (Ironically, this was at the same time as Duprez, back at the Opéra, was trying to acquire some of the "delicious head sounds and charm of Nourrit.")[14] In the wake of Duprez's success, Nourrit went in search of a makeover, one that required the abandonment of his instrument, as well as his friends, wife, and six children. But when, on arrival in Naples, Nourrit began to conduct a strange, uncanny relationship with his voice, all hope for emulating Duprez's Italian metamorphosis was lost. By April of that year his letters show him struggling with a voice that rebelled, that pleased him inexplicably, or that disobeyed and grew "veiled" on difficult nights. "I speak a language that is simply not my own," he confessed to an acquaintance in the Italian city.[15]

The more Nourrit listened to his new teacher Gaetano Donizetti, the more the dark life of that inner voice grew. His Italianization perpetuated a roller coaster ride: "Good God! I am French," he wrote to his brother-in-law on 15 October 1838. "What is so bad if they say that I have a French accent just so long as I sing well? To tell the truth, with the Italian inflection that I have cultivated, I have only one color at my disposal." "I used to have an almost feminine physiognomy (when I was young); now my face is covered by a black beard." Having lost weight and grown "manly," Nourrit by 1839 was apparently acting against nature, particularly while impersonating Pollione in Bellini's *Norma* at the San Carlo. His head voice was gone, his mezza voce gone too. "He is darkening [covering] it as Donizetti required," Nourrit's wife wrote. The singer himself intimated in a February letter to Quicherat that this was a role "where all tenors have come to grief in Naples." He continued, "To please the Italians [as Pollione] I have to adopt a certain kind of sonority that one cannot acquire except by sacrificing the fine and delicate nuances that permit a variety of effects and give each role a distinctive character."[16]

On 8 August 1839, the morning after a concert at which he had sung "Meco all'altar" and a duet from *Norma*, Nourrit climbed to the top floor of the Villa Barbaja and threw himself to his death in the courtyard below. His Parisian friends thought they knew why. His inner voice had killed him.

AGAINST VOCAL PRESENCE

Well, what I tried to do is to just listen to my voice, because my voice is my boss. She decides.

CECILIA BARTOLI, 1998

This chapter reflects upon the experience of *having a voice*—one voice—rather than simply *having voice*. It addresses that one voice found deep within the body, which must be located, listened to, and obeyed, because this voice is boss, according to soprano Cecilia Bartoli. It owns you. "She decides."[17] The sense, here, in other words, is of one being subject to one's voice and of having a relationship with it. Thus, we might argue, the modern injunction to "find your voice," and to privatize yourself like every good liberal self should.

But what does it mean to look for voice in the body? Figure 14 records a particular phase in the history of that search, a phase involving autoexperimentation. The images, from a late-century edition of Manuel García *fils's Traité complet de l'art du chant* (1847), show the master at work. Once thought the inventor of the laryngoscope, the nineteenth century's "Mr. Singing" supposedly made his scientific breakthrough with only a hand mirror and sunlight, becoming the first person to observe and study his own glottis in the act of vocalization.[18] These pictures show García searching, struggling, digging to find that dark voice, although—even in this later period—he was usually looking for several voices, as we shall see. Such self-reflection implies what we could call a political anatomy and identity politics. The voice here is embroiled in processes of self-discovery; the impulse is to know for oneself, to induce uncanny encounters with one's own voice by relating to the experience of it alone and in solitude. "Finding a voice" is difficult. But, once you

Fig. 2. — Ici la lumière est réfléchie du miroir concave sur le miroir laryngien ou pharyngien (guttural), et de celui-ci sur le petit miroir plan où l'image de la glotte se montre à l'observateur.

Fig. 1. — Le miroir à main dirige le rayon solaire contre le petit miroir guttural et reçoit de celui-ci l'image de la glotte.

Fig. 3. — Reçue d'abord par le miroir frontal (miroir concave), la lumière est ensuite réfléchie sur le miroir à main, et de celui-ci sur le miroir guttural.

Fig. 4. — L'observateur voit l'image de la glotte dans le miroir plan immédiatement au-dessus du trou rond par lequel passe la lumière qui éclaire le miroir laryngien.

FIGURE 14. Manuel García *fils* searches for voice in *Traité complet de l'art du chant,* 2 vols. (Paris, 1878), 1: 11.

locate it, you will be equipped to represent yourself. With a voice, for example, you can vote. The imperative, in other words, is to make your supposedly natural-born voice self-evident to yourself in order to know its dark biological power over you. "Find your voice!" is the romantic-modern battle cry.

In what follows, I examine settings in history before singers necessarily had one voice, where, instead of voices making people, people made voices. There was in fact a time when the best performers, the most celebrated singers in Europe, cultivated many voices—head voices, chest voices, feigned voices, flautino voices, white voices, falsetto voices, half voices, mixed voices, medium voices, nasal voices, inspirated voices, covered voices—as many voices, nuances, expressive registers, and colors as possible. Having just one voice was more often than not a sign of moral and physical poverty—or a plain lack of sociability. A voice was something you learned, as you would a language, through experience and education. The unwieldy, inexpressive thing you were born with (one of the first recognizably modern classifiers of voice, Giuseppe Concone, named this chimera the "voix inculte" in 1845) was hardly worthy of the name, and certainly unworthy of public

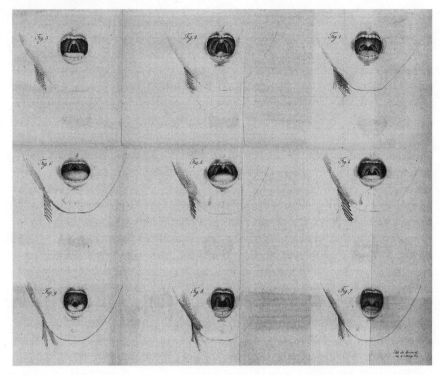

FIGURE 15. Francesco Bennati, *Recherches sur le mécanisme de la voix humaine* (Paris, 1832), 161. © BIU Santé (Paris).

display.[19] Even García *fils* knew that no voice was inborn. Children lacked voice, the son of the famous tenor wrote, because cultivation and puberty had yet to supply them with one. Even he—hailed in triumphalist accounts as the first to discover the immutable physiological principles of song—knew that voice only occurred when understood.[20]

To sketch the argument in crude terms, the basic historical shift in question here is the move from the outer, visible mouths of figure 15 (beautifully formed mouths as pictured by Bennati) to the "inside mouths" of figure 16 and approximately thirty years later, inner mouths that are pictured according to a laryngoscope, complete with the so-called *bocca ridente*, or sweetly smiling mouth. Opening a tutor of the early nineteenth century, singers could expect to be enjoined to form lips in this "gently smiling character."[21] These images suggest a story—that the singer's object of study was moving ever back: from external instruments or mouths in the early century, to the back of the throat, to the glottis, and then beyond, the voice eventually disappearing from ordinary view. A spectralization of

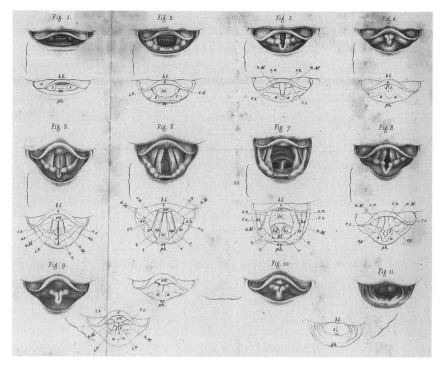

FIGURE 16. Johann Nepomuk Czermák, *Du laryngoscope et de son emploi en physiologie et en médecine* (Paris, 1860), plate II. © BIU Santé (Paris).

mouths, evidence suggests, attended this sense of a vanishing vocal source, alongside the vanishing sense that singers should cultivate several voices at once.

My argument here divides into three. After the so-called *voix sombrée* is described, a middle section brings to light the so-called "bari-tenor" voices of two Italians working in Paris, Domenico Donzelli and Bennati. A final part invokes the *voix mixte* of Adolphe Nourrit, an enigmatic voice tinged with French *grain* (to invoke the anachronistic language of Roland Barthes). Both of the latter discussions—on bari-tenors and mixed voices—intend the same: to seek out occluded truths, and to look otherwise and elsewhere, in search of alternative and yet no less objective ways of finding voice.

THE RULE OF THE MOUTH

Not so long ago, mouths were considered all-consuming. The stock vocal method issued to students at the Paris Conservatoire from 1804, for example, recommended that the master stand face-to-face with his pupil to prevent a "vicious" or uncultivated "position of all the parts that compose the mouth." The *Méthode de chant du conservatoire de musique* began by enumerating the "natural instruments" of tongue, palate, teeth, and lips. Formed mainly of material collected by Bernardo Mengozzi, the volume was issued with the same standardizing, nationalizing, and republican objectives as Louis Adam's *Méthode de piano du conservatoire,* printed that same year and described in the previous chapter.[22] By later standards, Mengozzi paid scant attention to what he called "the emission of sound." (According to etymologists, the French word *phonation* was coined only around 1824, three years after the conservatory inaugurated a class in "vocalization"—an enigmatic kind of song without words—to split from the traditional Italian course in "chant.") Mengozzi paid close attention to mouths. Voice, as ever, was firmly *of* the body, although it belonged less to the inscrutable facts of physiology than to the sociable truths of language.[23]

Mengozzi instructed his pupils to raise their heads and set their mouths as if smiling before opening to a vowel. Johann Adam Hiller and Luigi Lablache taught that the teeth should open enough to admit the tip of a forefinger.[24] Pushed-out lips, protruding jaws, knitted brows, blinking, rolling or twisting of the eyes, contortions of the neck, nodding of the head, the mouth opened too wide or too little, shaking of the mouth: all these were standard "defects" vilified in Italian, German, and French vocal tutors throughout the eighteenth century and beyond.[25] To beautify misshapen mouths and correct pronunciation, singing masters—Tosi, Hiller, Corfe, Tenducci, Marpurg, and García *fils* among them—enjoined students to sing before a mirror.[26] Why else the obsession that authors such as Tosi, Agricola, and Mancini had for teeth? Giovanni Battista Mancini's classic *Riflessioni pratiche sul canto figurato* (1777) devoted an entire chapter to the mouth, proposing, "To know well how to shape [the mouth] . . . can reasonably be kept as one of the essentials most important to the singer." Not only the significance of words, but "the resounding quality of the voice always depends . . . on the shaping of the position of the mouth." Mancini exhorted that the singing teacher should be ever ready to "illustrate his meaning by making himself an example, by assuming the different positions of the mouth."[27]

The eloquence of the singer depended on skill in solfeggi—do, re, mi—and messe di voce. Thus the encyclopedic early century collections of custom-made melodies, lexicons of solfeggi that fixed habits and equipped mouths with the flexibility and grammar required for comprehensible emotional display. The practice of solfeggi taught fluency in improvisation, educating ears, softening lips, preparing a stock figurative armory, and stirring the intellect.[28] In 1838 Andrea Costa counseled "a symmetrical and agreeable form and movement of the mouth," each vowel sounded according to "that exact conformation of the mouth and throat which respectively belongs to them."[29] Every *son filé,* or drawn-out thread, required direction in order

FIGURE 17. "Do" and "Re" as imagined in Gesualdo Lanza, *The Elements of Singing, Familiarly Exemplified: To Facilitate the Acquirement of the Science of Vocal Music, in the Italian and English Styles* (London, 1813), n.p. Courtesy of the University of St Andrews Library.

to find its proper place of articulation in the throat, palate, uvula, mouth, and nose. The messa di voce, or the practice of vocal swelling and dying, vouchsafed "placement" or "carriage" of sounds. (Later pedagogues such as Heinrich Panofka found the idea of "consummating" notes problematic and added to the old system of refractions and angles another system, which searched for voice in the body's sonorant cavities.) The beautiful mouth forged associations, shaping diverse currents of air, connecting notes across intervals by portamenti, uniting dissimilar vowels, binding sounds in intimacy, and drawing into relation. As Gesualdo Lanza, a London singing teacher of the early century, put it, "With respect to the form of the mouth, it is certain that even the least variation in the form of the mouth will give variation in the tone issuing from it."[30] A series of plates appeared in his tutor in order to exemplify these principles, the first two represented in figure 17.

This world of singing was certainly a far cry from the familiar later nineteenth-century scene, which ignored the mouth and often occluded the upper vocal tract entirely. "Always remember," wrote the great Italian pedagogue Giovanni Battista Lamperti (1839–1910), "that what 'goes on' above the throat are illusions no matter how real they may feel or sound." Teachers such as Lamperti sought to push sound back into the chest, preferring events inside the body and ideas of resonance over concepts of emission. The task was to cultivate one's dark inner voice instead of a myriad of outer ones by shutting sound within the body. Lamperti counseled that,

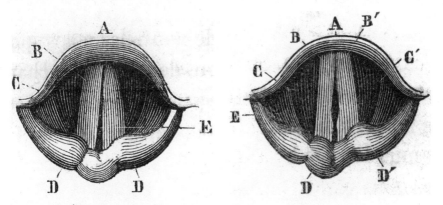

FIGURE 18. Édouard Fournié's view of glottis configurations for the low notes of the chest register appears to the left, alongside his view of the *voix mixte* to the right. A: Epiglottis. B: Vocal folds. C: Glottal cavity. D: Summit of the arytenoids. E: Aryepiglottic fold. In *Physiologie de la voix et de la parole* (Paris, 1866), 435 and 466.

far from projecting outward, one should "inhale" the voice. "When one sings well," he added, "one has the sensation of drinking."[31] In order to emancipate the voice, sounds needed to be rid of mouths and language. "The Italian singer has no throat," a disciple of Lamperti's illustrious father remembered being constantly reminded.[32] In his method without method, students were told to "let go," even of their sense of singing. The irrelevance of the upper parts was guaranteed only by the so-called "open throat" and supposedly unfiltered Italian vowels. Mouths got in the way.

We might go so far as to relate the "inner mouths" of figure 18 with this "new species of singing voice" supposedly discovered by two French doctors writing in 1840. Charles-Paul Diday and Joseph Pétrequin famously named their "discovery" (after the phrases singers used) the "voix sombrée, couverte, voix en dedans" (somber/submerged voice, covered voice, inside voice). (The visual link is strong in view of Édouard Fournié's enthusiasm for this voice's "musicality.")[33] The doctors claimed to hear this voice in the famously dark and reportedly homogenous vocal timbre of Duprez—a voice that was taken by those French commentators mindful of the fate of Nourrit to represent a "barbarous invasion" from northern Italy.[34] Achieved by heavy vowel modification and a low-fixed larynx, such voices were to be extracted from deep within: they were more felt than observed, and, as Diday and Pétrequin claimed, were self-expressive to the point of being socially dangerous. The emergence of this "new species of singing voice," the doctors wrote, "introduces a new element into the problem of phonation, and which would seem to demand a fundamental revolution in the execution and teaching of singing." The *voix sombrée*, as Gregory Bloch has shown, was associated with a lack of health: it had an annihilating effect on other voices. Diday and Pétrequin explained that the *voix sombrée* was antisocial, that it flattened, depersonalized, standard-ized, and covered faults in the voice. It caused "slowness in the renewing of fluids, sluggish blood, blockage of the arteries," permanent damage to "venous circula-tion," trouble with the "visceral lesions," burning sensations behind the sternum, fatigue, impotence, loss of vocal power, and—in extreme cases—vocal collapse. Worse, as Duprez's inability to express tenderness proved, the *voix sombrée* prom-ulgated the worst forms of liberal individualism and self-seeking materialism of the kind virulently under attack by social critics in late 1830s Paris.[35]

BENNATI'S GARDEN OF VOICES

A pioneer of self-exploration who knew nothing of these debates and nothing of this voice was Bennati—the same whose ideas we have repeatedly touched on. Francesco Bennati was at once a physician and a highly accomplished singer: to be specific, he was a "bari-tenor" (as he himself christened his "species of voice"). His medical education took place in Pavia; the castrato Pacchierotti oversaw his vocal training. In Paris the doctor was appointed house physician at the Théâtre Italien in the summer of 1830, a year before he published his study of Paganini, as described in the introductory pages of this book.[36] The appointment charged him with the health of the most celebrated singers in Europe (Sontag, Malibran, Lalande, Fodor, Rubini, Lablache, and Donzelli) and rendered the opera house at the Salle Favart his scientific laboratory. (In late 1832, Bennati advertised a "specu-lum" built by one of his patients; "glottiscopes" were common enough in the 1820s and '30s, decades before García *fils* claimed invention of the laryngo-scope.)[37] This said, Bennati did not delve as far as he might have in his search for voices, which is why his views—as pictured in figure 15—are interesting. Bennati ended up finding not an inner voice but—in deference to his venerable Paduan training—a whole botany of voices located closer to the surface. Though a key figure in the medicalization of voice types in the nineteenth century, Bennati favored the outer over the inner. He worked as much to make voices as to find them.[38]

In early 1830, for example, Bennati inserted a hollow tube up his nose in order to drive air down his throat. Thus he followed Nicolas Deleau, a medical doctor who worked with "deaf-mutes" at the Hospice des orphelins in Paris. Bennati was guided by words that Deleau had written only months previously in a letter to the Académie des sciences.

> Introduce through one nostril into the pharynx a hollow tube, which will permit the passage of a current of air contained in a vessel of moderate capacity; as soon as you feel the current of air strike upon the posterior walls, suspend the action of respira-tion and put the organs of speech in motion, as if you were acting upon the air of the lungs; you will speak in a soft voice, you will cause distinctly to be heard all the

elements of aphonic speech. Fearing to be deceived with regard to the power of interrupting the action of the chest, while I put in play the organs of speech, I attempted
to speak in a loud voice; the current of air established by the nose was in all its force;
at the instant two words could be heard in a manner so distinct and pure, that those
who assisted in the experiment thought they heard two individuals repeating the
same phrases.[39]

Struck by these words, Bennati sought out Deleau in order to test the procedure on
his singing self, that is, on the bari-tenor's three-octave instrument, described by
contemporaries as "one of the most beautiful and most wide-ranging voices
known."[40] His actions suggest that the talent for duplication—Sontag and Malibran come to mind—was hardly the sole preserve of women in this milieu. Once
again, two voices were heard. Once again, "two individuals" were self-evident, carried by two distinct streams of air.

What did the bellows-and-voice experiment prove? At the 10 May 1830 meeting
of the academy, Georges Cuvier, the most illustrious naturalist in France, presented his report on a memoir recently submitted to the institution by Bennati.
At this meeting the singing voice was considered as much a subject of natural
history—of biology and zoology—as of the human sciences. Cuvier lauded
Bennati's decentered conception: Bennati's research established that the vocal
organ was no single instrument, no cartilaginous accessory, no outside appendage
to take up and play. Nor was it a wind instrument (as Galen, Denis Dodart, or Félix
Savart had alleged) or a string instrument (as Antoine Ferrein had hoped) or a
reed (Magendie). These sounds instead were reproductive, in ways that had long
since determined Velluti's fate in London (see chapter 1). The vocal apparatus was
subject, Cuvier explained, to the invisible prerogatives of "organic and animal
life."[41] "The organ of the voice is an instrument sui generis," the naturalist summed
up, "an instrument inimitable by art."[42]

Bennati himself stepped back from Cuvier's obfuscations. Instead, his work
clung to clarity, claiming that, in cultivated singing subjects, voices were engineered
by a superinstrument, or rather a complex multiform shape-shifting assemblage.
For Bennati the bellows-and-voice experiment proved the universal truth of old
Italian two-register theories, at least for those trained singers classified—according
to the typology described for female contraltos in my first chapter—as "soprani
sfogati," "tenors-contraltini," and "basses-tailles." (Note the doctor's tendency to
think in twos.) High "falsetto" sounds, according to Bennati, linked to what he
called the "above-larynx" voice, formerly known as the head voice *(voix surlaryngienne)*.[43] Cuvier concurred that the falsetto was the product of a "new organ," or
separate physiological mechanism formed independently and higher in the body
than what Bennati called the "in-larynx voice" or "chest voice" *(voix laryngienne)*.

The Italian, in other words, observed *embranchements*, in the taxonomic style
of Cuvier's animal classifications. Bennati chided those who used such inaccurate

terms as "head" or "chest" and neglected simple observation (though they were, of course, looking just as hard as he was—just elsewhere). Take the high soprano sfogato voice—a voice with brilliant "above-larynx" facility—most famously acquired and displayed by a protagonist of chapter 2, Henriette Sontag. For Sontag, the tube formed a kind of inverted cone in the highest register, funneling sound in a stream from the base of the tongue. A narrow sphincter was seen to form at the back of the throat—the mouth pictured at the bottom left-hand corner of figure 15 imagined this—through which delicate streams of air were supposedly funneled (according to what is often derided today as a "garden hose" theory of voice). Bennati's intention was "to identify positive rules for the characterization of each voice [that is, each type of sound rather than type of singer], to understand its qualities, carriage, range, development and possible mutations." He determined to fix laws for every vocal species, such that life practices, medicants, and training methods might be proscribed for each.[44]

These strange ideas would be irrelevant were it not that Bennati's work pawned several historic extrapolations. A good example belonged to the founder of the first Orthophonic Institute in Paris, Marc Colombat de l'Isère. A man with a fiery revolutionary past, Colombat had in 1820 been imprisoned for two years in Grenoble after raising the tricolor over the citadel during a Jacobin uprising, and he was used to living under police surveillance. He held it his duty, in this era of the July Monarchy and what he (wishfully) called "representative government," to give voice to the voiceless—literally, in that mouths were educated to acquire eloquence. Colombat was famed for his "singing method" and metronome-like apparatus, the muthonome, which he devised to cure stuttering. Colombat, too, inserted Deleau's hollow tube up his nose in an effort to sing in falsetto and chest simultaneously (though he struggled to find the pure sounds experienced by his predecessors). Following Bennati, the pioneering speech therapist claimed that, during falsetto, a second "above-larynx" glottis—a *glotte pharyngienne* or *glotte superieur*—formed artificially at the back of throat by a constriction of the summit of the larynx, base of the tongue, pharyngeal wall, and uvula. This constriction, for Colombat, forced nothing short of the "birth of another instrument."[45]

The most prominent conservatory singing tutors—Auguste Panseron, Alexis de Garaudé, and Panofka—swallowed Colombat's bizarre "second glottis" notion whole.[46] In fact, an early report on García *fils*'s first public presentation of his vocal research suggests that the young García posited not two but *three* glottises in human existence. García identified, first, a voice formed by the vocal cords proper, then a falsetto head voice formed by the false vocal chords, and, third, a "voix arythéno-épiglottique," supposedly formed at the aryepiglottic folds.[47] No wonder, then, that the academy's report on García's first 1840 publication hailed the vocal organ as "a unique instrument" with the gift "of transforming itself into a multitude of different instruments."[48] For these scientists and singers, to be clear, switching from voice to voice—we would say from register to register—was analogous to exchanging or swapping one musical instrument for another. Such a thing as *a* voice hardly existed for these thinkers, since voices—even glottises—could be cultivated by a single individual in abundance and linked virtuosically to other voices. "The vocal organ is a mold," García summed up, "incessantly transforming itself according to the action of diverse passions."[49]

DONZELLI'S FRACTURED APPARATUS

The truth of such a multiplex conception of voice, Bennati implied, was confirmed night after night at the Théâtre Italien in the organ of the fellow "bari-tenor" Domenico Donzelli. Unlike virtuosic Italian contraltini in Paris (such as Giovanni David and Giovanni Battista Rubini), the celebrated Bergamasque singer lacked facility in managing shifts across registers or between each voice. He had no *passaggio*, or "passing voice." Donzelli himself admitted as much when he wrote to Bellini from Paris on 3 May 1831, describing (somewhat limited) options for the characterization of Pollione at the upcoming premiere of *Norma* at the Teatro alla Scala in 1832:

> The range of my voice is about two octaves, from low c to top c. The chest voice extends up to g, and it is in this part of my voice that I can declaim with even force, and sustain the declamation with the full power of the voice. From high g to top c I can make use of falsetto which, employed with skill and with power, provides an ornamental resource. I have sufficient agility, but find it considerably easier in descending than in ascending passages.[50]

Instead of moving between voices, one English critic observed, he descended (or ornamented) in falsetto and ascended in chest.[51] Donzelli's difficulty with the break might ordinarily have been grounds to dismiss his expressive scope as a singer. Not so for Bennati: the singer's flaw only confirmed the "truth" of violent discontinuity and multiple overlapping physiological systems.

The division struck through Donzelli's voice, according to Bennati, was a happy consequence of its natural history, and in particular the way in which his puberty had been managed. The dulcet "above-larynx voice" of his boy treble had been expertly shaped at Bergamo cathedral under the watchful eye of maestro di cappella Simon Mayr. At his coming-of-age, Donzelli had avoided throwing away this youthful instrument by discontinuing vocal exercise. The voice of fellow chorister Giuseppe Donizetti, younger brother of the composer, had not been so wisely silenced, which perhaps explained why he had been employed since 1828 at the court of Sultan Mahmud II in Istanbul, not as a singer but as instructor general of imperial Ottoman music. Donzelli, by contrast, emerged from his strenuous "second birth" (as Jean-Jacques Rousseau dubbed such mutations) with the beginnings of the finest "bari-tenor" in Europe. Donzelli's upper extension was a bonus, formed of an instrument of exquisite preadolescent provenance. As a bari-tenor himself, Bennati sensed the truth of this auxiliary apparatus intimately, since he had undergone a similar mutation and had cultivated a similarly compound physiology.[52]

Donzelli was a powerful falsettist, notwithstanding his reputation in modern scholarship as a kind of époque-making Neanderthal, a progenitor of the so-called Romantic "dramatic tenor."[53] According to the *Revue de Paris,* his voice had grown heavier in 1829–30, after a bad winter. But this is not to say that Stendhal's "ténor de poitrine"—Duprez especially—did not use falsetto. (Evidence suggests that Donzelli sang *everything* in the chest only for the title role in Rossini's *Otello,* a part that, in the surprising opinion of several critics, lacked melody and involved very little actual "singing.")[54] Donzelli could be attacked for being "admirable, if he did but abstain from falsetto more," or for being too "prodigal in the use of it." His voice had nothing of the uniformity of Duprez's sound, despite the fact that Quicherat later blamed Donzelli for first bringing "the system of the *voix sombrée,* that is, the corruption of Italian song" to the Théâtre Italien.[55]

Instead, Donzelli flourished in blackface roles or impersonating badly socialized outsiders who struggled for expression: Otello the Moor; Agorante the plaindealing Ethiopian (in Rossini's *Ricciardo e Zoraide,* 1818), Rodrigo the rugged Scot (in Rossini's *La donna del lago,* 1819), Corradino the Spanish tyrant (in Rossini's *Matilde di Shabran,* 1821), or Gualtiero the pirate (in Bellini's *Il pirata,* 1827). Recalling the Milanese premiere of *Ugo, conte di Parigi* (1832), in 1835, Donizetti mocked the idea of casting Donzelli as an *amoroso.* Some years earlier Bellini had complained about the "indolence" in Donzelli's sounds, anticipating such later Italian views as would vilify them for sluggishness or "impotence." For many French critics, Donzelli practiced "an art without seduction." He had cultivated the kind of unresponsive style, in short, that displayed—in the manner of the character of Rossini's Corradino—"a violent aversion to the [fair] sex."[56]

The trouble was the inexpressive way in which Donzelli shunted from emotion to emotion.[57] On his Parisian debut in 1825, Castil-Blaze lamented the "lacunae" in his voice. That same year, Ludovic Vitet, who would become an intimate and a liberal partisan of Nourrit at *Le Globe,* concluded that Donzelli "lacked art." Best suited to "ungrateful" roles such as Otello or Adriano in Meyerbeer's *Il crociato in Egitto,* the tenor was a useful acquisition for Paris. Yet he breathed too loudly, "scorned method," and failed to manage his transitions. If Donzelli's range had been smoothly regulated in his youth, "a shocking discrepancy had [now] established itself between chest and head sounds, the medium [or joining voice] having fallen into utter disgrace."[58] His later reputation as a dumb singer who took forever to learn new parts probably stemmed from this hole in his voice, an obstacle that consigned him to portrayals of the strong, the silent, or even the stupid. In short, Donzelli's double-voiced instrument, and powerful delivery drew as much criticism as praise in the press. Many said he sang like a bull or a wild elephant. When Castil-Blaze first heard him, he thought the Théâtre Italien on fire, such was the yelling. But just as often his bifurcated style would be praised as a "natural" exemplification of the physiological (or, better, sociocultural) limits of "masculine" song.[59]

This bifurcation was nowhere better displayed than in *Norma*, Bellini having tailored the male lead for Donzelli. Pollione is a divided protagonist, at once hero and tyrant, caught between his passion for Adalgisa and duty to Norma, his desire for a woman and love for his children, between savage Gaul and civilized Rome. A frightened man, he first creeps onstage after the barbarian druids have introduced the opera, announcing "Svanir le voci!" And, indeed, his "Meco all'altar di Venere" will not be sung in the usual style. "The opera had no arias," confirmed an English-language newspaper printed in 1833 in Paris.[60] Instead of directly singing the cantabile, Pollione-Donzelli slips into a schizophrenic narration, recounting a nightmare he cannot get out of his head.

It is a dream of two halves. Three eight-line strophes recount the protagonist's hallucinations of light and dark, the final strophe opposing the major-minor material of the first contrasting pair. Bellini's score follows Donzelli's prescriptions exactly. First, in C major, Adalgisa is imagined in lovely Rome, resplendent in white wedding dress before the altar of Venus. An exquisite lyric prototype (now so-called) unfolds above a breezy accompaniment, where, rounding off, the melody expands lugubriously, as the singer indulges the heady pleasures of "sensual transport." For his climax, here the proconsul crosses enthusiastically from a chesty G to a fermata on high C, the singer no doubt relishing his cadenza in "ornamental" falsetto. All is sweetness and light.

Second, in C minor, agitated strings—marked *sotto voce* and *tremolo*—interrupt. The Roman's voice darkens as a "veil falls." A "terrible shadow" divides the lovers. Day turns to night, and the woodwinds shift from illustrating nuptial rapture to thunderbolts. The switch induces vocal claustration; Donzelli-Pollione repeats the same figure over and over as the gloom deepens. The veil only lifts to introduce the third strophe, the singer awakening to reality. In this final stanza, the protagonist's C-major rapture is reprised perversely, the wedding scene recollected, but in Adalgisa's absence. The parallel minor interrupts earlier now, the fermata reached in double time, to be sung "with abandon" and probably in falsetto to mimic the sound of his children weeping ("de' figli al pianto"). For a final switch, the singer reverts back to animal sonority: *Norma così fa scempio d'amante traditor*. Here Donzelli-Pollione stops singing, intoning these final words tunelessly on a one-note D, "a terrible voice" imagined echoing from within the temple. Illusion and truth, onstage and offstage collide as a violent in-scene noise shatters the nightmare.[61]

THE INEFFABLE FRENCH PALATE

The primeval crash of Norma's awful druidic gong yields something of the darkness traced in this chapter: a move from day to night, from an instrumental to relational experience of voice, the voice apparently going "live." Both Donzelli's falsetto and Bennati's fixation on the back of the mouth, however, prove the virulence of the old ways. This was the case even as the vocal tract (now so-called) was identified, less as the "organ of voice" than the "organ of timbre," to use García's terms, and the mouth occluded—in scientific circles, at least—as a principal instrument of voice.[62] To be clear, the overarching narrative traced here—of drawing inward, of the voice's steady disappearance down the throat—is hardly the full story. In Paris, in particular, this trajectory was resisted, first, as we have seen, by Bennati's adherents, and second by advocates of the so-called *voix mixte,* or mixed voice—by those who sang with many voices at the same time.

The unrivaled master of singing with several instruments simultaneously—the doyen of vocal mixing—was Nourrit. The *Revue du Lyonnais* of 1839 hailed him in the year of his death "one of the most popular glories of France, idol of the nation, and apostle of noble passions and civic virtue." Ernest Legouvé recalled his "high, elevated, and brilliant voice, colored here and there with the singular sonorities of wind instruments, a *mélange* of flute and clarinet."[63] Nourrit was, in other words, a mixer who could sing with both chest and falsetto/head registers at the same time. And this without the assistance of horrible hollow tubes or artificial bellows.

The *voix mixte* was a thoroughly patriotic French voice, a voice first described in the second or 1826 edition of Garaudé's *Méthode,* probably the highest grossing vocal tutor at the time in France. Garaudé defined the voice as "a quality of sound" partaking of both chest and head, " little of one and of the other." To engender this voice, students were directed to a new exercise, one designed to unite the vibrant sounds of the chest with the sweetness of the head. It was a drill built on high chromatic scales, the tenor sliding imperceptibly between chest, mixed, and head voices and back again. (This third or mixed voice was new for the "ténor," itself a novel voice type for Frenchmen; since Mengozzi, only the soprano or *dessus* voices were allowed an additional third or "medium" voice.) Preferring vocalises over Mengozzi's dry solfeggi, Garaudé praised the "infinite charm" and *aplanissement* of these mixed tenor sounds.[64] They had a peculiar nuance gained of intimate (male) knowledge.

In his 1841 edition, Garaudé admitted that the voice was beyond description. He could only recommend that students listen to their master to experience its mystery. Here Garaudé relabeled the old *mixte* exercise, turning it from a functional drill (to pass between registers) into a means of engendering evocative timbral quality.[65] Mixture had a similar enchantment for Nourrit's defenders, Diday and Pétrequin, three years later. The doctors rebuked Bennati and Colombat for assuming that the falsetto began where the chest voice ended—that registers were stacked like building blocks one atop another. Instead, they observed *emplètement*, where, far from being "special domains," each register was woven into the next.[66] Another fan of sonic overlap, Panseron defended the *voix mixte* in 1840, despite the difficulty tenors had in finding it. He wrote of his personal experience of its enigmatic reality, which allowed him to discount the agnosticism of "physiologists and some professors of singing."[67]

From the standpoint of science, after acceptance of Bennati's hard registral theories, there was no such thing as a mixed voice. It was a charming lie. In 1830, Bennati called Garaudé's third register "imaginary." Cuvier followed suit.[68] The mixed voice, *voix mixte*, or *voce di mezzo petto*, according to García in 1847, was a misnomer. It was absurd to think that "the simultaneous action of two different mechanisms might assume the same note or two notes at the unison."[69] This was why García (and Concone) triggered such confusion in 1847 by renaming this "medium" (or "mixed" voice) the "voix de fausset."[70] The word "falsetto," to be clear, was used here in order to denigrate these in-between sounds so infected with Frenchness, mouths, and language. These mixtures were false ("falsetto" designating a deception), the illusion of a join between registers (here called "chest" and "head") where really there was discontinuity. "The *voix mixte* does not really exist in nature," summed up one Colombat-influenced commentator in 1844. "Sound comes from either one or the other register, from either one or the other glottis. To produce a *voix mixte*," the text continued, "it would be necessary to sing simultaneously with two glottises."[71]

The move to occlude mouths in singing, then, imbued these mouthy sounds with an as-if quality. The mixed voice, after all, was located between the visible truth of the mouth and the dark truth of the larynx. Those who remembered Nourrit's manner of issuing voice recalled how he focused attention on the space between filter and source, on the semishade of his palate, where sound could be bathed in half-light. In addition, Nourrit had frequently flaunted the roof of his mouth, apparently to jet air against it, by setting his head back in heroic style. Quicherat remembered his friend posing thus whenever he issued his trademark high "natural" or "blanche" voice. "There was a smile when [Nourrit] threw his head back to sing," noted a disapproving English critic in 1841, "or to launch a *mot* at someone behind him—a mincing elongation of his '*Oui*'—s and '*Patrie*'—s and the other sounds, which sung in French are intrinsically offensive, that annoyed my insular eyes and ears, as imparting to grace and sentiment and emphasis a touch of *make believe*."[72]

Nourrit was hardly alone in displaying the back of the throat, as evinced by the contemporaneous obsessions of Bennati, Malgaigne, Gerdy, Colombat, and others, who all searched for voices at the palate and uvula in the shadow of the July Revolution. An English expert on vocal matters, Richard Mackenzie Bacon explained this fascination for the roof of the mouth in view of Italian ideals in 1820: "We should say that there is a place near the back of the mouth, where the voice, whether from the head or the chest, must pass, and it seems as if the [Italian] method brings the tone to this spot previous to production, and sends it forth in its finished state, from that precise point, untainted either by the nose or the throat, the mouth or the lips."[73]

No less an authority than Rossini, Adolphe Nourrit's teacher and friend, recalled the importance of the soft palate as a "transmitter of sound" to the lost world of the mythic "bel canto" era, an era (of course) that never existed. The composer betrayed his nostalgia thus, according to Edmond Michotte: "The idea was to get to the stage when, as far as possible, the sound did not vary either in timbre or in intensity despite the movements of the tongue and the lips caused by changing vowels, now open, now closed. After the study of the vowels one passed to consonants, the diphthongs, articulation, breathing, etc. Above all one studied the sound created with the help of the roof of the mouth, which is the transmitter of beautiful sounds *par excellence*."[74] The roof of the mouth, in other words, was a principal "creator" of sound, a visible though increasingly inscrutable or occluded source for voice.

ARNOLD'S OVEREFFUSIVE SILENCE

The mysterious inaudibility of Nourrit's admixtures were nowhere more distinct than in the most acclaimed moment of Rossini's *Guillaume Tell*: the act 2 andantino of what became perhaps the most celebrated trio in all of French opera. It was in this impassioned scene, written for Nourrit and premiered less than a year before the 1830 uprisings, that the singer's supporters most identified sonic qualities of friendship in vocal sound. Here the *voix mixte* came into its own, cultivating beautiful masculinity in ways that clarify the question of *Guillaume Tell*'s relationship to revolutionary politics and the July Revolution, a topic much debated in opera studies by such scholars as Anselm Gerhard and Benjamin Walton.[75] The final pages of this chapter return to comparisons of Nourrit and Duprez, contrasting the perceived political effects of their acting styles and vocal sounds in this celebrated trio. For patriots, the emotional register of the *voix mixte* was precious, enough so that it became necessary to ensure its preservation via the national education system. This voice, as we shall see, would come to govern what it meant to be French.

"Ses jours qu'ils ont osé proscrire" motivated the celebrated *serment des trois suisses*, where three friends swear an oath to "independence or death" before the all-male act 2 finale among the revolutionaries of the cantons of Unterwalden, Schwyz, and Uri. At the end of the preceding *tempo d'attacco*, Arnold has just been informed of the death of his father, reported to him by comrades Walter and Tell. The event incites vocal, dramatic, and operatic breakdown. The youth falls to his

MUSICAL EXAMPLE 4. The trio "Ses jours qu'ils ont osé proscrire" with emotive tremoli and portamenti as notated by Manuel García *fils* in *Traité complet de l'art du chant* (Paris, 1847), 2: 53.

knees (probably) over a stuttering chromatic orchestral descent. "J'expire!" he chokes. The drama halted, movement is only restored—eventually—by the quiet appearance of an accompaniment figure. Reemerging on a higher, lyrical register, string palpitations bring to life a set piece in the oddly bright key of E major.

The cantabile begun, the repetition of the opening two lines of text ("Ses jours qu'ils ont osé proscrire") allowed Nourrit to color the same vowels a tone lower, as in the musical example above. Arnold's declamatory outbursts—"Je ne les ai pas défendus!"—also suited the singer. Quicherat reported Rossini presenting the score to Nourrit's wife in the run-up to the premiere with the words, "There are *des petites notes* here, which are for him."[76] Her husband's semitints, colorings, and half-lights, issued from various parts of the back of the throat, lent intimacy to the scene—intimate because, as the trio unfolds, it emerges that Arnold's cries are for the ears of his offstage listeners alone. Walter and Tell are strangely deaf to his highly emotional lament. His in-scene compatriots thus enter the cantabile late, only once Arnold's solo statement has finished, and the drama returns to its chaotic "reality." "He shudders," they then observe in voice-over, resuming their study of Arnold's "silent" agony. "He scarcely breathes," they report over bare pizzicato strings at the return of the real world of "J'expire."

Nourrit's inaudible and yet ardent "Ses jours" induced feelings of "tendresse filiale," male-male intimacy, and a weeping audience. The cantabile was "famous long before its appearance" according to *La France nouvelle*. During the full rehearsal of 24 July 1829, the "electrified assembly" rose at the end of the number, turned to

Rossini, and applauded. With *Guillaume Tell,* the preface to the original libretto announced, Rossini had become "a French composer."[77] Many commentators, Vitet among them, noted how during "Ses jours," "it was impossible to avoid feeling one's eyes welling up in tears." Others, Berlioz included, were so overwhelmed that they reported the moment as beyond analysis.[78] It was as if each listener had gained exclusive access to private feelings. These were rare, personal emotions, the audience drawn into a closed circle and bound by an electric force. "The illusion is complete and its effect electric," *La Gazette de France* summed up. "One is made to feel that the in-scene characters are for each spectator a brother and friend."[79]

By act 2 Nourrit's kinsmen-listeners had prior reason to feel privy to Arnold's "silent" singing. It is only in the stretto of this trio that the hero's at once mute and effusive interior will be ditched for the transparent purposes of liberty, equality, and fraternity. (The three soloists will even achieve full unison in their war cry at "son beau destin semble nous dire.") In the act 1 duo, Tell tests Arnold's partisanship in light of the latter's refusal to shape his melodic lines to those of his male brothers-in-arms. (By contrast, Arnold's love duet with Mathilde in the discrete world of act 2's "sombres forêts" is the model of vocal reciprocity: "Sa flamme répond à ma flamme.") In Arnold's face-off with Tell, the love-struck youth is so "mysterious" that his friend must resort to reading intentions from body language and trembling pantomime. Arnold launches, not once, but twice, into heart-wrenching "asides" that Tell cannot hear—"Ah! Mathilde, idole de mon âme!" These "inaudible" outpourings, which stand for the number's slow movement, occur first in a remote G♭ major before recurring—after more declamatory raging against Austrian occupation—a tone higher in A♭. "The fact is that in this opera there is only one voice that sings alone, that of Adolphe Nourrit," wrote *Le Corsaire,* all the other singers being "fenced in" by "duos, trios, quartets, quintets, ensemble pieces, and finales."[80]

Arnold's vocal bracketing (at figure 19) also struck d'Ortigue, who noted how much "Ah! Mathilde" had been colored for Nourrit's palate. "It is Nourrit himself who weeps, who sighs," wrote one Belgian commentator of the moment.[81] The reprise of Arnold's "aside," which launches several times up to high C, allowed tearful emotions to be tinted and retinted. (By contrast, Duprez smothered charm by blanketing both iterations in his uniform chest;[82] he nailed the fragment with "une sonorité métallique," recalled Quicherat, whereas Nourrit shaded it with "ineffable tenderness.")[83] "Again, you hear [Nourrit in] this small reprising fragment, which is like the imprint of an internal dialogue," wrote Vitet, a leading doctrinaire liberal who would soon—appropriately after the July Revolution—join Guizot's Ministry of the Interior (as inspector general of historical monuments).[84]

In the first performances of "Ses jours," to return to act 2, Nourrit failed to achieve the wrenching "mon père, tu m'as du maudire!" Tears suffocated him, according to Legouvé.[85] At the premiere, *L'Universel* reported, tears also overwhelmed the

FIGURE 19. Arnold disappears into the higher "Ah! Mathilde" in the Tell-Arnold duo from act 1, according to the first piano-vocal score of Rossini's *Guillaume Tell: opéra en quatre actes* (Paris, 1829). Courtesy of the Jean Gray Hargrove Music Library, University of California, Berkeley.

audience. Here Arnold, having begun and ended his first two phrases on G♯, pushes impossibly out to a G♮ an octave higher as he imagines his father cursing him. The pained C-major outburst (a declamatory injection of flat submediant) was, for Louis-François Lhéritier, "a new chord remarkably combined and applied at the limit of emotion." At the climactic "père" of this passage, Nourrit launched the *voix mixte* in its element. García *fils*'s *Traité complet*—in apparent tribute to the poet-artist—annotated the ascent to the G♮ of "mon père" with a decrescendo and added a tremolo to amplify his discussion of "trembling" and "emotion in the voice," as musical example 4 shows. By contrast, Duprez reputedly exploded sonorously onto the consonant "P." The Italo-French singer preferred open *a*'s or *o*'s to such high close vowels as "père," which, for Berlioz, attested to the young pretender's lack of *voix mixte* and lack of continuity across the break.[86] Arnold's cadence here segues into high Italianate convention, again perhaps to harness Nourrit's voices. For Lhéritier, the same critic who at the beginning of this book observed Paganini "merging" with his violin, Nourrit's lyrical close had ultramontane charm, "imitative of the elevation of the soul toward the sky."[87] Though "unheard," the poet-citizen was nothing if not effusive.

Nourrit edged further beyond hearing as he sang the impossibly high G♯s, A♯s, and Bs that brought this trio cantabile to its end. Here Arnold's pathetic cries of "O ciel! ô ciel! je ne te verrai plus" overlay the expanded commentary of Walter and Guillaume, a pair still oblivious to anything other than the hero's silent shuddering. Once again, Arnold's close vowels ("je ne te ver-") were tailored to Nourrit's overprominent mouth and nose. Castil-Blaze complained that if Duprez had bothered to cultivate the *voix mixte,* these high notes—which he "ripped from the throat"—might have had less of his gut-wrenching physicality and more of Nourrit's "infinite charm," sweetness, and tenderness, "which lends more satisfaction to the heart than the ear."[88] Nourrit's mouthiness, in other words, was better felt than heard. For such fans of Duprez as Gautier, by contrast, the young tenor had no need to artificially "suture" his voices together by the pretentious "trickery" of the *voix mixte.*[89] Whereas Duprez could do without such deception, Nourrit's sounds basked in the aura of implausibility, as if not really there at all.

Elsewhere Castil-Blaze wrote of Duprez's "discomfort" particularly with this cantabile's high Bs, notes issued by "coercive means" and a "constraint" that paled in comparison to Nourrit's sighs. "These cries allow you to be a little choked-up," he wrote, requiring, in other words, more than audible sonority.[90] In an 1837 text, later adapted to midcentury anxieties over the *ut de poitrine* and the famous anti-tenor tirade of *Les Soirées de l'orchestre* (1852), Berlioz described Duprez reworking the andantino as a scene less of filial love than of filial alienation. Berlioz mocked:

> Duprez, the daring artist, gives out, in *chest voice* and *accenting each syllable,* the high B naturals of the andante "O ciel! ô ciel! je ne te verrai plus!" with a resonance, an expression of heart-rending grief, and a beauty of tone that so far no one had been led to expect. Silence reigns in the stupefied house, people hold their breath, amazement and admiration are blended in an almost similar sentiment, *fear;* in fact, there is some reason for fear until that extraordinary phrase comes to its end; but when it has done so triumphantly, the wild enthusiasm of the audience may be guessed.[91]

In the mid-1840s, prints showing Duprez in the trio illustrate Tell holding Arnold back, restraining him by the wrists, as in figure 20. Nourrit-era images (figure 21), by contrast, picture men holding hands, as in the frontispiece that was featured on the title page of the original 1829 libretto—after a painting exhibited at the 1822 Salon by Charles-Guillaume Steuben—with three intimates, Nourrit, Henri-Bernard Dabadie, and Nicolas Levasseur, inclined toward each other in loving solidarity.[92]

THE EVER-DISAPPEARING FRENCH MOUTH

Instead of Duprez's sounds of desire, in other words, Nourrit cultivated sounds of love by directing attention to his mouth. In "Ses jours," a moment of excruciating closeness was also a moment of powerful bringing-together. Mixture was in fact endemic to *Guillaume Tell.* Just as Nourrit mixed nose and tongue, lips and teeth, mouth and palate, so the grand tableaux of the opera reconciled painting and

FIGURE 20. Antoine-Jean Weber's lithograph after Charles-Guillaume Steuben's *Le serment des troi suisses* (Paris, 1827), also copied for the frontispiece of the original libretto, and onstage in the original mise-en-scène of *Guillaume Tell*. Reproduced by permission of the Bibliothèque nationale de France.

FIGURE 21. Jules Rigo's lithograph of Célestin Deshay[e]s, *Guillaume Tell (2me Acte)*, shows Duprez restrained by Jean-Étienne-Auguste Massol as Tell and Levasseur as Walter (Paris, 1845). Reproduced by permission of the Bibliothèque nationale de France.

song, drama and tragedy, melody and words, Italian and French, voices and librettists, visual and aural, language and music. If Nourrit had given himself away by borrowing and combining from the catalogue of voices, Rossini's four-hour opera occasioned a universal cross-arts mélange. Even d'Ortigue, famously at the vanguard of rebranding "the swan of Pesaro" an aristocratic composer of "le code fashionable," had to modify his anti-Rossini opinions in view of *Guillaume Tell*. The work's fusion of literary, pictorial, and musical, d'Ortigue admitted, honored social cohesion and the immortal bonds of friendship.[93] As much idea as reality, this new superart manifested more than itself. It betrayed feelings of common cause and common humanity.

After all, "Ses jours"—by staging Arnold's farewell to his father—dramatized the painful break from the old patriarchal order to a new world, one founded on spiritual feeling. For reviewers such as Lhéritier, drawn to metaphors of "revolution" in 1829, this new "universe" of song heralded a moral order liberated from government, law, policy, or questions of franchise. The affective power of music, to be sure, was palpable in the invisible human unities formed in relation to this opera.[94] In this view, the art world made possible by *Guillaume Tell* was of the sort that would supersede in importance the all-too-present and all-too-real political one. As conservative liberal bias would have it, after all, the best revolutions are hidden: aesthetic rather that civic, lyric rather than governmental. If society was to be reformed, then this was ideally achieved from within, on the basis of the mass transformation of intimate realms rather than public violence. This liberal brand of noiseless revolution, critically speaking, implied a Jacobinism purged of revolutionary content. When power was devolved, apparently, the old top-down orders of obligation would fall into oblivion. The sphere of "the social" would be reformed from within, or rather would regenerate according to supposedly "natural" affinities or "natural" superiorities. If there were leaders, it was only because they had emerged freely, their spiritual mission being, as Nourrit put it, to "elevate thought and exalt love." In this sense song could be justified as a weapon of reform, and contemporaneous talk of *Guillaume Tell* explained as an instance of "musical revolution," since the opera itself provided a model for how *le peuple* might find voice.

Under the July Monarchy, Nourrit himself was closely allied with the search for ineffable French voice. An artist-citizen with impeccable political credentials, he mounted the barricades in July 1830—according to Fromental Halévy (who was appointed assistant *chef de chant* during preparations for *Guillaume Tell*)—sword in hand, to belt out "La Marseillaise" in the style of the trio's final call to arms. For later liberal opinion, however, Nourrit's republican zeal proved ill considered. The shouting, they said, caused permanent damage to his larynx.[95] Thank goodness, then, for Nourrit's retreat and later preference for *la vie intime,* the health of constitutional monarchy, and the tender mixtures of the trio cantabile. The old canard of the extent of political content in *Guillaume Tell,* to be clear, never had much to do with the immanent properties of the score. Rather, its meaning (as Benjamin Walton has suggested) depended on where—on which scenes and moments—listeners chose to pay attention.[96]

By mid-1830 Nourrit could be found collaborating with Joseph Mainzer's workers' choruses at the Association polytechnique, mobilizing the allusive power of song for the purposes not of public but of moral instruction. In the grainy throats of "the people," apparently, song carried a quasi-divine ethos. It taught virtue. It connected each to each. The value of soft power was nowhere better illustrated than by a multitude of voices mixing together, or by the affecting sight of bookbinders, engravers, silversmiths, stonemasons, joiners, and metal founders—all in their *bleu de travail*—united in love under Mainzer's directorship. The simple efficacy of song "to console, moralize, and discipline," as the German-born abbé put it, was never more affecting, or so usefully deployed as a nonviolent form of social control. In tandem with Mainzer, Nourrit envisaged a conservatory in Paris for popular instruction of song and drama, a plan thwarted only by the singer's untimely death. "Music with its intimate relationship with the soul, and with the interior life of man in society as it is at present," Mainzer wrote in 1836, "is an issue of the highest importance, and of an interest that is as moral as it is political."[97] Actual performance was never a necessity.

These plans served peculiarly French and peculiarly Orléanist conceptions of social health. The most evocative sounds were those imbued with enigma, those that conveyed the secret language of the soul in the style of Nourrit's celestial *voix mixte*. Neither the old brightly decorative nor newly willful modes of "Italian" expression cut it. "Music is the most intimate art," agreed Victor Cousin, member of Guizot's council of public instruction, expert on models of education in German states, and architect-in-chief of the first universal school system in France; and, what was more, "the less noise it makes, the more it touches." As well as requiring instruction in singing, the Cousin-inspired *Loi sur l'instruction primaire* of 28 June 1833 ordered the establishment of primary schools for boys in every French commune and made attendance compulsory. Guizot himself had been charmed by the moral effect of song when he heard the boys at the École Gautier in Paris, perhaps singing the first exercise in the solfège system of Guillaume-Louis Bocquillon (better known by his Germanized pseudonym, Wilhem): a simple eight-note rising scale on "Entends nos voix de haut des cieux" (listen to our voice of highest heaven). By the year of Bocquillon's death in 1842, the *Méthode Wilhem* had touched the lives of an estimated 4,000 children and some 1,200 adults in Paris alone. His system taught music literacy *(lecture musicale)*, theory *(grammaire musicale)*, and practice *(rhétorique musicale)*, the final "celestial attainment" being mastery of a "natural" language *(poésie musicale)*. Students were encouraged to sing as they read, listen from within, and learn from each other—to explore the twilight zone between speaking, writing, and singing. They were taught to seek the music of the words, to shape sounds to *le norme*, and to feel the grain of their collective French palates.

The education of the modern French mouth in fact began in earnest under Guizot's ministry.[98] Before the 1840s, it must be remembered, most French people did not speak French. The conservative-liberal imperative to seek unity as well as *intimité*, therefore, required the notion of an inner language, and indeed invented it—an academic French that no one actually spoke, an orality cleansed of argot, jargon, local dialect, or dirty inflection. Guizot's programs of educational reform attempted to install not only a standard of written and spoken language but a national modality of voice, as several historians have noted. Wilhem, whose *Méthode de lecture musicale et de chant élémentaire* was reprinted by Nourrit's brother-in-law according to a reformed system of "typographie musicale" in 1835, was explicit.[99] The goal was the achievement of "true national voice" as a bulwark for French unity by the "harmonization" of language and its intonations and by the occlusion of "vicious inflexion" and the "barbarous accents of our patois." The mission was to reform the people's mouth, harnessing poetry and song on the assumption that young minds would be attracted to the compelling mysteries of *la langue maternelle*. *Orality* is a good word here. Wilhem promulgated a purism—an elite standard of vocal hygiene—that was loath to disavow the legacy of French traditions of *"le dire,"* or the special mouthiness of the language.

Katherine Bergeron's recent book on the *mélodie* bathes the spectral origins of this idea of "French sound" in fascinating light. The *mélodie,* according to Bergeron, was less "a type of vocal piece" than "a vague and captivating quality of voice."[100] Legend has it that the first *mélodie* was formed around 1833 in the effusive mouth of Nourrit at the house of Josef Dessauer, where Liszt introduced Nourrit to his first Schubert song.[101] Since he knew no German, Nourrit sang the melody without words, as a vocalise. The artist's enthusiasm for these strange, foreign sounds was such that he would later organize several imaginative French paraphrases of many of Schubert's songs. The effect of Nourrit's pioneering Schubert performances must have been eerie, the charm of his uncanny translations spiced with a whiff of foreign authenticity. He sang "La jeune religieuse" ("Die junge Nonne" by Craigher), "Les astres" ("Die Sterne" by Fellinger), "Sois toujours mes seules amours" ("Sei mir gegrüsst" by Rückert), "Le roi des aulnes" ("Erlkönig" by Goethe). By the efforts of Nourrit in the 1830s, the story goes, the quintessentially patriotic and chamber ethos of the *mélodie* was born. And it was born, above all, of *intimité.*

Nourrit's "mélodies de Schubert," as Bergeron herself suggests, are usefully described in the same elegiac language employed by Roland Barthes in his celebrated lament for the *mélodie* in "The Grain of the Voice." It may be, in fact, that Barthes's elegy for a supposedly dead genre in 1972 ("the French are abandoning their language") represents an old way of mourning the disappearing French mouth; the essay remembers an ever-vanishing genre, one first formed, according to the creation myth, in the vocal tract of Nourrit. The mixed voice, Barthes suggests, involved an exclusively French articulation of the body. To listen to lieder and Dietrich Fischer-Dieskau, according to Barthes, was to listen only to "the lungs"; one heard the placelessness of a breath-obsessed, universalizing aesthetic. The art of the *mélodie,* on the other hand, lodged in the mouth and was steeped in Gallic materiality. Its *différence* was vouchsafed by "the grain of the throat" and a voice "lined with flesh." "The song must speak, must *write,*" urged Barthes. Instead of "bellows" (and I would add, chest, head, and lips), the place for the articulation of this voice was "the tongue, the glottis, the teeth, the mucous membrane, the nose." What one heard was not meaning but language, "the patina of consonants, the voluptuousness of vowels, a whole carnal stereophony." Barthes's position, in other words, was chauvinist (and racist). When artists sang, in his view, they betrayed truths, truths that were presymbolic, "the materiality of the body speaking its mother tongue." Thus the poignancy of the decline of the enigmatic vocal world of the *mélodie*. Because, for Barthes, the disappearance of the genre signified no more (and no less) than the disappearance of the French body.[102]

Barthes's unhappy farewell to his own mouth takes us backward, from the darkness of Duprez's "inside mouth," to the contrasts of Donzelli's multiplex instrument, to the visible mixtures of Nourrit's nose, palate, tongue, and teeth. We have moved against history and up the throat, from the familiar world of "my" voice to the less recognizable world of many. But what lessons can be drawn from illuminating these myriad and competing ways of locating voice? How might the bringing-to-light of so many sounds, mixtures, mouths, and voices help us think about questions of source, and—finally—about relations between voice and body? To revert to the first person and my own search, I want to reiterate that the voice belongs to much else besides the body. There is no absolute or natural relation between voices and bodies. The truth of what voices are depends on *where* observers look, on which part or aspect of the body is deemed essential: mouth, lips, tongue, vocal tract, larynx, lungs, cerebral cortex—one could go on and on. Voice depends, too, on language, on people, and on politics as much as it depends on "the body" so-called. Those nineteenth-century figures who went in search of voice—García, Bennati, Duprez, Donzelli, Nourrit—teach us at least this: that even the most self-evident truths are political, as much as they might be true.

6

Franz Liszt, Metapianism, and the Cultural History of the Hand

O, handle not the theme, to talk of hands,
Lest we remember still that we have none.

SHAKESPEARE, *TITUS ANDRONICUS*

THE CRIMINAL HAND

On 30 August 1832, Nicolas Theodore Frédéric Benoît became the first convicted parricide in Paris to be spared the *poing coupé:* amputation of the right hand immediately before execution by guillotine. Nineteen years of age, this son of a respected magistrate in the Ardennes had his *toilette* performed at the central asylum-prison at Bicêtre. The accoutrements of the old regime remained for this shy, mild-mannered, slightly built double murderer and pederast. His head was shaved, his clothes and shoes removed, his feet clamped in irons, a large white shroud placed over him, his head hooded in black. At 7 A.M., earlier than usual, a closed carriage left for the newly erected scaffold in a distant faubourg to the south of the city. There, half an hour later, the executioner and his assistants wrestled Benoît onto the platform—he refused to go quietly—and strapped him to the weigh-plank. The presiding officer read his sentence according to the provisions laid out in the not-yet-four-month-old penal code. The blade fell. As executions go, Benoît's was noisy but unspectacular.

However, for liberal commentators who had gathered there, a correspondent for *Gazette des tribunaux* among them, such haste betrayed the newly mythologized "dark side" of Paris: the dens of male prostitution, orgies, and vice that had come to light during Benoît's trial. The scene probably brought to mind less fortunate parricides, such as Angélique-Catherine Darcy, who had her hand and then head struck off in October 1828 by the same executioner on duty that morning, Henri Sanson. Victor Hugo, for one, was unimpressed by the new style of execution adopted in February 1832 for the sixty-four-year-old assassin Philippe-Marie

Desandrieux, the first person to be guillotined since the 1830 revolution. "They no longer dare after July to behead on the place de Grève," Hugo complained in his May preface to *Dernier Jour d'un condamné*, "because they are afraid, because they are cowardly, this is what they do. . . . [They] put him in a basket on two wheels, shuttered on all sides, padlocked and bolted; then, with a gendarme before and a gendarme behind, with hardly a sound and with no crowd in attendance, they delivered this parcel to the deserted barrière Saint-Jacques. It was . . . barely day-light. . . . Swiftly they drew the man from the basket, and, giving him no time to draw breath, furtively, slyly, shamefacedly they took off his head. This is what they call a public and solemn act of high justice."[1]

· · ·

Less than a month later, on 24 September 1832, a short story under the title "La Main de gloire (histoire macaronique)" appeared in the Parisian biweekly *Le Cabinet de lecture*. Its author was a close acquaintance of Hugo, Gérard de Nerval, a medical student who, instead of attending classes, fostered a reputation as the most ill-behaved poet in the city. Rumor had it that he could be found walking his pet lobster through the gardens of the Palais Royal on a blue silk ribbon. "Why is a pet lobster any more absurd than a cat, dog, gazelle, lion or any other creature," Théophile Gautier had Nerval explain in a later survey of the period. "Lobsters are quiet and serious; they neither bark nor bite, and they know the deepest secrets of the sea."[2]

"La Main de gloire" revels in such bourgeois disobedience. It recounts the tale of Eustache Bouteroue, a seventeenth-century Parisian clothier-apprentice, in a historical narrative Nerval concocted from a hodgepodge of early manuscript sources. Set in 1609, the story concerns what modern neuroscience would call "anarchic hand syndrome" (to my knowledge, it is the first example of the now-familiar genre of hand-gone-mad stories). In an ill-advised dispute over his bride-to-be, Eustache engages her jealous nephew, a soldier and expert swordsman, to a duel at dusk on the Pré-aux-Clercs. Knowing he has no chance to win by natural means, Eustache resorts to the occult: he consults a "skilful rogue" and fortune-teller at a stall on the Pont Neuf. The wily chiromancer, exploiting the situation, engages him in an impossible contract. In exchange for a potion to smear on his right hand that will guarantee victory, the desperate Eustache promises the gypsy-alchemist use of this same hand once he has been executed (as will surely happen once the duel is over). The title of the piece, "La Main de gloire," derives from this exchange. Nerval explains it by quoting the alchemical writings of the thirteenth-century Dominican and writer on music, Albertus Magnus:

> You take the severed hand of an executed man, purchased before his death; you sub-merge it meticulously, taking care to have it almost enclosed in a copper receptacle that contains cyma and saltpeter with *spondillis* grease. You place the receptacle in a

fire made of ferns and completely dry verbena until the hand, after a quarter of an hour, is completely dry and ready to be preserved. Later you make a candle with seal grease and Lapland sesame and you cause the hand to take hold of the candle as if it were a candlestick. Wherever you go, carrying it before you, all barriers will fall, all locks will open, and the people who come before you will remain motionless.[3]

The gypsy's intention, in other words, is to harvest Eustache's hand, prepare it in the old ways, and use it as a "criminal hand," that is, one that will continue to act, in death as in life, against the prevailing social and somatic order.

As the magic mixture is rubbed into Eustache's hand, he feels it twitch in disobedience: "At that, Eustache felt a kind of electric thrill that ran through his entire arm, and this frightened him a great deal. It seemed to him that his hand was swelling, and yet—strange to tell!—it clenched and stretched several times, cracking its joints, as when an animal awakens. Then he felt nothing more."[4] At first light the following morning, the hand once again thrills to life. On cue, as Eustache faces his rival on the Pré-aux-Clercs, his arm galvanizes into action, "dragging him forward, violently resisting any attempt to control it." The soldier—who had always intended to take pity on his dull, hapless opponent—is poignarded savagely to the floor by the previously weak, limp-wristed couturier. In the ensuing chaos, bewildered victor and both seconds grab what they can and scatter.

Several days later, Eustache decides to come out of hiding, master his morbid fear of capture and calm his nightmares. He reasons—wisely—that his best chance is to seek the help of a corrupt magistrate, Monsieur Chevassut, an acquaintance and long-time customer of the tailor's apprentice. To Eustache's relief, the corpulent official wastes little time in assuring him that nothing will come of that case, that the evidence against him will be buried in red tape and bureaucracy. But just as the relieved Eustache is being shown the door, the right hand's rebellious strength and elasticity returns. Once more, the "Hand of Glory" lashes out, slapping the magistrate hard across the face, rocking him back and streaking blue fingermarks across his flustered cheeks.

At this, Nerval's prose rushes quickly to Eustache's last moments on the scaffold and the final paragraphs, our hero having been arrested and locked in the Châtelet on the double accusation of homicide and assault of a magistrate. As with Benoît, the executioner on the scaffold summarily dispenses with his work, although this time more to satisfy the demands of Parisian spectacle than because of the shame such exhibitions might occasion. Seventeenth-century crowds, Nerval explains, did not like to wait.

The story would end here, but that Nerval's hand writes on. In an afterword, his writing describes Eustache's lifeless body, twisting limply on the hangman's noose, and the astonishment of the crowd as his right hand wistfully moves again. As anarchic fingers grow bolder and lift skyward, so the panicked master executioner starts cutting arteries and, when this fails, he severs the anarchic hand from the arm completely in two deft strokes. Nerval's pen, fired by the pandemonium of the scene, becomes agitated as events conclude: "[The hand] made a prodigious leap and fell, bloody, amid the crowd, which divided in shock. Then, making several more leaps, thanks to the elasticity of its fingers, and since everyone gave it a wide berth, it quickly found its way to the foot of the little tower of the Château-Gaillard. Then, scrambling with its fingers like a crab along the salients and the rough spots in the wall, it climbed to the little window where the gypsy was waiting for it."[5]

. . .

On 17 February 1832, eight months before Eustache's hand leapt free, Franz Liszt arrived at Paris's Hôtel d'Artois, on the rue Laffitte. Climbing the marble staircase to the first floor, he was received at the apartment of Caroline Boissier, a Swiss noblewoman visiting the city for the season.[6] The twenty-year-old pianist was there to continue the musical education of Caroline's nineteen-year-old daughter (she had received fifteen lessons already). The dedicatee of Liszt's *Fantaisie romantique sur deux mélodies suisses* (1835) was a good student: Valérie would soon acquire accomplishments enough to become a prolific writer, Christian moralist, and founder of the first ever school for nursing.[7] Liszt's lessons were intense: they took place every three or four days and usually lasted two hours. Her mother would sit in, both to chaperone and take notes for a now-famous lesson diary. Valérie's pianistic problem, identified in mid-January, was that her hands needed to be more "flexible and energetic."[8] Liszt prescribed octaves, at least three hours a day, for months—in scales modulating through every key and in all permutations, first "going from a *pianissimo* to a great *forte* and vice versa," then staccato filled in with diminished chords, then in broken patterns, repeated strokes, and so on. Whatever the variation, Liszt counseled, "the tones" should be "equal at all times, broadly stroked, and the wrist supple and flexible, the hand soft and falling." The key should never be struck with the extremity or nail of the finger, but "with the ball of the finger, which flattens the finger, of course, and allows it freedom." Liszt charged that the sound of the octaves be kept "pure, full, round, and complete." "He does this for hours on end," Caroline reported, "while at the same time reading to avoid boredom." "He wants one to play, without exception," she summed up on 17 February, "entirely with wrist action—playing with what is called 'la main morte.'"[9]

Liszt spent most of 1832 pursuing "dead hands." His ideal would anticipate several later developments in keyboard pedagogy: Sigismund Thalberg's rival notion of "la main désossée" (boneless hand);[10] Liszt acolyte Marie Jaëll's late-century technique of "la main dissociée"; or Mason, Deppe, and Leschetizky's concept of freeing or "emancipating" the playing hand by working toward its "devitalization."[11] When Liszt seemed in a bad mood during Valérie's 24 February lesson, her mother ascribed it to frustration with his hands: "It is astonishing to hear Liszt say that his fingers are heavy and clumsy," Valérie's mother wrote. In the ensuing month Liszt regularly railed against his pianistic rivals: their "rounded fingers" and "all the little musical affectations"—"enlevés," "plongés," the "showy contrasts" that characterized their playing. Instead he advocated "suffering" and "oppression" to give expression to his hands. Hans von Bülow, Liszt's most famous pupil, said of his practice, "I crucify, like a good Christ, the flesh of my fingers in order to make them obedient."[12] This was Liszt's idea: to seize living nature, unlock the gates of the material self, and transubstantiate flesh. His purpose was to attain levels where "one does not perceive the fingers, or the nails, or the instrument," levels only achievable (it would seem) by a maniacal devotion to octaves.[13]

On 6 March 1832 Valérie was presented with a "mahogany brace" or "hand guide" of the type that we have seen advocated by the celebrated Kalkbrenner.[14] This piece of machinery, which Liszt probably devised and constructed himself, forced Valérie to play octaves from the wrist (and not from the arm, as is generally assumed of Lisztian technique). And play them she did (plugged into her machine): short passages of octave crescendos and diminuendos "twenty, thirty, forty times," broken octave runs following the same pattern, full octave scales, "five, six, seven, eight times running through all twenty-four keys," and octave arpeggios in major, minor, and diminished sevenths. By the time of Valérie's final lessons, Liszt—now engaged in a similar octave regime—had pounded his fingers into such submission that he was finally on good terms with them. On 23 March Valérie's mother marveled at how pliable they were: "His fingers have neither a definite position nor form. They bend soft and pliant in all directions; the fingers, extended and recumbent, move in a weighty manner from one key to the next."[15] Indeed, they hardly resembled hands at all.

THE MAKEOVER EPISODE

The day after Caroline described Liszt's formless appendages, on 24 March, cholera officially broke out in Paris and the Boissiers returned to their residence in Geneva. Sweeping in from the East, the pandemic lingered until late September, causing eighteen thousand deaths in the city alone. Paganini's second tour famously coincided with its coming, the first display of his freakish or misshapen left hand occurring on the evening following the announcement of the first official death (25 March). By 19 April (three days before Liszt first heard the violinist at an Easter Sunday concert for the victims of the outbreak) Heine could moan at the inconvenience of it all: "I have been much disturbed in my work by the horrible screams of my neighbour, who died of cholera." There was everywhere a strong stench of chlorine, sloshed out in front of public buildings, mixed with that of camphor stuffed in pockets.[16] On 27 April, Liszt wrote to the Boissiers in Geneva, saying how he had been bedridden for ten days (in low spirits), how deeply he felt about having been "in the family" those past two months, and lamenting the "tristes et affligeantes raisons qui me retiennent et m'emprisonnent dans Paris," which had prevented him from traveling with them to Switzerland.[17]

Biographers record that Liszt plunged into an irregular lifestyle around this time, keeping dissolute hours and experimenting with emerging left-wing political theory. Exposing his mind to all it might crave, the virtuoso-in-training began to visit prisons to observe the habits of condemned men (Benoît perhaps?). He grew obsessed with death and dying. Not that he was in favor of capital punishment: "[It] is an abominable social crime. It is obvious we are all more or less guilty, deranged, or crazy, but it does not follow that we ought to be guillotined, hanged, or, as an act of mercy, shot."[18] As part of his newly chaotic routine, Liszt would pay impromptu visits to gambling dens, or to Salpêtrière hospital to play music to the insane.[19]

If the diary of Antoine Fontaney, a minor poet, is anything to go by, Liszt appeared regularly at Hugo's salon in these months, invariably to perform the funeral march from Beethoven's A♭ sonata (on 16 April, 18 April, and 19 June).[20] The Bibliothèque nationale de France holds Liszt's unpublished manuscript diary for 1832, a small leather-bound purple silk moiré pocketbook, the oblique ink jottings of which confirm at least the first of these appointments. Liszt's mostly illegible pencil scrawl—much of it emotional venting or quotations from Balzac, the Vulgate, Buffon, Hugo, Shakespeare, even Napoleon—might read as yet more evidence of his turbulent state. It seems likely that Liszt kept this sumptuous diary—a luxury item bought from Alphonse Giroux on the rue du Coq-St-Honoré, seller of miniatures, exotic objects, cabinets, and other items of fancy and fantasy—not so much for practical purposes as to incite in himself the volatile emotions proper to his developing notion of "the artist."[21] Almost every other evening in mid-1832, according to another source, Liszt would frequent Alexandre Dumas's intimate gatherings with his phalanstery: Henri Fourcade (writer), Victorine Collin (essayist), Louis Boulanger (painter), Étienne Cordelier-Delanoue (writer and poet), Auguste de Châtillon (poet and painter), Hugo, and often Nerval.[22] (Liszt had now become a devotee of Nerval's 1828 translation of Goethe's *Faust:* much later he planned an opera on the subject, in collaboration with Nerval and Dumas.)[23] Chez Dumas, Liszt might pound away on his host's out-of-tune upright; Hugo might recite verse; Dumas might show off his ambidexterity—he could write with both hands at the same time.[24] From there Liszt would generally return home, where, according to the memoirs of Gabrielle Anne de Courtiras, he would enrage the tenants in his building on the rue de Provence by playing the Dies Irae over and over, in countless variations, until dawn. (Eventually the tenants banded together to force his eviction.)[25]

By late April, though, Liszt was neglecting his diary, except for extreme outbursts such as the one on 25 May, in which he described himself as "in prison . . . burning

... crying ... without knowing why."[26] Pauline Pocknell argues, on the basis of this neglect and four ripped-out diary pages from 1–4 May, that "something else, mysterious but radical happened to Liszt's mindset towards the end of April 1832."[27] Whatever this "something else" may have been, Switzerland never left his thoughts, as evinced by a May letter to Valérie Boissier intimating plans to visit there with Dumas.[28] An earlier letter, also to Geneva, this time addressed to fellow pianist Pierre-Étienne Wolff, is more important still. Written on 2 May 1832, it would become the great musicological marker for this chaotic turning point in his artistic career:

> Here is a whole fortnight that my mind and fingers have been working like two lost spirits, = Homer, the Bible, Plato, Locke, Byron, Hugo, Lamartine, Chateaubriand, Beethoven, Bach, Hummel, Mozart, Weber, are all around me. I study them, meditate on them, devour them with fury; besides this I practice four to five hours of exercises (3rds, 6ths, 8ths, tremolos, repetition of notes, cadences, etc., etc.). Ah! Provided I don't go mad, you will find an artist in me! Yes, an artist such as you desire, such as is required nowadays![29]

Musicologists tend to agree that in these dark Parisian days Liszt reached deep inside himself, redoubled the struggle with his hands, rebuilt his technique from scratch, and staged the first of his trademark "makeovers." Apparently breaking from tradition, he submitted his hand to untold labors, thus embodying "the transition," as his first official biographer Lina Ramann would put it, "to a modern style of playing."[30] The études and characteristic pieces of the 1830s in view, Charles Rosen calls it "one of the greatest revolutions of keyboard style in history."[31] Others have referred no less effusively to the birth of "transcendental execution."

NEW BODIES

The talk of "reincarnation" has not been mythologized without cause, although it is debatable whether the familiar story I have rehearsed above (which was also Liszt's) stands much scrutiny. His words in that letter to Wolff have nevertheless seemed important because they suggest a novel, irrational "antimethod" in keyboard practice, an approach governed only by apparently superhuman acts of will. This is, after all, a paradigmatic example of the now-familiar "woodshed" experience (a quasi-monastic state that the player induces by isolating him- or herself in order to reemerge in transfigured form). Such "method" is, of course, anything but unmethodical. The trips to prisons, asylums, casinos, the "involuntary" submission to history and literature, the fearful embrace of criminality were just that: part of a self-consciously spontaneous attempt, not so much to reeducate fingers as to "transfigure" the self.

Liszt worked to cancel work. This chapter once again documents the material effort behind "transfiguration," less in order to demystify it (since ecstasy was palpable!) than to expose the historical conditions by which it took place. What I want to register here is the manual labor attendant on romantic conceits of musical mystification, and the terms by which it became possible to speak of "music" without the bodies and instruments that facilitated it. This will require revisiting debates reviewed in an earlier chapter over whether Thalberg's multihandedness betrayed crass athletic display or sleight of hand. The inspirited sense of handedness necessary to Lisztian realms of musical purity was extreme; it was cultivated by an elite group of pianists and pedagogues across Europe. Having reviewed philosophical and scientific debates about hand function and free will, the chapter returns to stories of Liszt's spectral hands, anecdotes to rival the tales of Benoît's unspectacular death and the horror of Eustache's disobedient appendage. The emergence of wayward hands bore out the shameful truth of doing. These were body parts, after all, that (by their very existence) both mocked human contingency in the world and conditioned engagement with it. At Liszt's piano, I argue, manual estrangement was cultivated in order to incarnate a newly untouchable kind of music, a "music" realized only by the denial of the fact of handedness itself.

Liszt's "making-over" involved both a new politics of the body and a new politics of performance. I say "politics" because the rebirthing practices he pioneered involved a remapping of the hand in relation to the rest of the performing body, a redrawing of mind-body-soul-hand relations in the name of higher and holier conceptions of artful performance. His students, though chained to keyboards, were induced to think and work in purer, "antisystematic," and less digital ways: beyond instruments, scores, their own fingers, and even music. In this didactic regime, there would no longer be a place for detailed methodical work, for small educative steps, the slow acquisition of skill, sensible knowledge, or sensitive fingers at the pianoforte. Rather, pupil and teacher would now seek transformative experiences. The end game was nothing less than to be born again—to be rewired as a new physiology, or at least to seek deeply instinctual modes of self-transformation. In this quest for perpetual conversion and reconversion, practice and pedagogy became newly invested in abstruse conceptions of body (or, to put this in emerging scientific terms, in ever-dynamic brain and nerve function). Invisible outcomes were targeted: desires, drives, instincts, intentions, volition. Higher forms of musical expression (read: Hungaro-German), in other words, could be sacralized by reconfiguring them in relation to higher or deeper cognitive functions. Lower-level efforts (read: Italo-French music making) could be construed oppositionally, as a mode of performance grounded in handed activities.[32] This was at least one of the effects of Liszt's "dead hand" technique. It was a practice that drew attention away from the player's fingers, reinforcing in her—through hours and hours at the piano—a persistent sense of personal alienation from the shameful work of her hands.

A radical conception of keyboard performance, in other words, was conse-
crated under the banner of a new physiology, a new body, and a higher set of forces
or antagonisms within the human form. This is not to say that, in this "born-again"
mythology, hands would be denied, disavowed, or disclaimed (how could they
be?). Rather, they were subsumed into a full-bodied and internally divided mor-
phology in which, as we shall see, the old pianistic tradition of celebrating them in
neo-Aristotlean terms as the "instrument of instruments" became intensely problematic.[33]

TALK TO THE HAND

The emergence of an anticlassical sense of handedness was borne out not only
in the experience of Liszt but in that of nearly every European pianist of the period.
The example that most readily comes to mind, of course, is Schumann's in far-off
Leipzig. At around the time Chopin was publishing his Op. 10 Études in Paris,
when Adolph von Henselt was resident in Vienna playing Bach ten hours a day on
a dummy keyboard (while reading the Bible) and when Alexander Dreyschock settled down in Prague to perfect his octaves (he practiced around sixteen hours a
day), Schumann famously declared war on his hands. On the day before Liszt apologized to Wolff, 7 May, Schumann penned what became one of the most celebrated
diary entries in Western music. His *Tagebuch* reported that he had begun to apply
a *Cigarrenmechanik* to the third finger of his right hand, a finger that he found by
turns "tolerable," "broken," "weak," "incorrigible," or "completely stiff." (He had
invented this gadget with his friend and fellow pianist Anton Töpken; his diary
entries in this period, mostly "notes to myself about my hand," document the extent
of his ongoing struggle with the manual companion.)[34] Two years previously, in
Heidelberg, Schumann had developed hand tremors, although his 1830 diary
seemed less concerned with his third finger than with the "lameness" of his "numb"
ring finger on the same hand.[35] His wife, Clara, later blamed Robert's right index
finger for the failure of his concert career, the third or fourth having little to do with
it![36] Schumann tried several therapies to regalvanize his hand: he turned his whole
house into "an apothecary shop" and experimented, for example, by inserting the
disobedient member into the carcass of freshly slaughtered animals *(Thierbäder)*,
or by having a doctor electrocute the muscles of his right arm, or by grasping the
metal rod of an electromagnetic bath machine. Nothing helped. Wilhelm Joseph
von Wasielewski, Schumann's first biographer, registered how anarchic things had
become: "The sinews of his third finger had lost their natural elasticity from excessive stretching; and the result was, that, instead of striking down, as desired, it
moved upwards. Conceive the terror of the bold experimenter when he saw this."[37]
    The anarchic hand has confounded explanation ever since. Musicologists have
long argued over Schumann's enforced turn from performance to composition,

from extroversion to creative introspection. John Daverio and more recently Eric Frederick Jensen lay blame for the musician's pianistic failure (and compositional ascent) with the "barbaric" hand strengthener; Eric Sams thought the hand injury was caused by mercury poisoning after treatments for syphilis; Alfred Meyer speculated that Schumann had cut the webbing between his fingers to supply them with more independence; Henson and Urich thought the problem was connected to damage of the "osterior interosseous nerve"; Peter Ostwald agreed but doubted whether the affliction was due to Schumann's "hypochondriachal neurosis," speculating that his hand might have been injured after he passed out on his right arm after a bout of heavy drinking; and Gerd Nauhaus thought the debility the result of a rupture of the *frenulum praeputii* caused by obsessive-compulsive masturbation.[38]

All these theories serve a basic misapprehension. Schumann's hand injury was far more than a medical or even psychosomatic condition. His affliction had only partially to do with the intimate mental details so beloved of recent, biographically fixated Schumann scholarship. To look for tiny neurotic tics or more biomedical evidence of a warped, introspective, asocial, internal, splintered fantasy life seems shortsighted in this context. Schumann's struggle was not merely his own. Rather, he was caught up in a large cultural shift, a pan-European change that involved nothing less than the social experience or somatic regulation of handedness.

This is not to say that Schumann merely decided to do without hands, although it is difficult to argue that he did not imagine outsourcing them. In a love letter to Clara in December of 1838, he wrote that his bond was strong enough to experience her as though she were a part of his body. And not just any part. She was his faithful right hand, a replacement or prosthetic member to which he would delegate manual activity: "I sometimes feel unhappy here [in Vienna], especially because I have an ailing hand. . . . I often complain to heaven and ask God, why did you do just this to me? It would be of such great value for me here. So much music is ready and alive inside of me, that I ought to be able to exhale it. And now I can bring it forth only with great difficulty, stumbling with one finger over the next. But now, of course, you are my right hand, and you must take good care of yourself so that nothing happens to you."[39] The extent of Schumann's dependence on his right hand was nowhere more evident than in his famous final moments at the sanatorium in Endenich. Incapacitated after his neurological meltdown, swimming in dementia and psychosis, weakened by pneumonia, unable to speak and barely conscious, he still apparently recognized "his" fingers. Brahms recorded how, for those final two days in late July 1856, Clara watched over her husband:

> I am sure I will never experience anything more moving than Robert and Clara's reunion. He lay there for some time with his eyes closed, and she knelt before him, more quietly than one would have thought possible. He recognized her later, and also

the following day. At one point he clearly wished to embrace her, threw one arm towards her. Of course he had not been able to speak for some time, one could only understand (or one thought one could understand) the occasional word.

He often refused the wine offered to him, then sometimes he would suck it from her finger so greedily and long and fervently, that one was convinced he knew the finger.[40]

These words leave us with a touching image of intimacy, a final picture of the myth of Robert-and-Clara. The widening rift between nineteenth-century composer and performer is beautifully encapsulated here in the increasingly distinct and heavily gendered set of values applied to each by midcentury: the mad composer-genius lost in hallucination and delirium on one hand, the marginalized editor-perfomer and faithful midwife to his creative fantasies on the other.

THE SCIENCE OF THE HAND

Pianistic contemporaries were not alone in their struggle against problematic hands. At least one nineteenth-century source recalls the comparable experience of no less a personage than Georges Cuvier, who succumbed to cholera on 13 May 1832 (in the same week as the crises of both Schumann and Liszt). Two nights before his death in rooms attached to the Jardin des Plantes, the great French naturalist—true scientist to the end—calmly observed the fingers on his right hand, which had begun to twitch involuntarily on his bed sheets. The ministrations of his doctors, who prescribed extensive leeching and cupping, failed to relieve his discomfort. The numbness and finally paralysis had spread to his left arm, respiratory system, and legs, having afflicted his right arm only days before. The founder of comparative anatomy and paleontology spoke slowly to his minders this night, indicating that "the nerves of the will are sick." These words were often recited in Cuvier's obituaries; they were his dying endorsement of recent work on the physiology of the nervous system, work that had distinguished so carefully between the nerves of sensibility and those of volition. Now, finally, the experimental findings of Charles Bell in London, François Magendie in Paris, and Antonio Scarpa in Pavia could be accepted.[41] The assumption that the physical size, fineness, coarseness, or shape of nerves accounted for the incredible range of nervous response could at last be laid to rest. Two nights before his death, in other words, Cuvier verified for posterity that every nerve obeyed function rather than form. There were tactile nerves, aural nerves, optical nerves, sensible nerves, motor nerves, and so on. The proof was there before him: he could feel his hand but could not move it.[42]

In these same years, Bell in London borrowed Cuvier's methods as he worked through his own obsession with handedness. Since August 1830 the Scottish surgeon, anatomist, and artist had been writing a treatise commissioned by the Royal Society. Issued as *The Hand, Its Mechanism and Vital Endowments, as Evincing Design* in 1833, the book was so popular that it would reach its fourth edition as early as 1837. This extraordinary text was written at the intersection of taxonomy, zoology, theology, physiology, fine art, comparative anatomy, and medicine. Bell preferred not to extol the hand as the visible sign of man's exaltedness, or as his privileged instrument. Rather, the nerve scientist "physiologized" this body part (in protoevolutionary terms) in less formative ways: as a complex structure, yes, but also one that had adapted itself to human function in the service of will and environment. The hand, in other words, was reconstrued to seem *incidental to* rather than *the cause of* mankind's superiority. Its actions were accessory to authentic human articulations of self. Thus Bell's monograph urged its readers to laud this member less for its miraculous visible endowments than for its equally miraculous "hidden" physiology:

> With the possession of an instrument like the hand there must be a great part of the organization, which strictly belongs to it, concealed. The hand is not a thing appended, or put on, like an additional movement in a watch; but a thousand intricate relations must be established throughout the body in connection with it—such as nerves of motion and nerves of sensation: and there must be an original part of the composition of the brain, which shall have relation to these new parts, before they can be put into activity. But ever with all this superadded organization the hand would lie inactive, unless there were created a propensity to put it into operation.[43]

The hand, in this view, functioned in the service of two larger and more fundamental organic systems. First, its merely visible activities were adapted to the dark inner workings of the body's nervous system. Second, its special capabilities were only the peripheral effect of its adaptation to the outer environment: it was little more than a by-product of the profound beauty of the two worlds to which it was subject. (The predominance of right-handedness could thus be explained in terms of the influence of such everyday human functions as opening parlor doors or unfolding penknives.) For Bell, hands merely exemplified the advanced extent to which man had adapted to inner and outer nature.

The sobriety of this hypothesis, appearing as it does toward the end of Bell's monograph, belies the strange reflexivity of his opening paragraphs, which struggle against Aristotle's dictum in *De anima* that "the soul is as the hand." "The human hand is so beautifully formed," Bell admits, "it has so fine a sensibility, that sensibility governs its motions so correctly, every effort of the will is answered so instantly, as if the hand itself were the seat of the will."[44] His central claim accounted for this difficult hypothesis by appealing to God. This is not to suggest that Bell was uncomfortable about strong theological arguments, but rather to argue that his treatise was hardly clothed in incorruptable righteousness. The illustrations, drawn by Bell himself, betray this moral ambiguity, as Ludmilla Jordanova has noticed.[45] Instead of depicting hands—not a single nonskeletal picture of a human hand appears—Bell sketched a child bouncing on a satyr's knee, an ape eating out of a bowl, a bear standing on its hind legs. These irreverent images are curious, Jordanova notes, as if Bell's hand—Nerval-like—were going its own playful way. If anything, they reinforce his insinuation that hands function independently of mind, that the seen might operate in opposition to the unseen, along with the activities of intending and doing, volition and action. Rather than belonging to man, and far from being expressive of his moral life, Bell concluded that the hand was the property of nature, or—more comfortingly—of God. "The complexity of [the hand's] structure," he repeated, "belongs to external nature and not to the mind." Myriad examples from the Cuvierian science of comparative anatomy buttressed this at once seditious and devoutly religious observance. Placing human hands alongside the paws, claws, hooves, and fins of vertebrates, mammals, and amphibians of every shape and size, Bell demonstrated how each animal instrument was beautifully molded, adapted, or designed—not to some inner personality, soul, intellect, or character, but to primitive necessity. "As for our hand," he wrote, "it is no more the freedom of its action which constitutes its perfection, than the knowledge which we have of these motions, and our consequent ability to direct it with the utmost precision."[46] The only reason we are able to control its actions, in other words, is because we possess knowledge of its current position, its movements being controlled—apparently—in retrospect. We might watch it go its own way. The rest was left to God.

LISZT'S FINGERPRINTS

Liszt was not primed to read such natural theology, although at least one of the books into which he threw himself while practicing octaves in 1832 suggested similar claims. At the time of the famous "makeover" letter to Wolff that year, Liszt was immersed in the *St. Petersburg Dialogues* (1821), by Catholic apologist Joseph de Maistre. On 8 May Liszt apologized to Wolff for the tone of his previous letter (quoted earlier) and drew on concepts from de Maistre's second dialogue to explain the balance of the spiritual and animal in him, ascribing his "delirium" and "madness" to recent overwork and "violent desire." Liszt's fascination with right-wing Catholicism, one imagines, extended to de Maistre's famous discussions of liberty in the sixth dialogue, in which the author lashed out at materialism, "those bothersome Ideologues" (who construed life as the by-product of physical sensation), and such "immoral" eighteenth-century predecessors as John Locke and Étienne Bonnot de Condillac. For sensationalist writers such as these, de Maistre observed, liberty had involved "the absence of obstacles," "the power of doing what one has not done or of not doing what one has done," a "pretty antithesis" that "dazzled the mind" and achieved nothing more. Liberty is not "the power to do," de Maistre countered, it is "the power to will." Rather than being about the action of hands, in other words, liberty was conceived as "unimpeded volition," an innate faculty anterior to sensuality or mere doing. To possess free will, de Maistre suggested, was not necessarily to possess free use of one's hands.[47]

Whatever Liszt's reading, his "crisis" certainly confirmed the gist of Bell's and de Maistre's intuitions: that virtuosi would no longer seek perfect control, that the old masterful display of hands before the keyboard would seem increasingly boring or unnecessary. Liszt's experience, in any event, was of a disengaged hand—one belonging less to himself than nature. Joseph d'Ortigue, influential anti-Rossini proselytizer, emphathized strongly with such theistic manual encounters in his pioneering, opinion-forming biography of Liszt in the *Gazette musicale* of June 1835. Lauding fleshly renunciations in the name of higher artistic, social, and religious missions, the critic exalted Liszt's hands:

> One has to see him, with his windblown hair, hurling his fingers from one end of the keyboard to the other to land on a note that explodes with a clamorous or silvery sound, like a bell struck by a bullet; his fingers seem to grow longer, like springs being released, as if at times freeing themselves from his hands. One has to see him raise his sublime eyes to the sky to search for insipration, then, gloomily, fix them on the ground; or see his radiant and inspired features, like those of a martyr, radiating in the joy of his tortures.[48]

After the mythic "makeover moment," Liszt's were not "feeling hands". They were hands that seemed to *have* feelings. Inwardly emotional, they were less instruments of intention than potential friends, aids, ambassadors, confidants, or imposters. (One is reminded of Sergei Rachmaninoff's words on his deathbed in 1943; racked with cancer, he lifted his fingers to his face and choked, "My dear hands; farewell my hands.")[49]

To sum up: around May 1832 it became newly possible in Europe to conduct a relationship with one's hands. This hand would not so much *learn* by doing as *become* by doing; a hand supplemental or "in addition to" self, a hand with identity, it would be a mobile, ever-shifting personality. Hands are construed in quite uncomfortable ways in these new contexts: as agents in likely opposition to self, as body parts to be acted against and disavowed if not entirely disclaimed. The encounter, in other words, was with a hand external to self, a rogue part or shard, at once agonizingly proximate to and set apart from its possessor, but also a member that he or she might command to play music or engender experiences as yet unknown.

This emerging sense of what we might call the criminal hand was nowhere more powerfully felt than in the extraordinary late-century work of one of Liszt's

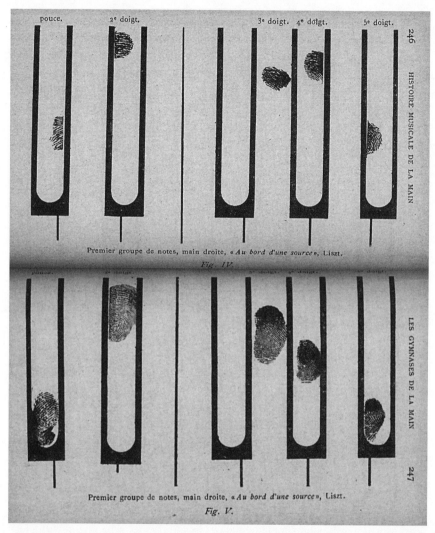

pouce.   2ᵉ doigt.   3ᵉ doigt.   4ᵉ doigt.   5ᵉ doigt.

Premier groupe de notes, main droite, «*Au bord d'une source*», Liszt.

Fig. IV.

Premier groupe de notes, main droite, «*Au bord d'une source*», Liszt.

Fig. V.

FIGURE 22. Jaëll-Liszt's *Au bord d'une source,* reprinted in Émile Gouget, *Histoire musicale de la main: son rôle dans la notation, la tonalité, le rythme et l'exécution instrumentale; la main des musiciens devant les sciences occultes,* 246–47. Image reproduced by permission of the Stanford Music Library, Stanford, California.

most zealous pupils, Marie Jaëll. The images of figure 22 represents her interpretation of how to play (and not to play) Liszt's *Au bord d'une source,* her identity here imprinted on the piano keys. This nineteenth-century association of the hand with criminality would of course be confirmed later in such new disciplines as forensic pathology, graphology, and biometric methods of criminal fingerprinting, where, as in Liszt's keyboard method, the open ball of the finger encoded identity. Jaëll's proposition was that pieces such as *Au bord d'une source* provided the opportunity for a detailed record of the pianist's individualized personality.[50]

Hands here obey no authorial or willful law other than, as we shall see, the God-given laws of nature and natural function. They are increasingly disobedient—having to be wrestled against, rehabilitated, coaxed into action, or addressed. And since no two hands were ever "identical," methodological systems began to seem useless. Every pupil, every physiology, every day, every mood, as we shall see, required special, unpredictable, individual treatment.[51]

AGAINST METHOD

Liszt never wrote a method. The closest he came to it was in 1835, when the Geneva Conservatoire of Music was founded with Wolff (whom we have met before) heading the piano department. Having eloped with Marie d'Agoult across the French border, Liszt was "ambushed," as he put it, by the administration and dragooned into teaching, an ironic occurence in light of the antiestablishment credentials he had garnered since he last encountered the Boissiers in 1832. (In May 1835, the *Gazette musicale* published Liszt's literary debut, "On the Position of Artists and Their Condition in Society," in which he exposed the *subalternité* of artist-musicians everywhere, encouraging them to unite in the name of their prophetic social responsibility to "the people.") Once more in right-wing circles, he was touted across the city by his faithful patron, Caroline Boissier, who introduced him at her salon at Rivage, a stately home on the banks of Lake Geneva.[52] Newly embroiled in the d'Agoult scandal—according to another Swiss admirer, Albertine de la Rive-Necker—Liszt now wore a ring with a silver skull set against a gold background on one of his index fingers, as if to advertise its "disobedience." Not that he wished to show his fingers off: Rive-Necker's account follows d'Ortigue in making one of the earliest descriptions of Liszt ignoring his hands in performance, apparently reading "invisible literature" in ways familiar to us from those ubiquitous nineteenth-century prints of the pianist staring into space. "While playing, he takes no notice of his hands, which he never looks at," Rive-Necker wrote in her diary. "His eyes wander upwards," she continued. "He seems to be reading invisible pages, or rather to be composing and playing according to the inspiration of the moment."[53]

Madame Boissier was not impressed by the newly "made-over" Liszt. The noble soul of the "poor young man," she wrote in her unpublished diary, had been "seduced" by Saint-Simonists on one hand and "perverted" by George Sand on the other. She lamented his rejection of "accepted beliefs and principles; I'm not too sure what he puts in their place."[54] Success had changed him: "He has surrendered himself to the left, but with a forthrightness, a credulousness, that is saddening and touching. It is distressing to see such a beautiful soul so abused, so misled."[55]

Whatever the truth of her characterization, Liszt did not thrive in Geneva. At the conservatory he frequently failed to turn up for work, preferring instead to take Alpine tours. Weeks after his appointment, he announced to the faculty that he lacked energy for male pupils, though he still found time for female ones. In a letter to Baron d'Eckstein, he complained of the administration's expectations, forced as he was "to regiment, discipline and *métronimiser* a legion of little ladies and young men, most of whom are still today of goodwill (peace be with them) and who make me—almost—regret the lack of mine."[56] He had already caused a stir early in his tenure by making his offer to teach conditional on his services being free of charge, a condition that the committee feared would harm the local music-teaching industry. (The news of Liszt's involvement with the conservatory was publicly announced in a local newspaper, Le Fédéral, on 13 October.) An equally "generous" gesture involved a proposal to write a tutor for the institution "at personal expense," although inevitably the bill for engraving would be sent to the institution. Evidence (or the lack of it) suggests that his "gift" came to nothing. (It is significant that, at around the same time, Chopin would also fail to complete a keyboard method. All that remains of his efforts is a tortured manuscript that struggles to formulate even the most basic of outlines.)[57]

Not that "nothing" prevented the Myth of the Absent Method from installing itself in the emerging music-historical imagination.[58] Absence has, of course, always been a keyword for Liszt. While pianist-pedagogues fantasize about these supposedly lost pages, they remain in one sense appropriately invisible, a goad to the seemingly endless stream of modern What-Would-Liszt-Do scholarship. Surely the best question is whether he had much of methodological substance to divulge. In his mature pedagogy platitudes such as "Technique should create itself from spirit, not mechanics" did the job. Whenever students asked for concrete advice, he would tell them, "Go to the conservatory!" Back in the mid-1830s, his position appeared no less abstract or evangelical, as perhaps best evinced by the musical supplement to the 7 June 1835 issue of the Gazette musicale de Paris. In this house publication, Liszt's publisher and chief publicist of the time, Maurice Schlesinger, took the bold step of reprinting the month-old plates of Harmonies poétiques et religieuses (S154) a week before releasing d'Ortigue's issue-length first biography of the performer-composer (see figure 23). The Gazette, moreover, was already between the third and fourth installments of "On the Position of Artists and Their Condition in Society."

This supplement was the first example of what a writer for Le Pianiste called "le

FIGURE 23. The opening of *Harmonies poétiques et religieuses* (Paris, 1835), 2, as printed by Schlesinger. This particular copy was once owned by Ferruccio Busoni. Reproduced by permission of the Bibliothèque nationale de France.

genre *spiritualiste*," a metanotational score for a methodless and manualless music.[59] For d'Ortigue and the musician himself, this earliest version of the *Harmonies poétiques et religieuses* represented a compositional début, since Liszt's output had so far consisted only of piano arrangements—Berlioz's *Grande symphonie fantastique* (S470), for example, and such "derivative" works as *Grande fantaisie sur la tyrolienne de l'opéra La Fiancée de Auber* (S385) or *Grande fantaisie di bravura sur La Clochette de Paganini* (S420). Instead of cobbling together preexisting music, the *Harmonies* borrowed name and character from a literary work and a literary style: the recently published collection of religious poems by *poète-législateur* Alphonse de Lamartine (1830) and his famously anticlassical or "styleless" verse. Writing to Marie d'Agoult on 30 October 1833, Liszt called it "my small Lamartian harmony without key or time" (ma petite harmonie lamartinienne sans ton ni mesure).[60] In the sketchbook he was working with from 16 May, Liszt—initially thinking in G minor—scribbled a passage from Schiller's unfinished *Der Geisterseher* (1789) over the opening stave, including these words: "Everything has been abandoned [such that] nothing remained, but the sad and piercing stare of a man consumed by the knowledge of man."[61]

By the time of Schlesinger's publication, two years later, the time signature and key signature of the sketch had indeed been abandoned. The printed score of *Harmonies poétiques et religieuses* was not so much "sans ton"—without sharps, flats, or barring—as without music. Paul Merrick interprets Liszt's first use of his trademark signatureless notation here as an attempt at "an impossible idea," a "visible invisibility"—"a vision of something he could not compose."[62] The words "senza tempo" (without tempo) and "avec un profound sentiment d'ennui" (perhaps best translated here as "with a deep sense of emptiness") only darken the veil. The opening off-kilter left-hand oscillations into and away from the C–F♯ tritone over ponderous offbeat accents further rebel against system. Liszt's iconoclastic notational style involves a strange, painstaking attention to every note, every sonority being represented by a welter of articulation, dynamic, pedaling, and verbal cues. The score's focus on detail extends to the barrage of textual instructions: "extremely slow," "heavy," "languid," "with sadness," "highly accented." The first bar line appears mysteriously at the bottom right-hand corner of the first page. What could be the function of this inexplicable line an eighth note before the end of the final system? These—and experiments in marking beats by number later in the piece—evince a highly methodical approach to the avant-garde task of being unmethodical. The purpose is apparently to depict Schiller's mood of abjection and world-weariness by being as incomprehensible as possible—by breaking the rules.

PLAYING AGAINST LAW

Liszt styled himself as the poet-prophet of this antiestablishment pianism, pioneering an experimental approach to hand position, pianistic register, texture, and sonority. Faced with the problem of locating the composer-performer's "position" at the keyboard, François-Joseph Fétis commented on the extent to which the pianist defied classification in 1841:

> Liszt, who allows himself to be guided by the impulse of the moment, and who possessed great powers of execution, is the only pianist who has no fixed position, and who according to the nature of the composition he is performing, places himself, sometimes more to the left, sometimes more to the right. Besides which his body is perpetually in motion.[63]

In an entry dated 15 January 1832, Valérie's lesson book remarked that not only did his hands observe "no fixed position," but also

> he has no touch at all, and, at the same time, he has all possible touches. His fingers are very long, and his hands are small and pointed. He does not keep them in a rounded position. He maintains that this position lends a feeling of dryness to one's playing and this horrifies him. Neither are they altogether flat.[64]

A month later, in February, Caroline expanded on this by remarking that she had been a privileged witness not only of "no method" and "no touch" but of "no piano":

> His small hands are at once delicate and tapering, and so flexible that they carry out whatever is demanded of them. With all that, they are powerful enough to break the keys at will. His touch is absolutely his own, and it transforms the sound of the instrument, which under hidden fingers becomes glittering or velvety as required. He coaxes it, possesses it, makes it resound to his heart. It is no longer a piano—but storms, prayers, songs of triumph, transports of joy, heart-rending despair.[65]

This metapianism, familiar to every critic who has ever followed d'Ortigue in praising Liszt for the "orchestrality" of his perfoming manner, achieved ultimate expression under the pen of pianophile Wilhelm von Lenz, who sought lessons in 1828:

> It is an accidental circumstance, of no importance, that Liszt happens to play the piano at all. Perhaps in a higher sense, this is not the case, . . . the piano being merely visible. . . . [Yet] it is altogether uncritical to say that Liszt does this or that differently from somebody else. Do not imagine that Liszt does anything—he "does" nothing at all; he "thinks," and what he thinks takes on this form. That is the process. Can it really be called piano-playing?[66]

The effects of dematerialization were as much a feature of his teaching as his playing. Liszt, in fact, anticipated several later-century pedagogical schemes, where, if fingerings or hand positions were chosen, they were not selected with the visible conformation of the five-digit hand in question. Instead, decisions were made on the basis of hidden functions: either in view of the external purpose of "the work" or the expressive potential of the student. Intangibles like the invisible weight of the arm, its transference from finger to finger, real legato (which, of course, can only be approximated on the pianoforte), and such unquantifiables as "energy" or "spirit" became new fascinations. Those familiar (and, on reflection, Byzantine) modern notions that the pupil play "from the arm," "toes," "back," or "stomach" emerged for similar reasons. Underscoring his turn from method, Liszt pioneered the practice of reading literature to his pupils, though for different reasons than Kalkbrenner, who was apparently the first to recommend enjoying a good novel while exercizing the fingers. In January 1832 Valérie Boissier, for one, had Victor Hugo's *Ode to Jenny* recited to her in an apparent attempt to improve her performance of a Moscheles étude.[67]

Liszt began to treat not so much the hands of his students as their souls, another reason why, particularly later in life, the master began to seem so messianic. In 1882 Carl Lachmund recalled, "Liszt's teaching cannot be codified; he strove for the spirit of the work; and music, like religion, has no language; he taught as Christ taught religion, in an allegorical way, or by metaphor. But magical was the effect of his influence. Those sufficiently advanced to undertand, acquired from the great master what they could not have found anywhere else in the world, then or now, at whatever price. Of plain technic he said little or nothing. Why should he have done?"[68] Liszt was merely chief witness to a new covenant that would supersede the old Hebraic law. (Kalkbrenner's father, after all, was Jewish.) His was a Catholic style of pedagogy, based not on rules, dictums, or orderings of the hand but on an intimate knowledge, indeed love, of each of his students.

If not priests, pianist-pedagogues might imagine themselves as doctors, such was their concern for the health of each of their students. Liszt's teacher Carl Czerny wrote in his *Letters to a Young Lady on the Art of Playing the Pianoforte* (1838) that "the fingers are little disobedient creatures, if they are not kept well-reined in; and they are apt to run off like an unbroken colt as soon as they have gained some degree of fluency."[69] Such afflictions, he clarified in his *Vollständige theoretisch-practische Pianoforte-Schule* of a year later, were best remedied in terms of the individual pathology of each patient:

> The Teacher who will honestly and assiduously apply himself to his calling, has quite as much occasion to reflect and to study, as the Pupil. He will find himself at the commencement of his career in the situation of a young Physician, who, after long study will still often be embarrassed at the bed-side of the sick. He must observe the character and capabilities of his Pupils, and act with them accordingly. He must by diligent practice cultivate more and more his [the Pupil's] own style of playing.[70]

These requirements demonstrated the extent to which teaching had moved from the goal of skills acquisition to such antimethods as would "normalize" students in the mode of the new health sciences. Another first-rate pupil of Czerny, Theodor Leschetizky famously toed the Lisztian line when he replied to a query from a friend in the United States in the following terms: "I have no technical method. . . . How is it possible one should have them? One pupil needs this, another that; the hand of each differs; the brain of each differs. There can be no rule. I am a doctor to whom my pupils come as patients to be cured of their musical ailments, and the remedy must vary in each case."[71] The duty of piano teachers, in other words, was to care for body and soul in ways that went beyond petty questions of material contingency.

BEYOND HANDS

Liszt's ideological triumph was sealed on 16 April 1832, when, at the height of his "makeover" struggles, he somehow managed to get through an important private performance of Carl Maria von Weber's *Konzertstück*, op. 79, despite a severely dislocated finger.[72] The story goes that his right thumb had been so badly injured while practicing that Liszt initially believed it broken. The whole event was a triumph of the will: "La divine Thérèse," indefatigable hostess for the occasion, refused to discontinue concert giving because of such trifling matters as cholera or revolution. Hers, indeed, was a premier salon in Paris, located within the high walls of the Austro-Hungarian embassy, on rue Saint-Dominique in the Faubourg Saint-Germain. This elite venue guarded its political conservatism jealously; the Count and Countess Antoine Apponyi (in defiance of circumstance) still refused to recognize titles bestowed during the Empire.

Liszt was no less defiant in his 1832 performance: the journal of Thérèse's son recorded how, in the section where he would have felt the most pain, at the climactic cadenza before the return of the theme, the pianist replaced Weber's glissando with a rapid double-octave run up the keyboard. "He is especially amazing in a passage, written entirely in octaves, which he plays with such rapidity and such force that the hands seem to multiply. It was impossible to follow with my eyes their rapid, inconceivable motions; they flew from one end of the piano to the other."[73] Dana Gooley interprets Apponyi's words to mean that Liszt improvised a chromatic scale at this point of thematic reentry, with "hands in alternating octaves" in patented style, "the constant repositioning of the hand between white and black keys, combin[ing] with the high velocity [to] create a dizzying visual effect." The audience, in other words, would have seen fingers disappearing in a blur.[74]

Many years later, in 1875, Count Apponyi's great-nephew Albert—before he became a Hungarian nationalist politician—reported a similar instance in which Liszt's hands vanished into insignificance. In this case the virtuoso was obliged to get through Beethoven's "Emperor" Concerto, op. 73, in Budapest, Hans Richter conducting, without the use of the third finger on his right hand.

> On the morning [of the concert] . . . to our dismay, we found [Liszt] with the third finger of his right hand bound up. "Yes," he said smiling, "as you see, I have cut myself."

We thought there would be no concert now, and asked the Master's opinion. "Why," he answered, "of course I shall play tonight!" "And your bad finger?" "Oh, I shall have to do without it" was all his reply.

That evening, he actually played the E-flat Major Concerto without using the third finger of his right hand, and not a soul detected it! Such was Liszt, the pianist. He played no less wonderfully than on the previous day.[75]

Such "beyond the hand" anecdotes were commonly told, lest we be tempted to think that they were only the effect of some strange quirk in the Apponyi family.

On 12 June 1841, to cite an English report, Liszt appeared for one of his marathon self-styled "recitals" in front of a packed audience at London's Willis's Rooms. Less than two weeks earlier, as everyone knew, he had suffered a serious coach accident while returning from dinner with German soprano Sophie Loewe and Austro-Hungarian diplomat Philipp von Neumann.[76] The horses bolted; the cab overturned; Liszt was dashed to the ground. The incident caused a "contusion" on his head, put his arm in a sling, and—most seriously—sprained his left wrist. Leeches were applied. "In spite of a weakness in the left hand, which, with anyone else would have amounted to disqualification," the *Athenaeum* reported of the recital, "his performance left all other pianoforte performance far behind it."[77] According to the *Times,* the "laurelled conqueror" might have been impressive in the three-stave "il canto espressivo ed appassionata assai" of *Fantaisie sur des motifs favoris de l'opéra La sonnambula* (S393), the left-hand thumb singing Elvino's despairing "Tutto è sciolto." But he truly shone at the appearance of the final joyous melody of the opera, "Ah! non giunge." Here Liszt trumped Thalberg's three-hand trick—sprained wrist and all—by mashing up two operatic themes, the celebratory finale and the viciously twisted cabaletta following Elvino's previous cantabile (where he confronts Amina for wrecking his life). "The most extraordinary [tour de force] was a variation, in which the theme and an accompaniment were distinctly heard in the middle octaves of the instrument while a brilliant trill [sic] in the treble and a powerful bass were kept up, thus producing all the effect of four hands."[78]

Three years later, still in metadigital mode, Liszt played his own piano version of Bach's A-minor Prelude and Fugue for organ, BWV 543 (S462/1) for the Montpellier artist, geologist, archaeologist, early music collector, organist, and Bach fanatic Jean-Joseph-Bonaventure Laurens. The difficulty of the transcription failed to prevent the enjoyment of a good cigar, apparently in the nonchalant keyboard-playing style of *opéra-comique* composer André-Ernest-Modeste Grétry.[79] Laurens's younger brother, Jules, remembered the conversation thus:

"How do you want me to play it?"
"How? But . . . the way it ought to be played."

"Here it is, to start with, as the author must have understood it, played it himself, or intended it to be played." And Liszt played. And it was admirable, the perfection itself of the classical style exactly in conformity with the original.

"Here it is a second time, as I feel it, with a slightly more picturesque movement, a more modern style and the effects demanded by an improved instrument." And it was, with these nuances, different . . . but no less admirable.

"Finally, a third time, here it is the way I would play it for the public—to astonish, as a charlatan." And, lighting a cigar which passed at moments between his lips to his fingers, executing with his ten fingers the part written for the organ pedals, and indulging in other *tours de force* and prestidigitation, he was prodigious, incredible, fabulous, and received gratefully with enthusiasm.[80]

Such "cigar" or "missing finger" stunts became ubiquitous. Berthold Kellermann, one of Liszt's latter-day acolytes (a pupil from 1873 to 1878), recalled how they had once attended an organ recital together. His master's favorite Bach Fugue for organ in G minor, BWV 542/2 (which Liszt published in piano transcription along with BWV 543 in 1852) was heard: "An organist who lacked the third finger of his right hand once gave a recital in a church, the chief item being Bach's great Fugue in G Minor. Liszt, the greatest player and connoisseur of Bach, said to me when the church was emptied: 'Kellermann, that missing middle finger trick I can do too. Look!' And before my eyes he played this difficult fugue while in *both* hands stretching out and avoiding the use of the middle finger."[81]

Liszt apparently cared little for playing Bach fugues and the "Emperor" Concerto with less than the full complement of fingers. His official biographer, Lina Ramann, remembered a conversation in October 1876 in which she dropped the name of Louis Böhner, E. T. A. Hoffmann's model for Kapellmeister Kreisler, the otherwise forgettable German composer-organist who had performed a fugue for her despite two lame fingers: "[Liszt] answered nothing; but with a certain tension of the muscles of the face, he seated himself at the piano and began to play a difficult fugue by Bach, with *three fingers* of each hand. The tension soon yielded to an evident satisfaction: he had tried if he could do anything similar, and having succeeded, he left off playing."[82] Another anecdote involved a charity concert for the Beethoven monument in Vienna on 16 March 1877. On the morning of the composer's half-century commemoration, Liszt apparently cut a finger while shaving. (The composer asserted the truth of this incident later in a letter to August Göllerich.) Ramann wrote:

A short time after this [three-finger] incident, Liszt had to learn that he could help himself with four fingers, even in long pieces of music, and that without the slightest prejudice to his execution. He had hurt the second finger of the left hand just at the time that he performed in public, at Vienna, Beethoven's Concerto in E Flat major, and his fantasia for choir, for the benefit of the Vienna Beethoven fund. This was in

March 1877, and though an old man of sixty-six, he played with a power and beauty that left everything behind, and no one perceived that all the parts for the left hand were executed without the second finger.[83]

Here again was proof of how little Liszt's hands mattered, how he lived beyond them, and how much they served art.

TOUCH, DON'T LOOK!

It seems disappointing to end this chapter by concluding that piano music cannot be played without hands, though this banal point seems to need iteration. The story of Liszt's long-suffering hands would be only mildly amusing, of course, were it not that twenty-first-century keyboard pedagogy and practice *tout court* is still so in thrall to the fiction, originally promulgated in relation to Liszt, that pianists must work beyond their hands. A whole raft of institutions, conservatories, music teachers, and even academic scholarship has long been devoted to this faintly ridiculous idea: that hands have little to do with pianistic expression, interpretation, or "the music itself."

Alan Walker perpetuates the old metapianism when he writes that "the last thing the supreme master of the keyboard was concerned with was the physical problems associated with the instrument."[84] The master would have been even more delighted with true believer Pauline Pocknell, who wrote, "Liszt well knew the source of exceptional musical performance on a keyboard instrument: it lay in the brain; it had nothing to do with lucky inheritance of a particular hand type. . . . He knew that hand dimensions were immaterial: true musically sensitive natures would adapt their technique to their own unique bodily structure in order to produce, somehow or another, beautiful sound as conceived in the mind."[85] Proclamations like this come dangerously close to implying that hands play no part in music making. Recall the words of the Viennese critic Heinrich Adami, in the *Allgemeine Theaterzeitung* of 5 May 1838, reviewing a 2 May midweek concert in Vienna's Vereinssaale: "Just as Lessing declared that Raphael would have become the greatest painter even had he come into the world without hands, so equally might this be said of Liszt as a pianist."[86]

The impulse to disavow handedness is, to be blunt, pure romantic mystification, just as any attempt to sanctify or deny the partisanship, possession, bias, or worldliness of one's actions is always already political. At a key moment in the emergence of the familiar idealist conceit of Art-Religion or Music-as-Literature, Liszt (and others) began to experience hands less as instruments of action than as creatures belonging to nature—relational, uncanny, occult, corrupting, even criminal. Operating at the threshold of the absolute, their very presence threatened not only the purity of the music but the truth of expression itself. Thus the shame of making a spectacle of one's hands; thus the Liszt-inspired practice of looking away from hands—reading "invisible literature" at the keyboard; thus the new, secretive, machine-operated mode of criminal execution adopted for parricides in Paris.

The plaster casts or molds of Liszt's hands now littering music museums in Europe (at least ten impressions were made during his lifetime) are eerie for these reasons, not because we have always been squeamish about the fact of our own handedness. The sight of a pianist's hands was just as nerve-racking for Liszt's contemporaries as it is for his disciples today. Amy Fay, one of the maestro's groupies in the 1870s, could observe that "[Liszt's] whole appearance and manner have a sort of Jesuitical elegance and ease." But then, with some unease, she continued, "His hands are very narrow, with long and slender fingers that look as if they had twice as many joints as other people's. They are so flexible and supple that it makes you nervous to look at them."[87] Camille Saint-Saëns was no less unsettled: "The fingers of Liszt were not human fingers."[88] American journalist Anne Hampton Brewster shone light into the gloom in 1878 when she performed a reading (in devilish detail) of one of his formless hands:

> It is a mixed [hand]; that is, the fingers are varied, some are round, some square and some flat or spatula; this is the true hand of an artist, for it betokens form and idea. The palm is covered with rays, betraying that his life has been an agitated, eventful one, full of passion and emotion—but the philosophic and material noeuds, or knots, on the Apollo and Mercury fingers, the logic and will on that wonderful long thumb, which extends beyond the middle joint of the forefinger shows how this remarkable man has been able to conquer instincts and govern temperament. . . . The Jupiter [forefinger] and Saturn [middle finger] are square; the ring, or Apollo, and little or Mercury fingers are spatula, flat and broad. The second phalange of the Jupiter finger is longer than the first. . . . The Saturn finger is full of knots. There is a wart on the Apollo finger of the right hand. The force of the little finger on both hands is tremendous; the knuckle seems as if made of iron.[89]

Liszt's hands were, in other words, diabolical. You could look, particularly if you had gained access to his inner circle, but it was better—or more righteous—to pretend you had not.

THE HAND WRITES ON

All this squeamishness has been lost in the recent musicological obsession with looking and spectacle in Liszt. The model for this style of scholarship traces back to Robert Schumann, who penned these all-too-famous words after an 1840 concert in Dresden:

> I had heard him before; but an artist is a different person in the presence of the public compared with what he appears in the presence of a few. The fine open space, the

glitter of light, the elegantly-dressed audience—all this elevates the frame of mind in giver and receiver. And now the demon's power began to awake; he first played with the public as if to try it, then gave it something more profound, until every single member was enveloped in his art; and then the whole mass began to rise and fall precisely as he willed it. . . . He must be heard—and also seen; for if Liszt played behind the scenes, a great deal of the poetry of his playing would be lost.[90]

Recent musicology has enjoyed rehearsing Schumann's backhanded compliment, this idea that the showman-virtuoso needed to be seen in order to be understood, as if Liszt were somehow special in this regard, as if looking had not been important to all music since time immemorial. At issue here are the supposedly hyperbolic body movements that Liszt brought to keyboard performance in the 1830s: his swaying, extravagant gestures before the instrument, his "expressive" facial features, and his "musical" stage persona.

Liszt scholarship seems unusually concerned with coding the visual as somehow abnormal. The very detail with which his life story has been wrenched from the past in recent biographical writings (my depiction of 1832 included) seems to derive in part from this compulsion to recover a sense of liveness, to reconstruct not only his aural but also his visual presence. As such, armed with not-altogether-unexaggerated nineteenth-century caricatures of the performer, recent scholarship has unmasked the virtuoso's supposedly excessive bodily movements as part of some kind of entrepreneurial strategy to manipulate "mass" markets, advertise "the Liszt brand," make money, and mastermind his unfolding career. The campaign of self-advertising, in other words, has been exposed as the product of emerging cultural phenomena with loose labels such as "modernity," consumer culture, or celebrity culture. Ever the social chameleon, ever the commodity, Liszt might be anything you wanted: sex god, strategist, entrepreneur, careerist, Catholic priest, fake.

There are, however, other ways to read Liszt's choreographic bodily gestures. In their best sense, as even Schumann begrudgingly implied, they were poetic, conceived less in service of spectacle or visual display than as a way of managing the body—of elevating, idealizing, purifying, or spiritualizing keyboard performance. Whether calculated or not, the artist-prophet performed a reborn conception of human physiology, one that would accord with his newly evangelical vision of artistic purity and high-minded concepts of human function. This he achieved, apparently, by extending expressiveness to parts of the body that literally do not "do" anything in performance. Deflecting attention from the hands, he pioneered social practices that placed expression in what were considered higher or more expressive physiological areas, in the process opening the way to what we now call "modern" pianism.

In his last days Liszt's fingers belonged so little to their possessor—they had become so much a function of their environment, so formless, malleable, and insignificant—that they took on the substance to which they had become best attuned. The old digits had apparently lost their natural coloring, or so, at least, was the observation of Mary King Waddington, wife of the prime minister of France. "It was very curious," she wrote after watching them "wander over the keys," break into a nocturne, and play a Hungarian march in 1879: "His fingers looked as if they were made of yellow ivory."[91]

Epilogue

The opening of this book described two iconic moments in which "pure voice" came into its own: at the literal shattering of Rubini's clavicle and the more figurative breaking of Paganini's hands. A later chapter pictured García *fils* with his laryngoscope, an instance mythologized as the historical juncture at which vocal knowledge was finally established upon the primordial bedrock of "modern" science. Then was the story of Liszt's makeover, recounted in the final chapter, where the virtuoso discovered the presence of his body and tapped the source of "modern" pianistic expression. Many more heroes of nineteenth-century performance had similar "Rubini moments," moments of breakthrough in which instruments were shattered and bodies erupted from within. Significantly, these eruptions suggested sexual emergence, hard bourgeois gender norms apparently bursting forth ecstatically.

An episode briefly touched upon was the famous tale of Gilbert-Louis Duprez's chest-high C, where the tenor finally found, according to his own vivid memoir, his primitive masculine self. At an 1831 performance of an Italian version of Rossini's *Guillaume Tell* in Lucca, Duprez reported being so emotionally overwhelmed that he—for lack of a better phrase—"came out." That earth-shattering C exploded at the summit of a famous octave-and-a-half rising scale, as Rossini's Arnold hurtled toward the close of his revolutionary act 4 cabaletta and call to arms, "Amis, amis, secondez ma vengeance." The old "tenorino," as Duprez called his former voice, was annihilated, but only by the concentration, apparently, of all the force of his moral and physical will.[1]

The familiar figure of the modern conductor, to gesture beyond the purview of this book, emerged in similar ways. If anyone most obviously embodied "*the* voice," it was this silent performer taking the stage when Louis Spohr, Carl Maria von Weber, and Felix Mendelssohn toured London in the 1820s. This was a figure who, in the early years, *faced* his audience rather than the band of players. From our point of view, he looked the wrong way.[2] His "unified body" (the true source of "the romantic song," as Barthes would have it) became a kind of focal point for the musical experience. The various voices of what was once a richly diversified ensemble were now united in him, which is to say that the conductor's pantomime and these first experiments in baton conducting were made possible only by an idealist conception of expressive voice. The conductor, in other words, was subject to a peculiar conception of subjective autonomy, his very existence predicated on the idea that vocal sound could be the projection of a single primordial force—the voice of the body, that is, coming to be. It turns out that alongside strange synecdochal notions of "the composer's voice" or "the composer's hand"—this sense of an invisible presence lurking behind musical events—there was another just-as-authoritarian phenomenon, one perhaps even more fundamental to the order of things: "the performer's voice" or "the performer's hand."

The first heroes of modern performance to "get it right," therefore, initially "got it wrong." All romantic origin myths notwithstanding, it was hardly that some inevitable standard of natural musical expression arose of its own accord. My claim is that the commonplace matters of musical understanding that we so triumphantly inherit are in fact crossed by contradiction. Many of the most orthodox assumptions about expressive performance—born of the earliest properly physiological approaches to vocal training, the first registral theories for voice, the beginnings of silent listening, the original "performer's voice," the first "modern" piano philosophies, the castrato's decline, and the emergence of divas—have disconcerting beginnings. A careful review of the evidence suggests that later musical norms emerge haphazardly, being founded, from later points of view, in error.

One prominent thread to draw from the chapters is the sense of musicians working to acquire multiple voices or multiple hands. It turns out that *the* recurring feature of exemplary musicianship in this period was the possession of not one voice but *several* expressive registers. Audiences for vocal music took pleasure in discerning several contrasting voices in the same mouth, or one voice in several mouths. In the case of pianists, a multiplicity of touches was preferred to one banal "inborn" touch or one congenital "voice." (The level of investment made by today's instrumentalists, listeners, recording engineers, and marketing executives in "*the* voice" is astounding, particularly given the blizzard of sound habitually listened through.) Three, four, or five hands would seem impossible for a single pianist to acquire in practice, though—from earlier points of view—this depended on where in the body you place expression. The insistence on "my own voice," in other words, is a phenomenon of very recent vintage.

The question of how musicians place expression in their bodies is key. This issue of placement becomes less than self-explanatory once it is understood that those paragons often thought to be on the cusp of our modernity—Rubini, Paganini, Mendelssohn, Duprez, Liszt—were not the first to tie expression to bodies. Their methods were certainly no more moral than rival techniques. It was just that they articulated different placements, or placed expression elsewhere—admittedly deeper in bodies, and admittedly in parts more abstruse. Whatever the case, it helps to think of their achievements less in the religious terms of transfiguration than in the worldly terms of *refiguration*. These artists cultivated expressive placements that were no more or less embodied or expressive than before. The point was that they were embodied and expressive in a different way.

Which is to say that the dream of unmediated expression or authentic utterance was just that: a dream, founded on just another form of rhetoric, another set of conventions, other matters of musical concern, alternate political ideologies, and competing strategies of training. The fallen angels of romantic performance were only fallen because of the age-old determination to wish the fact of mediation away. It was also why performers *tout court* suffered their "damaged" reputations. Their struggle, as much as any struggle against hands and voices, was as tragic as Heine, doyen of the most literary forms of musical purity, supposed. In a famous farewell to the subjects of these pages, Heine bade them good riddance: "And so the brief ephemeral fame of the *virtuoso* evaporates or vanished like a dying sound, without a trace or echo—like the cry of a camel in the desert."[3] Heine was just one of many serious-minded conservatives of the 1840s—Joseph d'Ortigue, Robert Schumann, Ludwig Rellstab, and J. W. Davison among them—who looked forward to a style of performance that eschewed improvisation, tinsel, flashiness, and "mechanism." Only, in their eagerness to cast spontaneity into the wilderness, these critics did not reckon that they were welcoming in a new kind of virtuosity, albeit a virtuosity of restraint and sleight of hand, by the back door.

These men failed to recognize that, if anything was vanishing, it was hardly "the performer" or "the virtuoso." What was more seriously under threat was the sense that "the music itself" could only ever emerge as a condition of labor. The lesson of history is that the mythic invisibility of music depends on physical effort. If music is an untouchable medium, which it may be, it is only because the means of production have conspired to make it so. Invisible music requires that audiences develop ears to look past what has become "superficial." Most of all, it demands that staged hands and voices cultivate inconspicuousness, which is why "serious" musicians were increasingly hidden in plain sight, and why they styled themselves as if to disappear.

One final thought: I have broached the difficult question of *musical materiality* by expounding on a series of performing situations or case studies, thickly described. I have introduced concert or operatic or pedagogical scenes—manifestations of hands and voices—not as static objects of study but as active sites where the matter of corporeality itself was contested and realized. Instead of taking nature at face value or as a given, then, this book has construed materiality itself as in a continual state of expressive flux. This is what I understand to make musical performance so exhilarating: because these events place the question of what you take as "mechanical," "human," "textual," "improvised," "vocal," "manual," "theatrical," "natural"—the stuff of materiality itself—under intense scrutiny. A close description of the fire and ice of "the given" at any particular moment can be informative on its own because it betrays how distinctions have been made, and what has been discriminated.

Few would deny that we are doing things with our bodies when we make music, that bodies make or index music, or that music comes from bodies. Fewer, I think, would venture that the reverse also applies: that bodies come from music. That when one is making music, one is also indexing a body, or rather that one's body is being indexed. The challenge is to show that when one is playing or singing, there are no stable essences, because what counts as "materiality" is constantly being negotiated. Any number of social factors might be at stake: one's eloquence, style, competence, restraint, expressivity, inconspicuousness, range, beauty, size, moral character, masculinity, individuality, nonindividuality, athleticism, race, sensitivity, nationality, sex, intelligence, and health, to name only a few possible qualities. When it comes to music, judgments are *always* being made and bodies are *always* being discriminated. We ought to be especially vigilant when bodies seem so "natural" as not to be noticed at all.

NOTES

INTRODUCTION

1. François-Henri-Joseph Blaze dit Castil-Blaze, "Le Piano," *Revue de Paris* 12 (1839), 174–96.

2. Francesco Bennati, "Notice physiologique sur Paganini," *Revue de Paris* 26 (May 1831), 52–60, which was a version of a paper read before the Académie des sciences in March 1831.

3. J. J. [Jules Janin], "Hoffman [sic] et Paganini—Conte fantastique," *Journal des débats,* 15 March 1831, 1–2. Louis-François Lhéritier wrote of "cette espèce de dislocation, qui s'opère sans efforts, ne peut être que le résultat d'une longue habitude" under his pseudonym Georges Imbert de Laphalèque, *Notice sur le célèbre violoniste Nicolo Paganini* (Paris, 1830), 54.

4. Gary Tomlinson, who elsewhere calls for a "cantology" or "carmenology" that would resist what he calls the "metaphysics" latent in the practice of musicology, opens his chapter "Modern Opera" with words pertinent to the "uncanny voice" of both Rubini's and Paganini's breaking body:

> The operatic voice had always been powerful, but before the early nineteenth century it was not so uncanny. . . . Unlike the voice of the Cartesian subject, which in its representation pointed beyond itself to a transhuman harmony, the modern voice is altogether human. Its revelation of mystery points not out but inward, toward the center of human knowledge that now encompasses its own supersensible realm. This voice consists, like the modern subject it describes, in a doubling over on itself of empirical and transcendental fields. It is a place where the phenomenal world extends itself to a noumenal margin, so it holds out the hope of embodying before our ears, finally, a transcendental object. Its most congenial space of operation is at the borders marking off phenomena from noumena, conditioned from unconditioned thought. Its operations in this space summon a sense of the uncanny.

For "cantology," see Gary Tomlinson, "Vico's Songs: Detours at the Origins of (Ethno) musicology," *Musical Quarterly* 83/3 (1999), 344–77, and Gary Tomlinson, *Metaphysical Song* (Princeton, 1999), 73, 83–84.

5. Carolyn Abbate, "Music: Drastic or Gnostic?" *Critical Inquiry* 30 (2004), 505–36; Elisabeth Le Guin, *Boccherini's Body: An Essay in Carnal Musicology* (Berkeley and Los Angeles, 2006). I have only been able to write as I do because of my drastic-carnal interlocutors, who blazed the trail for me here. The tone of their writing is powerfully reflected in mine.

6. Roland Barthes, *The Responsibility of Forms*, trans. Richard Howard (Berkeley, 1991), 286–92, 288.

7. Ibid., 289. In 1889 Friedrich Nietzsche famously wrote in praise of what I would call the "biology is destiny" position or the "just-there body"—history itself succumbing to the soma's shattering primordial force. See *The Will to Power*, trans. Walter Kauffmann and R. J. Hollingdale (New York, 1968), 358.

> Put briefly, perhaps the entire evolution of the spirit is a question of the body; it is the history of the development of a higher body that emerges into our sensibility. The organic is rising to yet higher levels. Our lust for knowledge of nature is a means through which the body desires to perfect itself. Or rather: hundreds of thousands of experiments are made to change the nourishment, the mode of living and of dwelling of the body: consciousness and evaluations in the body, all kinds of pleasure and displeasure, are signs of these changes and experiments. It is not a question of man at all: he is to be overcome.

8. Adriana Cavarero, *For More Than One Voice: Toward a Philosophy of Vocal Expression* (Stanford, 2005), 4; Wayne Koestenbaum, *The Queen's Throat: Opera, Homosexuality, and the Mystery of Desire* (New York, 1993), 155; Clemens Risi, "Opera in Performance: In Search of New Analytical Approaches," *Opera Quarterly* 27/2–3 (2011), 283–95, 286.

9. For Renée Fleming's "story of how I found my voice, of how I worked to shape it, and of how it, in turn, shaped me," see her *The Inner Voice: The Making of a Singer* (New York, 2004), n.p.

10. See, for example, Emily I. Dolan and John Tresch, "A Sublime Invasion: Meyerbeer, Balzac, and the Opera Machine," *Opera Quarterly* 27/1 (2011), 4–31; David Trippett, *Wagner's Melodies: Aesthetics and Materialism in German Musical Identity* (Cambridge, 2013); Benjamin Steege, *Helmholtz and the Modern Listener* (Cambridge, 2012); Lorraine Daston and Peter Galison, *Objectivity* (New York, 2007).

11. For a famous rumination on these matters, see Judith Butler, "Introduction," in *Bodies That Matter: On the Discursive Limits of Sex* (New York, 1993, 2011), xi–xxx. See also Bruno Latour, "How to Talk about the Body? The Normative Dimension of Science Studies," *Body and Society* 10/2–3 (2004), 205–29.

12. Shigehisa Kuriyama, *The Expressiveness of the Body and the Divergence of Greek and Chinese Medicine* (New York, 2002), 60.

13. Carolyn Abbate, *Unsung Voices: Opera and Musical Narrative in the Nineteenth Century* (Princeton, 1991).

14. Steven Feld, Aaron A. Fox, Thomas Porcello, and David Samuels, "Vocal Anthropology: From the Music of Language to the Language of Song," in *A Companion to Linguistic Anthropology,* ed. A. Duranti (Oxford, 2004), 321–46.

15. For the now standard phenomenological view in opera studies, see Clemens Risi, "Opera in Performance: In Search of New Analytical Approaches," *Opera Quarterly* 27/2–3 (2011), 283–95. Italian feminist writer Adriana Cavarero begins a recent book, *For More Than One Voice,* with Italo Calvino's biopolitical position on vocal materiality: "A voice means this: there is a living person, throat, chest, feelings, who sends into the air the voice, different from all other voices." For a thoughtful riposte, see Mary Ann Smart's review "Theorizing Gender, Culture and Music," *Women and Music: A Journal of Gender and Culture* 6 (2005), 106–10.

16. Susan Rutherford, *The Prima Donna and Opera, 1815–1930* (Cambridge, 2006); Dana Gooley, *The Virtuoso Liszt* (Cambridge, 2004).

17. Gooley does an admirable job of explicating Liszt's strategic ascension to myth in "Franz Liszt: The Virtuoso as Strategist," in *The Musician as Entrepreneur, 1700–1914: Managers, Charlatans, and Idealists,* ed. William Weber (Bloomington, 2004), 145–61.

18. Simon Schaffer, "Indiscipline and Interdisciplines: Some Exotic Genealogies of Modern Knowledge" (2010), www.fif.tu-darmstadt.de/aktuelles_2/vergangeneveranstaltungen/veranstaltungen_details_fif_4224.de.jsp. See also the introduction to the 2011 edition of Steven Shapin and Simon Schaffer, *Leviathan and the Air-Pump: Hobbes, Boyle, and the Experimental Life* (Princeton, 1985), xi–l.

19. Bruno Latour, *Reassembling the Social: An Introduction to Actor-Network-Theory* (Oxford, 2005).

20. Jennifer Hall-Witt, *Fashionable Acts: Opera and Elite Culture in London, 1780–1880* (Lebanon NH, 2007), 158.

21. In London the critical scuffle over Rubini broke out as early as June 1833. Taking up its familiar stance against "meritorious" ornament, the *Harmonicon* opposed the French press as well as Rubini's local supporters (the *Examiner,* for instance) by lambasting Rubini's performance of Argirio in Rossini's *Tancredi* as "a continued series of roulades." "With singers like Rubini," the writer mused, "the art of dramatic singing is a mere effort of the *muscles.*" "Of feeling he has not a particle," agreed the *Spectator.* See "The Drama," *Harmonicon* 11/6 (June 1833), 139. Five years later the scuffle turned nastier, with Rubini portrayed as a miserable insect: "Rubini, whose organ has declined, in point of volume, to the tone of a tolerably vigorous gnat in September, 'twiddled' away therewith, to the delight of the lieges, who indeed all but held their breath in order to hear it, because the slightest rustle would have rendered Rubini's voice inaudible." "The Morning Concerts of London/to the Editor of the Spectator," *Spectator* 469 (24 June 1837), 587. By 1837, news of Rubini's "twiddling" had reached even Paris. The tide was turning, as when Joseph d'Ortigue attacked Rubini for being vocally unclassifiable, that is, for not being "a true tenor," or for violating what the critic took to be the natural order of things, in "Du chant italien et chant parisien," *Journal de Paris,* 20 March 1837, 1–2.

22. The best account of "diva conduct" as indulgent resistance is still Wayne Koestenbaum's *The Queen's Throat.*

23. Nash converted New Street into Regent Street by widening the thoroughfare, building national and royal landmarks to mark its path, and erecting arcades, which arched like repeated mollusk shells down the hill toward Waterloo Place and the King's Theatre.

24. For a triumphalist account of this "transformation in behavior," see James H. Johnson, *Listening in Paris: A Cultural History* (Berkeley and Los Angeles, 1995). For a wonderful counterview, see Mary Ann Smart's review in *19th-Century Music* 20/3 (Spring 1997), 291–97.

1. "VELUTI IN SPECULUM"

1. The *Times* of the following day lauded Velluti's "powerful expression and elegance of ornament" in his aria and hailed Sontag for "that peculiar style of expression which the Germans denominate 'soul-singing,' and of which some critics have erroneously supposed her incapable." *Times,* 16 May 1829, 5b.

2. For the letter of 18 May 1829, see Eduard Devrient, *My Recollections of Felix Mendelssohn-Bartholdy, and His Letters to Me,* trans. Natalia MacFarren (London, 1869), 76; and Paul Jourdan, "Mendelssohn in England," Ph.D. diss. (University of Cambridge, 1998), 91.

3. *New Monthly Magazine and Literary Journal* 15/56 (1 August 1825), 344. The use of this entrance aria is interesting. For Meyerbeer's third version of *Il crociato,* given in Trieste in 1824, the role of Armando was not taken by Velluti but fell to mezzo Carolina Bassi. In this production, overseen by Meyerbeer, the entry of the ships into Damietta in the eighth scene did not introduce Felicia (as in the original Venetian production). Nor did it introduce Armando (as in the second Florentine version). Rather, it gave prominence to Adriano, the Grand Master of the Knights of Rhodes, tenor Nicola Tacchinardi, and his "Popoli dell'Egitto." For the later London production, probably on Meyerbeer's instruction, Velluti ditched "Cara mano dell'amore," the aria he preferred in Florence, and exchanged it for a transposed version of "Popoli dell'Egitto."

4. "Music," *New Monthly Magazine and Literary Journal* 24/88 (1 April 1826), 153–56, 155.

5. *La Pandore* recorded his arrival on 8 April 1825, noting that all the roles for his type were already occupied by women at the Salle Louvois (the company would move into the Salle Favart in November). "Théâtre-Italien," in *Le Théâtre-Italien de Paris 1801–1831: chronologie et documents,* ed. Jean Mongrédien (Paris, 2008), 6: 86–87. By the end of the month *Le Diable boiteux* remarked that, in Paris, the castrato had only been heard in private concerts. "Théâtre royal italien," in *Le Théâtre-Italien de Paris,* 6: 95.

6. More than this narrative rested on a castrato's provision. According to Stendhal, Velluti had been responsible not only for the success of many *prime donne,* but also for the whole historical trajectory of nineteenth-century song. By way of explaining the *canto d'agilità* of Rossini's *Semiramide,* the author described how the composer met Velluti in Milan for *Aureliano in Palmira* (1814). The male soprano was then at the height of his fame, "one of the handsomest men of his century." In rehearsal Velluti could be heard embroidering Arsace's second-act aria. Rossini found his original—"Perchè mai le luci aprimmo"—so buried in *gorgheggi* that he decided there and then to end such license. From *Aureliano* on, Stendhal has Rossini resolving, "Every scrap of ornamentation, every vestige of a *fioritura,* will constitute an integral part of the song itself, and the whole lot, without exception, will be noted down in the score." Thus, Stendhal explains, did Rossini wrest power away from the singer. Behind the veneer of Rossini's "second manner" and his "revolution" in vocal style (as witnessed in *Semiramide*), the anecdote suggests, there is pride, emptiness, and the uncanny presence of a eunuch; see Stendhal, *Life of Rossini,* trans. Richard N. Coe (London,

1985), 340. Although it is common knowledge that the anecdote's identification of a "revolution" does not bear scrutiny in Rossini's scores, audiences in the 1820s and '30s are likely to have believed Stendhal's story.

7. I have borrowed this notion of the castrato's "charge" from Heather Hadlock, *Mad Loves: Women and Music in Offenbach's "Les Contes d'Hoffmann"* (Princeton, 2000), 120.

8. Mladen Dolar, *A Voice and Nothing More* (Cambridge, MA, 2006), 31–32.

9. "[In terms of] the transmutation of spiritual narrative into psychological theory," Suzanne Kirschner has written, "Romanticism [specifically 'the literature and poetry of the likes of Schiller, Schelling, Fichte, Hegel, Hölderlin, Novalis, Kleist, Blake, Keats, Shelley, Coleridge, Wordsworth, and others'] was the great pivot-point in Western spiritual history." Kirschner, *The Religious and Romantic Origins of Psychoanalysis* (Cambridge, 1996), 1, 162.

10. Stinging attacks by John Dennis, Joseph Addison, and Richard Steele in the early eighteenth century are well known. Suzanne Aspden ascribes the vitriol to a "complex but gradually spreading concept in eighteenth-century Britain," "the belief that truth to one's own values comes before adherence to social values." For more on this "new solipsism," see Aspden, "'An Infinity of Factions': Opera in Eighteenth-Century Britain and the Undoing of Society," *Cambridge Opera Journal* 9 (1997), 1–19, 11. Todd S. Gilman traces such attacks to a 1653 treatise by John Bulwer; see Gilman, "The Italian (Castrato) in London," in *The Work of Opera: Genre, Nationhood, and Sexual Difference,* ed. Richard Dellamora and Daniel Fischlin (New York, 1997), 49–72, 50. For a more recent treatment, see Martha Feldman, "Denaturing the Castrato," *Opera Quarterly* 24/3–4 (2008), 178–99. John Rosselli's classic "The Castrati as a Professional Group and a Social Phenomenon, 1550–1850" appears in *Acta Musicologica* 60 (1988), 143–79.

11. *Atlas,* 4 January 1827, 12b.

12. Gregory W. Bloch, "The Pathological Voice of Gilbert-Louis Duprez," *Cambridge Opera Journal* 19/1 (2007), 11–31.

13. For James Rennie's and Richerand's *double mécanisme,* see *The Art of Improving the Voice and Ear; and of Increasing Their Musical Powers* (London, 1825), 27; *Nouveaux élémens de physiologie* (Paris, 1820), 2: 377; Félix Savart, "Mémoire sur la voix humaine," *Annales de chimie et de physique* 30 (September 1825), 64–87.

14. See Charles Wheatstone's review of Robert Willis et al. in C. W., *London and Westminster Review* 11 (1838), 27–41; John Barclay, *A New Anatomical Nomenclature* (London, 1803), 72.

15. Pierre Nicolas Gerdy, "Voix," in *Encyclopédie méthodique, médecine, par une société de médecins,* 16 vols. (Paris, 1830), 15: 479–93, 490.

16. Robley Dunglison, *Human Physiology,* 2 vols. (Philadelphia, 1832), 1: 378; Colombat de l'Isère, *Traité médico-chirurgical des maladies des organes de la voix* (Paris, 1834), 39; Guillaume Dupuytren, "Note sur le développement du larynx dans les eunuques," 143.

17. Thomas Laqueur famously argues that this period witnessed a move from a one-sex to a two-sex ordering of gender, where "the female body came no longer to be understood as a lesser version of the male's." This shift seems well borne out in Italian and French opera of the 1830s, in which the vocal personalities of the onstage male and female diverge sharply. See Laqueur, *Making Sex: Body and Gender from the Greeks to Freud* (Cambridge, MA, 1990), viii.

18. [William Lawrence], "Generation," in *Cyclopædia, or Universal Dictionary of Arts, Sciences, and Literature*, ed. Abraham Rees, 39 vols. (London, 1819), 16: n.p.

19. This is Barthes's extension of Kristeva's notion of a geno- and phenotext. See Roland Barthes, "The Grain of the Voice," in *Image, Music, Text*, trans. Stephen Heath (New York, 1977), 181; Julia Kristeva, *Revolution in Poetic Language*, trans. Margaret Waller (New York, 1984), 86.

20. Elizabeth Grosz, *Volatile Bodies* (Bloomington, 1994).

21. For more on this shift, see Richard Wistreich, "Reconstructing Pre-Romantic Singing Technique," *The Cambridge Companion to Singing*, ed. John Potter (Cambridge, 2002), 178–91.

22. Extract from the *Cork Southern Reporter*, quoted in *Harmonicon* 7 (1829), 140.

23. In 1966 Michel Foucault famously described the "early nineteenth-century" moment when "man" came to exist as an object of knowledge, "when natural history becomes biology, when the analysis of wealth becomes economics, when, above all, reflection upon language becomes philology." "To man's experience a body has been given," he wrote,

> a body which is his body—a fragment of ambiguous space, whose peculiar and irreducible spatiality is nevertheless articulated upon the space of things; to this same experience, desire is given as a primordial appetite on the basis of which all things assume value . . . the discovery that knowledge has anatomo-physiological conditions, that it is formed gradually within the structures of the body, that it may have a privileged place within it, but that its forms cannot be dissociated from its peculiar functioning; in short, that there is a nature of human knowledge that determines its forms and that can at the same time be made manifest to it in its own empirical contents. (*The Order of Things: An Archaeology of the Human Sciences*, trans. Alan Sheridan (New York, 1994), 312)

24. François Magendie distinguished this "native voice" from the true "voix proprement dite ou acquise" in *Précis élémentaire de physiologie*, 2 vols. (Paris, 1816), 1: 226.

25. See Alan Richardson, *British Romanticism and the Science of the Mind* (Cambridge, 2000).

26. Signor Pergetti sung his own "Quel tuo girar del ciglio" at a Società Armonica concert in the Hanover Square Rooms; see *Musical World* 19/19 (9 May 1844), 158–59. Later in the century he produced a vocal tutor striking for its "Grammar of Singing," a series of miniature compositions based on selected ornaments. See Paolo Pergetti, *Treatise on Singing Forming a Complete School of the Art* (London, 1858).

27. Honoré de Balzac, "Sarrasine," in Roland Barthes, *S/Z*, trans. Richard Miller (London, 1975), 221–54, 229.

28. For more on the move from a mechanistic/dualistic universe to biological/embodied particularity, see Richardson, *British Romanticism and the Science of the Mind*, 152, 179. Richardson argues that the sensationalist, David Hartleyian, "blank slate" or mechanistic conceptions of the mind were replaced by biological approaches to material psychology influenced by early radicals such as Franz Joseph Gall. Richardson surveys turn-of-the-century discourse on Africans, women, children, mutes, and so on in terms of the "turn to

the body that marks the larger field of Romantic discourse." He writes of this turn that "a conception of human nature that refuses to transcend or deny the body—that *begins* in the body and its brain—can help to affirm a common humanity or to engineer a systematic hierarchy of human differences." See also Edward S. Reed, *From Soul to Mind: The Emergence of Psychology* (New Haven, 1997).

29. *London Magazine* 2 (1 July 1825), 474. Silke Leopold has described how the castrato (in voice and figure) perfectly embodied the manly virtues and courtly ideals of the ancien régime. The corrective move here has been to eschew the preoccupation, begun in the nineteenth century, with the castrato's (atypical) sexuality. Leopold, "'Not Sex but Pitch': Kastraten als Liebhaber—Einmal 'über' der Gürtellenie betrachtet," *Provokation und Tradition: Erfahrungen mit der alten Musik*, ed. Hans-Martin Linde and Regula Rapp (Stuttgart-Weimar, 2000), 219–40. For a classic overview, see Rosselli, "The Castrati as a Professional Group."

30. Quoted and discussed in Philippe Lacoue-Labarthe, *Typography: Mimesis, Philosophy, Politics*, ed. Christopher Fynsk (Cambridge, MA, 1989), 259.

31. John Ebers, *Seven Years of the King's Theatre* (London, 1828), 271.

32. Malibran failed to follow the advice of her brother Manuel García, who suggested that singers "should avoid excesses of all kinds: of diet, habits or conduct," including dried fruits and "exciting drinks." See Manuel García, *École de Garcia. Traité complet de l'art du chant* (1840), trans. Donald Paschke, 2 vols. (New York, 1975), 1: 5.

33. The poem appeared as the lead article or "advertisement" on the front page of "Velluti to His Revilers." The six-column defense argued that to "load him personally with abuse" was unfair. "Why with curses load the sufferer? / Was I the cause of what I mourn? Did I / Unmake myself, and hug deformity? / Did I, a smiling and trusting child . . . / Call for the knife? And not resist in vain, / With shrieks, convulsive and a fiery pain, / That second baptism, bloody and profane." *Examiner* 914 (7 August 1825), 495.

34. *Athenaeum* 39 (23 July 1828), 621.

35. Rennie, *The Art of Improving the Voice and Ear*, 67–74.

36. Nowhere was the castrato's potent mutability better proved than by an anecdote that began to circulate during the last decade of the eighteenth century. This incident, observed around 1765 and told by Johann Wilhelm von Archenholz in *A Picture of Italy*, trans. Joseph Trapp (London, 1791), is quoted in Angus Heriot, *The Castrati in Opera* (London, 1960), 47. In it, a musico experiences the essential fluidity of sex while "live" on stage. "This man [Balani] was born without any visible signs of those parts which are taken out on castration; an opinion, which was even confirmed by his voice. . . . One day, he exerted himself so uncommonly in singing an arietta, that all of a sudden those parts, which had so long been concealed by nature, dropped into their proper place. The singer at this very instant lost his voice, which became even perceptible in the same performance, and with it he lost every prospect of a future subsistence." Balani, not a true castrato, suffered a case of what Richard C. Sha calls "wandering testes." Even in 1830s London, one's maleness was often observed to drop into place in such unforeseen ways. One's sex, according to the influential mid-eighteenth-century observations of John Hunter, shifted according to one's shifting testes, which might descend from the abdomen in some persons, be absorbed, or indeed move against gravity according to the vicissitudes of sexual disposition. Vocal sound, this story suggested, was key to establishing one's place along the female-male continuum. Sex was fluid,

never merely here or there. Richard C. Sha, *Perverse Romanticism: Aesthetics and Sexuality in Britain, 1750–1832* (Baltimore, 2009), 96.

37. For the derivation of the term *musico,* see Marco Beghelli, "Il ruolo del musico," in *Donizetti, Napoli, l'Europa,* ed. Franco Carmelo Greco and Renato Di Benedetto (Naples, 2000), 323–35.

38. Rossini used these words in a letter of 26 August 1868 to the Italian music critic Filippo Filippi. See Rodolfo Celletti, *A History of Bel Canto,* trans. Frederick Fuller (Oxford, 1991), 136.

39. The work of Heather Hadlock grounds much of this discussion of the female contralto. See, for example, her portraits of Pasta, Pisaroni, and Brambilla in "Women Playing Men in Italian Opera, 1810–1835," in *Women's Voices across Musical Worlds,* ed. Jane A. Bernstein (Boston, 2004), 285–307. For the fate of the musico after 1830, see Hadlock, "On the Cusp between Past and Future: The Mezzo-Soprano Romeo of Bellini's *I Capuleti,*" *Opera Quarterly* 17/3 (2001), 399–422.

40. Francesco Bennati, *Recherches sur le mécanisme de la voix humaine* (Paris, 1832), xii.

41. Mercedes Merlin, *Memoirs of Madame Malibran,* 2 vols. (London, 1844), 64.

42. "King's Theatre," *Times,* 22 May 1835, 3c. See also Jennifer Hall-Witt, *Fashionable Acts: Opera and Elite Culture in London, 1780–1880* (Lebanon, NH, 2007), 55.

43. In the 1820s Pasta was known as much for her female impersonations (Paisiello's Nina or Rossini's Semiramide) as for her trouser interpretations (Tancredi or Romeo in Zingarelli's *Giulietta e Romeo*).

44. *Quarterly Musical Magazine and Review* 9 (1827), 54.

45. Stendhal's tendency in his famous essay on Pasta was to laud her as an actress for her "ideal beauty," technical mastery, the "microscopic detail," and the faithfulness of her characterizations, "which never deteriorate from the plainest and most natural modes of simplicity." Her greatness hinged not on unconscious expressions of self but on controlled acts of imitation. See Stendhal, *Life of Rossini,* 371–86.

46. Her letter, signed "Anglo-Italicus," was dated 29 May 1826; see *Examiner* 958 (11 June 1826), 372. Shelley's mother, Mary Wollstonecraft, had notoriously disdained attempts to naturalize hard sexual distinction, writing, "Girls and boys, in short, would play harmlessly together, if the distinction of sex was not inculcated long before nature makes any difference." *A Vindication of the Rights of Woman: With Strictures on Political and Moral Subjects* (London, 1792), 79.

47. Ebers, *Seven Years of the King's Theatre,* 219–20.

48. Quoted in Enid M. Standring, "Rossini and His Music in the Life and Works of George Sand," *Nineteenth-Century French Studies* 10/1–2 (1981–82), 17–27, 21.

49. *Examiner* 953 (7 May 1826), 292.

50. Stendhal, *Life of Rossini,* 373–83.

51. *New Monthly Magazine and Literary Journal* 18 (1 February 1826), 57.

52. On Rossini's recommendation Meyerbeer recomposed *Il crociato in Egitto* for Pasta in a Parisian version that premiered at the Théâtre Italien on 25 September 1825. Pasta brought this production to London in 1828, a Pisaroni number from Meyerbeer's *L'esule di Granata* (Milan, 1821), "Ah, come rapida," interpolated as her second-act aria. This interpolation had already been made for Carolina Bassi in Trieste in autumn 1824, but now the

number boasted a new recitative, "Eccomi giunto," a new cabaletta, "L'aspetto adorabile," probably by Nicolini, and a new position in the act. See Don White, "Meyerbeer in Italy," the booklet accompanying Opera Rara's recording of *Il crociato in Egitto* (London, 1991).

53. *Harmonicon* 6 (1828), 155. In 1828 Velluti played Armando only a few weeks after Pasta's benefit in the same role. At least one journal argued for Velluti's superiority "both in respect to the polish of vocal art and of his acting," all the while hinting that "Pasta undertook the part with reluctance." "We have before observed that Madame Pasta confides too much in mere volume of voice when urged to any trial of skill," the critic continued, "but Velluti's peculiar tone is not to be overwhelmed, and his polish only appears the more beautiful by the contrast with the comparative coarseness which attends any preternatural exertion of the voice." *Quarterly Musical Magazine and Review* 10 (1828–30), 72–73.

54. *Athenaeum* 5 (29 January 1828), 76. Ludovic Vitet's opinion of Pasta around 1826 was similar: like Rossini, she relied on formula and a model of singing based on the routine imitation of instruments. See Benjamin Walton, "The Professional Dilettante: Ludovic Vitet and 'Le Globe,'" *Reading Critics Reading: Opera and Ballet Criticism in France from the Revolution to 1848*, ed. Roger Parker and Mary Ann Smart (Oxford, 2001), 69–85, 81–82.

55. *Harmonicon* 7 (1829), 150.

56. Harriet Granville was the wife of the British ambassador in Paris in 1828. The letter was dated 28 May 1827. See *A Second Self: The Letters of Harriet Granville (1810–45)*, ed. Virginia Surtees (Salisbury, 1990), 220. Stories that Pisaroni had undergone a version of false puberty in 1813 or had been disfigured by smallpox proliferated in the late 1820s; see Hadlock, "Women Playing Men," 293.

57. See Bennati, *Recherches sur le mécanisme*, 26.

58. There is little doubt that the castrato and his manager, Giovanni Fradelloni, traveled with this work to England in 1825. In John Ebers's words, Velluti had "brought with him, from Florence, designs for the scenery, dresses, &c." See Ebers, *Seven Years of the King's Theatre*, 266. Meyerbeer had written this duet for Florence's Teatro della Pergola to substitute for "Ah! che fate," Armando's original rondò finale composed for Velluti at the Venice premiere.

59. *New Monthly Magazine and Literary Journal* 15 (1 August 1825), 345.

60. See Richard Mackenzie Bacon, his signature collection, Cambridge University Library, Manuscripts Add. 6,245, 18v. On 19 July 1828 Velluti again assumed the role of teacher when he sang the same duet with Sontag in a new production of *Il crociato*. The press criticized, among other things, Palmide's "immense turban." "We must protest against the stage being made a *conservatorio*, or Armando d'Orville being reduced to a singing master," one critic added. "Signor Velluti's exertions towards the good order of the performance were incessant; the choruses, the principal personages, nay, Mademoiselle Sontag herself, had the full benefit of his assistance, to which even his prayers to heaven formed no interruption, as, with his hands clasped and his eyes turned upwards, he, nevertheless, continued to beat time most perceptibly." *Athenaeum* 39 (23 July 1828), 621.

61. *London Magazine* 4 (1 March 1826), 316.

62. See a commentary in *London Magazine* 2 (1 August 1825), 517. The print title recalls the classic denunciation of Nicolini that appeared in Joseph Addison's *Spectator* in 1711: "Squire *Squeekum*, who by his voice seems (if I may use the Expression) to be 'cut out' for

an *Italian* Singer." The literature on British opposition to the castrato and his emasculating popery is vast. For an example, see Richard Leppert, "Imagery, Musical Confrontation and Cultural Difference in Early 18th-Century London," *Early Music* 14/3 (1986), 323–45, 331.

63. *New Times*, 1 July 1825, 2e.

64. Mustafà was born in a village near Perugia on 14 April 1829. He was just over a month old on the night Mendelssohn dreamed about Velluti in London.

65. According to Ebers, Velluti wanted to appear in Morlacchi's *Tebaldo e Isolina* on his debut. Ayrton, who was director at the time, persuaded him to favor Meyerbeer; see Ebers, *Seven Years of the King's Theatre*, 260. Ayrton's enthusiasm for Meyerbeer was probably encouraged by Wellington himself. "The Duke of W-, we have reason to know," *London Magazine* reported, "sent for Mr Ayrton into his box at the Opera, and threatened to shut up the House, if *Il crociato* was not got up with all speed." *London Magazine* 2 (1 July 1825), 475.

66. *London Magazine* 2 (1 August 1825), 517. Before translation, the original included, "His shameless patrons have dared to insult, not only the British nation, but even humanity itself, by thrusting forward this non-creature upon the stage. . . . But women; can women too, attend the scene? Can British matrons take their daughters to hear the portentous yells of this disenfranchised of nature, and will they explain the cause to the youthful and uninformed mind? . . . The British people are content to seek for entertainment within the confines of nature." *Times*, 30 June 1825, 3a.

67. *Examiner* 909 (3 July 1825), 417.

68. *Times*, 1 July 1825, 3d.

69. This account is compiled from *New Times*, 1 July 1825, 2e; *London Magazine* 2 (1 August 1825), 517; *Times*, 1 July 1825, 3d; Ebers, *Seven Years of the King's Theatre*, 268; and *New Monthly Magazine and Literary Journal* 15 (1 August 1825), 344. Lord Mount Edgcumbe's words appear in Heriot, *The Castrati in Opera*, 195–96.

70. *Examiner* 909 (3 July 1825), 417.

71. In 1829 the *Harmonicon* printed "Observations on Song" by a Dr Beattie, who, apart from opposing the male and female voice, was drawn into discussing "a third species of musical sound." "For may it not be affirmed with truth, that no person of uncorrupted taste ever heard, for the first time, the music I allude to," the doctor questioned, "without some degree of horror; proceeding not only from the disagreeable ideas suggested by what was done before his eyes, but also from the thrilling sharpness of tone that had startled his ear?" *Harmonicon* 7 (1829), 156.

72. *Times*, 2 July 1825, 3e.

73. *London Magazine* 4 (1 March 1826), 315.

74. *Atlas*, 18 June 1826, 74.

75. *Harmonicon* 4 (1826), 164.

76. See Heriot, *The Castrati in Opera*, 192.

77. See George Hogarth, *Memoirs of the Opera in Italy, France, Germany, and England*, 2 vols. (London, 1851), 1: 311. The *Morning Post* featured an exchange of letters between the parties on 10, 11, and 21 July 1826, while the *Harmonicon* railed against his "contemptuous and oppressive conduct." *Harmonicon* 4 (1826), 103 and 164–65.

78. *Atlas*, 23 July 1826, 155a.

79. Ibid., 154c.

80. *Atlas*, 11 June 1826, 58c.

81. *London Magazine* 4 (1 March 1826), 316.

82. See William Cobbett, *Advice to Young Men* (London, 1829), n.p. Cobbett scorned wasting money on "the decoration of the body." His utilitarian views emerged in such statements as "Men are estimated by other *men* according to their capacity and willingness to be *useful.*" He had a high regard for female tolerance: "Female eyes are . . . very sharp: they can discover beauty though half hidden by a beard, and even by dirt, and surrounded by rags." See also David Kuchta, "The Making of the Self-Made Man: Class, Clothing, and English Masculinity, 1688–1832," *The Sex of Things*, ed. Victoria de Grazia and Ellen Furlough (Berkeley and Los Angeles, 1996), 54–78.

83. *Courier* 10,568 (3 October 1825), 3b; *Times*, 3 October 1825, 2e.

84. *Examiner* 909 (3 July 1825), 417.

85. Balzac, "Sarrasine," 252.

86. The well-known story of the increasing absorption of listeners has been given a familiar though triumphalist account by James Johnson: "If the Rossini-dominated decade of the 1820s was an apprenticeship in listening for the sheer thrill of the music, the 1830s was the time of mastering the new perspective, of exploring its implications and experimenting with ways of capturing and conveying music's meaning." Johnson, *Listening in Paris: A Cultural History* (Berkeley, 1995), 270.

87. For an archaeology of musical depth and "deep" subjectivity in German intellectual history (as opposed to general European or specifically British cultural history), see Holly Watkins, "From the Mine to the Shrine: The Critical Origins of Musical Depth," *19th-Century Music* 27/3 (2004), 179–207. My sense is that, for a brief period only, an exteriorizing rather than interiorizing mode of "deep" listening appeared in the cosmopolitan capitals of Europe around 1830. See my "Dancing the Symphonic: Beethoven-Bochsa's *Symphonie Pastorale,* 1829," *19th-Century Music* 27/1 (2003), 25–47.

88. Quoted in Richardson, *British Romanticism and the Science of the Mind,* 431.

89. The gendered voice of this period, of course, has received much recent critical attention. The familiar Kristevian identification of the voice with the maternal (and hence female/sexual) grounds much current work on power and voice. For a reading of *Sarrasine* via Barthes in this mold, see Carolyn Abbate, "Opera; or, the Envoicing of Women," in *Musicology and Difference: Gender and Sexuality in Music Scholarship,* ed. Ruth A. Solie (Berkeley and Los Angeles, 1993), 1–22. For a survey of the literature on the performance of sexuality (where *Sarrasine* reappears), see the editor's introduction to *Siren Songs: Representations of Gender and Sexuality in Opera,* ed. Mary Ann Smart (Princeton, 2000), 3–16.

90. That Velluti featured in García's textbook of vocal technique at all might surprise given how wedded the compiler was to the new pathology of song. However, the famous inventor of the double laryngoscope still possessed a strong antiquarian streak, as the performance indications in all of his "demonstration" numbers and the arguments of my chapter 5 attest.

91. The moonlight scene in the last act is so excellent, not only in itself, but in the opportunities it afforded of theatrical display, that those who have witnessed it must yet retain a lively impression of its power and beauty. In this scene, the prominent object is a castle illuminated by the rays of the moon. . . . Such

had been the skill of the painter, that a pale gleaming light seemed to pervade every part of the stage. . . . If ever the attention of an audience was enchained, enthralled, bound, as it were, by a spell, it was when Velluti sang the *Notte tremenda.* The stillness of the scene was communicated to the house; and not a word was spoken, not a breath heard:—was this wonderful? When not to the eye and ear only, but to the heart and soul. (Ebers, *Seven Years of the King's Theatre,* 292–93)

92. A comparison of the early printed editions of Meyerbeer's *Il crociato* with the manuscript preserved in the archives of La Fenice reveals similar findings in Velluti's part: in the manuscript, unadorned fermatas and a simple melodic framework are ripe for embellishment; see Giacomo Meyerbeer, *Il crociato in Egitto: melodramma eroico* (1824), ed. Philip Gossett (New York, 1979). Unmetered sections and *arbítri* also litter the castrato's part in *Aureliano in Palmira;* see Celletti, *A History of Bel Canto,* 141.

93. Significantly, this phrase does not recur in the second stanza. Moreover, in the early printed editions a much simpler vocal line retains the harp accompaniment at this point; see Francesco Morlacchi and Gaetano Rossi, *Tebaldo e Isolina: A Facsimile Edition of the Printed Piano-Vocal Score (c. 1825),* ed. Philip Gossett (New York, 1989), 234. Revealingly, Stendhal's extended reading of Velluti's romanza deflected attention from the singer toward the object of song: "Beauty herself in all her delicate shapeliness and entrancing fascination." Stendhal, *Life of Rossini,* 263.

94. For scored inhalations and exhalations, see mm. 28, 33, 55, 57, 59, 60, and 61.

95. Compared to other operatic extracts reproduced in his treatise, Velluti's romance only exaggerates the norm in terms of the fussiness of its text. García's tutor is a complex weave of the innovative present and preserved past. Old-fashioned aspects in this confusion are belied by both the author's choice of didactic repertoire (two arias by Cimarosa, a Crescentini number by Zingarelli, and a florid bass aria from *Semiramide*) and his aesthetic nostalgia, as exemplified in "Caro suono lusinghier." García introduces Velluti's piece thus: "The aria which follows belongs to the style of the past century and offers a remarkable example of it. I got it from Giovanni Batista *[sic]* Velluti who is the only person today who possesses the secrets of that extinct school." García, *École de Garcia,* 2: 237. The 1841 issue of Alexis de Garaudé's *Méthode complète de chant* is the earliest vocal work that I know of to be preoccupied with timbre. Garaudé altered the 1809 and 1826 editions by adding a new introductory exercise designed for teachers to "recognize the timbre, qualities and faults" of the voice. *Méthode complète de chant* (Paris, 1841), 7.

96. In a letter to Luigi Crisostomo Ferrucci of 23 March 1866, Rossini wrote, "Those mutilated boys, who could follow no other career but that of singing, were the founders of the *cantar che nell'anima si sente,* and the horrid decadence of Italian *bel canto* originated with their suppression." Quoted in Herbert Weinstock, *Rossini: A Biography* (London, 1968), 338.

97. *Atlas,* 18 June 1826, 74.

98. *London Magazine* 2 (1 August 1825), 518.

99. García, *École de Garcia,* 1:55.

100. For more on this, see John Rosselli, "Song into Theatre: The Beginnings of Opera," *The Cambridge Companion to Singing,* 83–95, 88.

101. *New Monthly Magazine and Literary Journal* 18 (1 April 1826), 150. The *Harmonicon* argued that Morlacchi's opera existed only to "gratify the vanity of the musico." The critic defended the composer on the basis that he had adapted his original to suit a weak summer company. The opera was apparently "surpassed in poverty of design and feebleness of execution by drivelling compositions of Nicolini, Pacini, Pavesi, Mercadente, and id genus omne. So ignorant, indeed, does the composer seem of the real object of music, that he has thought only of the words and neglected the ideas. Thus the heroine, when lamenting her lost felicity, launches into an air of tumultuous gaiety." *Harmonicon* 3 (1826), 86.

102. *Examiner* 943 (5 March 1826), 148.

103. Ibid. Isaac Robert Cruikshank's satirical print "The Living Skeleton" of 1825 (British Museum Satires 14882) has one of his oglers declare, "He is a greater curiosity than Senior Velluti." Seurat appeared at the behest of the radical attorney Mr. Pearson, who exhibited him from late 1825 to 1826 at the height of Velluti mania. "No Englishman can look upon the French Apollo," one commentator remarked, "without thanking his stars he is an Englishman." *European Magazine* 1 (September 1825), 77. A Mr. Boyle contributed a full anatomical analysis of Seurat in the *Medical and Physical Journal* for September/October; see extracts in the *Courier* 10,568 (3 October 1825), 4d. Another article described him as "a man in the last stage of some chronic disease," twenty-eight years of age, and five foot seven. "Sexual passion exists," the writer noted, "but has never been indulged." *London Medical Repository and Review* 1 (June–December 1825), 379–80.

104. *London Magazine* 2 (1 June 1825), 269.

105. By emphasizing his nothingness, Velluti recalled earlier castrati who might, for example, actively encourage the myth that they had been born from an egg. Interestingly, the castrato's "unmetred" existence expressed itself musically. Velluti's part in *Aureliano*, for example, is striking for the way it features additions sung "out of time"—passages strewn with unmetered grace notes, *arbítri*, triplet/duplet interplay, and so on.

106. Balzac, "Sarrasine," 252.

107. *Morning Herald*, 10 June 1829, 3f. Less than a week later, when Velluti repeated Welsh's composition, one journalist wrote that "though he displayed great vocal powers and execution, they were not such as are quite suitable to an English air, nor are the tones of his voice of that kind which are likely to please the lovers of genuine English music." *Morning Herald*, 16 June 1829, 3e.

108. He had acquired the villa in 1822; see Ermanno Illuminati, *Giovan Battista Velluti, cantante lirico (1780–1860)* (Corridonia, 1985), 20.

2. REFLECTING ON REFLEX

1. L'organe de l'ouïe provoque quelquefois des sympathies très-bizarres qui, selon toutes les apparences, ont leur source dans le système ganglionnaire. . . .

Je connais un pianiste distinguée, d'un temperament très-nerveux; il éprouve souvent des difficultés d'uriner, et subit quelquefois toutes les peines du monde sans pouvoir satisfaire à ce besoin; alors le sifflement ou quelques accords du piano le débarrassent à l'instant de cette incommodité.

L'intime connexion qui a lieu entre l'oreille interne et les viscères abdominaux par les neufs sympathiques permet à ces organes d'avoir à leur tour une influence marquée sur l'organe de l'ouïe. (J. Matuszyński, *De l'influence du nerf sympathique sur les fonctions des sens* (Paris: Faculté de médecine, 1837), 32)

2. For more on these occasions, see Florent Palluault, *Medical Students in England and France 1815–1858: A Comparative Study* (Oxford, 2003), 252.

3. J. Matuszyński, *Ueber die Natur und Behandlung des Weichselzopfes* (Tübingen, 1834).

4. Honoré de Balzac, *The Wrong Side of Paris*, trans. Jordan Stump (New York, 2005), 178. Balzac was directly charmed by Polish nervousness in 1833, when he met his future wife and another frail creature of the species, Eveline Rzewuska, the Countess Hańska. *The Initiate* appeared in serialized form in *Le Spectateur républicain* of 1847. For information on the "disease," Balzac consulted Madame Hańska's physician, one Dr. Knothe, an expert in alchemy, playing the violin, and Polish folk medicine. *Plica polonica, trichoma,* or, as it is more generally known today, *plica neuropathica,* is a still-bewildering neurological affliction now thought to be more psychiatric than ethnic in nature. For *plica polonica's* relation to (as one eighteenth-century traveler put it) "itchings, swellings, eruptions, ulcers, intermitting fevers, pains, even convulsions, palsy and madness," see Larry Wolff, *Inventing Eastern Europe: The Map of Civilization on the Mind of the Enlightenment* (Stanford, 1994), 30.

5. Bronislaw Edward Sydow, ed., *Correspondance de Frédéric Chopin*, 3 vols. (Paris, 1953–60), 2: 130–31.

6. Ibid., 1: 249–50.

7. For more on the Chopin-Matuszyński relationship, including the letter written by Chopin's father on 9 January 1836 thanking Matuszyński for his care, see Pierre Azoury, *Chopin Through His Contemporaries: Friends, Lovers, and Rivals* (Westport, CT, 1999), 22–32.

8. Letter from George Sand to Pauline Viardot of 29 April 1842. See George Sand, *Correspondance*, ed. Georges Lubin, 25 vols. (Paris, 1964–72), 5: 647–48.

9. Keith Barry, *Chopin and His Fourteen Doctors* (Sydney, 1934) (Chopin actually had thirty-three doctors!); Édouard Ganche, *Souffrances de Frédéric Chopin: essai de médecine et de psychologie* (Paris, 1935); Franz Hermann Franken, *Die Krankheiten grosser Komponisten,* 4 vols. (Wilhelmshaven, 1986), 1: 186–235; John O'Shea, *Music and Medicine: Medical Profiles of Great Composers* (London, 1990), 140–54.

10. Lucyna Majka, Joanna Gozdzik, and Michal Witt, "Cystic Fibrosis: A Probable Cause of Frédéric Chopin's Suffering and Death," *Journal of Applied Genetics* 44/1 (2003), 77–84, 80.

11. These are Moscheles's words according to Henley; see Czesław Sieluzycki, "On the Health of Chopin: Truth, Supposition, Legends," *Chopin Studies* 6 (1999), 99–155. D'Agoult wrote, "Il n'ya chez lui que la toux de permanente" in a letter to George Sand on 8 April 1837. See *Marie d'Agoult–George Sand: correspondance,* ed. Charles F. Dupêchez (Paris, 2001), 147. Midcentury French critic Hippolyte Barbedette wrote that Chopin was "a sick man who enjoyed suffering, and did not want to be cured." Quoted in Richard Taruskin, *Oxford History of Western Music,* 8 vols. (Oxford, 2005), 5: 355. Marmontel remembered Chopin in these terms: "Sous les doigts agiles et nerveux de Chopin, les traits les plus

ardus, les plus subtils, les contours les plus fins, étaient nuancés, modulés avec une exquise délicatesse. Sous sa main à la fois émue et savante, les phrases de chant élégantes ou expressives se détachaient lumineuses, colorées; en l'écoutant, on restait sous le charme d'une emotion communicative, qui prenait sa source dans l'organisation délicate, le tempérament maladif et impressionable de l'artiste: véritable sensitive musicale, qu'Auber définnissait d'un mot en disant 'qu'il se mourait toute sa vie.' " Antoine Marmontel, *Les Pianistes célèbres* (Paris, 1878), 3. The myth that Chopin was only ever "barely in existence" is, as Jeffrey Kallberg has suggested, largely the work of his late and posthumous reception. See *Chopin at the Boundaries: Sex, History, and Musical Genre* (Cambridge, MA, 1996), 66.

12. Marshall Hall summarized the problem of "sympathetic movement" as follows: "[Such movements] have been supposed the function of the rational (Stahl) or irrational soul (Whytt). By some, these movements are attached to the brain; by others as attached to the brain and spinal marrow (Müller, Soemmering, Alison, Whytt); by others as attached to segments in the spinal marrow (Flourens, Mayo), by others as a function of the sympathetic (Tiedemann, Lobstein) or of the pneumogastric nerve (Ball, Shaw)." Marshall Hall, "Memoir II: On the True Spinal Marrow and the Excito-Motory System of Nerves," in *Memoirs on the Nervous System* (London, 1837), 43.

13. Xavier Bichat, *Physiological Researches on Life and Death*, trans. F. Gold (Manchester, NH, 1977); the original French edition appeared in 1800. See also Michael Goss, "The Lessened Locus of Feelings: A Transformation in French Physiology in the Early Nineteenth Century," *Journal of the History of Biology* 12/2 (1979), 231-71.

14. For a full account of this reception of Bichat's system, see Edwin Clarke and L. S. Jacyna, *Nineteenth-Century Origins of Neuroscientific Concepts* (Berkeley and Los Angeles, 1987), 332-41. Also useful are J. F. Lobstein, *A Treatise on the Structure, Functions and Diseases of the Human Sympathetic Nerve* (Philadelphia, 1831), originally published in 1823 as *De nervi sympathetici humani fabrica;* and François-Joseph-Victor Broussais, "Réflexions sur les fonctions du système nerveux en général, sur celles du grand sympathique en particulier, et sur quelques autres points de physiologie," *Journal universel des sciences médicales* 12 (1818), 5-43, 129-67.

15. François-Joseph-Victor Broussais, "On the Organ and Propensity of Amativeness," in *On the Functions of the Cerebellum,* ed. and trans. George Combe (Edinburgh, 1838), 132.

16. *Tableau décennal du commerce de la France, 1827-1836* (Paris, 1838), 95.

17. For more on the history of "sympathy," see Edward Shorter, *From Paralysis to Fatigue: A History of Psychosomatic Illness in the Modern Era* (New York, 1992), 12-24, where the author argues that "sympathy" was steadily replaced by the modernized notion of "consensus." See also Alison Winter, *Mesmerized: Powers of Mind in Victorian Britain* (Chicago, 1998); and Evelyn Forget, "Evocations of Sympathy: Sympathetic Imagery in Eighteenth-Century Social Theory and Physiology," *History of Political Economy* 35 (2003), 282-308.

18. George Cuvier, *Le Règne animal distribué d'après son organisation,* 4 vols. (Paris, 1817), 1: 17.

19. Matuszyński, *De l'influence du nerf sympathique,* 30-31.

20. According to Sand, in a letter of 18 June 1846 to Marie de Rozières, Chopin was disturbed by the extent of his sweating: "He's quite upset by it and claims that, however much he

washes, he still *stinks!* . . . We laugh to the point of tears to see such an *ethereal* creature refusing to sweat like everyone else, but don't ever mention it." Sand, *Correspondance,* 7: 379.

21. *E. H. Weber on the Tactile Sense,* ed. and trans. Helen E. Ross and David J. Murray, 2nd ed. (Hove, 1996), 87.

22. Jim Secord's *Victorian Sensation* (Chicago, 2000) makes this point more broadly for British culture, suggesting that "sensation" took on a wider meaning in the nineteenth century, having more to do with the "occasion" of perception rather than its physical impress. For another suggestive angle on the history of piano "touch," see Myles W. Jackson, "Measuring Musical Virtuosity: Physicists, Physiologists, and the Pianist's Touch in the Nineteenth Century," *JALS: The Journal of the American Liszt Society* 61-62 (2010), 13–40.

23. J. Müller, *Elements of Physiognomy,* trans. William Baly, 2 vols. (London, 1842), 1: 1068, 1081.

24. Quoted in Jean-Jacques Eigeldinger, *Chopin: Pianist and Teacher as Seen by His Pupils,* ed. Roy Howat, trans. Krysia Osostowicz, Roy Howat, and Naomi Shohet (Cambridge, 1986), 195.

25. Harold C. Schonberg, *The Great Pianists* (New York, 1963), 106.

26. J. N. Hummel, *A Complete Theoretical and Practical Course of Instructions on the Art of Playing the Piano Forte Commencing with the Simplest Elementary Principles and Including Every Information Requisite to the Most Finished Style of Performance* (London, 1828), Part 3, 40–42.

27. Eigeldinger, *Chopin,* 27. In Adagios, Hummel counseled, one should depend on "the most delicate withdrawing of the fingers from the key, and on the nice sensibility of the fingers themselves." When one played ornaments, he called for "tenderness and attraction." "When [the student] has obtained this delicate feeling so far as to be able to produce these various gradations," he explained, "this power will manifest itself not only by its advantageous effect upon his ear, but, by degrees, it will also shed its influence upon his sensibility, becoming by its means purer and more delicate, and thus implant in his soul the seeds of a true, beautiful and expressive style of performance." Hummel, *A Complete Theoretical and Practical Course,* iii, and Part 3, 40–42.

28. Antoine de Kontski, *L'Indispensable du pianiste, édition nouvelle et augmentée, Op. 100* (St. Petersburg, ca. 1851), 16–17. See also Jonathan Bellman, "Frédéric Chopin, Antoine de Kontski and the *Carezzando* Touch," *Early Music* 29/3 (2001), 399–407, 403–4.

29. Eigeldinger, *Chopin,* 44–45.

30. Chopin wrote, "No one will notice the inequality of sound in a very fast scale, as long as the notes are played in equal time—the goal isn't to learn to play everything with an equal sound. A well-formed technique, it seems to me, [is one] that can control and vary *[bien nuancer]* a beautiful sound quality. . . . As many sounds as there are fingers—everything is a matter of knowing good fingering. Hummel was the most knowledgeable on this subject." Ibid., 195.

31. Leslie David Blasius, "The Mechanics of Sensation and the Construction of the Romantic Musical Experience," in *Music Theory in the Age of Romanticism,* ed. Ian Bent (Cambridge, 1996), 3–24.

32. "We humans are instruments gifted with sensation and memory. Our senses are merely keys that are struck by the natural world around us, keys that often strike them-

selves—and this, according to my way of thinking, is all that would take place in a harpsichord." Denis Diderot, *Rameau's Nephew and Other Works,* trans. Jacques Barzun and Ralph H. Bowen (Indianapolis, 2001), 101. In a letter to Jullan Fontana from Britain on 18 August 1848, Chopin wrote:

> You are my old cembalo on which time and circumstance have played their dismal tremolo. Yes; two *old cembali*—though you will object to such companionship. That is without prejudice to wither beauty or virtue; *la table d'harmonie* is excellent, but the strings have snapped and some of the pegs are missing. The worst is that we are the work of a fine instrument maker: some Stradivarius sui generis, who is no longer here to repair us. We can't give out new notes under clumsy hands, and we choke down in ourselves all that which, for the want of an expert, no one can get out of us. For me, I scarcely breathe; *je suis tout prêt à crever.* (Sydow, ed., *Correspondance de Chopin,* 3: 363–64)

33. Quoted in Franklin Fearing, *Reflex Action: A Study in the History of Physiological Psychology* (London, 1930), 85.

34. Quoted in ibid., 79.

35. Étienne Bonnot de Condillac, *La Logique,* trans. W. R. Albury (New York, 1980), 165.

36. Jan Goldstein, *The Post-Revolutionary Self: Politics and Psyche in France, 1750–1850* (Cambridge, MA, 2005), 60–138.

37. "Epilogue: Obituary and Funeral of Frederic Chopin," *Revue et gazette musicale,* 408–13, quoted in William G. Atwood, *The Parisian Worlds of Frédéric Chopin* (New Haven, 1999), 409.

38. Robert Schumann, *On Music and Musicians,* trans. Paul Rosenfeld (New York, 1946), 136.

39. Quoted in Eigeldinger, *Chopin,* 277.

40. Charles Rosen, *The Romantic Generation* (Cambridge, MA, 1995), 383.

41. By 1844 the high-society English newspaper the *Morning Post* could write that these études were "undoubtedly the most ingenious and beautiful" of Chopin's compositions, "more in vogue now than those of any other master," and "the *sine quâ non* in the education of all pianists who aspire to public display." Quoted in *Musical Examiner* 112 (12 December 1844), 87. When Chopin's études were negatively received, as by Ludwig Rellstab in his Berlin journal *Iris im Gebiete der Tonkunst,* it was generally because they peddled a violence only profiteering physicians would properly understand:

> As long as he [Chopin] goes on hatching such deformities as the above-mentioned études—a source of much amusement for all my friends, including the pianists among them—we will go on laughing at them. . . . Let us spare ourselves a special review of each of the twelve apostles, which Mr. Chopin has sent into the world in these twelve pieces, and content ourselves with the more useful remark that a person with crooked fingers may well find the means to straighten them in these études, but that a less handicapped person ought to beware, and refrain from playing them except in the company of Messrs. Von

Gräfe or Diefenbach [two Berlin doctors], who may indeed find, if this sort of piano playing comes into fashion, that a whole new practice will open up to them as assistants to famous piano teachers.

Contemporary reaction to these pieces, in other words, recognized in all sorts of ways the "subtlety" of what Rosen calls "Chopin's sadism." I have based my translation of Rellstab's 1834 review on Harriet Goodman's translation in Dieter Hildebrandt, *Pianoforte: A Social History of the Piano* (New York, 1988), 76.

42. Kallberg, it must be admitted, isolates "supernatural" rather than "illness" tropes. See his *Chopin at the Boundaries*, 66.

43. I have borrowed from Cyril and Rena Clarke's translation in Alfred Cortot, *In Search of Chopin* (New York, 1951), 8.

44. From 1832, as Jan Goldstein has argued, the entire lycée system and French bureaucracy *tout court* was reorganized to reflect the concerns of a new area of knowledge called "psichologie." Goldstein stresses that the ascendant bourgeois world of the July Monarchy oriented itself around practices of introspection, self-searching, and a reinvigorated concept of the *moi*. At the head of this movement was Victor Cousin and the "unwitting progenitor" of his movement, Maine de Biran. In his Sorbonne lectures of 1828, Cousin asked, "What is psychological analysis? It is the slow, patient, and meticulous observation, with the aid of consciousness, of phenomena hidden in the depths of human nature. These phenomena are complicated, fleeting, obscure, rendered almost indiscernible *(insaissable)* by their very closeness. The consciousness which applies itself to them is an instrument of extreme delicacy: it is a microscope applied to things infinitely small. . . . And this art is not learned in a day. One does not fold back upon oneself easily without long practice, sustained habit, and a laborious apprenticeship." Goldstein, *The Post-Revolutionary Self* (Cambridge, MA, 2005), 130, 168.

45. Raoul von Koczalski's two recordings of supposedly the most "heroic" work of them all, the Polonaise, op. 53, makes this clear. According to tradition these performances are of priceless documentary value, Koczalski having been charged with carrying the legacy left to him by his teacher, Chopin's pupil Karol Mikuli. The 1923 recording was issued on Polydor 62441, and the 1938 version appeared on HMV DA 4431.

46. Chopin's O'Meara annotations are reprinted in Chopin, *Sämtliche Etüden*, ed. Paul Badura-Skoda (Vienna, 2005); and Chopin, *Etiudy op. 10, 25; Trzy etiudy, Méthode des méthodes*, ed. Jan Ekier (Warsaw, 2000).

47. Sydow, ed., *Correspondance de Chopin*, 3: 365. Chopin apparently called his third finger the "grand chanteur." Sophie Adelung remembered how Chopin, late in life, would teach while lying down in an adjoining room, coughing, taking opium drops or sugar and gum water, and rubbing his forehead with eau de cologne. "But this did not prevent him from attentively following [my] playing," Adelung recalled. "Even from a distance, and out of sight, not the slightest detail of her playing escaped him. 'Fourth finger on F♯', he would call out; his ear, sensitive to the slightest nuance, knew immediately, from the sound, which fingers had played each note." Quoted in Eigeldinger, *Chopin*, 48, 167.

48. Felix Salzer performed an exhaustive analysis of this study in "Chopin's Étude in F Major, Opus 25, No. 3: The Scope of Tonality," *Music Forum* 3 (1973), 281–90.

3. THE SONTAG-MALIBRAN STEREOTYPE

1. See *Atlas*, 7 June 1829, 381a. When Mendelssohn visited Turner's exhibition, he dismissed the art as "the most hideous smearing" *(greulichste Schmierereien)*. See R. Larry Todd, *Mendelssohn: A Life in Music* (Oxford, 2003), 209.

2. James Elmes's *Annals of the Fine Arts* (1820) included an informative account of the building (numbered 240–52 Regent Street), erected in 1818 to house the Royal Harmonic Institution. The grand concert room was described as "a parallelogram, elongated at one end by the orchestra, and at the other end by four tiers of boxes. The side walls of this saloon are decorated by fluted pilasters of the Corinthian order, and the apertures to the orchestra and boxes are terminated by four majestic columns of the same description. The cornice is ornamented by modillions, the ceiling arched, forming the segment of a circle, and enriched in octagular *[sic]* Mosaic panels, and with large embossed flowers in each panel." Quoted in Robert Elkin, *Royal Philharmonic: The Annals of the Royal Philharmonic Society* (London, 1947), 21.

3. For an early description of the rooms, see *Quarterly Musical Magazine and Review* 2 (1820), 385–86. My report of the concert derives from *Morning Herald*, 1 June 1829, 3f; and *Times*, 1 June 1829, 2c.

4. *Times*, 22 May 1829, 3f. On this occasion Malibran and Sontag provided a foretaste of what was to come at the Argyll Rooms by singing a duet by Mercadente, the orchestral parts having been arranged by Alexander Lee. See the *Courier* 11701 (20 May 1829), 4a.

5. *Examiner* 914 (7 August 1825), 495b.

6. "There was, however, a difficulty remaining—she is a minor, and the consent of her mother and her guardian was necessary. The mother had no objection, but the guardian, M. Kemowsky, refused his consent. The Ambassador has, therefore, applied to the King, and by a Cabinet order, the consent is declared unnecessary." See *Times*, 14 June 1827, 3a.

7. This was in a letter addressed to her husband. See April Fitzlyon, *Maria Malibran, Diva of the Romantic Age* (London, 1987), 127.

8. See, for example, *Atlas*, 1 March 1829, 137b: "[Sontag] has just recovered the effects of her last decadence (a slight roulade down the stairs, caused it is said, by treading on a piece of orange-peel), and is singing Rode's variations as gaily as ever" (Catalani had popularized the singing of these violin variations). For Gautier's words of 1852, see Janet Johnson, "The Musical Environment in France," in *The Cambridge Companion to Berlioz*, ed. Peter Bloom (Cambridge, 2000), 36.

9. Sontag left Paris on 2 April. For her debut, see W. T. Parke, *Musical Memoirs; Comprising an Account of the General State of Music in England*, 2 vols. (London, 1830), 2: 272. Laporte engaged Malibran at the King's Theatre at seventy-five guineas a night. The following evening (22 April), "Otello was introduced to the most crowded (though we cannot say fashionable) audience we have witnessed this season [because of] the much-talked-of Malibran." See *London Literary Gazette and Journal of Belle Lettres, Arts and Sciences* 640 (25 April 1829), 276.

10. The *Harmonicon* devoted a whole paragraph to the venue:

> This room, the finest in London for music, had been altered, repaired, and fitted up. The orchestra is now stationed where the royal boxes were placed, and two semi-circular rows of small boxes have been built at the opposite end.

One half of the floor has been raised into an amphitheatre, which with the other half is filled with cross benches, but there are no side ones, for want whereof the appearance of the room suffers materially. The predominant clothing is light blue, the ornamental part being executed in a cheap theatrical manner, and very French. The whole is illuminated by one lustre, suspended from the centre of the ceiling, which is decorated in good taste, and diffusing an agreeable light. The orchestra is much too perpendicular, and wants depth in the lower part. The proscenium also, which is a flimsy affair, gives it more the appearance of a portable stage, than is usual or becoming in a concert-room. (*Harmonicon* 7 (1829), 145)

11. *Quarterly Musical Magazine and Review* 10 (1828–30), 301; and *Harmonicon* 7 (1829), 140. Reports of Sontag's 5 May debut were contradictory. The *Harmonicon* found her voice "much improved in quality, having acquired more fullness, become more mellow." See *Harmonicon* 7 (1829), 15. As a foil to this, Harriet Countess Granville, who attended this performance, wrote to the Duke of Devonshire the following day that Sontag,

thinner than anybody I ever saw, looking as if she had cried her eyes out, sang beautifully sometimes, sometimes false, which she never used. There is more effort, weaker in health. She has had a baby, but she is married and has been so two years. She has sworn to conceal it, but trod upon a peach-stone, was known to *accoucher,* and therefore now is obliged to confide the truth to a few. Madame Appony [Madame la Comtesse d'Apponyi, the wife of the Austrian ambassador in Paris to whom Chopin dedicated the op. 27 nocturnes] has received her since with the highest honour, the French ditto. The husband she will not name because of her oath, but nobody doubts it being Count Clam. The mystery necessary because old Clam has promised to shoot himself if his son marries her. (Harriet Granville, *Letters of Harriet Countess Granville 1810–45,* ed. F. Leveson Gower, 2 vols. (London, 1894), 2: 40)

12. *Harmonicon* 7 (1829), 145.

13. *Quarterly Musical Magazine and Review* 10 (1828–30), 301–2.

14. Reviews of these concerts appear in the *Times,* 23 May 1829, 5c; *Times,* 1 June 1829, 2c; and *Morning Journal* 1 June 1829, 3d.

15. For these benefits, see *Courier* 11719 (10 June 1829), 3c; and *Courier* 11724 (16 June 1829), 3c. Duet performances in London included Moscheles's benefit (8 May, King's Concert Room, "Ebben, a te: ferisci"), Anderson's benefit (13 May, Argyll Rooms, "Ebben, a te: ferisci"), Laporte's benefit (15 May, King's Theatre, *Tancredi*), Fourth Grand Concert (30 May, Argyll Rooms, "Lasciami, non t'ascolto"), Eighth Philharmonic Society Concert (8 June, Argyll Rooms, "Ebben, a te: ferisci"), Velluti's benefit (9 June, Argyll Rooms, "Ebben: a te ferisci"), Welsh's benefit (15 June, Argyll Rooms, both duets), Sontag's benefit (18 June, King's Theatre, *Tancredi*), opera performance (20 June, King's Theatre, *Tancredi*), Ella's benefit (24 June, Mrs. Henshaw's, "Ebben, a te: ferisci"), and more opera performances (13 and 14 July, King's Theatre, *Tancredi*).

16. Anonymous, *A Memoir of the Countess de Rossi (Madame Sontag)* (London, 1849), 37.

17. For more on Bauer's memoirs (1883–84), see Fitzlyon, *Maria Malibran,* 68.

18. Mercedes Merlin, *Memoirs of Madame Malibran,* 2 vols. (London, 1840), 2: 54.

19. This performance was far from the first. Fétis was in London in 1829 to ply his trade as a music critic and piano accompanist. His report describes this performance as having taken place at Lord Saltoun's house in London for the benefit of John Ella. (Here Ella directed the Società Lirica, or Saltoun Club, a group of aristocrat amateurs who met to perform together.) The story that Fétis effected a reconciliation between Sontag and Malibran after nasty incidents at the King's Theatre in 1829 is wishful thinking. Ella's 1829 benefit featuring "Ebben, a te: ferisci" actually took place on 24 June at Mrs. Henshaw's house at 26 Wimpole Street; see the advertisement in the *Athenaeum* 81 (24 June 1829), 400c. See also Arthur Pougin, *Marie Malibran: The Story of a Great Singer* (London, 1911), 65.

20. The Epsom Races began on 2 June, months after Sontag and Malibran first met. The anecdote described Lord Burghersh, Sir George Warrender, and De Beriot in Malibran's entourage, Rossi and de Benkhausen in Sontag's. See Julie de Margueritte, "Souvenirs of the Opera in Europe," in *Life of Henriette Sontag, Countess de Rossi with Interesting Sketches* (New York, 1852), 61–63, 63. Mendelssohn also went to the races on 4 June with his friend Goldschmidt. See the composer's diary for 1829 in M. Denecke Mendelssohn Collection, Bodleian Library, Oxford, pocket diaries g. 1–10.

21. This story appears in Pontmartin's *Souvenirs d'un vieux melomane;* see Howard Bushnell, *Maria Malibran: A Biography of a Singer* (University Park, 1979), 88.

22. Tickets rose to twenty-four francs. The *Times* article involved a long discussion of "*engouement,* and of which the English word infatuation conveys but a faint and imperfect idea. Instances of infatuation are known and seen in England in individuals only; it closely borders on insanity of mind, and amounts to a sudden but transient deprivation of reason. But the *engouement* of the Parisians is a sort of epidemic which attains a whole community; it is a magic spell." See *Times,* 14 September 1829, 6e.

23. This article noticed how Sontag was "not so often guilty of the fault of pitching it below the note, in order to replace it afterwards, a vicious habit which has been visible since her return from London." See translations of *La Revue musicale* 5 (1829): 102–3, in Bushnell, *Maria Malibran,* 89, and in *Harmonicon* 7 (1829), 96. Evidence recurs in the *Times,* 14 September 1829, 6f.

24. The reviewer took the opportunity to cut both Malibran and Sontag down to size, perhaps to reinforce the idea of their mutual dependence: "In all the duets, Madame Malibran has not equal success. . . . In the second duet with Argirio, some want of agility and some feebleness of organ are betrayed in the second movement, 'Ecco la trombe', where the trumpet accompaniment is heard from without. . . . [Sontag's] dramatic action and recitative are, it must be owned, liable to the ordinary reproach of languor; but some sparks of feeling, giving hope of better things, burst forth." See *Morning Chronicle,* 22 June 1829, 2e.

25. Paul Scudo, "Henriette Sontag," in *Life of Henriette Sontag,* 39–46, 42. In a classic piece of vitriol, Berlioz waded into Scudo and Rossini, who was "this trimmer," "this great abscess," with "the air of a retired satyr [who] poses every evening on the Boulevard Italien, attended by Scudo and all the little Scudi who crawl about Paris." See Hector Berlioz, *Evenings in the Orchestra,* trans. C. R. Fortescue (Harmondsworth, 1963), 335.

26. Heather Hadlock, "*Tancredi* and *Semiramide,*" in *The Cambridge Companion to Rossini,* ed. Emanuele Senici (Cambridge, 2004), 139–58, 151.

27. After *Semiramide*—on 20 October 1823, to be precise—Rossini had taken up his belongings and his wife (or rather his wife had taken *him*, since she earned the higher salary) and departed Bologna for London and Paris. Settling in the French capital, so the story goes, Rossini toned down the *canto fiorito* at its peak in *Semiramide,* apparently as an accommodation to the more declamatory manner of French singing. In the late 1820s, we hear, "syllabication," a slowed-down line, and a type of vocalization perhaps placed forward in the mouth—*dans la masque*—began to replace the Italianate melismas of *Semiramide.* Though convincing, this story seems less compelling when we turn attention away from the study of operatic scores to the study of newspapers and journals. According to critics on the ground, a singer such as Pasta, far from restraining herself, turned her supposedly plain, noble style into something more florid by 1829 (as when Chorley hailed the "immovable beauty" and beau ideal as "fierce, masterful, Oriental"). Henry Chorley, *Thirty Years' Musical Recollections,* 2 vols. (London, 1862), 1: 41. Bear in mind that, even in 1829, Pasta's style of ornamentation was tame by Malibran's "wild" standards. Laure Cinti-Damoreau certainly was not holding back either, apparently introducing ever more roulades, arpeggios, trills, and portamenti, particularly into the already ornate parts of vocal writing. For more on ornamentation trends at the time, see Austin Caswell, "Mme Cinti-Damoreau and the Embellishment of Italian Opera in Paris: 1820–1845," *Journal of the American Musicological Society* 28/3 (1975): 459–92.

28. Ignaz Moscheles, *Gems à la Malibran, Book 2* (London, 1829).

29. *Times,* 9 May 1829, 6c.

30. *Harmonicon* 7 (1829), 146–47.

31. For the debate over Abramo Basevi and form, see, for example, Harold S. Powers, "'La Solita Forma' and 'The Uses of Convention,'" *Acta Musicologica* 59/1 (1987), 65–69; or Roger Parker, "'Insolite Forme,' or Basevi's Garden Path," in *Leonora's Last Act* (Princeton, 1997), 42–60.

32. Hilary Poriss, *Changing the Score: Arias, Prima Donnas, and the Authority of Performance* (Oxford University Press, 2009).

33. For example, Sontag's Cenerentola, one of her more accomplished roles, involved omitting "one or two pieces," interpolating heavily, ratcheting the part up from contralto, and singing in G. "[Sontag] is very fond of singing in G. This, indeed, appears to be the key in which she can mostly display the extent and power of her voice. One of her most successful transpositions is that in her cavatini *[sic]* in the finale, which, from E, she raises a tone and a half to G. . . . [In this cavatina] she descends to G below the lines, sliding over, in the prettiest manner possible, a chromatic scale of great extent, with a grace and neatness that are absolutely irresistible." *Athenaeum* 22 (8 April 1829), 348a.

34. The writer (probably Edward Taylor) continued, "The duet Lasciami non t'ascolto *[sic],* which they also sang yesterday, is admirably suited for them, and may compete in every respect with the former." See *Courier* 11724 (16 June 1829), 3c.

35. The critic wrote earlier, "Malibran, who is highly-talented as a pianiste and writer, composes those she has sung with Sontag, &c. herself; and very clever, ingenious, and appropriate effusions they are." See *Athenaeum* 100 (23 September 1829), 601.

36. *Athenaeum* 86 (17 June 1829), 380.

37. Cited in Pougin, *Marie Malibran,* 282.

38. *Athenaeum* 82 (20 May 1829), 317.

39. Cited in Eric Bentley, ed., *Shaw on Music* (New York, 1983), 55.

40. *Le Globe* 6/92 (6 September 1828), 682. The writer, reporting on Malibran's debut in Paris, attacked her for "la lenteur dans tous les mouvements [including strettos], le manque de contraste, le défaut de progression dans la vivacité de la mesure, ou, en d'autres termes, le défaut d'entraînement, voilà ce qui rend si souvent l'exécution de notre pauvre Théâtre-Italien si pale, si glaciale, si décolorée, . . . [The reviewer would prefer her to sacrifice] ces petites notes piques qu'elle lance de temps en temps comme une balle à la volée. Cette espèce d'agréments métalliques." Elsewhere, the *Times* criticized her Rosina in similar terms: "[Malibran] never sympathizes with the audience, and the accent of true nature must of necessity be frequently lost amongst these convulsive shrieks and this display of violent gesticulation." *Times,* 14 September 1829, 6e.

41. Ibid., 6f.

42. X.X.X. [Castil-Blaze], "Chronique musicale," *Journal des débats,* 30 January 1829, 1c; also translated and misdated in James Johnson, *Listening in Paris: A Cultural History* (Berkeley and Los Angeles, 1995), 225–26.

43. See *Times,* 14 September 1829, 6f. By mid-1829 Ayrton had finally had enough of "her eternal descending run of semitones." Reviewing a performance of Mozart's *Le nozze di Figaro,* he was appalled by her "Porgi, amor": "[It] almost makes one wish that her pretty mouth were closed by the padlock fastened upon Papageno's for a much more pardonable offence." See *Harmonicon* 7 (1829), 178.

44. See Jean-Jacques Eigeldinger, *Chopin: Pianist and Teacher as Seen by His Pupils,* ed. Roy Howat, trans. Krysia Osostowicz, Roy Howat, and Naomi Shohet (Cambridge, 1986), 114.

45. The quotes and programs are taken from the *Times,* 23 May 1829, 5c; *Times,* 1 June 1829, 2c; and *Morning Journal,* 1 June 1829, 3d.

46. *Quarterly Musical Magazine and Review* 10 (1828–30), 300.

47. *Athenaeum* 85 (10 June 1829), 379–80.

48. The editor, William Ayrton, reminded his readers that the *Herald* critic was "a native of the emerald isle." See *Harmonicon* 7 (1829), 141. This particular Irishman was often ridiculed in 1829. The *Times* (probably Alsager) lambasted him at one point for lauding Sontag's "polyphonic powers." See the report in *Harmonicon* 7 (1829), 113.

49. Thomas Laqueur, "Orgasm, Generation, and the Politics of Reproductive Biology," in *The Making of the Modern Body: Sexuality and Society in the Nineteenth Century,* ed. Catherine Gallagher and Thomas Laqueur (Berkeley and Los Angeles, 1987), 1–41.

50. The writer, reviewing the 20 June performance of *Tancredi* at the King's Theatre, had just written of "the hazy lustre in which [Malibran's Tancredi] moves." See *Athenaeum* 87 (24 June 1829), 395.

51. John Keats, *Endymion: A Poetic Romance* (London: Taylor and Hessey), 166.

52. Sally Shuttleworth, *Charlotte Brontë and Victorian Psychology* (Cambridge, 1996), 85.

53. Translated in Rodolfo Celletti, *A History of Bel Canto,* trans. Frederick Fuller (Oxford, 1991), 141. Baer presented his theory of ovulation, challenging the ancient view that conception occurred at points of orgasm, in *De ovi mammalium et homini genesi* (Leipzig, 1827).

54. See Théophile Gautier, "Albertus, or the Soul and Sin," in *The Works of Théophile Gautier,* trans. Agnes Less, ed. F. C. de Sumichrast, 24 vols. (London: George Harrap, 1903), 24: 227.

55. See my "Gautier's 'Diva': The First French Uses of the Word," in *The Arts of the Prima Donna in the Long Nineteenth Century,* ed. Rachel Cowgill and Hilary Poriss (Oxford, 2012), 123–46.

56. In a letter of 5 June 1829; see Paul Jourdain, "Mendelssohn in England," Ph.D. diss. (University of Cambridge, 1998), 100.

57. Sam George, *Botany, Sexuality, and Women's Writing, 1760–1830* (Manchester, 2007).

58. *Trésor de la langue française,* ed. Paul Imbs, 16 vols. (Paris: Éditions du Centre national de la recherche scientifique, 1979–94).

59. Quoted in Maurice Cranston, *The Romantic Movement* (Oxford, 1994), 18.

60. See Herbert Weinstock, *Vincenzo Bellini: His Life and Operas* (London, 1972), 145. Malibran apparently could not get beyond her Amina personality. Reality and illusion were supposedly confused for her. Bellini kept an oval miniature of the singer, her right hand raised to her hair, which he wore at the knot of his cravat. The maestro referred to her as "that diavoletta of a Malibran, who between evening and morning can learn a whole opera for you," such was their affinity and her identification with the characters she played, according to a letter to Florimo of 5 January 1835. The authenticity of this letter is in dispute. Florimo probably "edited" the letters that Bellini wrote to him before having them published. See ibid., 144–46.

61. In his *Portraits et Salons;* see Bushnell, *Maria Malibran,* 230.

62. Quoted in William Henry Husk, ed., *Templeton and Malibran* (London, 1880), 34.

63. Isaac Nathan, *Musurgia Vocalis: An Essay on the History and Theory of Music, and on the Qualities, Capabilities, and Management of the Human Voice,* 2nd ed. (London, 1836), 267–68.

64. Louis Borne wrote this in 1830–31 in his *Briefe aus Paris;* cited in Pougin, *Marie Malibran,* 116.

65. See Fitzlyon, *Maria Malibran,* 79.

66. Théophile Gautier, "Past and Present," in *Life of Henriette Sontag,* 51–52, 52.

67. Hector Berlioz, "How Sontag Sings," in *Life of Henriette Sontag,* 53.

68. *Harmonicon* 6 (1828), 120.

69. *Athenaeum* 25 (18 April 1828), 395. A reviewer attending a musical soirée under the auspices of Bohrer and Pixis in Paris found Sontag's charms overrated:

> Never was a singer gifted with a voice more pure, equal, and flexible, than this young lady, and never were qualities, so rarely found in unison, so lamentable abused. The air of Mercadante, composed expressly for her, and which is nothing but a tissue of passages fitted to display the flexibility of her organs, and the variations to a Swiss air, which terminated the concert, contain such a profusion of notes devoid of all meaning, of every moral intention, that in spite of the perfection and precision displayed in executing them, it was impossible to resist the ennui they occasioned. (*Harmonicon* 6 (1828), 119)

70. See *Athenaeum* 41 (6 August 1828), 653.

71. *Quarterly Musical Magazine and Review* 9 (1827), 482. These words are paraphrased in John Edmund Cox, *Musical Recollections of the Last Half-Century,* 2 vols. (London, 1872), 1: 163.

72. Quoted in X, "From My Study," in *Musical Times* 35/615 (1 May 1894), 299–304, 303–4.

73. *Athenaeum* 22 (8 April 1828), 347. This was a preview extracted from Augustus Bozzi Granville, *St Petersburgh: A Journal of Travels to and from That Capital,* 2nd ed., 2 vols. (London, 1829), 1: 276.

74. See Louis Borne, "Henriette Sontag in Frankfurt," in *Life of Henriette Sontag,* 46–51, 49. These stories had several variations. According to one journal, "Passing through Göttingen, several of the students, envious of the happiness enjoyed by the horses in dragging the lovely form of Madlle Sontag, took out the unremonstrating animals from the carriage, and hauled it in." See *Atlas,* 10 January 1830, 28c.

75. Alan Walker, *Franz Liszt I: The Virtuoso Years, 1811–1847,* 3 vols. (London, 1983), 1: 184.

76. See the advertisements for engravings of Sontag by Albert Hoffay and J. Brocker in *Athenaeum* 28 (7 May 1828), 442; and *Athenaeum* 25 (18 April 1828), 394.

77. *Athenaeum* 28 (7 May 1828), 440.

78. See Pisanus Fraxi, *Bibliography of Prohibited Books,* 3 vols. (London, 1962), 3: 316–17. Rumors also circulated at the time that Sontag had been the mistress of the chancellor of the exchequer, Gouldburn. See "Leo Sacks—One of the Charity Crabs," in *Catalogue of Political and Personal Satires,* ed. Mary D. George, 11: 163.

79. The existence of this popular publication had been ascertained only from its many reviews in periodicals of 1829, but it was typical of its type.

80. Borne, "Henriette Sontag in Frankfurt," 48.

81. *Athenaeum* 22 (8 April 1828), 347. This passage was extracted from Granville, *St Petersburgh,* 276.

82. *Harmonicon* 6 (1828), 120. This passage was paraphrased in Cox, *Musical Recollections of the Last Half-Century,* 1: 160. Sontag is generally accepted to have been born in 1806, which would have made her twenty-one at the time of her marriage. It seems likely this date was fabricated to clean up the somewhat sordid past in her family of entertainers. Her mother had twelve children, only three of whom were fathered by Sontag's father.

83. George Hogarth, *Memoirs of the Musical Drama,* 2 vols. (London, 1838), 2: 406.

84. Margueritte, "Souvenirs of the Opera in Europe," 59.

85. *Athenaeum* 25 (18 April 1828), 394.

86. *Athenaeum* 28 (7 May 1828), 437. This passage was extracted from Edward Holmes, *A Ramble among the Musicians of Germany, Giving Some Account of the Operas of Munich, Dresden, Berlin, etc.* (London, 1828).

87. *Le Globe* 6/89 (1828), 658.

88. From "To a Young Lady/Who had been reproached for taking long walks in the country" (1805), and quoted in *Literary Magnet* 1 (January 1826), 21.

89. In a letter to Eugene dated "Monday night, 1827." See Howard Bushnell, *Maria Malibran,* 39.

90. See *Times,* 27 April 1829, 2f; and *Times,* 14 September 1829, 6e.

91. *Times,* 14 September 1829, 6e. Comparisons of Pasta and Malibran were frequently made. The 23 June 1828 issue of *Le Figaro* claimed that "despite the depth of her acting and the power of her effects, despite the majesty of her poses and the sublime expression of her features, Mme Pasta would envy her young rival for her abandon, her artlessness, her freedom, which always makes something inspired of what she does, something unexpected, improvised. Possessing in addition a decidedly superior voice, Mme Malibran is capable of embellishing her singing with all the charm of the ornaments." Quoted in Bushnell, *Maria*

Malibran, 75. "Malibran has the unforeseen," Delacroix once recorded in his diary. "Her singing and her action changed from day to day." Quoted in Pougin, *Marie Malibran*, 291–92. "[Pasta] was always present for herself on the stage," the painter wrote elsewhere, while "[Malibran] forgot to find herself before a public." Quoted in Bushnell, *Maria Malibran*, 175.

92. Hector Berlioz, *The Art of Music and Other Essays (A travers chants)*, trans. Elizabeth Csicsery-Rónay (Bloomington, IN, 1994), 3–4.

93. See *L'Eco*, 28 November 1834; quoted in Bushnell, *Maria Malibran*, 179.

94. This fascination with eyes extended to Sontag too: "Mademoiselle Sontag!—Yes, Mademoiselle Sontag!—We are actually about to inflict a few sobering remarks on the reader respecting this lovely import. . . . Her hair is light and elegant, and her floating eyes—'—Oh! they resemble/Blue water lilies, when the breeze/Is making the stream around them tremble!'" See *News*, 15 April 1828. A copy of this can be found in the 1828 file for the King's Theatre in the Enthoven Collection, Theatre Museum, London.

95. Quoted in Fitzlyon, *Maria Malibran*, 91.

96. Stendhal, *Life of Rossini* [1823], trans. Richard N. Coe (London, 1985), 354–83.

97. In a letter to Carlo Severini of 22 September 1829. See Albert Soubies, *Le Théâtre-Italien de 1801 à 1913* (Paris, 1913), 44.

98. In a 27 February 1835 letter now in the Brussels Conservatory. See Fitzlyon, *Maria Malibran*, 190–91.

99. Ibid., 253.

100. Irigaray's struggle to pin down this active, productive subject echoes Étienne de Jouy's words with which this chapter began:

> Experienced as all-powerful where "she" is most radically powerless in her indifferentiation. Never here and now because she is that everywhere else-where from whence the "subject" continues to draw his reserves, his resources, yet unable to recognize them/her. Not uprooted from matter, the earth, the mother, and yet, at the same time dispersed. . . . Woman remains this nothing at all [ce rien du tout], this whole of nothing yet [ce tout de rien encore] where each (male) one comes to seek the means to replenish resemblance to self (as) to same. And so she is displaced. . . . That sex (of) nothing at all in its absolute fluidity, its plasticity to all metamorphoses, its ubiquity in all its compossibilities, its invisibility. . . . All water must become a mirror, all seas, a glass. . . . Everything, then, should be rethought in terms of volute(s), helix(es), diagonal(s), spiral(s), curl(s), turn(s), revolution(s), pirouette(s). (Luce Irigaray, "Volume without Contours," in *Irigaray Reader*, ed. Margaret Whitford (Oxford, 1991), 53–68)

101. Margaret Fuller, *Woman in the Nineteenth Century*, ed. Larry J. Reynolds (New York, 1998), 61.

102. Descriptions of the charge or electricity of the Sontag-Malibran sonority were routine. *Le Globe* responded to the first time Sontag and Malibran ever sang "Ebben: a te ferisci" by marveling:

> All that remains is to talk about *Semiramide*'s duos, but it would be difficult to describe the effect produced. The audience was electrified: Mademoiselle Sontag

had us admire her beautiful voice, Madame Malibran her expression, her dramatic verve, and the richness of an imagination that infused fermatas with ravishing novelty and originality. (*Le Globe* 7/24 (1829), 190)

The press had similar reactions in London, for example at the Argyll Rooms for Velluti's benefit on 9 June: "The Concert closed with Rossini's *Ebben a te ferisci*, by Sontag and Malibran, which had a truly electrifying effect, and sent the company away in ecstasy." *Courier* 11719 (10 June 1829), 3c.

103. *Atlas*, 14 June 1829, 96.

104. Quoted and discussed in Heather Hadlock, "The Career of Cherubino, or the Trouser Role Grows Up," in *Siren Songs: Representations of Gender and Sexuality in Opera*, ed. Mary Ann Smart (Princeton, 2000), 67–92, 73.

105. Gautier's assessment of the Sontag-Malibran stereotype is extreme. The witch revealed, the hero is propelled into hell. The fullness of the past broken, he witnesses a "wondrous symphony" played by "virtuosi [who] with their dried, thin fingers made the strings of the Stradivarii sing again. Souls seemed to sound in the voices of the grave; cavernous gongs like thunder rumbled." Responding to a sneeze in the audience with "God bless you," he is attacked by devils, and the story ends, "On that morn, near Rome, peasants found upon the Appian Way the body of a man stone dead, his back broken, his neck twisted." See Gautier, "Albertus, or the Soul and Sin," 24: 217–79, 227, 270, and 279.

4. BONELESS HANDS / THALBERG'S READY-MADE SOUL / VELVET FINGERS

1. The young Thalberg had appeared at the Argyll Rooms a decade earlier. But the 17 May 1826 concert passed by without notice. See his advertisement in the *Times*, 16 May 1826, 2c. For more on "visual listening" and the importance of the Pastoral in this milieu, see my "Dancing the Symphonic: Beethoven-Bochsa's *Symphonie pastorale*," *19th-Century Music* 27/1 (2003), 25–47. Sir George "presided at piano," making corrections, filling out harmonies, and aiding the band when necessary. In his finicky way, he penned in his personal concert program that the symphony had lasted "40 min."

2. "Philharmonic Concerts," *Spectator* 411 (14 May 1836), 465.

3. Francesco Bennati's "Mémoire sur un cas particulier d'anomalie de la voix humaine pendant le chant" was read at the Académie des sciences on 30 September 1833 and published in an offprint the following year (Paris, 1834). According to the *Musical World*, Ivanoff's performance was encored not because of the singer, but because such music "should always be heard twice, for itself." "Concerts," *Musical World* 9 (13 May 1836), 141.

4. Malibran was engaged in an English-language version of *Fidelio*. "Music and Musicians; Philharmonic Society," *Atlas*, 15 May 1836, 311.

5. "Concerts of the Month," *Court Magazine and Monthly Critic and Lady's Magazine* 8/6 (June 1836), 272. At its foundation in 1813, the Philharmonic Society was opposed to showing off, admitting only "the best and most approved instrumental music" for its concerts. Inevitably, the ban on vocal solos and duets eased in 1816, the restriction on concertos lifting in 1819.

6. "Philharmonic Concerts," *Spectator* 411 (14 May 1836), 465.

7. Thalberg spent much of his career playing without an orchestra and endorsing Érards, although early on, particularly in Paris, he alternated between Pleyel and Érard, as at his benefit in Paris on 16 April 1836. See also the story of Thalberg accepting Érard's "gift" of a fine instrument. "Revue du Monde musical," *Revue de Paris* 27 (April 1836), 263–64. Late in his career Thalberg penned a written endorsement of Érard's new metal frame at the London's Great Exhibition of 1851, reprinted as "Notes on Pianofortes," *Hogg's Instructor* 8 (1852), 182–85.

8. Herz played on 5 May 1834. Mendelssohn wrote of the Semiquaver King in a letter to Moscheles on 26 June 1834: "He certainly is a characteristic figure of these times, of the year 1834; and as Art should be a mirror reflecting the character of the times,—as Hegel or some one else probably says somewhere,—he certainly does reflect most truly all salons and vanities, and a little yearning, and a deal of yawning, and kid gloves, and musk; a scent I abhor." Ignaz Moscheles, *Letters of Felix Mendelssohn to Ignaz and Charlotte Moscheles,* ed. Felix Moscheles (Boston, 1888), 112. When Mendelssohn premiered his Piano Concerto in D Minor, op. 40, at the Birmingham Festival in 1837, one critic took hand watching to be a sign of musical cultivation in the city, noting how Mendelssohn "had ventured onto the same ground as Thalberg": "The angle commanding a view of the keys of the pianoforte was thronged with sturdy occupants, who resisted all attempts of intruders, and every square foot was contested with an eagerness which spoke volumes for the amateurs and their love of classical composition." *Musical World* 7/81 (29 September 1837), 40.

9. The confusion betrays how fraught public solo keyboard performance was before the 1840s. See especially the letters from W. Watts to Thalberg, British Library Manuscripts, RPS MS. 328 f. 67 (8 June 1836). In March of 1823, Kalkbrenner and Smart squared off over the rule that barred remuneration for that season. Kalkbrenner never again played for the Philharmonic. See Cyril Erlich, *First Philharmonic: A History of the Philharmonic Society* (Oxford, 1995), 28. This reminds one also of the quarrels between Kalkbrenner (*inspecteur-contrôleur de la salle* for Conservatoire Concerts) and Habeneck at the Assemblée générale preceding the 1832 season. They fought over the relative merits of solo virtuosity and Beethoven symphonies. See *La Musique à Paris en 1830–1831* (Paris, 1983), Article 4, 121. Once again, it was Thalberg's 1836 talents, as Berlioz noted, that forced a relaxation of Habeneck's and the society's insistence that virtuosi be kept at bay. Hector Berlioz, "Premier concert du Conservatoire," *Revue et gazette musicale de Paris* 3/5 (31 January 1836), 38–39.

10. "Philharmonic Concerts," *Spectator* 411 (14 May 1836), 464.

11. "Music and Musicians; Philharmonic Society," *Atlas,* 15 May 1836, 311.

12. August Lewald's fascinating description of the event appeared in his *Aquarelle aus dem Leben,* 6 vols. (Mannheim, 1837), 4: 181–85.

13. "[In the beginning,] I ventured to extemporize before a few persons only, some connoisseurs, others unacquainted with the science, and while so doing, observed quietly how they received it, and what effect my Fantasia produced on both portions of my little, assembled, and mixed public." J.N. Hummel, *A Complete Theoretical and Practical Course of Instructions on the Art of Playing the Piano Forte* (London, 1827), 74.

14. "Musical Table-Talk: Views of Celebrated Composers," *Atlas,* 13 March 1836, 171.

15. The correspondent for the *Morning Post* noted that the pianist had preluded in the same way during rehearsal, Thalberg having apparently arrived with no intention of playing. "Sir George Smart, however, persuaded him just to step into the orchestra, 'and run his

fingers over the keys'; he did so, and was loudly applauded both by the band and the company on his appearance. He sat down, preluded a little, then struck into a beautiful thema with variations—but we must not anticipate the treats which the subscribers have in store; suffice it to say, that his style is unique." "Musical, &c.," *Morning Post*, 9 May 1836, 3f.

16. "Music and Musicians, Philharmonic Society," *Atlas*, 15 May 1836, 311.

17. "Concerts of the Month," *Court Magazine and Monthly Critic and Lady's Magazine* 8 (1836), 272.

18. "The advent of M. Thalberg will, if we mistake not, form an era in the history of our piano-forte playing. His performance is *sui generis;* he can be compared with none we have ever heard; he seems gifted with three hands, for he plays more notes, and those at a greater distance from each other, than we hitherto have thought could be commanded by the number of fingers and thumbs usually bestowed by nature." "Philharmonic Concerts," *Musical Library: Monthly Supplement* 27 (June 1836), 93.

19. "Concert de M. Sigismund Thalberg," *Gazette des salons* 5 (15 March 1837), 578–79, 578. The review accounted for the 12 March Conservatoire Concert, Thalberg's soloistic rival on this occasion being Lambert Massart on violin.

20. Smart's annotations are collected under *Philharmonic Society Concerts,* vol. 3 (1831–44), shelf mark K.6.d.3 in the British Library.

21. *La Phalange* 5/54 (6 May 1842), 889–90.

22. "Memoir of Sigismund Thalberg," supplement to *Musical World* 5 (17 March 1837), vii–xvi, xi.

23. Vera Mikol quotes Schumann, "So far as solo-playing is concerned, the fourth decade of this century saw it at its highest pitch of executive brilliancy and at its lowest of purpose and feeling—indeed, it may be comprehensively designated as the epoch of Thalberg." See "The Influence of Sigismund Thalberg on American Musical Taste, 1830–1872," *Proceedings of the American Philosophical Society* 102/5 (20 October 1958), 464–68, 466.

24. "Thalberg," *Le Ménestrel* 15/119 (13 March 1836), 4.

25. "Le piano d'aujourd'hui ne connaît, à vrai dire, que le Thalberg simple, le Thalberg amendé et le Thalberg exagéré; grattez ce qui s'écrit pour le piano, vous verrez Thalberg." Wilhelm von Lenz, *Beethoven et ses trois styles* (St. Petersburg, 1852), 8.

26. *La Méthode des méthodes de piano* (Paris, 1840), 9. "Of the pianoforte-players, Thalberg is really the most interesting. . . . In his combinations, capricious and fantasia-like as they are, all follows and develops itself so naturally that one easily overlooks the lack of unity and a certain Italian mannerism. In 1826 I gave him some instruction." Moscheles went on to lament how he now apparently required new hands:

> I find that at my age my fingers require to practise most carefully the exercises of former years, in order to keep pace with the times. I can manage them pliable and elastic, but I cannot make them any longer than they are; and that is just the road that modern pianists, like Chopin, Thalberg, etc., have taken, in order to develop their technique. To play your music, I have also to stretch my fingers to the fullest extent; but there they obey more naturally, because the mechanical construction of your passages is of secondary importance, as compared to the spirit which dictates them. (*Letters of Felix Mendelssohn,* 153–54)

27. "Monsieur Sigismund Thalberg," *Morning Herald,* 23 May 1836, 3d.

28. "Music and the Drama: M. Thalberg's Concert," *Athenaeum* 448 (28 May 1836), 386.

29. "Music," *Sunday Times* 713 (19 June 1836), 3b.

30. "Musical: Berrettoni and J. Bennett's Concert," *Morning Post,* 24 June 1836, 4c.

31. See reports in *Morning Post,* 8 May 1837, 6; "Music and the Drama," *Athenaeum* 498 (13 May 1837), 347; and "Music/Mori's Concert," *Sunday Times* 760 (14 May 1837), 5d.

32. *Morning Herald,* 9 May 1837, 5c.

33. *Musical World* 5/61 (12 May 1837), 139.

34. "Music and Musicians; Mr Mori's Concert," *Atlas,* 14 May 1837, 307. For Lablache's jaw issues, see "Musical Intelligence," *Age* 92 (1 October 1843), 6.

35. *Morning Herald,* 9 May 1837, 5c.

36. "Music and Musicians; Mr Mori's Concert," 307. Thalberg was, according to the *Sunday Times,* "certainly the most brilliant pianoforte player we have ever heard." The *Musical World* called him "a meteor," "perfectly incomprehensible to little creatures."

37. *Musical World* 5/61 (12 May 1837), 139–40.

38. "Concerts, Musical Soirees of the Nobility," *World of Fashion and Continental Feuilletons* 159 (1 June 1837), 124.

39. "Concert Room—King's Theatre," *Morning Herald,* 18 May 1837, 3c.

40. "M. Thalberg's Concert," *Morning Post,* 18 May 1837, 3f.

41. For a survey of Schumann's writings on Thalberg, see Leon B. Plantinga, *Schumann as Critic* (New Haven and London, 1967), 207–14.

42. Moscheles wrote these words in 1821, adding that he would never forgive Cramer for disfiguring those "thin, well-shaped fingers" by his inveterate use of snuff, which so often "clogg[ed] the action of the keys." *Life of Moscheles with Selections from His Diaries and Correspondence,* ed. A. D. Coleridge, 2 vols. (London and Hurst, 1873), 1: 51.

43. Robert Schumann, *On Music and Musicians,* trans. Fanny Raymond Ritter (London, 1877), 60. The original appeared as a journal supplement—*Musikalische Haus- und Lebensregeln* (Musical House Rules to Live By)—in an issue of *Neue Zeitschrift für Musik* 36 (3 May 1850), supplement 3, although it was initially meant for inclusion in his *Album für die Jugend.* One-handed keyboard music for "la mano sinistra" was already commonly in use in the early nineteenth century. The last of the three solfeggios in A major (W117:3) by C. P. E. Bach, for either hand, is a familiar example.

44. Heinrich Heine, "The Musical Season of 1843: Second Paper," in *The Works of Heinrich Heine,* trans. Charles Godfrey Leland (London, 1894), 4: 384–86. The "pharaoh" accusation, along with the famous line "[Herz] has been long dead; and fortunately also just got married" ([Herz] ist längst tot und hat kürzlich auch geheiratet), first appeared in "Musikalische Saison in Paris," an article supplement to *Allgemeine Zeitung* 85 (26 March 1843), 11b. The "sa mise élégante et tirée à quatre épingles," or "dressed to kill," accusation appears to have been inserted for the 1855 French version. *Lutèce: lettres sur la vie politique, artistique et sociale de la France* [1855] (Paris, 1892), 311–14. In each translation, then, Kalkbrenner grows increasingly colorful.

45. For Mendelssohn's "patty" and "sausage," see his letter of 5 September 1835 in Moscheles, *Letters of Felix Mendelssohn,* 139.

46. Robert Schumann, "Etüden für des Pianoforte," *Neue Zeitschrift für Musik* 11/29 (8 October 1839), 113–14.

47. The hand had an illustrious past. Since Anaxagoras and the fifth century B.C., at least, it was an emblem of agency, meaningful intention, and human purpose—proof of the supervening authority of man. In the classic Aristotelian or Galenic account, mankind's seat in the natural order, his placement above every living creature, was due to the use of his hands, to their exquisite organization and sensory capabilities. The ten fingers of the trained hand opened experiential highways to human sensory perception and physical knowledge in one sense; and, in another, the fingers were capable of altering, manipulating, and reshaping physical space.

48. In *De anima* Aristotle argued that "knowledge and sensation are in a manner identical with their respective objects. . . . It is not the stone which is in the soul, but the form of the stone. So that there is an analogy between the soul and the hand; for, as the hand is the instrument of instruments, so the intellect is the form of forms and sensation the form of sensibles. . . . It is in the sensible forms that intelligible forms exist." Aristotle, *De anima,* trans. R. D. Hicks (Salem, 1988), 145, 91.

49. "Every hand in its natural state, that is, with the exception of extraordinary accidents, is in perfect analogy with the body of which it constitutes a part. The bones, the nerves, the muscles, the blood and the skin of the hand, are only the continuation of the bones, the nerves, the muscles, the blood and skin of the rest of the body. The same blood circulates in the heart, in the head, and in the hand." Johann Kaspar Lavater, *Essays on Physiognomy Designed to Promote the Knowledge and the Love of Mankind,* trans. Henry Hunter, 3 vols. (London, 1789–98), 3: 419.

50. D'Arpentigny was particularly enthusiastic about the thumb, going so far as to misattribute these words to Isaac Newton: "'In default of other proofs', said Newton, 'the thumb would convince me of the existence of God.' Just as, without the thumb, the hand would be defective and incomplete, so, without moral force, logic, and decision [faculties of which the thumb in different degrees affords the indications] the most fertile and brilliant spirit would be a gift entirely without value." M. Le Capitaine C. S. d'Arpentigny, *The Science of the Hand; or the Art of Recognizing the Tendencies of the Human Mind by the Observation of the Formation of the Hands,* ed. Heron-Allen (London, 1886), 138–39.

51. "Memoir of Mr Frederick Kalkbrenner," *Quarterly Musical Magazine and Review* 24/6 (1824), 503.

52. "[In my school of fingering], too, I shall build upon Nature, for a natural fingering devoid of unnecessary strain and extension is clearly the best. The shapes of our hand and the keyboard teach us how to use our fingers. The former tells us that the three interior fingers are longer than the little finger and the thumb. From the latter we learn that certain keys are longer and lie lower than the others." Carl Philipp Emanuel Bach, *Essay on the True Art of Playing Keyboard Instruments,* trans. William J. Mitchell (London and New York, 1949), 44–45.

53. Bach's work certainly anticipated the enlightened encyclopedias, being unusual for its length, its attempt to systematize a "True Art," and its comprehensiveness. I list these compendia only because they represent such a dramatic departure from the thin volumes circulated by such early century keyboardists as Saint Lambert (1702), François Couperin (1716), and Friedrich Wilhelm Marpurg (I'm thinking of his twenty-four-page first edition of 1750).

54. Diruta's *Il transilvano* espoused a system of fingering apparently used in German lands at the time:

Now it remains for me to say which are the good and the bad fingers, which will similarly play the good and bad notes, for this is as necessary to the organist as to the virginal player. This knowledge is really the most important thing of all. There are five fingers in each hand, the thumb being accounted the first . . . and the little finger the fifth. The first plays a bad note *(la nota cattiva),* the second a good note *(la buona),* the third a bad note, the fourth a good note, and the fifth a bad note. The second, third and fourth fingers do most of the work; what I say about one hand applies equally to the other. (Girolamo Diruta, *Il transilvano* (Venice, 1597), 13; translated in Reginald R. Gerig, *Famous Pianists and Their Technique* (London, 1974), 12)

55. Examples include Juan Bermudos's *El libro llamado Declaración de instrumentos musicales* (Osuna, 1555) and Tómas de Santa Maria's *Arte de tañer fantasía* (Valladolid, 1565).

56. Türk felt it necessary, for example, to discuss every part of his clavichord in minute detail: strings, bass tangent, pins, cloth loops, keys, springs, casings. At the very outset of his "school," he made long lists of such apparent "irrelevancies" as the panoply of keyboard instruments available to him: "klavier, organ, harpsichord, spinet, pianoforte, pedal *(Fussklavier),* pantalon, hämmerpantalone, klaviorganum, cembal d'amour, piano-violin, Bogenflügel, Bogenhammerklavier, Hurdy-Gurdy, Lute-harpsichord, theorbo-harpsichord, pandoret, harfenklavier, virginal, Fortbien, Claveçin Roial, Bellesonorereal, Harmonica." Daniel Gottlob Türk, *School of Clavier Playing or Instructions in Playing the Clavier for Teachers and Students,* trans. Raymond H. Haggh (Lincoln and London, 1982), 9.

57. "Die Perle schwimmt nicht auf der Fläche; sie muss in der Tiefe gesucht werden, selbst mit Gefahr. Klara ist eine Taucherin." Florestan's 1833 words are reprinted in Robert Schumann, *Gesammelte Schriften über Musik und Musiker,* ed. Martin Kreisig, 2 vols. (Leipzig, 1914), 1: 21.

58. In a letter to Titus Woyciechowski dated 12 December 1831. *Selected Correspondence of Fryderyk Chopin,* trans. Arthur Hedley (London, 1962), 98–99.

59. Frédéric Kalkbrenner, *Method of Learning the Pianoforte, with the Aid of the Manual-Guide; containing the principles of music, a complete system of fingering, a classification of authors to be studied, rules on expression, on manners of phrasing, on musical punctuation* (1831), trans. Sabilla Novello (London, 1862), 12. "Voyez Kalkbrenner, lorsqu'il touche le piano.—Ce n'est pas sans raison que je dis voyez;—vous ne vous apercevez, ni à son corps ni à son visage, des immenses difficultés qui passent sous ses doigts. Kalkbrenner est l'exécutant-modèle." "De l'Étude," *Le Pianiste* (1833), 39.

60. Dussek showed off his "interesting profile" and "singing fingers" in Václav Tomásek, "Selbstbiographie," in *Libussa: Jahrbuch* 4 (1845), 349–98, 393.

61. "Kalkbrenner and Thalberg," *Musical World* 8/107 (29 March 1838), 213.

62. "As polished as a billiard ball . . . undisturbed, unexcited, with a gracious smile, he controlled his obedient fingers as a captain a company of well-drilled soldiers." Ernst Pauer, quoted in Harold C. Schonberg, *The Great Pianists* (New York, 1963), 112.

63. British Library, Manuscripts Add. 52337 A ff. 118–20; letter from Kalkbrenner to William Ayrton (1831).

64. Kalkbrenner, *Method of Learning the Pianoforte,* 4.

65. Heller quotes Kalkbrenner, "Je ferai non seulement votre éducation musicale, mais je m'efforcerai de vous décrotter, de vous rendre présentable à Paris." Stephen Heller, "Une visite à Kalkbrenner (1838)," *S.I.M Revue musicale mensuelle (Bulletin français de la S.I.M.)* 6 (December 1910), 690–95, 691.

66. Henri Blanchard, "Revue critique," *Revue et gazette musicale de Paris* 5/32 (1838), 325–26, 326. Fétis hailed Kalkbrenner's first edition for its straightforwardness, economy, and rationality. His only reservation involved the author's insinuation (denied by Kalkbrenner in a letter to the journal of a month later) that a student's engagement with art should proceed only once the technical groundwork had been laid. Fétis, "Publications élémentaires," *Revue musicale* 11/46 (24 December 1831), 368–70.

67. *Modern German Music: Recollections and Criticisms* (London, 1854), 231.

68. Mlles. Carbeault, Darroux, and Sarrauton were awarded the joint first prize. "École Royale de musique, Concours annuels," *Revue musicale* 4/6 (August 1829), 60–67, 63.

69. "Effusio Musica," *Quarterly Musical Magazine and Review* 6/21 (1824), 135–39, 139.

70. Antoine Marmontel, *Les Pianistes célèbres* (Paris, 1878), 102.

71. "De l'Étude," 39.

72. Saint-Saëns, who trained with Kalkbrenner's "musical son" Camille Stamaty, remembered:

> I also was put upon the regime of the *guide-mains*. It was a bar fixed in front of the keyboard, upon which the forearm rested, in such a fashion as to get rid of all muscular action except that of the hand itself. This system is excellent for forming the young pianist in the execution of works written for the clavecin and for the earliest pianofortes, of which the notes spoke without effort on the player's part, though insufficient for modern works and instruments. It is thus, however, that we should begin developing first firmness of touch and finger, and suppleness of wrist, and adding progressively the weight of the forearm and that of the arm. It was not only strength of finger that one acquired by this method, but also the production of tone-quality by the finger only, a precious expedient that has become rare in our days. (Quoted in Gerig, *Famous Pianists and Their Technique*, 136)

73. Kalkbrenner, *Method of Learning the Pianoforte*, 4.

74. "Kalkbrenner's Apotheose," *Neue Zeitschrift für Musik* 18 (1843), 18.

75. By the 1840s the success of this machine shocked even such good friends as Ignaz Moscheles, who had frequented Vienna's Ludlamshöhle with him twenty years previously and was later a regular guest at Kalkbrenner's country estate at Château de Praslin near Nogent-sur-Vernisson. In 1841 Moscheles felt the apparatus was "quite unnecessary," since, when one practices "with the 'hand-guide' (as Kalkbrenner recommends, and still daily uses), all feeling must be dormant," according to a letter quoted in *Life of Moscheles with Selections from His Diaries and Correspondence*, ed. A. D. Coleridge, 2 vols. (London and Hurst, 1873), 94.

76. Constance Malpas, "Jules Guérin Makes His Market: The Social Economy of Orthopaedic Medicine in Paris, c. 1825–1845," *Cultural Approaches to the History of Medicine*, ed. Willem de Blécourt and Cornelie Usborne (New York, 2004), 148–70.

77. Jules Janin, *735 Lettres à sa femme*, ed. Mergier-Bourdeix, 3 vols. (Paris, 1973), 1: 154.

78. D. W. F. Hardie, "The Macintoshes and the Origins of the Chemical Industry," *Science, Technology, and Economic Growth in the Eighteenth Century,* ed. A. E. Musson (London, 1972), 168–94, 188.

79. The prospectus was reproduced with a different list of instructors as "Institution de Mme Daubrée," *Revue de Paris* 9 (1834), 1–4.

80. See Heinrich Panofka, "Madame Polmartin," *Revue et gazette musicale de Paris* 7/11 (6 February 1840), 88–89.

81. "In 1829," explained Berlioz, "I had the honor to teach the guitar (I have been attracted to terrible instruments) in a well-known school for young ladies in the Marais." Music was hardly the sole attraction: "Three times a week I would emerge from my garret in the rue de Richelieu and wend my weary way along endless boulevards to near the Place de la Bastille to teach Carulli's Divertissements. My pupils were scarcely more than infants, almost all of them as timid as lambs and as intelligent as guinea-fowls." One or two of these guinea fowls, according to Berlioz, suggested dropping guitar in favor of "music lessons." Berlioz preferred talking to his pupils, who—released from "visible" pursuits—at last began to "progress." "Young and old thus acquired a rather less vague idea of the art of music," Berlioz recalled, "than they would have got from arpeggios on the guitar." Hector Berlioz, "Théatre de l'opéra-comique," *Journal des débats,* 8 June 1855, 1–2, 1d, translated in David Cairns, *Berlioz 1830–1832: The Making of an Artist* (London, 1989), 438.

82. "A Violent Distraction—F—H—Mademoiselle M—," in *The Memoirs of Hector Berlioz,* trans. David Cairns (London, 1969), 129–30, 130. Berlioz reports that he had been invited to teach by Madame d'Aubrée herself.

83. Érard purchased the esteemed pavilion (and soon-to-be orthopedic clinic) with its eleven hectares of park on 12 August 1820. Less than a hundred years previously on the estate, in November 1763, Pilâtre de Rozier and Marquis d'Arlandes made the first successful flight in a hot air balloon built by the Montgolfier brothers. Since the seventeenth century, La Muette had been royal land, Louis XVI having spent years at the château with his young bride, Marie-Antoinette.

84. *Institut orthopédique de Paris, pour le traitement des difformités de la taille et des membres, chez les personnes des deux sexes / Dirigé par MM. Les Docteurs Pravaz et Jules Guérin* (Paris, ca. 1835), 7. See also the feuilleton "Visite a l'Institut orthopédique de Paris," *Gazette médicale de Paris* 3/26 (17 June 1835), 401–5.

85. Valentine Mott, *Travels in Europe and the East* (New York, 1842), 55. Guérin argued for the place of physical fitness and nutrition in orthopedic practice, and was a particular fan of cheese and onions.

86. Guérin eventually fell victim to his own arguments, and his lack of formal surgical qualifications came back to haunt him. In 1848 an enquiry into Guérin's experiments in subcutaneous tenotomy drew the wrath of the Académie des sciences. Orthopedic practitioners such as Jean François Malgaigne and Bouvier were increasingly keen to establish boundaries between surgery and orthopedics. Guérin thence lost his appointment at the Hôpital des enfants malades, and the institute at Passy collapsed in 1849 before he returned—tail between legs—to Belgium.

87. Moke-Pleyel practiced "never less than four or five hours a day, not counting the time spent giving lessons," according to a letter Berlioz wrote to his sister in June of 1830. Hector Berlioz, *Correspondance générale,* ed. Pierre Citron, 8 vols. (Paris, 1972), 1: 336. For

Kalkbrenner's austere daily regime—he used a watch to make sure he practiced long enough, and read books while playing, mostly hands separately—see "Memoir of Mr Frederick Kalkbrenner," 505–6.

88. "Der Thalberg-Apparat," *Neue Zeitschrift für Musik* 26 (1847), 209; Félix Levacher d'Urclé, *De l'anatomie de la main considérée dans ses rapports avec l'exécution de la musique instrumentale* [with long recommendations by Auzias-Turenne, Sigismund Thalberg, and Jean Cruveilhier] (Paris, 1846).

89. Hector Berlioz reviewed this *"appareil orthopédique"* in "Revue musicale: Nouvelle Méthode," *Journal des débats*, 7 June 1846, 3c–e.

90. D'Urclé, *De l'anatomie de la main*, 21.

91. Sigismund Thalberg, *L'Art du chant appliqué au piano*, 2 vols. (London, 1853), 1: ii.

92. Auzias-Turenne, "Sur les analogies des members supérieurs avec les inférieurs," *Comptes rendus hebdomadaires des séances de l'Académie des sciences* 23 (28 December 1846), 1148–50. See also Flourens, "Nouvelles observations sur le parallèle des extrémités dans l'homme et les quadrupèdes," *Annales des sciences naturelles* 10 (1838), 35–41.

93. Joseph d'Ortigue, "Concert de M. Sigismund Thalberg," *Revue et gazette musicale de Paris* 4/12 (19 March 1837), 96–98. In hyperbolic style, d'Ortigue lauded how Thalberg penetrated the listener's soul before exalting that listener progressively and spiritually.

94. S., "Music and Musicians; Mr Mori's Concert," *Atlas*, 14 May 1837, 307.

95. "Impressions of Thalberg," *Morning Post* 20743 (15 June 1837), 3d.

96. On 6 March 1839, George Mifflin Dallas observed Thalberg perform with Sontag in St. Petersburg at the Assemblée de la noblesse: "He seems a young man of twenty-five, of rather slender figure, florid complexion, light chestnut hair, and a distinct Grecian profile. His personal deportment was modest, deferential, but perfectly composed and calm. Dressed in full black, with white cravat and maintaining a mild but imperturbable serenity, he took his seat at the piano, with the preoccupied air of a young clergyman full of his most interesting sermon." *Magazine of Music* 8/7 (1891), 126.

97. François-Joseph Fétis, "Concert de M. Thalberg," *Le Temps*, 1 March 1836, 1–2.

98. "Avec un gout parfait, il s'est borné à rendre avec une perfection absolue les pensées du grand musicien dont il était l'interprète." Ibid., 2a.

99. In April 1848, Thalberg played Beethoven (the C-minor concerto) and selections from *Lieder ohne Worte* by the recently deceased Mendelssohn at Her Majesty's Theatre. One critic wrote that the performance "may be called his *début* in this country as a classical pianist." *Times*, 18 April 1848, 5b. In fact, Thalberg had frequently played music by dead composers.

100. Henri Blanchard wrote, "C'est l'ame expansive de Thalberg qui erre sur cet ivoire. . . . Sous ce calme apparent, sous ce phlegme germanique, bouillonne un incessant besoin de création; et ce besoin, ce démon familier de Socrate est dans Thalberg un stryge qui dévore, détruit sourdement le système physiologique le plus exquis qui fut jamais." "Thalberg," *Revue et gazette musicale de Paris* 3/19 (8 May 1836), 153.

101. For more on the triumph of Cousinian metaphysics in France after around 1832, see Jan Goldstein, *The Post-Revolutionary Self: Politics and Psyche in France, 1750–1850* (Cambridge, MA, 2005).

102. Translated in John Knowles Paine, *Famous Composers and Their Works* 4 (1891), 814.

103. Lenz, *Beethoven,* 9.

104. "Young and Delcambre's Type-Composing Machine," *Mechanics' Magazine* 36/985 (25 June 1842), 497–501, 497; "Rosenberg's Type-Composing and Distributing Machines," *Mechanics' Magazine* 37/1003 (29 October 1842), 401–5; "Industrie. Des Claviers typographiques," *L'Illustration* 4/1 (25 March 1843), 59–61.

105. "Nothing is so lady-like as a well formed hand; it is tacitly understood to be the privilege of women of fashion.... A well-made hand must be delicate, rather long, and dimpled. The hand requires a great deal of care." Antoine Martin Bureaud-Riofrey, *Physical Education; Specially Adapted to Young Ladies* (London, 1838), 481–82.

106. "Philharmonic Society," *Times,* 7 June 1836, 3g. This article described the firm's Apollonicon, a mammoth finger-and-barrel chamber organ encased in Grecian style with Doric pilasters surmounted by paintings of Apollo (music), Erato (poetry), and Clio (history). According to Rachel Cowgill, the ossification of a nineteenth-century "classical" canon in London was in part due to the Apollonicon's somewhat haphazard, though influential, executions of a core of works by Bach, Mozart, and Haydn. "The London Apollonicon Recitals, 1817–32: A Case-Study in Bach, Mozart and Haydn Reception," *Journal of the Royal Musical Association* 123/2 (1998), 190–228.

107. See the report in "Philharmonic Society," *Morning Post,* 28 June 1842, 5; and MacFarren senior's defense of "candor" in *Musical World* 16/26 (30 June 1842), 201–2. See also Cyril Erlich, *First Philharmonic: A History of the Royal Philharmonic Society* (Oxford, 1995), 40. Davison wrote that Thalberg's *Andante* op. 32 was "an affliction! We heard nothing so maudlin or monotonous, so lachrymose and lackadaisical, so pitifully puling and positively paralytic, or whining, whooping, whizzing, whirring, wishy-washy, wallowing and warm-waterish, since the dear, delightful, dead-for-durance days when dear old Aunt Tabitha seated herself at the harpsichord." He has similar things to say about Chopin. See Charles Reid, *The Music Monster: A Biography of James William Davison* (London, 1984), 15–16.

108. Schumann lambasted Thalberg for turning music into a kind of sport or athletics. He mocked the pianist for being "accustomed to wealth and elegance" and for mistaking his piano for a horse, an animal to be tamed, groomed, saddled, and then ridden on a steeplechase, from one obstacle to another. Robert Schumann, "Pianofortemusik [2nd article]," *Neue Zeitschrift für Musik* 17/43 (25 November 1842), 175–77, 176. Dana Gooley characterizes the Thalberg-Liszt rivalry as a battle between operatic vocality and instrumental orchestrality in *The Virtuoso Liszt* (Cambridge, 2004), 35.

109. F. Liszt, "Revue critique: M. Thalberg.—Grande Fantaisie," *Revue et gazette musicale de Paris* 4/2 (6 January 1837), 17–20, 19. In a letter to d'Agoult of 13 February 1837, Liszt noted Chopin's suspicion that "un Dietrichstein" had bribed Fétis to laud Thalberg. Liszt's claim that Thalberg was more aristocratic than liberal has stuck, supposedly because the patronage of the Count and Countess Apponyi proved it. (The Apponyis were apparently responsible for easing Thalberg into the public eye, his first Parisian appearance occurring at the Austro-Hungarian embassy in November 1835.) Liszt wrote to d'Agoult in March of 1837 that "Les Apponyi cabalent (le mot est exact) pour Thalberg et contre moi." *Correspondance de Liszt et de la comtesse d'Agoult, 1833–1840,* ed. Daniel Ollivier, 2 vols. (Paris, 1933), 1: 198.

110. Curille's sixteen-year-old automaton is described in "Wiener—Neuigkeite: Liszt als Automat," *Wiener Courier (ein polit. Journal)* 220 (17 September 1856), 2b.

111. François-Joseph Fétis, "MM. Thalberg et Liszt," *Revue et gazette musicale de Paris* 4/17 (23 April 1837), 141. For "Thalberg-Hongrois," see "Concerts: Monument de Beethoven," *Le Ménestrel* 8/22 (2 May 1841), 2–3, 2.

112. "Tout ce que j'ai pu distinguer, *en fait de mécanisme neuf*, dans ces choeurs infinis naissant sous les doigts de Liszt." Hector Berlioz, "Premier concert du Conservatoire," *Revue et gazette musicale de Paris* 3/5 (31 January 1836), 38–39.

5. IN SEARCH OF VOICE

1. Jane Fulcher, *The Nation's Image: French Grand Opera as Politics and Politicized Art* (Cambridge, 1987), 100; Maurice Agulhon, *1848 ou l'apprentissage de la République* (Paris, 1973), 9; Louis Quicherat, *Adolphe Nourrit: Sa vie, son talent, son caractère, sa correspondance*, 3 vols. (Paris, 1867), 2: 143.

2. This is from Goncourt's journal of 18 November 1860, which is cited in a suggestive study of shifting friendship politics in this era, Sarah Esther Horowitz, "States of Intimacy: Friendship and the Remaking of French Political Elites, 1815—1848," Ph.D. diss. (University of California at Berkeley, 2008), 267.

3. See, for example, Nourrit's letter of 19 October 1836 intimating details of the wrangle with Duprez in Quicherat, *Adolphe Nourrit*, 3: 23–24.

4. Heinrich Heine called Duponchel "ein hagerer, gelbblasser Mann," in "Über die Französische Bühne," *Allgemeine Theater-Revue* 3 (May 1837), 155–248, 236.

5. Ange-Henri Blaze, "Revue musicale," *Revue des deux mondes* 24 (15 December 1840), 873–83, 881.

6. Léon Escudier, *La France musicale*, 3 January 1841, 5–6, 6; Quicherat, *Adolphe Nourrit*, 2: 201.

7. Léon Escudier called Duponchel "un directeur d'une incapacité incontestable" in "La vérité sur l'Opéra," *La France musicale* 4/1 (3 January 1841), 5–6, 6; Quicherat, *Adolphe Nourrit*, 2: 201; Heine, "Über die Französische Bühne," 239.

8. Frédéric Soulié, "Opéra.—Nourrit, Dupré," *La Presse* 270 (10 April 1837), 1c. Théophile Gautier's words of 31 July 1837 appear in "État actuel du thèatre," *Histoire de l'art dramatique en France depuis vingt-cinq ans*, 6 vols. (Paris, 1858–59), 1: 18.

9. Blaze wrote of "une monotonie insupportable" in H. W., "Revue musicale," *Revue des deux mondes* 26 (1 May 1841), 485–95, 493. "En somme, une voix de poitrine, et toujours une voix de poitrine, inflexible aux désirs des situations, aux mouvements divers de la scène, au goût national." Charles Maurice, *Histoire anecdotique du théâtre* (Paris, 1856), 2: 163.

10. Quicherat, *Adolphe Nourrit*, 2: 42.

11. Joseph Mainzer questioned his capacities as an "artist" in J. M . . . er, "Début de Duprez, role de Mazaniello," *Le National*, 28 September 1837, 2; Joseph d'Ortigue, "Début de M. Duprez.—*Guillaume Tell*," *Journal de Paris* 70 (19 April 1837), 1–2; J. d'O, "Représentation de retraite de d'Ad. Nourrit," *Revue et gazette musicale de Paris* 4/15 (9 April 1837), 123–25, 125.

12. Hippolyte Fortoul's words appear in *Le Monde*, 24 April 1837; and Quicherat, *Adolphe Nourrit*, 2: 495.

13. Auguste Laget, "La voix sombrée," *Le Guide musical* 3/33–34 (15 and 22 August 1867), 1–4, 1. Laget also blamed Duprez for "urlomanie," for separating song from speech, and for destroying French prosody. *La France* is quoted in Quicherat, *Adolphe Nourrit*, 2: 270. En.

M., "Débuts de Duprez dans *Guillaume Tell*," *Revue et gazette musicale de Paris* 4/17 (23 April 1837), 142–44, 143.

14. Blaze lamented this ill-fated attempt to "creuser les registres de sa voix" in H. W., "Adolphe Nourrit," *Revue des deux mondes* 18 (1 April 1839), 145–52, 151. Dessalles-Régis, "Duprez," *La France littéraire* 38 (1838), 477–90, 488.

15. Henry Pleasants translates a conversation between the singer and a friend (probably Guillaume Cottrau) reported in *Omnibus pittoresco* (28 March 1839), in *The Great Tenor Tragedy: The Last Days of Adolphe Nourrit* (Portland, 1995), 120.

16. Pleasants, *The Great Tenor Tragedy*, 105, 77, 103.

17. Interview with Elizabeth Farnsworth, *PBS NewsHour*, November 9, 1998. Bartoli's words echo those of her alter ego, Maria Malibran, particularly as mythologized by Ernest Legouvé in his memoirs: "My throat and I know one another. We are often at loggerheads." *Soixante ans de souvenirs*, 2 vols. (Paris, 1886), 1: 245.

18. James Stark, *Bel Canto: A History of Vocal Pedagogy* (Toronto, 2003), xxii.

19. An Italian teaching in Paris from 1837 to 1848, Concone pioneered modern classifications of voice. Having bound each "voice type" to its "timbre naturel," he advocated the development of "homogenous sonority" by "free and pure" vocalization in ways that resonate remarkably with practice today. His lessons are still widely in use. Giuseppe Concone, *Introduction à l'art de bien chanter* (Paris, 1845), 324.

20. García *fils* followed ancient precedent by dedicating a section of his tutor to the "manner of disposing mouth." *Traité complet de l'art du chant*, 2 vols. (Paris, 1847), 1: 25.

21. "In the interior of the larynx is a body which resembles no other part of the animal structure," Galen wrote of such inner mouths. "This is the first and most important organ of voice [which I] call the glottis, or tongue of the larynx." Quoted in William Gordon Holmes, *A Treatise on Vocal Physiology and Hygiene* (London, 1881), 102.

22. Bernardo Mengozzi, as presented by a committee comprising Richer, Garat, Gossec, Mehul, Cherubini, and others, in *Méthode de chant du conservatoire de musique* (Paris, 1804), 7, 8.

23. French teachers such as Alexis de Garaudé were assigned "vocalization," where vocalises (raw sound) were taught instead of solfeggi, as if to confirm that song and language, source and filter, and the arts of singing and speech were separating.

24. J. A. Hiller, *Anweisung zum musikalisch-richtigen Gesange* (Leipzig, 1774), 6; Domenico Corri, *The Singer's Preceptor* (London, 1811), 5; Louis Lablache, *Méthode complète de chant* (Paris, 1840), 2.

25. Examples include G. B. Mancini's *Riflessioni pratiche sul canto figurato* (Milan, 1774), 103–19, 117; F. W. Marpurg, *Anleitung zur musik überhaupt und zur Singkunst besonders* (Berlin, 1763); and Jean Paul Egide Martini, *Mélopée moderne; ou l'art du chant, réduit en principes* (Paris, ca. 1792), 4.

26. The common injunction to sing before a mirror extends from Rule 10 in castrato *Mr.* [Giusto Fernando] *Tenducci's Instructions to His Scholars* (London, 1785) to Manuel García *fils, Hints on Singing*, ed. Beata García (London, 1894), 13.

27. Giambattista Mancini, *Practical Reflections on the Figurative Art of Singing*, trans. Pietro Buzzi (Boston, 1912), 90, 92.

28. Gesualdo Lanza, *The Elements of Singing Abridged* (London, 1819), 70. Robert O. Gjerdingen's "Monuments of Solfeggi" offers a glimpse into the dimly recollected world of

instructional melodies and schematic bass movements. See http://faculty-web.at.north-western.edu/music/gjerdingen/solfeggi/index.htm.

29. Andrea Costa, *Analytical Considerations on the Art of Singing* (London, 1838), 30.

30. Lanza's words appear in an informative review of "Treatises on Singing," *Quarterly Musical Magazine and Review* 1/3 (1818), 351–70, 356.

31. As reported by William Earl Brown in *Vocal Wisdom: Maxims of Giovanni Battista Lamperti* (Marlboro, NJ, 1957), 39, 129.

32. William Shakespeare, *The Art of Singing: Based on the Principles of the Old Italian Singing-Masters* (Boston, 1905), 26.

33. Paul Diday and Joseph Pétrequin announced their discovery in "Mémoire sur une nouvelle espèce de voix chantée," *Gazette médicale de Paris* 8/20 (16 May 1840), 305–14. In a letter of response, Manuel García *fils* scoffed at this idea of "a new species of voice." The pedagogue protested that Duprez's "new voice," far from being self-indulgent, "new," or even "a voice," was a common or garden-variety "fundamental timbre." He used the term *"timbre sombre"* in "Au Rédacteur," *Gazette médicale de Paris* 8/26 (27 June 1840), 407, and defended this so-called "artifice" as a fully natural and time-honored Italian resource in "Correspondance," *Compte rendu des séances de l'Académie des sciences* 12 (19 April 1841), 692–93. Édouard Fournié also hailed this *"timbre sombre"* in *Physiologie de la voix et de la parole* (Paris, 1866), 488. For an excellent analysis of these debates, see Gregory W. Bloch, "The Pathological Voice of Gilbert-Louis Duprez," *Cambridge Opera Journal* 19/1 (2007), 11–31.

34. Friend of Berlioz Stéphen de la Madeleine—though he thought the *voix sombrée* "probably as old as the flood"—attacked *"le système sombré"* as an "eccentric" imposition that revolutionized the French scene in 1836 and against which he had "crusaded" for fifteen years. The public had surrendered to "a first-class artist, whose triumphs have been more prejudicial to French art than the invasion of barbarians on the exasperated splendors of the later Roman Empire." *Théories completes du chant* (Paris, 1852), 192, 276. August Laget repeated descriptions of barbarous attack twenty years later in *Le Chant et les chanteurs* (Paris and Toulouse, 1874), 199.

35. Diday and Pétrequin, "Mémoire sur une nouvelle espèce," 305, 313.

36. According to *Le Figaro*, the appointment of Bennati as "docteur dilettante" was a win-win situation for him, because he was equipped both to order a tenor to rest and then to sing his role. "Théatre Italien," *Le Figaro* 5/270 (29 September 1830), 2.

37. García was hardly alone in probing for voice, as evidenced by Cagniard de Latour's "double mirror" (1825), B. G. Babington's glottiscope (1829), and Pierre Nicolas Gerdy's "mirror" (1830). At the Académie des sciences on 21 December 1832, "M. Bennati adresse un paquet cacheté, contenant le dessin et la description d'un appareil nouveau destiné à éclairer et a rendre accessible à la vue la partie supérieure du larynx avec ses alentours." *Gazette médicale de Paris* 3/130 (29 December 1832), 896.

38. Francesco Bennati, *Recherches sur le mécanisme de la voix humaine* (Paris, 1832).

39. Deleau's discovery was probably made accidentally while tinkering with an air-driven instrument for catheterizing Eustachian tubes. Ibid., xii–iv, and translated in Colombat de l'Isère, *A Treatise upon the Diseases and Hygiene of the Organs of the Voice*, trans. J. F. W. Lane (Boston, 1857) 56–57.

40. Charles-Joseph-Frédéric Carron du Villards, "Notice nécrologique sur le Docteur Bennati," *Recherches pratiques sur les causes qui font échouer l'opération de la cataracte* (Paris, 1834), 419–24, 420.

41. Musical instruments are not necessarily "artificial," of course, and were once, it seems, entirely "natural" objects. The summary occurred, for example, in the *Revue musicale*'s third installment of "*Du mécanisme de la voix pendant le chant*, par M. le docteur Bennati (suite et fin)," *Revue musicale* 9/3 (28 August 1830), 65–75, 71.

42. Cuvier's report, presented on behalf of himself, M. de Prony, and Savart, was published in *Le Globe* two days after Bennati's presentation as "Sur le mécanisme de la voix humaine dans le chant par M. Bennati: Séance du 10 mai," *Le Globe* 6/86 (12 May 1830), 1. Three days later the same report was published in several scientific periodicals and the *Revue musicale*. "Rapport sur un mémoire de M. Bennati, intitulé: *Du mécanisme de la voix humaine dans le chant,*" *Revue musicale* 8/2 (15 May 1830), 33–40.

43. Bennati—though he advocated the widest possible range and defended the sweetest masculine sounds—ended up infantilizing the falsetto voice here. Inadvertently, falsetto sounds were quarantined for their later pathologization. Bennati, *Recherches sur le mécanisme de la voix humaine*, x.

44. Ibid., xviii. Composer and friend Nicola Vaccai even wrote to Bennati in 1832 in order to discuss a new *metodo pratico,* one that would shun the "single type of exercises for different types of voices" and invent exclusive training programs targeted to each sounding mechanism. Vaccai's tutor never included that theoretical section, but it is still in print as *Metodo pratico di canto* (Milan, 2001). Vaccai's letter to Bennati on the subject of his *Metodo* is reproduced in Mauro Uberti, "Il *Metodo practico di canto* di Nicola Vaccai," *Nuova Rivista Italiana* 8 (2004), 43–67, 45–46.

45. Borrowing the language of Joseph-François Malgaigne and Pierre Nicolas Gerdy, Colombat made his description of vocal function in *Traité médico-chirurgical des maladies des organes de la voix* (Paris, 1834), 78–79. His views were well circulated in musical circles, and these same words were reprinted in "Du faucet, ou voix pharyngienne," *Revue musicale* 9/27 (5 July 1835), 212–34, 214. For the later involvement of his son in mainstream music instruction, see Émile Colombat, *L'Enseignement orthophonique au Conservatoire national de musique et de déclamation de Paris* (Paris, 1873).

46. Panseron discussed Colombat's "voix pharyngienne" in his 1840 tutor *Méthode de vocalisation en 2 parties* (Paris, 1840), 3. Garaudé discussed a "seconde voix" caused by a pseudoglottis or "nouvelle ouverture vocale" in the second edition of his *Méthode complète de chant ou théorie pratique de cet art* (Paris, ca. 1841), 8. A "second voice" formed in the pharynx when the tenor crossed into the [falsetto] "head voice." Garaudé observed: "The soft palate contracts suddenly, the soft palate lifts and tightens," and "a new vocal aperture opens which could almost name itself *glotte pharyngienne.*" François-Joseph Fétis, meanwhile, wrote in 1837 of "un second voix factice" working "without the direct participation of the ordinary vocal organ" in "Recherches sur la théorie de la voix," *Revue et gazette musicale de Paris* 4/39 (24 September 1837), 419–22, 420.

47. At the 16 November 1840 séance of the Académie des sciences, García *fils* observed three apertures "placées les unes au-dessus des autres," each linked to a separate voice. Anonymous, "Mémoire sur la voix; par M. Manuel García," *Gazette médicale de Paris* 8/46 (1840), 748–49. García based his description of "la voix arythéno-épiglottique" on Bennati's

1833 description of Nicolai Ivanoff's anomalous Russian bass register in *Mémoire sur un cas particulier d'anomalie de la voix humaine pendant le chant* (Paris, 1834). A second paper, García's "Mémoire sur la voix humaine," appeared in *La France musicale* 4/19 (9 May 1841), 161–63; 4/20 (10 May 1841), 173–75; and 4/21 (23 May 1841), 181–82. This memoir, evidence suggests, was not the 16 November 1840 report but another read at the Académie des sciences on 12 April 1841 on García's behalf, which formed the template for the physiological "Études physiologiques sur la voix humaine" of his famous vocal tutor of 1847. This 1847 version (altered from 1841 to emphasize resonance concepts over "garden hose" ideas) expanded the discussion of the "production of registers," García actually defending two-glottis conjectures against Johannes Peter Müller's theory that the vocal cords only vibrate at their edges for falsetto. He pointed to the huge volume Wilhelmine Schröder-Devrient achieved in her "falsetto-head" (which surely could never be the product of edges alone), and the overtone singing of the Turkic Bashkir people to counter Müller's one-glottis view. García, *Traité complet de l'art,* 1: 12–14.

48. The reporting scientists declared themselves "struck by the multiplicity of changes to which the [vocal] mechanism is susceptible." Echoing Cuvier's words on Bennati, they wrote that "this organ can truly and itself alone be considered to represent an assemblage of instruments differing one from another." Magendie presented the report on behalf of Henri Dutrochet on 12 April 1840, lauding the vocal organ in "Travaux académiques. Académie des sciences," *Gazette médicale de Paris* 9/17 (24 April 1841), 269–70, 270, and later in García, *Traité complet de l'art,* 1: 3–4.

49. García, *Traité complet de l'art,* 2: 54. An 1843 memoir by Diday and Pétrequin offered a variation on the theme by theorizing "the transformation of the glottis." For them, the larynx was a double instrument: falsetto notes sounded when the lips of the glottis acted as if the *embouchure* of a flute, chest notes when the cords turned back into a reed. Again, the upper register was feminine and abnormal, according to the doctors, since reed instruments were "vital," flutes "mechanical." Diday and Pétrequin, "Mémoire sur le mécanisme de la voix de fausset," *Gazette médicale de Paris* 12/8 (24 February 1844), 115–20; and 12/9 (2 March 1844), 133–39, 135–36.

50. David Kimbell translated the letter in *Vincenzo Bellini: "Norma"* (Cambridge, 1998), 12.

51. "The King's Theatre," *Quarterly Musical Magazine and Review* 10/38 (1828), 261–73, 272.

52. Bennati, *Recherches sur le mécanisme,* 50–52.

53. Historians have identified many such progenitors, including Matteo Babbini and Giacomo David. On Donzelli, see Maurizio Modugno, "Domenico Donzelli e il suo tempo," *Nuova rivista musicale italiana* 18/2 (1984), 200–216; Giorgio Appolonia, *Le voci di Rossini* (Turin, 1992), 225–41, 225. Donzelli's reputation has developed out of Alberto Mazzucato's 1842 expert delineation of the six characteristics of his style: 1) his use of the *timbre sombre;* 2) his overexploitation of long notes in recitative; 3) his exaggerated slides on ascending portamenti; 4) his frequent use of the *messe di voce;* and 6) his skillful "clear and true gruppetto" that he interpolated in slow melodies. "Preliminari ad un esame critico sul *Metodo di canto* di García," *Gazzetta musicale di Milano* 1/14 (3 April 1842), 55–56, 56. See also David Lawton's introduction to the Ricordi critical edition of Giuseppe Verdi, *Il trovatore* (Chicago and Milan, 1993), xxxi.

54. A role lacking a love duet, Otello was a character "prone to silence," jealousy being an emotion beyond the reach of musical expression. "With melody," one English critic wrote, "[the role] is at open war." "Review of Music," *Harmonicon* 1/6 (June 1823), 79–84, 82. Castil-Blaze thought Donzelli suited to Otello because "il y a peu à chanter." X.X.X. [Castil-Blaze], "Début de Donzelli," *Journal des débats*, 2 May 1825, 1–3, 3a; "The Drama," *Harmonicon* 7/3 (March 1829), 69–70, 70.

55. "Album, 10 October 1830," *Revue de Paris* 19 (1830), 103–4; Quicherat, *Adolphe Nourrit*, 2: 214.

56. In an 1835 letter Donizetti wrote, "What? Donzelli in love? But you know that Donzelli must be fifty! And with fifty years on his back to play the impassioned one, or, *per Bacco*, even at my age [thirty-seven], no! I know that Donzelli in 1822 in Rome was already playing tyrants. I know that in Milan in *Norma* he was already over the hill as he seemed in *Ugo* [*conte di Parigi*]." In Guido Zavadini, *Donizetti: vita, musiche, epistolario* (Bergamo, 1943), 375, and translated in William Ashbrook, *Donizetti and His Operas* (Cambridge, 1982), 633. On 2 August 1828 Bellini lamented "dell'indole del suo canto" and complained that, for Donzelli, he would have to transpose Gualtiero (in *Pirata*) three tones lower. Vincenzo Bellini, *Epistolario*, ed. Luisa Cambi (Milan, 1943), 141. *Le Diable boiteux* spoke of his "l'art sans séduction" on 28 April 1825 in *Le Théâtre-Italien de Paris 1801–1831: chronologie et documents*, ed. Jean Mongrédien (Paris, 2008), 6: 97; "The Drama," *Harmonicon* 8/5 (May 1830), 221–24, 221.

57. "Donzelli does not nuance his singing enough; he delivers almost everything with equal force; he took several notes in the chest that are usually taken with the head voice." In "Feuilleton de 28 Avril," *Journal de Paris* 118 (28 April 1825), 1. *Le Corsaire* of 30 April 1825 complained that Donzelli failed to "melt the heart" because his "transitions between pride and love, love and fury were not skillfully rendered." In *Le Théâtre-Italien de Paris*, ed. Mongrédien, 6: 100. Le Dilettante lamented his "ports de voix" in *L'Aristarque français* (8 May 1825) and *Le Théâtre-Italien de Paris*, ed. Mongrédien, 108.

58. Castil-Blaze worried about Donzelli's "lacunae" in X.X.X., "Début de Donzelli," 1a. *Le Globe* accused Donzelli of ignoring "l'art de manier sa voix" in "Reprise de *la Donna del lago*.—Mlle Sontag," 3/18 (27 June 1826), 428. For Vitet, see Benjamin Walton, "The Professional Dilettante: Ludovic Vitet and *Le Globe*," *Reading Critics Reading*, ed. Roger Parker and Mary Ann Smart (Oxford, 2001), 69–85.

59. *La France musicale* reported Donzelli's difficulty with new parts in "The Opera in Italy," translated in *Musical World* 8/247 (17 December 1840), 388. "The very idea of W. Knyvett and Donzelli being coupled together in the same piece [by Mozart], like a tame and wild elephant (the one with a mere thread of a voice, but always in tune and always correct; the other with a volume of sound, sometimes absolutely startling, but sadly deficient in judgment), may be easily conceived. We hope never so to hear it again." "The Ancient Concerts," *Harmonicon* 8/6 (June 1830), 259–62, 260. Castil-Blaze's words are reported by B[enoît] Jouvin, "Hérold: sa vie et ses oeuvres," *Le Ménestrel* 33/51 (18 November 1866), 401–2, 402.

60. *Galignani's Messenger* is quoted in Kimbell, *Vincenzo Bellini*, 48. The *Court Journal* reported that "Donzelli had but little scope for exertion, except in the opening scene of the first act." "Theatres," *Court Journal* 5/218 (29 June 1833), 457b.

61. This reminds one of Melina Esse's work on Bellini's "poetics of restraint," a stripped-down declamatory manner that pressed male emotion into an at once submerged and powerfully passionate level, redefining operatic expressivity along explicitly gendered lines.

"Speaking and Sighing: Bellini's Canto Declamato and the Poetics of Restraint," *Current Musicology* 87 (Spring 2009), 7–45.

62. Anonymous, "Mémoire sur la voix," 748.

63. Legouvé, *Soixante ans de souvenirs*, 2: 126.

64. A. de Garaudé, *Méthode complète de chant* (Paris, 1826), 22. A comparison of the 1809, 1826, and 1841 editions is instructive.

65. Garaudé identified the drill, which previously had functioned to "reunite" the tenor's chest and head, as an exercise for the "employment" of the mixed voice in his *Méthode complète de chant* (Paris, 1841), 17.

66. Diday and Pétrequin, "Mémoire sur le mécanisme de la voix de fausset," *Gazette médicale de Paris* 12/9 (2 March 1844), 133–39, 134.

67. Auguste Panseron, *Méthode de vocalisation en 2 parties* (Paris, 1840), 7.

68. Bennati attacked Garaudé's "third [mixed] register" idea in the paper that Cuvier reported on 10 May 1830, "Du mécanisme de la voix pendant le chant." His words, before they appeared in *Recherches sur le mécanisme de la voix humaine*, were printed in *Revue musicale* 8/6 (24 July 1830), 353–67, 356. For Cuvier's agreement, see "Rapport sur un mémoire de M. Bennati," 356.

69. García, *Traité complet de l'art du chant*, 2: 58.

70. Ibid., 1: 8.

71. Terence Joseph O'Donnelly, *Académie de musique élémentaire contenant une exposition claire de la théorie*, trans. A. D. de Cressier (Paris, 1844), 332.

72. Quicherat, *Adolphe Nourrit*, 2: 364. Quicherat described Nourrit's head-back stance in ibid., 1: 400. Henry Fothergill Chorley, *Music and Manners in France and Germany*, 3 vols. (London, 1841), 1: 62. Diday and Pétrequin—undeterred by those questioning Nourrit's "oversweetness" or masculinity—discussed the effect of his thrown-back head on the legibility of acting style. The *voix blanche* apparently raised the larynx, lifted the narrowed throat, and straightened the windpipe, its ricocheting sounds setting the body upright. The *voix sombrée*, by contrast, allowed for a dynamic rather than a static posture, where actor-singers followed their own selfish exigencies. For the *voix blanche*, apparently, the funneling of the sound facilitated the formal style of dialogic pantomime that Nourrit was famous for. Diday and Pétrequin, "Mémoire sur une nouvelle espèce de voix chantée," 307.

73. Timotheus [Bacon], "Elements of Vocal Science: Of Tone," *Quarterly Musical Magazine and Review* 2/7 (1820), 255–63, 261.

74. Edmond Michotte, *Richard Wagner's Visit to Rossini (Paris 1860)*, trans. Herbert Weinstock (Chicago, 1968), 115.

75. Anselm Gerhard, "Rossini and the Revolution," in *The Urbanization of Opera* (Chicago, 1998), 63–120; Benjamin Walton, "Looking for the Revolution in *Guillaume Tell*," in *Rossini in Restoration Paris: The Sound of Modern Life* (Cambridge, 2007), 257–92. For operatic masculinities, see Karen Henson, "Introduction: Divo Worship," *Cambridge Opera Journal* 19/1 (Special Issue: "The Divo and the Danseur") (2007), 1–9.

76. Quicherat, *Adolphe Nourrit*, 2: 305.

77. See the preface of the original 1829 libretto, Étienne de Jouy and Hippolyte Bis, *Guillaume Tell, opera en 4 actes* (Roullet, 3 August 1829).

78. "Première representation de *Guillaume Tell*," *La France nouvelle* 734 (5 August 1829), 1–3, 2; "Boîte de Journal," *Le Voleur* 41 (25 July 1829), 4; *Le Globe* 7/63 (8 August 1829),

499–501, 501; Berlioz, "Guillaume-Tell," *Gazette musicale de Paris* 1/43 (29 October 1834), 341–43, 343.

79. "Deuxième representation de *Guillaume Tell*," *La Gazette de France* 586 (9 August 1829), 1–2, 1.

80. *Le Corsaire* 7/2368 (5 August 1829), 2.

81. The *Journal du commerce d'Anvers* is quoted in Quicherat, *Adolphe Nourrit*, 2: 321.

82. J. d'O [Joseph d'Ortigue], "Début de M. Duprez.—Guillaume Tell," *Journal de Paris* 70 (19 April 1837), 1–2, 1.

83. Quicherat, *Adolphe Nourrit*, 2: 307.

84. Ludovic Vitet, "Musique. Académie royale de musique," *Le Globe* 7/63 (8 August 1829), 499–501, 500.

85. According to Legouvé, "Les larmes le suffoquaient" at "mon père." *Soixante ans de souvenirs*, 2: 157.

86. For the explosion, see Ségond, *Hygiène du chanter, influence du chant sur l'économie animale* (Paris, 1846), 130. H***** [Hector Berlioz], "Débuts de Duprez dans *les Huguenots*," *Journal des débats*, 17 May 1837, 1b.

87. Georges Imbert de Laphalèque [Louis-François Lhéritier], "De la musique en France [III]," *Revue de Paris* 5 (August 1829), 253–68, 260.

88. Castil-Blaze, "Duprez," *Revue de Paris* 40 (April 1837), 348–54, 349.

89. Théophile Gautier, *Histoire de l'art dramatique en France*, 6 vols. (Paris, 1858–59), 1: 130.

90. Castil-Blaze, "Variétés," *Revue de Paris* 1 (13 July 1844), 365.

91. H***** [Hector Berlioz], "*Guillaume Tell*.—Début de Duprez," *Journal des débats*, 19 April 1837, 1c. The later 1852 framing of this passage represented a 180-degree about-face for Berlioz, who wrote in 1837 that he could scarcely breathe in anticipation of Duprez. Alexandre Dumas, who had heard Duprez in Italy, was seated beside him.

92. M. Elizabeth C. Bartlet, *Guillaume Tell di Gioachino Rossini: fonti iconografiche* (Pesaro, 1996), 115, 118.

93. Joseph d'Ortigue began to revise his position in his "Post-scriptum" for *De la guerre des dilettanti*, reprinted in *Le Balcon de l'opéra* (Paris, 1833), 64–80. For d'Ortigue's shifting views, see Olivier Bara, "Les Voix dissonantes de l'anti-rossinisme français sous la Restauration," *Chroniques italiennes* 77/78 (2006), 107–25, 123.

94. Lhéritier, a proponent of the idea of "réforme musicale" or "révolution" in 1829, went so far as to picture Rossini as God, throwing the "worlds" of "his choruses, his masses, his orchestra" together in a vast "universe" of competing elements. Laphalèque, "De la musique en France [III]," 267.

95. Fromental Halévy, *Derniers souvenirs et portraits* (Paris, 1863), 156. Quicherat, by contrast, depicted Nourrit exhausted by the public chores of revolution, in *Adolphe Nourrit*, 1: 83.

96. Walton, "Looking for the Revolution," 257–92.

97. Mainzer, *Le National*, 12 October 1836, and translated in Kerry Murphy, "Joseph Mainzer's 'Sacred and Beautiful Mission': An Aspect of Parisian Musical Life of the 1830s," *Music and Letters* 75/1 (February 1994), 33–46, 38.

98. Jean-Benoît Nadeau and Julie Barlow, *The Story of French* (London, 2006), 174.

99. Wilhem [Guillaume-Louis Bocquillon], *Guide de la méthode, ou Instructions pour l'emploi simultané des tableaux de lecture musicale et de chant élémentaire*, 3rd ed. (Paris, 1835).

100. Katherine Bergeron, *Voice Lessons: French Mélodie in the Belle Epoque* (Oxford, 2010), 6.

101. Quicherat, *Adolphe Nourrit,* 2: 32.

102. Roland Barthes, "Grain of the Voice" (1972), in *Image-Music-Text,* trans. Stephen Heath (New York, 1978), 179–89.

6. FRANZ LISZT, METAPIANISM, AND THE CULTURAL HISTORY OF THE HAND

1. On 15 March 1832, Hugo signed off on these words for the revised preface to his novel: "Préface: Dernier Jour d'un condamné," *Oeuvres complètes,* ed. Jacques Seebacher (Paris, 1985), 1: 401–16, 409. The law of 28 April 1832 discontinued mutilation of the hand, branding, and the iron collar. For more on Benoît, see Louis Chevalier, *Labouring Classes and the Working Poor* (London, 1973), 83–84, from whence I have borrowed my translation. See also Michel Foucault, *Discipline and Punish: The Birth of the Prison,* trans. Alan Sheridan (London, 1977), 14; Henri Sanson, *Memoirs of the Sansons: From Private Notes and Documents (1688–1847)* (London, 1876), 279; *Gazette des tribunaux* 2070 (1 April 1832), 563; and *Gazette des tribunaux* 2199 (31 August 1832), 1075.

2. Théophile Gautier, "Gérard de Nerval," in Johann Wolfgang von Goethe, *Faust et le second Faust de Goethe,* trans. Nerval (Paris, 1868), i–xxvii, xvi.

3. The translation is Calvino's. See Gérard de Nerval, "The Enchanted Hand," in *Fantastic Tales,* ed. Italo Calvino (London, 2001), 175–76.

4. Nerval, "The Enchanted Hand," 169; Gérard de Nerval, "La Main de gloire (histoire macaronique)," *Le Cabinet de lecture* 3/214 (24 September 1832), 5a.

5. Nerval, "The Enchanted Hand," 180; and Nerval, "La Main de gloire," 6c.

6. C. Barbey-Boissier, *La comtesse Agénor de Gasparin et sa famille: correspondance et souvenirs 1813–1894,* 2 vols. (Paris, 1902), 1: 147.

7. Valérie would later wed Count Agénor de Gasparin, French statesman, religious evangelical, and human rights activist famous for his work on the purity and sanctity of marriage. Later she became known as an abolitionist and belles-lettres novelist under the pseudonym Antoine Goru. In 1835 her mother recorded the moment of dedication in an unpublished journal: "[Liszt] demanda la permission de dédier à Valérie un beau morceau qu'il fait graver en ce moment et qu'il a compose ici." Quoted in Robert Bory, *Une Retraite romantique en Suisse: Liszt et la comtesse d'Agoult* (Paris, 1930), 33.

8. Madame Auguste Boissier, *Liszt pédagogue: leçons de piano données par Liszt à Mademoiselle Valérie Boissier à Paris en 1832* (Geneva, 1976), 22.

9. Ibid., 48.

10. Sigismond Thalberg, *L'Art du chant appliqué au piano op. 70* (Leipzig, 1853), 2.

11. For more on Marie Jaëll's ideal of freeing the hand, see Vladimir Jankélévitch, *Liszt et la rhapsodie. Essai sur la virtuosité* (Paris, 1979), 58. Edwin Hughes, one of Leschetizky's army of *Vorreiters,* or assistant teachers, sensed a powerful link between playing and criminality: "After pupils have once gotten this foundation they branch off in every direction: each has his own peculiarities and no one method will answer for all any more; the teaching must become individual. The enforcement of strict rules cannot be insisted upon. It is just as in law. Not everyone who kills his fellow-man is hanged or guillotined

or electrocuted." Quoted in Reginald R. Gerig, *Famous Pianists and Their Technique* (London, 1974), 278.

12. In a letter to his father of 25 October 1851, he confessed to practicing exclusively on technique for "four to five hours daily." For this and more on his ideas of "crucifixion," see *Hans von Bülow: Briefe*, 8 vols. (Leipzig, 1895), 1: 381.

13. Madame Boissier, *Liszt pédagogue*, 56. His favorite piece, for both Valérie and himself, was a brutal octave study by the now-forgotten Bohemian pianist and composer Joseph Christoph Kessler.

14. Kalkbrenner's contraption was not the only such device of the era. Related designs included Logier's Chiroplaste (1814), Kalkbrenner's Guide-mains (1831), Herz's Dactylion (1836), Martin's Chirogymnaste (1840), Guérin's Sténochire (1844), Magner's Digital (1845), Lahousse's Clavi-grade (1855), Ziegler's Gymnase des doigts (1848), Lemoine's Baguler (1864), Melle Faivre's Velocemano (1866), and more. See Paul Raspé, "Pianos: virtuoses et instruments de torture à l'époque romantique," *Clés pour la musique* 31/32 (1971), 11–14.

15. Madame Boissier, *Liszt pédagogue*, 90.

16. Chlorine was dispensed twice daily on both the interior and exterior stairs of the Salle Le Peletier, which housed the Opéra. Vases in the foyer and corridors were filled with the same chemical, while a powerful ventilator operated continually in the auditorium. See *Le Figaro* 7/92 (1 April 1832), 3b. Heine recorded his experience of the epidemic in a letter of 19 April 1832 to Varnhagen von Ense. See *Heinrich Heine's Memoirs: From His Works, Letters and Conversations*, ed. Gustav Karpeles, trans. Gilbert Cannan, 2 vols. (New York, 1910), 1: 272. Later the German famously remembered the cholera in these words:

> Its arrival was officially announced on the 29th of March; and as this was the Mi-Câreme [mid-Lent], and a bright and sunny day, the Parisians swarmed more gaily than ever on the Boulevards, where masks were even seen mocking the fear of the cholera and the disease itself in off-color and misshapen caricature. That night, the balls were more crowded than ever; hilarious laughter all but drowned the louder music; one grew hot in the chahut, a fairly unequivocal dance, and gulped all kinds of ices and other cold drinks—when suddenly the merriest of the harlequins felt a chill in his legs, took off his mask, and to the amazement of all revealed a violet-blue face. It was soon discovered that this was no joke; the laughter died, and several wagonloads were driven directly from the ball to the Hotel-Dieu, the main hospital, where they arrived in their gaudy fancy dress and promptly died, too. . . . Those dead were said to have been buried so fast that not even their checkered fool's clothes were taken off them; and merrily as they lived they now lie in their graves. (Heinrich Heine, *Works of Prose*, ed. Hermann Kesten, trans. E. B. Ashton (New York, 1943), 66)

17. Robert Bory, "Diverses lettres inédites de Liszt," in *Schweizerisches Jahrbuch für Musikwissenschaft* 3 (Aarau, 1928), 5–25, 6. Liszt may have been trying to avoid contact with his lover in Switzerland, the rich, alluring, thirtysomething Countess Adèle de Laprunarède.

18. Liszt wrote this later in life (in January 1882) in a letter to Baroness Meyendorff; see *The Letters of Franz Liszt to Olga Von Meyendorff, 1871–1886* (Washington, DC, 1979), 418.

19. For the 7 February lesson, Caroline Boissier wrote, "He struggles with a suffering nature and so he analyzes the language of all pains. He visits hospitals, gambling casinos, asylums for the insane. He goes down into the dungeons, and he has even seen those condemned to die!" Madame Boissier, *Liszt pédagogue*, 39–40. In January 1835 Liszt endorsed the rogue science of phrenology by visiting the asylum at Salpêtrière to perform for a remarkable sixty-year-old female *idiote*. The woman had become the centerpiece of a heated debate over the emerging discipline, the controversy involving her uncanny neurocognitive ability to sing back any melody presented to her without error. She attracted a frenzy of comment in music and scientific writings of the period. Because her "organ of tone" (located in the area of the temporal lobes, which modern neuroscience still localizes as the "seat of musical activity") was more a depression than a bump, she had become useful to such opponents of "organology" as Dr. François Leurat, a noted advocate of moral, humane, or persuasive therapies in the treatment of the insane. His nemesis, Dr. Jean Fossati, however, countered that her cerebral organ was less a case for phrenology than pathology since it was not the *size* or *volume* but the *texture* of that cerebral part that appeared active in this case. The woman's reaction to Liszt's pianism was striking. Unable to repeat the showers of notes the virtuoso presented to her, according to Leurat, she "vibrated with each chord and responded to the music as if it were an electrical discharge." "L'idiote dilettante," *Vert-Vert: Journal politique du matin et du soir*, 23 January 1835, 1b, and 24 January 1835, 1a. Leurat's lead article appeared as "Phrénologie: observation d'un cas de sentiment musical très-développé chez une idiote," *Gazette médicale de Paris* 3 (3 January 1835), 1a. A shortened version of Leurat's text was republished as "L'idiote mélomane," *Le Pianiste* 2/7 (5 February 1835), 53b.

20. Antoine Fontaney, *Journal intime*, ed. René Jasinski (Paris, 1925), 133, 135, and 148.

21. "Carnet de Marie d'Agoult. Année 1832: de la main de Franz Liszt," Bibliothèque nationale de France, Manuscripts, NAF 14319. For more, see Pauline Pocknell, "Franz Liszt's Unpublished Pocket-Diary for 1832—A Guide to His Memories," *Liszt 2000: Selected Lectures Given at the International Liszt Conference in Budapest, May 18–20, 1999*, ed. Klára Hamburger (Budapest, 2000), 52–77. Alphonse Giroux is best remembered these days for making and selling the first camera manufactured after Daguerre's famous design.

22. Alexandre Dumas, *Mes Mémoires (1830–1833)*, ed. Pierre Josserand (Paris, 1989), 718.

23. Three years before the poet's suicide in 1853, the pianist provided the poet with material for his famous review of the premiere of Wagner's *Lohengrin*. For more on Liszt's fascination with *Faust*, the opera, and his relations with Nerval, see Eric Frederick Jansen, "Liszt, Nerval and *Faust*," *19th-Century Music* 6/2 (1982), 151–58.

24. See Émile Gouget, *Histoire musicale de la main: Son rôle dans la notation, la tonalité, le rythme et l'exécution instrumentale. La main des musiciens devant les sciences occultes* (Paris, 1898), 113.

25. De Courtiras wrote under a pseudonym: Countess Dash, *Mémoires des autres*, 6 vols. (Paris, 1896–97), 4: 149.

26. "Carnet de Marie d'Agoult," 39v.

27. Pocknell, "Franz Liszt's Unpublished Pocket-Diary," 60.

28. The letter of 24 May 1832 from Ecouteboeuf is printed in Bory, "Diverses lettres inédites de Liszt," 6–8.

29. See *Letters of Franz Liszt* [1894], ed. La Mara, trans. Constance Bache I (New York, 1969), 8. This idea of a "makeover" was probably derived from Berlioz's comments in "Liszt,"

Revue et gazette musicale de Paris 3/5 (31 January 1836), 198–200: "The Liszt that we all knew, the Liszt of last year, has been left behind by the Liszt of today. All that I have been able to distinguish in the way of new technique, in these infinite choruses born under the fingers of Liszt, is limited to nuances and accents that have been unanimously declared to be, and have in fact remained until now, inaccessible to the piano. There were broad and simple melodies, sustained and perfectly linked phrases, and whole sheaves of notes, hurled in some cases with extreme violence, yet without coarseness and losing nothing of their harmonic luxuriousness." Translated in Paul Metzner, *Crescendo of the Virtuoso* (Berkeley and Los Angeles, 1998), 145. In 1834 Liszt echoed a similar experience in a letter to his mistress, Marie d'Agoult: that he had been seized with "an immense need to learn, to know, to deepen myself" (un immense besoin [immense est bien ambitieux] de savoir, de connaître, d'approfondir) and that he would do this by practicing "cadenzas, octaves, and tremolos—enough to crack my head. I have the études of Hiller, Chopin and Kessler" (de cadences, d'octaves, de tremolos— cela me casse le tête. J'ai là des études de Hiller, de Chopin, et de Kessler). *Correspondance de Liszt et de la comtesse d'Agoult*, ed. Daniel Ollivier (Paris, 1933), 82.

30. For a counterview on the myth that Paganini caused Liszt to "relearn" the piano, see Alan Davison, "Franz Liszt and the Development of Nineteenth-Century Pianism: A Rereading of the Evidence," *Musical Times* 147/1896 (2006), 33–42. Liszt first saw Paganini on 9 March 1831.

31. Charles Rosen, *The Romantic Generation* (Cambridge, MA, 1995), 491.

32. This, in a nutshell, would sum up my problem with the increasingly prominent and well-funded fields of music psychology and neuroscientific approaches to music in general. Their theoretical frameworks seem to me to be arch-romantic (or phrenological) in conception, with their denial of politics and their "all the world's a brain" conception of music.

33. In *De anima*, Aristotle wrote, "The soul is as the hand; for the hand is an instrument with respect to instruments, the intellect is a form with respect to forms, and sense-perception a form with respect to things perceived." Quoted in Katherine Rowe, "'God's handy worke': Divine Complicity and the Anatomist's Touch," in *The Body Parts*, ed. David Hillmen and Carlo Mazio (London, 1997), 285–309. Galen echoed these words—that hands participate in a vast, circulating mimetic order—when he discussed the usefulness of various body parts in *De usu partium*:

> Now, just as the man's body is bare of weapons, so is his soul destitute of skills. Therefore, to compensate for the nakedness of his body, he received hands, and for his soul's lack of skills, reason, by means of which he arms his body in every way. . . . For though the hand is no one particular instrument, it is the instrument for all instruments because it is formed by Nature to receive them all, and similarly, although reason is no one of the arts in particular, it would be an art for arts because it is naturally disposed to take them all unto itself. Hence man, the only one of all the animals having an art for arts in his soul, should logically have an instrument for instruments in his body. (Quoted in Katherine Rowe, *Dead Hands: Fictions of Agency, Renaissance to Modern* (Stanford, 1999), 5)

34. Schumann wrote, "Mit dem dritten [Finger] geht's durch die Cigarrenmechanik leidlich." Robert Schumann, *Tagebücher I (1827–1838)* (Leipzig, 1971), 386.

35. Peter F. Ostwald, "Florestan, Eusebius, Clara, and Schumann's Right Hand," *19th-Century Music* 4/1 (1980), 17–31, 22.

36. Eric Sams, "Schumann's Hand Injury," *Musical Times* 112/1546 (1971), 1156–59, 1156.

37. Wilhelm Joseph von Wasielewski, *Life of Robert Schumann*, trans. A. L. Alger (London, 1878), 65. In a letter to his mother on 9 August 1832, Schumann wrote,

> My whole house has been turned into an apothecary shop [Apotheke]. I really got quite uneasy about my hand, but carefully avoided asking an anatomist [Anatomen], because I was so afraid he would say the damage was irretrievable. I had begun to make all sorts of plans for the future, and had almost resolved to study theology (not law), and peopled an imaginary parsonage with real people, yourself and others. At last I went to Professor Kühl, and asked him to tell me truthfully whether my hand would heal. After shaking his head a lot, he said: "Yes, but not for some time, not for about six months." As soon as I heard these words, a weight was taken off my heart, and I quickly promised to do all that he required. It was traumatic enough, namely to take *Tierbäder*—let Schurig describe them to you—to bathe my hand in warm brandy-and-water all day long, to put on a herb poultice at night, and to play the piano as little as possible. The remedies are not exactly pleasant, and I fear very much that the cattle-essence might pass into me; but on the whole these treatments appear to be beneficial. And I feel so much strength and spirit in every limb, that I really would like to beat someone up! (*Early Letters of Robert Schumann*, trans. May Herbert (London, 1888), 179–80; and *Robert Schumann "Schlage nur eine Weltsaite an": Briefe 1828–1855*, ed. Karin Sousa (Frankfurt am Main and Leipzig, 2006), 39–40)

38. Ostwald, "Florestan, Eusebius, Clara," 21.

39. In a December 1838 letter to Clara, quoted in ibid., 31.

40. Quoted in Dieter Hildebrandt, *Piano Forte: A Social History of the Piano*, trans. Harriet Goodman (London, 1985), 134–35.

41. Four of Antonio Scarpa's fingers are now on display in the University History Museum in Pavia.

42. Charles Bell, *Letters of Sir Charles Bell* (London, 1870), 314; Sarah Wallace Bowditch Lee, *Memoirs of Cuvier* (London, 1833), 177.

43. Charles Bell, *The Hand, Its Mechanism and Vital Endowments, as Evincing Design* (London, 1833), 211.

44. Ibid., 13.

45. Ludmilla Jordanova, "The Hand," *Visual Anthropology Review* 8/2 (1992), 2–7. Jordanova comments equally on how self-conscious Bell was about his hands, as evinced in a tongue-in-cheek letter to his brother in August 1830 in which he played around with the idea of himself as a "handy fellow":

> Behold with what I point! [he then drew a hand on a shield]—This hand, how exquisite in form and motion. But first turn over—use it to learn to admire!
>
> I have a letter this morning from the President of the Royal Society, who, with the counsel and approbation of the Archbishop of Canterbury have pro-

posed to me to write on the *Human Hand*. . . . I think I know now what to engrave on my seal—a hand. I shall introduce it on all occasions, sometimes doubled . . . as implying the pugnacious nature of the man—sometimes smooth and open, as ready to receive—sometimes pointing, as from the master. In short, I shall make use of this hand until they acknowledge me a handy fellow! (Bell, *Letters of Sir Charles Bell*, 314)

46. Bell, *The Hand*, 198. In the glory days of the *Liszt Society Journal*, extraordinarily, Dudley Newton still appealed to comparative anatomy in his attempt to dispel various myths: that Liszt's fingers had no webbing, that his third and fourth were of equal length, and that the length of his index fingers proved he was higher up on the evolutionary plane. Passages such as this would pass for Liszt scholarship in 1990:

One of the most important purposes for which the hand evolved was for gripping branches for swinging from branch to branch, usually in search of food in the form of fruit, leaves, or buds. This, known as brachiation, was quite a normal form of locomotion, and it still is for some animals. The long flexor muscles which are used to close the fingers for this purpose pass through the wrist and are attached to the underside of the forearm near the elbow, as they still are today, giving the fingers a tremendous strength which they would not otherwise have. All modern primates were derived from an arboreal stock. (Dudley Newton, "Liszt's Hands," *Liszt Society Journal* 15 (1990), 9–14, 13)

47. Joseph de Maistre, *St Petersburg Dialogues*, trans. and ed. Richard A. Lebrun (Montreal, 1993), 172–73.

48. Joseph d'Ortigue, "Études biographique: Franz Listz [sic]," *Gazette musicale de Paris* 2/24 (14 June 1835), 197–204, 202b. Ben Walton comments on d'Ortigue's portrayal of "Liszt as pure living, breathing, performing *Zeitgeist*" in his introduction to Vincent Giroud's translation of the biography, which I have borrowed from, in "The First Biography: Joseph d'Ortigue on Franz Liszt at Age Twenty-Three," in *Franz Liszt and His World*, ed. Christopher Gibbs and Dana Gooley (Princeton, 2006), 303–34.

49. Harold C. Schonberg, *The Great Pianists* (London, 1963), 376.

50. For Marie Jaëll, see Gouget, *Histoire musicale de la main*, 246–47. Elsewhere, commenting on Liszt's "dissociated fingers," Jaëll wrote, "Et c'est précisément la prodigieuse dissociation des doigts de Liszt, intimement reliée à la transcendante cérébralité de son jeu, qui a provoqué le perfectionnement momentané de ma mémoire, et par conséquent de ma pensée musicale. . . . Liszt possédait chacun de ses doigts un *état de conscience* distinct." See her *Les Rythmes du regard et la dissociation des doigts* (Paris, 1906), 5.

51. Liszt's contemporary and fellow pupil of Czerny was probably most vociferous on this point. Leschetizky wrote, "I *have* no method and I *will have* no method. Go to concerts and be sharp-witted, and if you are observing you will learn tremendously from the ways that are successful and also from those that are not. Adopt with your pupils the ways that succeed with them, and get away as far as possible from the idea of a method. Write over your music-room the motto: 'NO METHOD.'" Gerig, *Famous Pianists*, 273.

52. A series of letters published in 1928 indicates the extent to which Liszt and the Boissiers had kept in touch since 1832. See Bory, "Diverses lettres inédites de Liszt," 5–25.

53. "Liszt est bien mis. Il a des mains charmantes. A l'index il porte une bague, sur laquelle est représentée une tête de mort en argent sur fond d'or." From the journal of Albertine de la Rive-Necker of 9 August 1836, quoted in Bory, *Une Retraite romantique,* 36. In the *Courrier de la Gironde* of September 1844, Saint-Rieul Dupouy wrote:

> Liszt is undoubtedly the greatest pianist of this age and of all time. . . . Liszt is a great poet. His soul leads his hands, and indeed he plays more with his heart, his intelligence, his whole being than with his fingers. At times he leans backwards and seems to be reading, in the air, music that is dreamed, or to be translating something that is sung up there in the region of harmonies. Then he leans his head over the keyboard as if to bring it to life; he grasps it bodily, struggles with it, tames it, embraces it, magnetizes it with his powerful hands. Then it is no longer a piano that you hear; it is an orchestra of a thousand voices. (Quoted in Bertrand Ott, *Lisztian Keyboard Energy: An Essay on the Pianism of Franz Liszt,* trans. Donald H. Windham (New York, 1992), 16)

54. Bory, *Une Retraite romantique,* 31.

55. Ibid., 32.

56. Rémy Campos, *Instituer la musique: les premières années de Conservatoire de Musique de Genève (1835–1859)* (Geneva, 2003), 247.

57. Frédéric Chopin, *Esquisses pour une méthode de piano,* ed. Jean-Jacques Eigeldinger (Paris, 1993).

58. Liszt told his biographer Lina Ramann that no such *méthode* ever existed, though the mention of it in several letters to his mother and committee minutes at the conservatory suggest otherwise. The late Robert Bory, for one, speculated that the printer lost the finished manuscript and was then obliged to pawn the remaining engraving plates, which have now been lost. See Adrian Williams, *Portrait of Liszt: By Himself and His Contemporaries* (Oxford, 1990), 73–74.

59. The enthusiastic writer reported that "le genre *spiritualiste*" heralded that Liszt had "entered into a new way" (il entre dans une voie nouvelle), citing d'Ortigue to argue that the music made one soar close to God. "Annonces motivées," *Le Pianiste* 2 (1835), 129–30, 129.

60. *Correspondance de Liszt,* 48. For d'Ortigue's 1835 assessment of Liszt as a composer, see d'Ortigue, "Études biographique," 203. Liszt invested heavily in *Harmonies poétiques et religieuses,* publishing it with fanfare simultaneously in Paris and Leipzig, reworking the material obsessively over the course of his career, and writing to d'Agoult in 1833 that "he set great store in these few pages." *Correspondance de Liszt,* 48. See also Joan Backus, "Liszt's *Harmonies poétiques et religieuses:* Inspiration and the Challenge of Form," *Liszt Society Journal* 21 (1987), 3–21.

61. Liszt's 1829–33 sketchbook is held at the Goethe- und Schiller-Archiv (GSA 60/N 6). The leaf in question reproduced in facsimile by Rezsö Kókai, *Franz Liszt in seinen frühen Klavierwerken* (Basel, 1968), 140. Liszt probably picked up the inscription from Victor Hugo, who had quoted Schiller's words to introduce the fifth chapter of his first novel, *Hans d'Islande* (1823): "On eût dit que toutes les passions avaient agité son coeur, et que toutes l'avaient abaondonné *[sic]*; il ne lui restait rien que le coup d'oeil triste et perçant d'un homme consommé dans la connaissance des hommes, et qui voyait d'un regard où tendait chaque chose." Victor Hugo, *Hans d'Islande* (Paris, 1868), 47.

62. Paul Merrick, "Liszt's *sans ton* Key Signature," *Studia Musicologica Academiae Scientiarum Hungaricae* 45/3–4 (2004), 281–302, 286.

63. F. J. Fétis and I. Moscheles, *Complete System of Instruction for the Piano-Forte; being a treatise on the art of playing that instrument based on an analysis of the best works that have been written on the subject* (London, 1841), 13.

64. Madame Boissier, *Liszt pédagogue*, 16.

65. C. Barbey-Boissier, *La comtesse Agénor de Gasparin et sa famille*, 1: 186.

66. Wilhelm von Lenz, *The Great Piano Virtuosos of Our Time* [1872], ed. Philip Reder (London, 1983), 8–9. Heine's words come to mind here too: "Next to him [Liszt], all pianists disappear. . . . In truth, all other piano players . . . are just that: piano players; they excel in the accuracy with which they handle the stringed wood. But with Liszt one no longer thinks of the difficulty overcome; the piano disappears and Music is revealed." Heinrich Heine, *Sämtliche Schriften*, ed. Klaus Briegleb, 12 vols. (Munich, 1978), 5: 358.

67. In the preface to his *Méthode*, Kalkbrenner writes, "After a few days I understood all the advantage that this new working method [the *guide-mains*] gave me; my hand-position could no longer be incorrect, I had nothing more to occupy me, playing only five-finger exercises. Soon I decided to try reading, while feeding my fingers their daily nourishment. For the first few hours it seemed difficult, [but] by the next day I was already accustomed to it. Since then I have always read while practicing." Quoted in Jean-Jacques Eigeldinger, *Chopin: Pianist and Teacher as Seen by His Pupils* (Cambridge, 1986), 96; Madame Boissier, *Liszt pédagogue*, 23.

68. From his recollection of his first lesson on 22 April 1882; see *Living with Liszt: From the Diary of Carl Lachmund, an American Pupil of Liszt*, ed. Alan Walker (1995), 14. A year later, in October 1883, Lachmund developed a troubled relationship with his hands, being obliged to practice with three fingers on each: "My hands bother me beyond all endurance. A lame finger on one that has tormented me now for nearly a month, something like a felon on the other hand." Ibid., 381.

69. Carl Czerny, *Letters to a Young Lady on the Art of Playing the Pianoforte* (London, 1838), 23.

70. Carl Czerny, *Complete Theoretical and Practical Piano Forte School, Op. 500*, 3 vols. (London, 1839), 3: 130.

71. Annette Hullah, *Theodor Leschetizky* [1905] (London, 1923), 41–42.

72. On 18 April a young admirer wrote in his diary, "The day before yesterday, the ambassador got Liszt to come, and he played us a Weber concerto with the rarest perfection. A few days ago when at home practicing for the occasion, he dislocated the thumb of his right hand, and even thought he had broken it." Rudolph Apponyi, *Vingt-cinq ans à Paris*, 4 vols. (Paris, 1913), 2: 179.

73. Ibid.

74. Dana Gooley, *The Virtuoso Liszt* (Cambridge, 2004), 104.

75. *The Memoirs of Count Apponyi* (London, 1935), 88.

76. Neumann left an account of the 31 May misadventure in a diary entry of the following day. See *The Diary of Philipp von Neumann, 1829 to 1850*, ed. and trans. E. Beresford Chancellor, 2 vols. (New York, 1928), 2: 168.

77. "Concerts of the Week," *Athenaeum* 712 (19 June 1841), 478a.

78. *Times*, 14 June 1841, 5f.

79. For Grétry, see Gouget, *Histoire musicale de la main*, 250.

80. See Jean Jacques Eigeldinger, "Liszt trascrittore e interprete de Bach," *L'organo* 11 (1973), 171–83, 176. Jules Laurens remembered this of the winter of 1844. I have borrowed Charles Rosen's translation from *The Romantic Generation* (Cambridge, MA, 1996), 510–11. Jules Laurens's manuscript recollections can be found at Bibliothèque Inguimbertine de Carpentras Ms. 2.173 (17).

81. "Ein Orgelspieler, dem an der rechten Hand der dritte Finger fehlte, gab einmal ein Konzert in der Kirche. Die große G-moll Fuge von Sebastian Bach war die Hauptnummer des Konzertes. Liszt, der größte Bach-Kenner und Bach-Spieler, sagte zu mir, als die Kirche leer war: 'Kellermann, das mit dem fehlenden Mittelfinger kann ich auch, gib mal acht!' Und er spielte vor menin Augen diese schwierige Fuge, indem er an beiden Händen den Mittelfinger ausstreckte, onhe ihn jemals zu benützen." Berthold Kellermann, *Erinnerungen: Ein Künstler leben* (Leipzig, 1932), 44.

82. Lina Ramann, *Franz Liszt, Artist and Man*, trans. E. Cowdery, 2 vols. (London, 1882), 1: 261–62.

83. Ibid., 1: 262. For a performance that (for commercial purposes) Liszt advertised as his last, the piano was decorated in wreaths. "Étranger," *Revue et gazette musicale de Paris* 44/12 (25 March 1877), 95. The eleven-year-old Ferruccio Busoni reported the performance cold and uninspiring, while Austrian composer Wilhelm Kienzl thought differently:

> Appearing as a man resurrected from the dead, he was now indeed transfigured and purified, a spirit far removed from mere virtuosity, one for whom the outer expression of his inner interpretation was facilitated by sovereign mastery of every technique made possible by the hand, all expressed exactly as desired. The Lisztian incarnation of the E-flat Concerto of Beethoven left an indelible impression on me. Here was a totally personal interpretation, yet without any violation of the Artwork, the essence of the Spirit of Beethoven. Liszt played the work in such a free, improvisatory manner that it was as if the composer were before one's very eyes. (Wilhelm Kienzl, *Meine Lebenswanderung* (Stuttgart, 1926), 44–45)

84. Alan Walker, *Franz Liszt: The Final Years, 1861–1886* (Ithaca, 1997), 228–29. For more on Liszt's authoritarianism and disdain of method, see Alan Walker, *Reflections on Liszt* (Ithaca, 2005), especially 51–59.

85. Pauline Pocknell, "Reading Liszt's Hands: Molds, Casts and Replicas as Guides to Contemporary Creative Representations," *Journal of the American Liszt Society* 54–56 (2003–5), 171–90, 180.

86. "Mit demselben Rechte, als *Lessing* von *Raphael* behauptete, dass er der grösste Maler hätte werden müssen, selbst wenn er ohne Hände zur Welt gekommen wäre, mit demselben Rechte könnte man ein Gleiches auch von *Lisst [sic]* als Clavierspieler sagen." Press reprint in Dezsö Legány, *Franz Liszt: Unbekannte Presse und Briefe aus Wien 1822–1886* (Budapest, 1984), 35.

87. Entry of 1 May 1873, Amy Fay, *Music Study in Germany* (Chicago, 1891), 205–6.

88. "Ses doigts n'étaient pas des doigts humains; mais rien n'est plus facile que de marcher dans la voie qu'il tracée et, de fait, tout le monde y marche, qu'on en ait conscience ou non. . . . A l'encontre de Beethoven, méprisant les fatalités de la physiologie et imposant

aux doigts contrariés et surmenés sa volonté tyrannique, Liszt les prend et les exerce dans leur nature, de manière à en obtenir, sans les violenter le maximum d'effet qu'ils sont susceptibles de produire." Camille Saint-Saëns, *Portraits et souvenirs* (Paris, 1900), 18.

89. "Roman Notes," *Dwight's Journal of Music* 38/2 (27 April 1878), 220.

90. Robert Schumann, *Music and Musicians, Essays and Criticisms,* ed. and trans. Fanny Raymond Ritter (London, 1877), 145–46.

91. Mary Alsop King Waddington, *My First Years as a Frenchwoman* (New York, 1914), 91.

EPILOGUE

1. Duprez described harnessing "la concentration de toute la volonté, de toutes les forces morales et physiques," in *Souvenirs d'un chanteur* (Paris, 1880), 74.

2. For the conductor as pantomime figure, see my "Dancing the Symphonic: Beethoven-Bochsa's *Symphonie Pastorale,* 1829," *19th-Century Music* 27/1 (2003), 25–47.

3. Heine's leave-taking appeared in *Lutetia* (1854). For a translation and comparison with the earlier 1844 version of that year's "Music Season in Paris," see "Heinrich Heine on Liszt," ed. Rainer Kleinertz, trans. Susan Gillespie, in *Franz Liszt and His World,* ed. Christopher H. Gibbs and Dana Gooley (Princeton, 2006), 441–65.

WORKS CITED

NEWSPAPERS AND MAGAZINES

The Age
Allgemeine Theater-Revue
Allgemeine Zeitung
Annales de chimie et de physique
Annales des sciences naturelles
The Athenaeum
The Atlas
Le Cabinet de lecture
Comptes rendus hebdomadaires des séances de l'Académie des sciences
Le Corsaire
The Courier
The Court Journal: Court Circular and Fashionable Gazette
The Court Magazine and La Belle Assemblée
The Examiner
Le Figaro
La France littéraire
La France musicale
La France nouvelle
La Gazette de France
Gazette des salons
Gazette des tribunaux
Gazette médicale de Paris
Gazette musicale de Paris
Gazzetta musicale di Milano
Le Globe

Le Guide musical
The Harmonicon
Hogg's Instructor
L'Illustration
Journal de Paris
Journal des débats
Journal universel des sciences médicales
The Literary Magnet
The London and Westminster Review
The London Literary Gazette and Journal of Belle Lettres, Arts and Sciences
The London Magazine
The London Medical Repository and Review
Magazine of Music
The Mechanics' Magazine, Museum, Register, Journal
Le Ménestrel
Le Monde
The Morning Chronicle
The Morning Herald
The Morning Journal
The Morning Post
The Musical Examiner
Musical Library: Monthly Supplement
The Musical Times
The Musical World
Le National
Neue Zeitschrift für Musik
The New Monthly Magazine and Literary Journal
The News
The New Times
La Phalange
Le Pianiste
La Presse
The Quarterly Musical Magazine and Review
Revue des deux mondes
Revue de Paris
Revue et gazette musicale de Paris
Revue musicale
The Spectator
The Sunday Times
Le Temps
The Times
Vert-Vert
Le Voleur
Wiener Courier
The World of Fashion and Continental Feuilletons

ARTICLES AND BOOKS

Abbate, Carolyn. "Music: Drastic or Gnostic?" *Critical Inquiry* 30/3 (2004): 505–36.

———. "Opera; or, the Envoicing of Women." In *Musicology and Difference: Gender and Sexuality in Music Scholarship,* edited by Ruth A. Solie, 1–22. Berkeley: University of California Press, 1993.

———. *Unsung Voices: Opera and Musical Narrative in the Nineteenth Century.* Princeton, NJ: Princeton University Press, 1991.

Agulhon, Maurice. *1848 ou l'apprentissage de la République.* Paris: Éditions du Seuil, 1973.

Appolonia, Giorgio. *Le voci di Rossini.* Turin: Eda, 1992.

Apponyi, Albert. *The Memoirs of Count Apponyi.* London: William Heinemann, 1935.

Apponyi, Rudolf. *Vingt-cinq ans à Paris.* 4 vols. Paris: Plon-Nourrit, 1913.

Archenholz, Johann Wilhelm von. *A Picture of Italy.* Translated by Joseph Trapp. London: G. G. J. & J. Robinson, 1791.

Aristotle. *De anima.* Translated by R. D. Hicks. Salem: Ayer, 1988.

Ashbrook, William. *Donizetti and His Operas.* Cambridge: Cambridge University Press, 1982.

Aspden, Suzanne. "'An Infinity of Factions': Opera in Eighteenth-Century Britain and the Undoing of Society." *Cambridge Opera Journal* 9/1 (1997): 1–19.

Atwood, William G. *The Parisian Worlds of Frédéric Chopin.* New Haven: Yale University Press, 1999.

Azoury, Pierre. *Chopin Through His Contemporaries: Friends, Lovers, and Rivals.* Westport: Greenwood Press, 1999.

Bach, Carl Philipp Emanuel. *Essay on the True Art of Playing Keyboard Instruments.* Translated by William J. Mitchell. New York: Norton, 1949.

Backus, Joan. "Liszt's *Harmonies poétiques et religieuses:* Inspiration and the Challenge of Form." *Liszt Society Journal* 21 (1987): 3–21.

Baer, Karl Ernst von. *De ovi mammalium et hominis genesi.* Leipzig: Voss, 1827.

Balzac, Honoré de. "Sarrasine." In Roland Barthes, *S/Z,* 221–54. Translated by Richard Miller. London: Jonathan Cape, 1975.

———. *The Wrong Side of Paris.* Translated by Jordan Stump. New York: Modern Library, 2005.

Bara, Olivier. "Les Voix dissonantes de l'anti-rossinisme français sous la Restauration." *Chroniques italiennes* 77/78 (2006): 107–25.

Barbey-Boissier, C. *La comtesse Agénor de Gasparin et sa famille: correspondance et souvenirs 1813–1894.* 2 vols. Paris: Plon-Nourrit, 1902.

Barclay, John. *A New Anatomical Nomenclature.* Edinburgh: Ross and Blackwood, 1803.

Barry, Keith. *Chopin and His Fourteen Doctors.* Sydney: Australasian medical publishing company, 1934.

Barthes, Roland. *Image, Music, Text.* Translated by Stephen Heath. New York: Noonday Press, 1977.

———. *The Responsibility of Forms.* Translated by Richard Howard. Berkeley: University of California Press, 1991.

Bartlet, M. Elizabeth C. *Guillaume Tell di Gioachino Rossini: fonti iconografiche.* Pesaro: Fondazione Rossini, 1996.

Beghelli, Marco. "Il ruolo del musico." In *Donizetti, Napoli, l'Europa*, edited by Franco Carmelo Greco and Renato Di Benedetto, 323–35. Naples: Edizioni scientifiche italiane, 2000.

Bell, Charles. *The Hand: Its Mechanism and Vital Endowments as Evincing Design*. London: Pickering, 1833.

———. *Letters of Sir Charles Bell*. London: J. Murray, 1870.

Bellini, Vincenzo. *Epistolario*. Edited by Luisa Cambi. Milan: A. Mondadori, 1943.

Bellman, Jonathan. "Frédéric Chopin, Antoine de Kontski and the *Carezzando* Touch." *Early Music* 29/3 (2001): 399–407.

Bennati, Francesco. *Mémoire sur un cas particulier d'anomalie de la voix humaine pendant le chant*. Paris: H. Dupuy, 1834.

———. *Recherches sur le mécanisme de la voix humaine*. Paris: Ballière, 1832.

Bentley, Eric, ed. *Shaw on Music*. New York: Applause, 1983.

Bergeron, Katherine. *Voice Lessons: French Mélodie in the Belle Epoque*. Oxford: Oxford University Press, 2010.

Berlioz, Hector. *The Art of Music and Other Essays (A travers chants)*. Edited and translated by Elizabeth Csicsery-Rónay. Bloomington: Indiana University Press, 1994.

———. *Correspondance générale*. Edited by Pierre Citron. 8 vols. Paris: Flammarion, 1972.

———. *Evenings in the Orchestra*. Translated by C. R. Fortescue. Harmondsworth: Penguin Books, 1963.

———. *The Memoirs of Hector Berlioz*. Translated by David Cairns. London: Gollancz, 1969.

Bichat, Xavier. *Physiological Researches on Life and Death*. Translated by F. Gold. London: Longman, 1815.

Blasius, Leslie David. "The Mechanics of Sensation and the Construction of the Romantic Musical Experience." In *Music Theory in the Age of Romanticism*, edited by Ian Bent, 3–24. Cambridge: Cambridge University Press, 1996.

Bloch, Gregory W. "The Pathological Voice of Gilbert-Louis Duprez." *Cambridge Opera Journal* 19/1 (2007): 11–31.

Boissier, Mme Auguste. *Liszt Pédagogue: leçons de piano données par Liszt à Mademoiselle Valérie Boissier à Paris en 1832*. Paris: H. Champion, 1976.

Bory, Robert. "Diverses lettres inédites de Liszt." *Schweizerisches Jahrbuch für Musikwissenschaft* 3 (1928): 5–25.

———. *Une Retraite romantique en Suisse: Liszt et la comtesse d'Agoult*. Lausanne: SPES, 1930.

Bourgery, Jean Baptiste Marc. *Traité complet d'anatomie de l'homme*. 8 vols. Paris: C. A. Delaunay, 1844.

Brewster, Anne Hampton. "Roman Notes." *Dwight's Journal of Music* 38/2 (1878), 220.

Broussais, François-Joseph-Victor. *On the Functions of the Cerebellum*. Edited and translated by George Combe. Edinburgh: Maclachlan & Stewart, 1838.

Brown, William Earl. *Vocal Wisdom: Maxims of Giovanni Battista Lamperti*. Marlboro, NJ: Taplinger, 1957.

Bülow, Hans von. *Briefe*. 8 vols. Leipzig: Breitkopf, 1895.

Bureaud-Riofrey, Antoine Martin. *Physical Education; Specially Adapted to Young Ladies*. London: Longman, 1838.

Bushnell, Howard. *Maria Malibran: A Biography of a Singer*. University Park: Pennsylvania State University Press, 1979.

Butler, Judith. *Bodies That Matter: On the Discursive Limits of "Sex."* 1993. Reprint, New York: Routledge, 2011.

Cairns, David. *Berlioz, 1830–1832: The Making of an Artist.* London: Deutsch, 1989.

Campos, Rémy. *Instituer la musique: les premières années de Conservatoire de Musique de Genève (1835–1859).* Geneva: Éditions Université-Conservatoire de musique-Genève, 2003.

Carron du Villards, Charles-Joseph-Frédéric. "Notice nécrologique sur le Docteur Bennati" In *Recherches pratiques sur les causes qui font échouer l'opération de la cataracte*, 419-24. Paris: Author, 1834.

Caswell, Austin. "Mme Cinti-Damoreau and the Embellishment of Italian Opera in Paris: 1820–1845," *Journal of the American Musicological Society* 28/3 (1975): 459–92.

Cavarero, Adriana. *For More Than One Voice: Toward a Philosophy of Vocal Expression.* Stanford: Stanford University Press, 2005.

Celletti, Rodolfo. *A History of Bel Canto.* Translated by Frederick Fuller. Oxford: Clarendon Press, 1991.

Chevalier, Louis. *Labouring Classes and the Working Poor.* London, 1973.

Chopin, Frédéric. *Esquisses pour une méthode de piano.* Edited by Jean-Jacques Eigeldinger. Paris: Flammarion, 1993.

———. *Etiudy op. 10, 25; Trzy etiudy, Méthode des méthodes.* Edited by Jan Ekier. Warsaw: Fundacja Wydania Narodowego, 2000.

———. *Sämtliche Etüden.* Edited by Paul Badura-Skoda. Vienna: Wiener Urtext Edition, 2005.

———. *Selected Correspondence of Fryderyk Chopin.* Translated by Arthur Hedley. London: Heinemann, 1962.

Chorley, Henry F. *Modern German Music: Recollections and Criticisms.* London: Smith, Elder and Co., 1854.

———. *Music and Manners in France and Germany.* 3 vols. London: Longman, 1841.

———. *Thirty Years' Musical Recollections.* 2 vols. London: Hurst & Blackett, 1862.

Clarke, Edwin, and L. S. Jacyna. *Nineteenth-Century Origins of Neuroscientific Concepts.* Berkeley: University of California Press, 1987.

Cobbett, William. *Advice to Young Men.* London: Author, 1829.

Coleridge, A. D., ed. *Life of Moscheles with Selections from His Diaries and Correspondence.* 2 vols. London: Hurst and Blackett, 1873.

Colette, Marie-Noëlle, et al. *La Musique à Paris en 1830–1831.* Paris: Bibliothèque nationale, 1983.

Colombat, Émile. *L'Enseignement orthophonique du Conservatoire national de musique et de déclamation de Paris.* Paris: Asselin, 1873.

Colombat de l'Isère, Marc. *A Treatise upon the Diseases and Hygiene of the Organs of the Voice.* Translated by J. F. W. Lane. Boston: Redding, 1857.

———. *Traité médico-chirurgical des maladies des organes de la voix.* Paris: Mansut, 1834.

Concone, Giuseppe. *Introduction à l'art de bien chanter.* Paris: S. Richault, 1845.

Condillac, Étienne Bonnet de. *La Logique.* Translated by W. R. Albury. New York: Abaris Books, 1980.

Corri, Domenico. *The Singer's Preceptor.* London: Chappell, 1811.

Cortot, Alfred. *In Search of Chopin.* New York: P. Nevill, 1951.

Costa, Andrea. *Analytical Considerations on the Art of Singing.* London: Sherwood, Gilbert and Piper, 1838.

Countess Dash [Gabrielle Anne De Courtiras]. *Mémoires des autres.* 6 vols. Paris: Librairie illustrée, 1896–1897.

Cowgill, Rachel. "The London Apollonicon Recitals, 1817–32: A Case-Study in Bach, Mozart and Haydn Reception." *Journal of the Royal Musical Association* 123/2 (1998): 190–228.

Cox, John Edmund. *Musical Recollections of the Last Half-Century.* London: Tinsley Bros., 1872.

Cranston, Maurice. *The Romantic Movement.* Oxford: Blackwell, 1994.

Cuvier, George. *Le Règne animal distribué d'après son organisation.* 4 vols. Paris: Déterville, 1817.

Czermák, Johann Nepomuk. *Du laryngoscope et de son emploi en physiologie et en médecine.* Paris: J. B. Baillière, 1860.

Czerny, Carl. *Complete Theoretical and Practical Piano Forte School, Op. 500.* 3 vols. London: R. Cocks, 1839.

———. *Letters to a Young Lady on the Art of Playing the Pianoforte.* London: R. Cocks, 1838.

D'Arpentigny, M. Le Capitaine C. S. *The Science of the Hand; or the Art of Recognizing the Tendencies of the Human Mind by the Observation of the Formation of the Hands.* Edited by Heron-Allen. London: Ward, Lock & Co., 1886.

Daston, Lorraine, and Peter Galison. *Objectivity.* New York: Zone Books, 2007.

Davies, J. Q. "Dancing the Symphonic: Beethoven-Bochsa's *Symphonie pastorale.*" *19th-Century Music* 27/1 (2003): 25–47.

———. "Gautier's 'Diva': The First French Uses of the Word." In *The Arts of the Prima Donna in the Long Nineteenth Century,* edited by Rachel Cowgill and Hilary Poriss, 123–46. Oxford: Oxford University Press, 2012.

Davison, Alan. "Franz Liszt and the Development of Nineteenth-Century Pianism: A Re-Reading of the Evidence." *Musical Times* 147/1896 (2006): 33–42.

Delpech, Jacques. *De l'orthomorphie par rapport à l'espèce humaine.* Paris: Gabon, 1828.

Devrient, Eduard. *My Recollections of Felix Mendelssohn-Bartholdy, and His Letters to Me.* Translated by Natalia MacFarren. London: Richard Bentley, 1869.

Diderot, Denis. *Rameau's Nephew and Other Works.* Translated by Jacques Barzun and Ralph H. Bowen. Indianapolis: Hackett, 2001.

Diruta, Girolamo. *Il transilvano.* Venice: Vincenti, 1597.

Dolan, Emily I., and John Tresch. "A Sublime Invasion: Meyerbeer, Balzac, and the Opera Machine." *Opera Quarterly* 27/1 (2011): 4–31.

Dolar, Mladen. *The Voice and Nothing More.* Cambridge, MA: MIT Press, 2006.

D'Ortigue, Joseph. *Le Balcon de l'opéra.* Paris: Eugène Renduel, 1833.

Dumas, Alexandre. *Mes Mémoires (1830–1833).* Edited by Pierre Josserand. Paris: Laffont, 1989.

Dunglison, Robley. *Human Physiology.* 2 vols. Philadelphia: Carey & Lea, 1832.

Duprez, Gilbert-Louis. *Souvenirs d'un chanteur.* Paris: Calmann Lévy, 1880.

D'Urclé, Félix Levacher. *De l'anatomie de la main considérée dans ses rapports avec l'exécution de la musique instrumentale.* Paris: Mme Laude, 1846.

Ebers, John. *Seven Years of the King's Theatre.* London: W. H. Ainsworth, 1828.

Ehrlich, Cyril. *First Philharmonic: A History of the Philharmonic Society.* Oxford: Clarendon, 1995.

Eigeldinger, Jean-Jacques. *Chopin: Pianist and Teacher.* Edited by Roy Howat and translated by Krysia Osostowicz, Roy Howat, and Naomi Shohet. Cambridge: Cambridge University Press, 1986.

———. "Liszt trascrittore e interprete de Bach." *L'organo* 11 (1973): 171–83.

Elkin, Robert. *Royal Philharmonic: The Annals of the Royal Philharmonic Society.* London: Rider, 1947.

Esse, Melina. "Speaking and Sighing: Bellini's *canto declamato* and the Poetics of Restraint." *Current Musicology* 87 (2009): 7–45.

Fay, Amy. *Music Study in Germany.* Chicago: A. C. McClurg, 1891.

Fearing, Franklin. *Reflex Action: A Study in the History of Physiological Psychology.* London: Balliere, Tindall & Cox, 1930.

Feld, Steven, Aaron A. Fox, Thomas Porcello, and David Samuels. "Vocal Anthropology: From the Music of Language to the Language of Song." In *A Companion to Linguistic Anthropology,* edited by A. Duranti, 321–46. Malden, MA: Blackwell, 2004.

Feldman, Martha. "Denaturing the Castrato." *Opera Quarterly* 24/3–4 (2008): 178–99.

Fétis, François-Joseph. *La Méthode des méthodes de piano.* Paris: Schlesinger, 1840.

Fétis, François-Joseph, and Ignaz Moscheles. *Complete System of Instruction for the Piano-Forte; being a treatise on the art of playing that instrument based on an analysis of the best works that have been written on the subject.* London: Chappell, 1841.

Fitzlyon, April. *Maria Malibran, Diva of the Romantic Age.* London: Souvenir Press, 1987.

Fleming, Renée. *The Inner Voice: The Making of a Singer.* New York: Viking, 2004.

Fontaney, Antoine. *Journal intime.* Edited by René Jasinski. Paris: Les Presses françaises, 1925.

Forget, Evelyn. "Evocations of Sympathy: Sympathetic Imagery in Eighteenth-Century Social Theory and Physiology." *History of Political Economy* 35 (2003): 282–308.

Foucault, Michel. *Discipline and Punish: The Birth of the Prison.* Translated by Alan Sheridan. London: Allen Lane, 1977.

———. "Nietzsche, Genealogy, History (1977)." In *The Foucault Reader,* edited by Paul Rabinow. New York: Pantheon, 1984.

———. *The Order of Things: An Archeology of the Human Sciences.* Translated by Alan Sheridan. New York: Vintage Books, 1994.

Fournié, Édouard. *Physiologie de la voix et de la parole.* Paris, 1866.

France, Direction Générales des Douanes. *Tableau décennal du commerce de la France, 1827–1836.* Paris: Government publication, 1838.

Franken, Franz Hermann. *Die Krankheiten grosser Komponisten.* 4 vols. Wilhelmshaven: Noetzel, 1986.

Fraxi, Pisanus. *Bibliography of Prohibited Books.* 3 vols. London: Jack Brussel, 1962.

Fulcher, Jane. *The Nation's Image: French Grand Opera as Politics and Politicized Art.* Cambridge: Cambridge University Press, 1987.

Fuller, Margaret. *Woman in the Nineteenth Century.* Edited by Larry J. Reynolds. New York: W. W. Norton, 1998.

Ganche, Édouard. *Souffrances de Frédéric Chopin: essai de médecine et de psychologie.* Paris: Mercure de France, 1935.

Garaudé, Alexis de. *Méthode complète de chant.* Paris: Author, 1826.

———. *Méthode complète de chant ou théorie pratique de cet art.* Paris: Author, ca. 1841.

García, Manuel Patricio Rodríguez. *Hints on Singing.* Edited by Beata García. London: Ascherberg, 1894.

———. *Traité complet de l'art du chant.* 2 vols. Paris: Author, 1847.

Gautier, Théophile. "Albertus, or the Soul and Sin." In *The Works of Théophile Gautier,* translated by Agnes Less and edited by F. C. de Sumichrast, 24: 217–79. 24 vols. London: George Harrap, 1903.

———. "Gérard de Nerval." In Johann Wolfgang von Goethe, *Faust et le second Faust de Goethe,* translated by Nerval, i–xxvii. Paris: Lévy, 1868.

———. *Histoire de l'art dramatique en France depuis vingt-cinq ans.* 6 vols. Paris: Édition Hetzel, 1859.

George, Sam. *Botany, Sexuality, and Women's Writing, 1760–1830.* Manchester: Manchester University Press, 2007.

Gerdy, Pierre Nicolas. "Voix." In *Encyclopédie méthodique, médecine, par une société de médecins,* 15: 479–493. 16 vols. Paris: Panckoucke, 1830.

Gerhard, Anselm. *The Urbanization of Opera.* Chicago: University of Chicago Press, 1998.

Gerig, Reginald R. *Famous Pianists and Their Technique.* Washington: R. B. Luce, 1974.

Gibbs, Christopher H., and Dana Gooley, eds. *Franz Liszt and His World.* Princeton, NJ: Princeton University Press, 2006.

Gilman, Todd S. "The Italian (Castrato) in London." In *Genre, Nationhood, and Sexual Difference,* edited by Richard Dellamora and Daniel Fischlin, 49–72. New York: Columbia University Press, 1997.

Gjerdingen, Robert O. "Monuments of Solfeggi." Accessed May 13, 2013. http://faculty-web. at.northwestern.edu/music/gjerdingen/solfeggi/index.htm.

Goldstein, Jan. *The Post-Revolutionary Self: Politics and Psyche in France, 1750–1850.* Cambridge, MA: Harvard University Press, 2005.

Gooley, Dana. "Franz Liszt: The Virtuoso as Strategist." In *The Musician as Entrepreneur, 1700–1914: Managers, Charlatans, and Idealists,* edited by William Weber,145–61. Bloomington: Indiana University Press, 2004.

———. *The Virtuoso Liszt.* Cambridge: Cambridge University Press, 2004.

Goss, Michael. "The Lessened Locus of Feelings: A Transformation in French Physiology in the Early Nineteenth Century." *Journal of the History of Biology* 12/2 (1979): 231–71.

Gouget, Émile. *Histoire musicale de la main: son rôle dans la notation, la tonalité, le rythme et l'exécution instrumentale; la main des musiciens devant les sciences occultes.* Paris: Fischbacher, 1898.

Granville, Augustus Bozzi. *St. Petersburgh. A Journal of Travels to and from that Capital.* 2 vols. London: Colburn, 1829.

Granville, Harriet. *Letters of Harriet Countess Granville 1810–45.* Edited by F. Leveson Gower. 2 vols. London: Longmans, 1894.

Grosz, Elizabeth. *Volatile Bodies.* Bloomington: Indiana University Press, 1994.

Hadlock, Heather. "The Career of Cherubino, or the Trouser Role Grows Up." In *Siren Songs: Representations of Gender and Sexuality in Opera,* edited by Mary Ann Smart, 67–92. Princeton, NJ: Princeton University Press, 2000.

———. *Mad Loves: Women and Music in Offenbach's "Les Contes d'Hoffmann."* Princeton, NJ: Princeton University Press, 2000.

———. "On the Cusp between Past and Future: The Mezzo-Soprano Romeo of Bellini's *I Capuleti*." *Opera Quarterly* 17/3 (2001): 399–422.

———. "*Tancredi* and *Semiramide*." In *The Cambridge Companion to Rossini*, edited by Emanuele Senici, 139–58. Cambridge: Cambridge University Press, 2004.

———. "Women Playing Men in Italian Opera, 1810–1835." In *Women's Voices across Musical Worlds*, edited by Jane A. Bernstein, 285–307. Boston: Northeastern University Press, 2004.

Halévy, Fromental. *Derniers souvenirs et portraits*. Paris: Michel Lévy, 1863.

Hall, Marshall. *Memoirs on the Nervous System*. London: Sherwood, Gilbert & Piper, 1837.

Hall-Witt, Jennifer. *Fashionable Acts: Opera and Elite Culture in London, 1780–1880*. Durham: University of New Hampshire Press, 2007.

Hardie, D. W. F. "The Macintoshes and the Origins of the Chemical Industry." In *Science, Technology, and Economic Growth in the Eighteenth Century*, edited by A. E. Musson, 168–94. London, Methuen: 1972.

Heine, Heinrich. *Heinrich Heine's Memoirs: From His Works, Letters and Conversations*. Edited by Gustav Karpeles. Translated by Gilbert Cannan. 2 vols. New York: John Lane, 1910.

———. *Lutèce: lettres sur la vie politique, artistique et sociale de la France*. Paris: Clamann Lévy, 1892.

———. *Sämtliche Schriften*. Edited by Klaus Briegleb. 12 vols. Munich: Hanser, 1978.

———. *Works of Prose*. Edited by Hermann Kesten. Translated by E. B. Ashton. New York: L. B. Fischer, 1943.

Heller, Stephen. "Une visite à Kalkbrenner (1838)." *S.I.M. Revue musicale mensuelle (Bulletin français de la S.I.M.)* 6 (1910): 690–95.

Henson, Karen. "Introduction: Divo Worship." *Cambridge Opera Journal* 19/1 (2007): 1–9.

Heriot, Angus. *The Castrati in Opera*. London: Calderbooks, 1960.

Hildebrandt, Dieter. *Pianoforte: A Social History of the Piano*. Translated by Harriet Goodman. London: Hutchinson, 1988.

Hiller, J. A. *Anweisung zum musikalisch-richtigen Gesange*. Leipzig: Johann Friedrich Junius, 1774.

Hogarth, George. *Memoirs of the Musical Drama*. 2 vols. London: R. Bentley, 1838.

———. *Memoirs of the Opera in Italy, France, Germany, and England*. 2 vols. London: R. Bentley, 1851.

Holmes, Edward. *A Ramble among the Musicians of Germany, Giving Some Account of the Operas of Munich, Dresden, Berlin, etc.* London: Hunt and Clarke, 1828.

Holmes, William Gordon. *A Treatise on Vocal Physiology and Hygiene*. London: Churchill, 1881.

Horowitz, Sarah Esther. *States of Intimacy: Friendship and the Remaking of French Political Elites, 1815–1848*. Ph.D. diss., University of California at Berkeley, 2008.

Hugo, Victor. *Oeuvres completes*. Edited by Jacques Seebacher. 16 vols. Paris: R. Laffont, 1985.

Hullah, Annette. *Theodor Leschetizky*. 1905. Reprint, London: J. Lane, 1923.

Hummel, Johann Nepomuk. *A Complete Theoretical and Practical Course of Instructions on the Art of Playing the Piano Forte Commencing with the Simplest Elementary Principles and Including every Information Requisite to the Most Finished Style of Performance*. London: T. Boosey, 1828.

Husk, William Henry, ed. *Templeton and Malibran*. London: W. Reeves, 1880.

Illuminati, Ermanno. *Giovan Battista Velluti, cantante lirico (1780–1860).* Corridonia: Comune di Corridonia, 1985.

Imbs, Paul, ed. *Trésor de la langue française.* 16 vols. Paris: Éditions du Centre national de la recherche scientifique, 1979–1994.

Institut orthopédique de la Muette. *Institut orthopédique de Paris, pour le traitement des difformités de la taille et des membres, chez les personnes des deux sexes. Dirigé par MM. Les Docteurs Pravaz et Jules Guérin.* Paris: A. Everat, ca. 1835.

Irigaray, Luce. *This Sex Which Is Not One.* Translated by Catherine Porter and Carolyn Burke. Ithaca: Cornell University Press, 1985.

———. "Volume without Contours." In *Irigaray Reader,* edited by Margaret Whitford, 53–68. Oxford: Blackwell, 1991.

Jackson, Myles W. "Measuring Musical Virtuosity: Physicists, Physiologists, and the Pianist's Touch in the Nineteenth Century." *The Journal of the American Liszt Society* 61–62 (2010): 13–40.

Jaëll, Marie. *Les Rythmes du regard et la dissociation des doigts.* Paris: Fischbacher, 1906.

Janin, Jules. *735 Lettres à sa femme.* 3 vols. Paris: C. Klincksieck, 1973.

Jankélévitch, Vladimir. *Liszt et la rhapsodie. Essai sur la virtuosité.* Paris: Plon, 1979.

Jansen, Eric Frederick. "Liszt, Nerval and *Faust.*" *19th-Century Music* 6/2 (1982): 151–58.

Johnson, James H. *Listening in Paris: A Cultural History.* Berkeley: University of California Press, 1995.

Johnson, Janet. "The Musical Environment in France." In *The Cambridge Companion to Berlioz,* edited by Peter Bloom, 20–40. Cambridge: Cambridge University Press, 2000.

Jordanova, Ludmilla. "The Hand." *Visual Anthropology Review* 8/2 (1992): 2–7.

Jourdan, Paul. "Mendelssohn in England, 1829–37." Ph.D. diss., University of Cambridge, 1998.

Kalkbrenner, Frédéric. *Method of Learning the Pianoforte, with the Aid of the Manual-Guide; Containing the Principles of Music, a Complete System of Fingering, a Classification of Authors to be Studied, Rules on Expression, on Manners of Phrasing, on Musical Punctuation* (1831). Translated by Sabilla Novello. London: Novello, 1862.

Kallberg, Jeffrey. *Chopin at the Boundaries.* Cambridge, MA: Harvard University Press, 1996.

Keats, John. *Endymion: A Poetic Romance.* London: Taylor and Hessey, 1818.

Kellermann, Berthold. *Erinnerungen: Ein Künstler leben.* Leipzig: E. Rentsch, 1932.

Kienzl, Wilhelm. *Meine Lebenswanderung.* Stuttgart: Engelhorn, 1926.

Kimbell, David. *Vincenzo Bellini: "Norma."* Cambridge: Cambridge University Press, 1998.

Kirschner, Suzanne. *The Religious and Romantic Origins of Psychoanalysis.* Cambridge: Cambridge University Press, 1996.

Koestenbaum, Wayne. *The Queen's Throat: Opera, Homosexuality, and the Mystery of Desire.* New York: Poseidon Press, 1993.

Kókai, Rezsö. *Franz Liszt in seinen frühen Klavierwerken.* Basel: Bärenreiter Kassel, 1968.

Kontski, Antoine de. *L'Indispensable du pianiste, édition nouvelle et augmentée, op. 100.* St. Petersburg: Bernard, ca. 1851.

Kristeva, Julia. *Revolution in Poetic Language.* Translated by Margaret Waller. New York: Columbia University Press, 1984.

Kuchta, David. "The Making of the Self-Made Man: Class, Clothing, and English Masculinity, 1688–1832." In *The Sex of Things,* edited by Victoria de Grazia and Ellen Furlough, 54–78. Berkeley: University of California Press, 1996.

Kuriyama, Shigehisa. *The Expressiveness of the Body and the Divergence of Greek and Chinese Medicine.* New York: Zone Books, 2002.

Lablache, Louis. *Méthode complète de chant.* Paris: Canaux, 1840.

Lachmund, Carl. *Living with Liszt: From the Diary of Carl Lachmund, an American Pupil of Liszt.* Edited by Alan Walker. Stuyvesant, NY: Pendragon Press, 1995.

Lacoue-Labarthe, Philippe. *Typography: Mimesis, Philosophy, Politics.* Edited by Christopher Fynsk. Cambridge, MA: Harvard University Press, 1989.

Laget, August. *Le Chant et les chanteurs.* Paris and Toulouse: Heugel, 1874.

Lanza, Gesualdo. *The Elements of Singing, Familiarly Exemplified.* London: Button & Whitaker, 1813.

Laphalèque, Georges Imbert de [Louis-François Lhéritier]. *Notice sur le célèbre violoniste Nicolo Paganini.* Paris: E. Guyot, 1830.

Laqueur, Thomas. *Making Sex: Body and Gender from the Greeks to Freud.* Cambridge, MA: Harvard University Press, 1990.

———. "Orgasm, Generation, and the Politics of Reproductive Biology." In *The Making of the Modern Body: Sexuality and Society in the Nineteenth Century,* edited by Catherine Gallagher and Thomas Laqueur, 1–41. Berkeley, CA: University of California Press, 1987.

Latour, Bruno. *Essays on Physiognomy Designed to Promote the Knowledge and the Love of Mankind.* Translated by Henry Hunter. 3 vols. London: John Murray, H. Hunter and T. Holloway, 1789–1798.

———. "How to Talk about the Body? The Normative Dimension of Science Studies." *Body and Society* 10/2–3 (2004): 205–29.

———. *Reassembling the Social: An Introduction to Actor-Network-Theory.* Oxford: Oxford University Press, 2005.

Lawrence, William. "Generation." In *Cyclopedia, or Universal Dictionary of Arts, Sciences, and Literature,* edited by Abraham Rees, 16: n.p. 39 vols. London: Longman, Hurst, Rees, Orme & Browne, 1819.

Lawton, David. Introduction to Giuseppe Verdi, *Il trovatore.* 2 vols. Chicago and Milan: University of Chicago Press and Ricordi, 1993.

Lee, Sarah Wallace Bowdich. *Memoirs of Cuvier.* London: Longman, 1833.

Legány, Dezsó. *Franz Liszt: Unbekannte Presse und Briefe aus Wien 1822–1886.* Budapest: Corvina Kiadó, 1984.

Legouvé, Ernest. *Soixante ans de souvenirs.* 2 vols. Paris, 1886.

Le Guin, Elisabeth. *Boccherini's Body: An Essay in Carnal Musicology.* Berkeley: University of California Press, 2006.

Lenz, Wilhelm von. *The Great Piano Virtuosos of Our Time.* Edited by Philip Reder. London: Kahn & Averill, 1983.

———. *Beethoven et ses trois styles.* St. Petersburg: Bernard, 1852.

Leopold, Silke. "'Not Sex but Pitch': Kastraten als Liebhaber—Einmal 'über' der Gürtellenie betrachtet." In *Provokation und Tradition. Erfahrungen mit der alten Musik,* edited by Hans-Martin Linde and Regula Rapp, 219–40. Stuttgart-Weimar: Metzler, 2000.

Leppert, Richard. "Imagery, Musical Confrontation and Cultural Difference in Early 18ᵗʰ-Century London." *Early Music* 14/3 (1986): 323–45.

Lewald, August. *Aquarelle aus dem Leben.* 6 vols. Mannheim: Hoff, 1837.

Liszt, Franz. *Correspondance de Liszt et de la Comtesse d'Agoult, 1833–1840.* Edited by Daniel Ollivier. 2 vols. Paris: B. Grasset, 1933.

———. *Letters of Franz Liszt.* Edited by La Mara. Translated by Constance Bache. 2 vols. New York: Charles Scribner's Sons, 1894.

———. *The Letters of Franz Liszt to Olga Von Meyendorff, 1871–1886.* Washington: Dumbarton Oaks, 1979.

Lobstein, J. F. *A Treatise on the Structure, Functions and Diseases of the Human Sympathetic Nerve.* Philadelphia: J. G. Auner, 1831.

Madeleine, Etienne-Jean-Baptiste-Nicolas. *Théories complètes du chant.* Paris: Amyot, 1852.

Magendie, François. *Précis élémentaire de physiologie.* 2 vols. Paris: Méquignon-Marvis, 1816.

Maistre, Joseph de. *St. Petersburg Dialogues.* Translated and edited by Richard A. Lebrun. Montreal: McGill-Queens University Press, 1993.

Majka, Lucyna; Joanna Gozdzik and Michal Witt, "Cystic Fibrosis: A Probable Cause of Frédéric Chopin's Suffering and Death." *Journal of Applied Genetics* 44/1 (2003): 77–84.

Malpas, Constance. "Jules Guérin Makes His Market: The Social Economy of Orthopaedic Medicine in Paris, ca. 1825–1845." In *Cultural Approaches to the History of Medicine,* edited by William de Blécourt and Cornelie Usborne, 148–70. New York, 2004.

Mancini, Giambattista. *Riflessioni pratiche sul canto figurato.* Milan: G. Galeazzi, 1777.

Marmontel, Antoine. *Les Pianistes célèbres.* Paris: Heugel et fils, 1878.

Marpurg, F. W. *Anleitung zur musik überhaupt und zur Singkunst.* Berlin: Wever, 1763.

Martini, Jean Paul Egide. *Mélopée moderne; ou l'art du chant, réduit en principes.* Paris: Boyer, ca. 1792.

Mascagni, Paolo. *Tavole figurate di alcune parti organiche del corpo umano.* Florence: Marenigh, 1819.

Matuszyński, Jan. *De l'influence du nerf sympathique sur les fonctions des sens.* Paris: Faculté de médecine, 1837.

———. *Ueber die Natur und Behandlung des Weichselzopfes.* Tübingen: Osiander, 1834.

Maurice, Charles. *Histoire anecdotique du théâtre.* 2 vols. Paris: H. Plon, 1856.

Mengozzi, Bernardo, et al. *Méthode de chant du Conservatoire de musique.* Paris: À l'Imprimerie du Conservatoire de musique, 1804.

Merlin, María de las Mercedes Santa Cruz y Montalvo. *Memoirs of Madame Malibran.* 2 vols. London: H. Colburn, 1844.

Merrick, Paul. "Liszt's *sans ton* Key Signature." *Studia Musicologica Academiae Scientiarum Hungaricae* 45/3–4 (2004): 281–302.

Meyerbeer, Giacomo. *Il crociato in Egitto: melodramma eroico (1824).* Edited by Philip Gossett. New York: Garland, 1979.

Michotte, Edmond. *Richard Wagner's Visit to Rossini (Paris 1860).* Translated by Herbert Weinstock. Chicago: University of Chicago Press, 1968.

Mikol, Vera. "The Influence of Sigismund Thalberg on American Musical Taste, 1830–1872." *Proceedings of the American Philosophical Society* 102/5 (20 October 1958): 464–68.

Mitchell, John, ed. *A Memoir of the Countess de Rossi (Madame Sontag).* London: Mr. Mitchell, 1849.

Modugno, Maurizio. "Domenico Donzelli e il suo tempo." *Nuova rivista musicale italiana* 18/2 (1984): 200–216.

Mongrédien, Jean, ed. *Le Théâtre-Italien de Paris 1801–1831: chronologie et documents.* 8 vols. Lyon: Symétrie, 2008.

Morlacchi, Francesco, and Gaetano Rossi. *Tebaldo e Isolina: A Facsimile Edition of the Printed Piano-Vocal Score (ca. 1825).* Edited by Philip Gossett. New York: Garland, 1989.

Moscheles, Ignaz. *Gems à la Malibran, Book 2.* London: Mori & Lavenu, 1829.

———. *Letters of Felix Mendelssohn to Ignaz and Charlotte Moscheles.* Edited by Felix Moscheles. Boston: Ticknor, 1888.

Mott, Valentine. *Travels in Europe and the East.* New York: Harper, 1842.

Müller, Johannes Peter. *Elements of Physiology.* Translated by William Baly. 2 vols. London: Taylor and Walton, 1842.

Murphy, Kerry. "Joseph Mainzer's 'Sacred and Beautiful Mission': An Aspect of Parisian Musical Life of the 1830s." *Music & Letters* 75/1 (1994): 33–46.

Nadeau, Jean-Benoît, and Julie Barlow. *The Story of French.* London: Portico, 2008.

Nathan, Isaac. *Musurgia Vocalis: An Essay on the History and Theory of Music, and on the Qualities, Capabilities, and Management of the Human Voice.* London: Fentum, 1836.

Nerval, Gérard de. "The Enchanted Hand." In *Fantastic Tales,* edited by Italo Calvino, 143–80. London: Penguin, 2001.

Neumann, Philipp von. *The Diary of Philipp von Neumann, 1829 to 1850.* Translated and edited by E. Beresford Chancellor. 2 vols. New York: Houghton Mifflin, 1928.

Newton, Dudley. "Liszt's Hands." *Liszt Society Journal* 15 (1990): 9–14.

Nietzsche, Friedrich. *The Will to Power.* Translated by Walter Kauffmann and R. J. Hollingdale. New York: Vintage Books, 1968.

O'Donnelly, Terence Joseph. *Académie de musique élémentaire contenant une exposition claire de la théorie.* Translated by A. D. de Cressier. Paris: Grue, 1844.

O'Shea, John. *Music and Medicine: Medical Profiles of Great Composers.* London: Dent, 1990.

Ostwald, Peter F. "Florestan, Eusebius, Clara and Schumann's Right Hand." *19th-Century Music* 4/1 (1980): 17–31.

Ott, Bertrand. *Lisztian Keyboard Energy: An Essay on the Pianism of Franz Liszt.* Translated by Donald H. Windham. New York: E. Mellen Press, 1992.

Paine, John Knowles. *Famous Composers and Their Works.* Boston: J. B. Millet, 1891.

Palluault, Florent. *Medical Students in England and France 1815–1858: A Comparative Study.* DPhil diss., University of Oxford, 2003.

Panseron, Auguste. *Méthode de vocalisation en 2 parties.* Paris: Author, 1840.

Parke, William Thomas. *Musical Memoirs; Comprising an Account of the General State of Music in England.* London: H. Colburn and R. Bentley, 1830.

Parker, Roger. *Leonora's Last Act.* Princeton, NJ: Princeton University Press, 1997.

Pergetti, Paolo. *Treatise on Singing Forming a Complete School of the Art.* London: R. W. Ollivier, 1858.

Plantinga, Leon B. *Schumann as Critic.* New Haven and London: Yale University Press, 1967.

Pleasants, Henry. *The Great Tenor Tragedy: The Last Days of Adolphe Nourrit.* Portland: Amadeus Press, 1995.

Pocknell, Pauline. "Franz Liszt's Unpublished Pocket-Diary for 1832—A Guide to His Memories." In *Liszt 2000*, edited by Klára Hamburger, 52–77. Budapest: Hungarian Liszt Society, 2000.

———. "Reading Liszt's Hands: Molds, Casts and Replicas as Guides to Contemporary Creative Representations." *Journal of the American Liszt Society* 54–56 (2003–5): 171–90.

Poriss, Hilary. *Changing the Score: Arias, Prima Donnas, and the Authority of Performance.* Oxford: Oxford University Press, 2009.

Pougin, Arthur. *Marie Malibran: The Story of a Great Singer.* London: E Nash, 1911.

Powers, Harold S. "'La solita forma' and 'The Uses of Convention.'" *Acta Musicologica* 59/1 (1987): 65–69.

Quicherat, Louis. *Adolphe Nourrit: sa vie, son talent, son caractère, sa correspondence.* 3 vols. Paris: Hachette, 1867.

Ramann, Lina. *Franz Liszt, Artist and Man.* Translated by E. Cowdery. 2 vols. London: W. H. Allen, 1882.

Raspé, Paul. "Pianos: virtuoses et instruments de torture à l'époque romantique." *Clés pour la musique* 31/32 (1971): 11–14.

Reed, Edward S. *From Soul to Mind: The Emergence of Psychology.* New Haven: Yale University Press, 1997.

Reid, Charles. *The Music Monster: A Biography of James William Davison.* London: Quartet, 1984.

Rennie, James. *The Art of Improving the Voice and Ear; and of Increasing Their Musical Powers.* London: S. Prowett, 1825.

Richardson, Alan. *British Romanticism and the Science of the Mind.* Cambridge: Cambridge University Press, 2000.

Richerand, Balthasar-Anthelme. *Nouveaux éléments de physiologie.* 2 vols. Paris: Caille et Ravier, 1820.

Risi, Clemens. "Opera in Performance: In Search of New Analytical Approaches." *Opera Quarterly* 27/2–3 (2011): 283–95.

Rosen, Charles. *The Romantic Generation.* Cambridge, MA: Harvard University Press, 1995.

Rosselli, John. "The Castrati as a Professional Group and a Social Phenomenon, 1550–1850." *Acta Musicologica* 60 (1988): 143–79.

———. "Song into Theatre: The Beginnings of Opera." In *The Cambridge Companion to Singing*, edited by John Potter, 83–95. Cambridge: Cambridge University Press, 2002.

Rowe, Katherine. *Dead Hands: Fictions of Agency, Renaissance to Modern.* Stanford: Stanford University Press, 1999.

———. "'God's handy worke': Divine Complicity and the Anatomist's Touch." *The Body in Parts*, edited by David Hillmen and Carlo Mazio, 285–309. London: Routledge, 1997.

Rutherford, Susan. *The Prima Donna and Opera, 1815–1930.* Cambridge: Cambridge University Press, 2006.

Saint-Saëns, Camille. *Portraits et souvenirs.* Paris: Société d'édition artistique, 1900.

Salzer, Felix. "Chopin's Étude in F Major, opus 25, no. 3: The Scope of Tonality." *Music Forum* 3 (1973): 281–90.

Sams, Eric. "Schumann's Hand Injury." *The Musical Times* 112/1546 (1971): 1156–59.

Sand, George. *Correspondance.* Edited by Georges Lubin. 25 vols. Paris: Garnier, 1964–1972.

———. *Marie d'Agoult-George Sand: correspondance.* Edited by Charles F. Dupêchez. Paris: Bartillat, 2001.

Sanson, Henri. *Memoirs of the Sansons: From Private Notes and Documents (1688–1847).* London: Chatto and Windus, 1876.

Schaffer, Simon. "Indiscipline and Interdisciplines: Some Exotic Genealogies of Modern Knowledge." Last modified April 26, 2010. www.fif.tu-darmstadt.de/aktuelles_2/vergangeneveranstaltungen/veranstaltungen_details_fif_4224.de.jsp.

Schonberg, Harold C. *The Great Pianists.* New York: Simon and Schuster, 1963.

Schumann, Robert. *Early Letters of Robert Schumann.* Translated by May Herbert. London: G. Bell, 1888.

———. "Etüden für das Pianoforte." *Neue Zeitschrift für Musik* 11/29 (8 October 1839): 113–14.

———. *Gesammelte Schriften über Musik und Musiker.* Edited by Martin Kreisig. 2 vols. Leipzig: Breitkopf & Härtel, 1914.

———. *Music and Musicians.* Translated by Fanny Raymond Ritter. London: William Reeves, 1877.

———. *Robert Schumann "Schlage nur eine Weltsaite an": Briefe 1828–1855.* Edited by Karin Sousa. Frankfurt am Main, Leipzig: Insel-Verlag, 2006.

———. *Tagebücher I (1827–1838).* Leipzig: Deutscher Verlag, 1971.

Scudo, Paul, Hector Berlioz, Louis Boerne, Adolphe Adam, Marie Aycard, Julie de Margueritte, Prince Puckler-Muskau, and Théophile Gautier. *Life of Henriette Sontag, Countess de Rossi.* New York: Stringer & Townsend, 1852.

Secord, Jim. *Victorian Sensation.* Chicago: University of Chicago Press, 2000.

Ségond, Louis Auguste. *Hygiène du chanteur, influence du chant sur l'économie animale.* Paris: Labé, 1846.

Sha, Richard C. *Perverse Romanticism: Aesthetics and Sexuality in Britain, 1750–1832.* Baltimore: Johns Hopkins University Press, 2009.

Shakespeare, William. *The Art of Singing: Based on the Principles of the Old Italian Singing-Masters.* Boston: Ditson, 1905.

Shapin, Steven, and Simon Schaffer. *Leviathan and the Air-Pump: Hobbes, Boyle, and the Experimental Life.* 1985. Reprint, Princeton, NJ: Princeton University Press, 2011.

Sherwood, H. H. *The Motive Power of Organic Life.* New York: Chapin, 1841.

Shorter, Edward. *From Paralysis to Fatigue: A History of Psychosomatic Illness in the Modern Era.* New York: Free Press, 1992.

Sieluzycki, Czeclaw. "On the Health of Chopin: Truth, Supposition, Legends." *Chopin Studies* 6 (1999): 99–155.

Smart, Mary Ann. Introduction to *Siren Songs: Representations of Gender and Sexuality in Opera.* Edited by Mary Ann Smart, 3–16. Princeton NJ: Princeton University Press, 2000.

———. Review of *Listening in Paris: A Cultural History,* by James H. Johnson. *19th-Century Music* 20/3 (1997): 291–97.

———. "Theorizing Gender, Culture and Music." *Women and Music: A Journal of Gender and Culture* 6 (2005): 106–10.

Soubies, Albert. *Le Théâtre-Italien de 1801 à 1913.* Paris: Fischbacher, 1913.

Standring, Enid M. "Rossini and His Music in the Life and Works of George Sand." *Nineteenth-Century French Studies* 10/1–2 (1981–82): 17–27.

Stark, James. *Bel Canto: A History of Vocal Pedagogy.* Toronto: University of Toronto Press, 2003.

Steege, Benjamin. *Helmholtz and the Modern Listener.* Cambridge: Cambridge University Press, 2012.

Stendhal [Marie-Henri Beyle]. *Life of Rossini.* Translated by Richard N. Coe. London: J. Calder, 1985.

———. *Scarlet and Black.* Translated by Margaret R. B. Shaw. London: Penguin Books, 1953.

Stephens, Frederic George, and Mary Dorothy George. *Catalogue of Political and Personal Satires.* 11 vols. London: British Museum, 1952.

Sydow, Bronislaw Edward, ed., *Correspondance de Frédéric Chopin.* 3 vols. Paris: Richard-Masse, 1953–1960.

Taruskin, Richard. *Oxford History of Western Music.* 8 vols. Oxford: Oxford University Press, 2005.

Tenducci, Giusto Fernando. *Mr. Tenducci's Instructions to His Scholars.* London: Longman & Broderip, 1785.

Thalberg, Sigismund. *L'Art du chant appliqué au piano.* Leipzig: Breitkopf & Härtel, 1853.

Todd, R. Larry. *Mendelssohn: A Life in Music.* Oxford: Oxford University Press, 2005.

Tomásek, Václav. "Selbstbiographie." *Libussa: Jahrbuch* 4. Edited by Paul Alois Klar. Prague: Calve, 1845.

Tomlinson, Gary. *Metaphysical Song.* Princeton, NJ: Princeton University Press, 1999.

———. "Vico's Songs: Detours at the Origins of (Ethno)musicology." *The Musical Quarterly* 83/3 (1999): 344–77.

Trippett, David. *Wagner's Melodies: Aesthetics and Materialism in German Musical Identity.* Cambridge: Cambridge University Press, 2013.

Türk, Daniel Gottlob. *School of Clavier Playing or Instructions in Playing the Clavier for Teachers and Students.* Translated and introduced by Raymond H. Haggh. Lincoln: University of Nebraska Press, 1982.

Uberti, Mauro. "Il *Metodo practico di canto* di Nicola Vaccai." In *Nuova Rivista Italiana* 8 (2004): 43–67.

Vaccai, Nicola. *Metodo pratico di canto.* Milan: Ricordi, 2001.

Waddington, Mary Alsop King. *My First Years as a Frenchwoman.* New York: C. Scribner, 1914.

Walker, Alan. *Franz Liszt I: The Virtuoso Years, 1811–1847.* 3 vols. London: Faber & Faber, 1983.

———. *Franz Liszt III: The Final Years, 1861–1886.* 3 vols. London: Faber & Faber, 1997.

———. *Reflections on Liszt.* Ithaca: Cornell University Press, 2005.

Walton, Benjamin. Introduction to "The First Biography: Joseph d'Ortigue on Franz Liszt at Age Twenty-Three." In *Franz Liszt and His World*, edited by Christopher Gibbs and Dana Gooley, 303–34. Princeton, NJ: Princeton University Press, 2006.

———. "The Professional Dilettante: Ludovic Vitet and *Le Globe*." In *Reading Critics Reading: Opera and Ballet Criticism in France from the Revolution to 1848*, edited by Roger Parker and Mary Ann Smart, 69–85. Oxford: Oxford University Press, 2001.

———. *Rossini in Restoration Paris: The Sound of Modern Life.* Cambridge: University of Cambridge, 2007.

Wasielewski, Wilhelm Joseph von. *Life of Robert Schumann*. Translated by A. L. Alger. London: W. Reeves, 1878.

Watkins, Holly. "From the Mine to the Shrine: The Critical Origins of Musical Depth." *19th-Century Music* 27/3 (2004): 179–207.

Weber, Ernst Heinrich. *E. H. Weber on the Tactile Sense*. Edited and translated by Helen E. Ross and David J. Murray. Hove: Erlbaum, 1996.

Weinstock, Herbert. *Rossini: A Biography*. London: Oxford University Press, 1968.

———. *Vincenzo Bellini: His Life and Operas*. London: Weidenfeld & Nicolson, 1972.

White, Don. "Meyerbeer in Italy." Opera Rara's *Il crociato in Egitto*. ORC 10. London, 1991.

Wilder, Burt, G. "The Hand as an Unruly Member." *The American Naturalist* 1/8 (1867), 414–23.

Wilhem [Guillaume-Louis Bocquillon]. *Guide de la méthode, ou Instructions pour l'emploi simultané des tableaux de lecture musicale et de chant élémentaire*. Paris: E. Duverger, 1835.

Williams, Adrian. *Portrait of Liszt: By Himself and His Contemporaries*. Oxford: Clarendon, 1990.

Winter, Alison. *Mesmerized: Powers of Mind in Victorian Britain*. Chicago: University of Chicago Press, 1998.

Wistreich, Richard. "Reconstructing Pre-Romantic Singing Technique." In *The Cambridge Companion to Singing*, edited by John Potter, 178–91. Cambridge: Cambridge University Press, 2002.

Wolff, Larry. *Inventing Eastern Europe: The Map of Civilization on the Mind of the Enlightenment*. Stanford: Stanford University Press, 1994.

Wollstonecraft, Mary. *A Vindication of the Rights of Woman: With Strictures on Political and Moral Subjects*. London: J. Johnson, 1792.

MANUSCRIPTS AND ARCHIVES

Bacon, Richard Mackenzie. His signature collection. Cambridge University Library. Manuscripts Add. 6,245, 18v.

Liszt, Franz. "Carnet de Marie d'Agoult. Année 1832." Bibliothèque nationale de France. Manuscripts. NAF 14319.

M. Denecke Mendelssohn Collection. Bodleian Library, Oxford.

Royal Philharmonic Society Archive. The British Library. Manuscripts.

INDEX